CLUED IN TO POLITICS

CQ Press, an imprint of SAGE, is the leading publisher of books, periodicals, and electronic products on American government and international affairs. CQ Press consistently ranks among the top commercial publishers in terms of quality, as evidenced by the numerous awards its products have won over the years. CQ Press owes its existence to Nelson Poynter, former publisher of the *St. Petersburg Times,* and his wife Henrietta, with whom he founded Congressional Quarterly in 1945. Poynter established CQ with the mission of promoting democracy through education and in 1975 founded the Modern Media Institute, renamed The Poynter Institute for Media Studies after his death. The Poynter Institute (*www.poynter.org*) is a nonprofit organization dedicated to training journalists and media leaders.

In 2008, CQ Press was acquired by SAGE, a leading international publisher of journals, books, and electronic media for academic, educational, and professional markets. Since 1965, SAGE has helped inform and educate a global community of scholars, practitioners, researchers, and students spanning a wide range of subject areas, including business, humanities, social sciences, and science, technology, and medicine. A privately owned corporation, SAGE has offices in Los Angeles, London, New Delhi, and Singapore, in addition to the Washington DC office of CQ Press.

CLUED IN TO POLITICS

A Critical Thinking Reader in American Government

Fourth Edition

Christine Barbour
Indiana University

Matthew J. Streb
Northern Illinois University

Editors

Los Angeles | London | New Delhi
Singapore | Washington DC

Los Angeles | London | New Delhi
Singapore | Washington DC

FOR INFORMATION:

CQ Press

An Imprint of SAGE Publications, Inc.

2455 Teller Road

Thousand Oaks, California 91320

E-mail: order@sagepub.com

SAGE Publications Ltd.

1 Oliver's Yard

55 City Road

London EC1Y 1SP

United Kingdom

SAGE Publications India Pvt. Ltd.

B 1/I 1 Mohan Cooperative Industrial Area

Mathura Road, New Delhi 110 044

India

SAGE Publications Asia-Pacific Pte. Ltd.

3 Church Street

#10-04 Samsung Hub

Singapore 049483

Printed in the United States of America

Library of Congress Cataloging-in-Publication Data

Clued in to politics : a critical thinking reader in American government / Christine Barbour, Indiana University, Matthew J. Streb, Northern Illinois University, editors.——Fourth edition.

pages cm.

Includes bibliographical references

ISBN 978-1-60871-794-1 (pbk. : alk. paper) 1. United States——Politics and government. I. Barbour, Christine, 1955- II. Streb, Matthew J. (Matthew Justin), 1974–

JK21.B27 2014

320.973——dc23   2013030669

This book is printed on acid-free paper.

Acquisitions Editor: Charisse Kiino

Editorial Assistant: Davia Grant

Production Editor: Laura Barrett

Copy Editor: Talia Greenberg

Typesetter: C&M Digitals (P) Ltd.

Proofreader: Ellen Howard

Cover Designer: Gail Buschman

Marketing Manager: Amy Whitaker

Permissions Editor: Jennifer Barron

SUSTAINABLE FORESTRY INITIATIVE

Certified Chain of Custody
Promoting Sustainable Forestry
www.sfiprogram.org
SFI-01268

SFI label applies to text stock

13 14 15 16 17 10 9 8 7 6 5 4 3 2 1

Contents

Contents

Contents

Preface to the Instructor

Sometimes in our efforts to get students to think critically about the texts they read, we resemble nothing so much as tourists in a foreign land, convinced that if we only make our requests louder and more insistent, we will suddenly be understood by uncomprehending native shopkeepers. "NO, NO," we say loudly. "Don't just report what the author is saying. ANALYZE it." If repeating the word *ANALYZE* in stentorian tones were enough to do the trick, all of our students would have been ace critical thinkers long ago. It isn't enough.

The reason it's not enough is that many, if not most, of our students don't really understand what it means to analyze, or to evaluate, or to assess—in short, to think critically. It isn't something that comes naturally, and we have learned the hard way that if we don't model it for students, they will be stuck at a level of descriptive understanding.

In this book we present the CLUES model—a tool for prodding students out of that descriptive rut. CLUES is an acronym (fully defined in the Preface to the Student) for the five essential steps of critical thinking that students need to internalize so that they can get the hang of thinking critically in their academic and everyday lives. We use these steps to help students work through readings together in class and, eventually, at home on their own.

In this reader we teach students to think critically about important substantive areas of American politics by means of the following features:

- Engaging, contemporary articles from a variety of sources—newspapers, magazines, and the Internet—that illustrate American government at all levels.
- Consistent end-of-reading questions that walk students through the CLUES method of critical thinking, helping to model the process for them so that they can learn to do it automatically.
- Classic readings, such as John F. Kennedy's inaugural address and *Federalist* No. 51, that close each chapter and help students understand and observe the changes or constants in key political arguments over time.
- Readings that are balanced between objective and opinion-based points of view and vary in length and format to provide instructors with maximum flexibility.
- Chapters that correspond with the chapters of a typical introductory American politics text for easy incorporation into course syllabi.

How to Use the Book in the Classroom

There are several ways *Clued in to Politics* can be incorporated in the classroom. These suggestions work for small classes or large lecture classes with discussion sections, but most of them are applicable for large lecture classes without discussion sections as well (see below for more on how to use the reader in large lecture classes without discussion sections). Certainly, one does not have to use all these pedagogical approaches, nor is this list exhaustive.

Answering/Creating CLUES Questions

This assignment is an excellent starting point to teach students critical thinking skills. It works well in all sizes of classes because instructors have a variety of options available to them. In a smaller class, students can begin by answering the CLUES questions for the assigned article on their own as homework or in small groups in class. The work can be given a numerical grade for the assignment or a pass/fail. The class should review the answers to the CLUES questions, especially early in the semester when students are getting familiar with the method.

In large classes, individual assignments usually work best. The instructor can collect the assignments and grade them pass/fail or use the assignments as a way to take attendance. As in smaller classes, the instructor should walk the class through the answers for the first few readings.

As the students become more advanced and independent, they can choose their own articles, figuring out what argument the author is making and creating their own questions to fit each step of the model (it is helpful early on if the instructor approves the student's article to be sure there is a clear argument to analyze). They can then answer their own questions. Getting students to apply the CLUES framework to articles on their own will help them develop immensely as critical thinkers.

Class Discussion/Class Debate

This pedagogical approach is best suited for small classes and classes that hold discussion sections. The instructor can take a variety of approaches. The class can work as a whole, or in small groups, deconstructing the author's argument. This pedagogical approach works especially well in discussing the political implications (the "S" in the CLUES framework) of the author's argument.

Even in larger classes, instructors can ask students to work with the person sitting next to them to come up with answers to the CLUES questions and then share them with the class. These "pair and share exercises" need only take a few minutes, but they can break up a lecture format and get students engaged in the readings.

Minute Reaction Papers

The use of short reaction papers to the articles is an excellent way to make sure students are both completing and understanding the readings. Instructors have a few options here. Students could write a paragraph or two simply discussing their reactions to the readings, relating the article to a concept discussed in lecture, or just responding to one of the CLUES questions.

Minute reaction papers are successful because they allow the instructor to measure whether the class grasped the author's argument and how the students' critical thinking skills are progressing. This type of assignment is particularly effective in large classes because it can be used to take attendance. Minute reaction papers are typically graded pass/fail.

Rebuttal Papers

Once students have finished several CLUES assignments on their own and are beginning to use the CLUES framework automatically, we raise the degree of difficulty a notch. Perhaps we ask students to find an editorial they disagree with and ask them to write their own editorial in opposition, using the CLUES model to guide their writing (for example, cautioning them to be aware of their audience, to set out their values and argument clearly, to supply evidence). The instructor should approve each student's article so that the student does not choose one that is too difficult to analyze.

By this point, students should have a solid understanding of evaluating evidence; this assignment will help them learn to rebut arguments with which they do not agree. Again, an assignment such as this one should be done well into the semester after the students have had much practice working through several articles using the CLUES framework. This assignment works well in all types of classes (although large lecture classes without discussion sections would need graders).

Persuasive Papers

This assignment is similar to the rebuttal paper. Instead of focusing on one article, choose a topic that is discussed in the reader (for example, third parties, nonpartisan redistricting commissions) and have the students take a side. Students should go beyond simply analyzing the author's argument. Instead, they should bring in many different points of view on the topic, make an argument, and refute the opposition.

Like the rebuttal paper, this assignment should be given later in the semester once students have had more experience analyzing arguments. This assignment works well in all types of classes (although large lecture classes without discussion sections would need to have graders).

Classic Reading Papers

Each chapter in *Clued in to Politics* contains a classic reading designed to help students understand and observe the changes or constants in key political arguments over time. As a way to integrate the classic readings in class, students could choose or be assigned a classic reading and then write a paper relating the classic to current-day government. For example, students who read *Federalist* No. 78 could examine whether Alexander Hamilton was correct. This assignment will make students contemplate history and think critically about how important arguments of the past apply or don't apply to American politics today.

Large Lectures without Discussion Sections

Many of us find ourselves teaching larger and larger classes solely based on lecture and with little opportunity for class discussion. This can make the use of a reader difficult.

As stated before, students will learn a great deal from *Clued in to Politics* simply by reading on their own. That said, students will benefit even more from additional instruction and help in learning to think critically. This can seem daunting for the instructor of such a large class (and in many cases without any help from teaching assistants), but *Clued in to Politics* can still be easily incorporated into this kind of class.

Instructors should explain the CLUES concept to the class early in the semester. This will help reinforce what students have read and will clear up any areas of confusion. At the beginning of each chapter, instructors might briefly highlight some of the questions they want students to contemplate as they are reading. Instructors can also tie in some of the major concepts of the class to the readings. For example, when discussing the partisan polarization in a lecture on Congress, an instructor might mention the *Politico* article written by former representative Steve LaTourette regarding his belief that the Republican Party is nominating unelectable Senate candidates. This instruction will help students understand the reading and tie it in to the "big picture."

To further help students grasp the concept of critical thinking, instructors might assign each student a partner or to a small group. Students can walk through the CLUES questions together, or later in the semester they can develop their own CLUES questions and answers in response to an article they have found. The instructor can then randomly collect the assignments to make sure they are being completed.

Other assignments that work well in a large lecture setting—and that were mentioned previously—are minute reaction papers and answering CLUES questions. These assignments can be used to monitor how well the class comprehends the readings and to take attendance. The instructor may randomly read a few of the reaction papers to see whether the students are grasping the concepts behind critical thinking.

Acknowledgments

Several people have helped us with this project, and we are grateful for their assistance. In particular, we would like to thank Gerald Wright of Indiana University; Michael Genovese and Evan Gerstmann of Loyola Marymount University (LMU); Brian Frederick of Bridgewater State College; David Kessler of the Bancroft Library at the University of California, Berkeley; and Carol Briley of the Truman Presidential Museum and Library. We are also indebted to research assistants Caroline Guidi, Jennie Haubenschild, and Tim Marquez for their good work on this project.

We would also like to thank David Pace and Joan Middendorf of the Freshman Learning Project (FLP) at Indiana University for reminding us that students cannot learn to think like we do unless we model it for them. The FLP experience, and particularly David's own work with modeling critical thinking for students, has been invaluable in the conception of this book.

We are grateful to Jean Woy for her help in developing this project and to all the folks at CQ Press who helped put this edition together: Brenda Carter and Charisse Kiino for their vision, patience, and support; Davia Grant for coordinating the work—gathering permissions and keeping us on track; Talia Greenberg for her gentle and able editing; and Laura Barrett for her excellent work managing production.

Preface to the Student

This is a book of readings about politics. Although politics has its tedious moments, it also has an exhilarating side. It can be exciting, challenging, and even inspiring. It touches all of our lives much more often and more deeply than we may think. The readings in this book, although they will inevitably cover some heavy ground, were chosen to showcase the dramatic, fun, quirky, personal side of politics.

This is also a book about critical thinking. There's just no point in reading about politics if we aren't going to do it with a laser-like vision that cuts through the fog and sees the light, as it were, that separates myth from reality, lies from truth, stupidity from intelligence. If we don't think critically, we risk becoming the dupes of politicians and the system. Where's the sense in that?

So this book has two goals: first, to assemble readings on American politics that capture the excitement, drama, and interest of the political world; and second, to model the kind of critical thinking about that world that will give you the tools you need to deal with it.

What Kind of Readings Are We Using?

In our search for selections for this book, we combed a variety of news sources, from mainstream newspapers and news magazines, to opinion journals, to the Internet. It is both our good fortune and our curse to be living in an age when so much information about politics is available to us: our good fortune because it truly is possible for us to become informed on most matters today, and our curse because there is so much more work to be done in sorting the trustworthy from the unreliable, the true from the fraudulent, the reality from the spin. Long gone are the days when the words from a single trusted news source like Walter Cronkite could sway or soothe a nation. Today, we have to dig deeper, ask tougher questions, and raise a more skeptical eyebrow to understand our world.

The news items we have selected show many faces of politics: idiosyncratic and amusing, as well as serious, weighty, and consequential. They show the good that government can do as well as its darker side. Our goal is to shake the image you may have of politics as totally irrelevant, hopelessly corrupt, or just deadly dull, and give you a healthy appreciation for what it is: a vibrant and important activity that reflects all sides of human nature and that affects our lives in many ways.

Why Bother with Critical Thinking When It's So Much Easier Not To?

Critical thinking sounds like work, and it sounds like fault-finding—two potentially unpleasant activities. It may be hard work at first (what skill worth having isn't difficult to begin with?), but what we mean by critical thinking has nothing to do with fault-finding or being negative. *Critical* in this case means careful evaluation and vigilant judgment. It means being wary of the surface appearance of what we hear and read and digging deeper to look for the subtext—what a person means and intends, whether that person has evidence for his or her conclusions, and what the political implications of the conclusions really are.

Becoming adept at critical thinking has a number of benefits:

We become much better students. The skills of the critical thinker are not just the skills of the good citizen; they are the skills of the scholar. When we read we figure out what is important quickly and easily, we know which questions to ask to tease out more meaning, we can decide whether what we are reading is worth our time, and we know what to take with us and what to discard.

We are better able to hold our own in political (or other) arguments. We think more logically and clearly, we are more persuasive, and we impress people with our grasp of reason and fact. There is not a career in the world that is not enhanced by critical thinking skills.

We learn to be good democratic citizens. Critical thinking helps us sort through the barrage of information that assails us regularly and teaches us to process this information thoughtfully. Critical awareness of what our leaders are doing and the ability to understand and evaluate what they tell us is the lifeblood of democratic government.

Although it sounds like a dull and dusty activity, critical thinking can be vital and enjoyable. When we are good at it, it empowers and liberates us. We are not at the mercy of others' conclusions and decisions; we can evaluate facts and arguments for ourselves, turning conventional wisdom upside down and exploring the world of ideas with confidence.

How Does One Learn to Think Critically?

The trick to learning how to think critically is to do it. It helps to have a model to follow, however, and in this book we provide one. The focus of critical thinking here is the understanding of political argument. *Argument* in this case doesn't refer to a confrontation or a fight, but rather to a political contention, based on a set of assumptions, supported by evidence, leading to a clear, well-developed conclusion with consequences for how we understand the world.

Critical thinking involves constantly asking questions about the arguments you read: Whose argument is it? What is the basic case and what values underlie it? What evidence is used to back it up? What conclusions are drawn? What difference does the whole thing make? On the assumption that it will be easier for you to remember the questions to ask if you have a little help, we present here a mnemonic device that creates an acronym from the five major steps of critical thinking. Eventually, asking these questions will become second nature, but in the meantime, thinking of them as CLUES to critical thinking about American politics will help you to keep them in mind as you read.

This is what CLUES stands for:

Consider the source and the audience

Lay out the argument, the values, and the assumptions

Uncover the evidence

Evaluate the conclusion

Sort out the political implications

We'll investigate each of these steps in a little more depth.

Consider the Source and the Audience

Who is writing the news item? Where did the item appear? Why was it written? Toward what audience is it directed? What must the author or publisher do to attract and keep the audience? How might that affect content?

Knowing the source and the audience goes a long way in helping you understand where the author is coming from, what his or her intentions are. If the person is a mainstream journalist, he or she probably has a reputation as an objective reporter to preserve and will at least make an honest attempt to provide unbiased information. Even so, knowing the actual news source helps you nail that down. Even in a reputable national paper like the *New York Times* or the *Wall Street Journal*, if the item comes from the editorial pages, you can count on its having an ideological point of view—usually (but not exclusively) liberal in the case of the *Times*, conservative in the case of the *Journal*. Opinion magazines have even more blatant points of view. Readers go to these sources looking for a particular perspective, and that perspective may affect the reliability of the information you find.

Lay Out the Argument, the Values, and the Assumptions

What is the basic argument the author wants to make? What assumptions about the world does he or she make? What values does the author hold about what is important and what government should do? Are all the important terms clearly defined?

If these points aren't clear, the author may be unclear on them as well. A lot of substandard thinking can be found out there, and being able to identify and discard it is a valuable skill. Often we are intimidated by a smart-sounding argument, only to discover on closer examination that it is just a piece of fuzzy thinking. A more insidious case occurs when the author is trying to obscure the point in order to get you to sign on to something you might not otherwise accept. If the argument, values, and assumptions are not perfectly clear and upfront, there may be a hidden agenda you should know about. You don't want to be persuaded by someone who claims to be an advocate for democracy, only to find out that, by *democracy*, he or she means something completely different than you do.

Uncover the Evidence

Has the author done basic research to back up his or her argument with facts and evidence? Good arguments cannot be based on gut feelings, rumor, or wishful thinking. They should be based on hard evidence—either empirical, verifiable observations about the world or solid, logical reasoning. If the argument is worth being held, it should stand up to rigorous examination, and the author should be able to defend it on these grounds. If the evidence or logic is missing, the argument can usually be dismissed.

Evaluate the Conclusion

Is the argument successful? Does it convince you? Why or why not? Does it change your mind about any beliefs you held previously? Does accepting this argument require you to rethink any of your other beliefs?

Conclusions should follow logically from the assumptions and values of an argument, if solid evidence and reasoning support it. What is the conclusion here? What is the author asking you to accept as the product of his or her argument? Does it make sense to you? Do you "buy" it? If you do, does it fit with your other ideas, or do you need to refine what you thought previously? Have you learned from this argument, or have you merely had your own beliefs reinforced?

Sort Out the Political Implications

What is the political significance of this argument? What difference does this argument make to your understanding of the way the political world works? How does it affect who gets what scarce resources, and how they get them? How does it affect who wins in the political process and who loses?

Political news is valuable if it means something. If it doesn't, it may entertain you, but essentially it wastes your time if it claims to be something more than entertainment. Make the information you get prove its importance. If it doesn't, find a different news source on which to rely.

So, How Does This Book Work?

Each chapter of this book focuses on one of the main topics in a typical introductory American politics course. In each chapter we provide a selection of articles, transcripts, and other forms of political information. There are endless possibilities to include in the reader, so at the beginning of each piece we discuss our thought process in including the particular selection. Although our goal is to provide new and current information, the last selection in each chapter is typically much older, presenting a classic perspective on the subject. These classics can be as vitally relevant as the current daily news, and it is crucial that we be able to bring the same critical thinking skills to bear on them.

Sometimes the best way to learn how to do something is to watch someone else doing it. While that might be easy when it comes to tying a knot or chopping an onion, it is difficult when it comes to thinking. To model the way the CLUES steps work, we conclude each article with a CLUES box that sets out several questions you should be asking yourself as you take each step. Don't just gloss over these questions. Think about them, and answer each of them carefully. As you do, your understanding of the article will deepen, you will see more clearly what its strengths and weaknesses are, and you will be able to evaluate it more thoroughly. Eventually you will figure out what questions you should be asking on your own. When you get to that point, feel free to leave the CLUES boxes behind. You will be well on your way to being a critical thinker in your own right—an effective citizen and a promising scholar.

About the Editors

Christine Barbour teaches in the political science department and the Honors College at Indiana University, where she has become increasingly interested in how teachers of large classes can maximize what their students learn. At Indiana, Professor Barbour has been a Lilly Fellow, working on a project to increase student retention in large introductory courses, and a member of the Freshmen Learning Project, a university-wide effort to improve the first-year undergraduate experience. She has served on the *New York Times* College Advisory Board, working with other educators to develop ways to integrate newspaper reading into the undergraduate curriculum. She has won several teaching honors. The two awarded by her students mean the most to her: the Indiana University Student Alumni Association Award for Outstanding Faculty and the Indiana University Chapter of the Society of Professional Journalists Brown Derby Award. She is the author, with Gerald Wright, of *Keeping the Republic: Power and Citizenship in American Politics*, 4th edition (2009). When not teaching or writing textbooks, Professor Barbour enjoys playing with her dogs, traveling, and writing about food. She is the food editor for *Bloom Magazine* and a coauthor of *Indiana Cooks!* (2005) and *Home Grown Indiana* (2009). She is currently working on a textbook about food politics and a book about local politics, development, and the fishing industry in Apalachicola, Florida.

Matthew J. Streb is professor and chair in the department of political science at Northern Illinois University. His most recent research examines the effects of the politicization of judicial elections. He is the author of *The New Electoral Politics of Race* (2002) and *Rethinking American Electoral Democracy* (2011) and the editor or coeditor of several other books, including *Polls and Politics* (2004), *Academic Freedom at the Dawn of a New Century* (2006), *Running for Judge* (2007), and *Law and Election Politics* (2013). Professor Streb has published articles in such journals as *Political Research Quarterly*, *Public Opinion Quarterly*, *Political Behavior*, *Election Law Journal*, and *American Politics Research*. In 2008 he received the NIU Foundation Award for Faculty Excellence. He specializes and teaches in the areas of parties, elections, polling and public opinion, Congress, civil rights movements, and research methods, and regularly teaches sections of Introduction to American Government.

1

Introduction to American Politics

It's a riddle fit for a sphinx:

What is both an inspiring pursuit and a mind-numbing turn-off? A noble calling to serve an interest greater than oneself, and a degrading scramble for personal advantage? A spellbinding spectacle of the human passion for excellence, and a tedious litany of scandal and corruption?

The newest reality show on TV? Hardly. It's *politics* . . . the oldest reality show on earth.

How can politics embody so many contradictions? Politics is a reflection of human nature, itself a strange brew of opposites and incongruities. After all, politics is the process by which we distribute scarce resources like power and influence. Everybody wants them, but not everybody can have them. The stakes are high, and the methods are often cutthroat. But politics is also the means by which we come together to do what we cannot do alone—to build governments, construct highway systems, feed the poor, work for peace, and explore the skies. The same process of politics exploits our worst nature, and embraces our best nature.

As such, politics is a distinctively human activity, and in many ways it is our saving grace. Watch the family dogs when they want the same bone—they bite and snarl and pull each other away by the throat. Never once do they stop, call a meeting, attempt to reason or compromise or share. The strongest wins by violence and intimidation—every time. Human beings sometimes resort to the same tactics, but politics offers us an alternative—a way to resolve disputes without fighting and without coercion. Politics is the process of making decisions about who should get what valued resources, through discussion and debate, compromise and cooperation, bargaining, trade-offs, even bribery and graft sometimes, but always through human interaction that offers the possibility of a peaceful resolution.

American Government: The Democratic Experiment

In the United States we are fortunate to be living in the midst of a grand democratic experiment. In democracies, the people who are governed have rights that government cannot infringe upon, and what's more, they have a voice in the way they are governed. To the extent that they make their voice heard through the political process, their rights are expanded and protected. To the extent that they keep silent, they are often ignored by the system. Their rights can shrink or be trumped by the demands and concerns of more vocal citizens.

The United States is the first case of democracy being practiced for such a long time, on such a large scale. We call it an experiment because, like all experiments, we really do not know how it will turn out, although we have hopes and expectations. It is tempting to think that it will last for all time—that human beings, in America anyway, have solved the myriad problems that have afflicted societies through the ages and discovered the key to living in freedom and peace forever. But that is not likely. The founders themselves warned that they had put together a system requiring careful maintenance. Benjamin Franklin adjured a woman outside Constitution Hall that they had created a republic, "if you can keep it."

Democracies take time and effort, and lots of it, if they are to survive. They require that those who live in them be vigilant and careful, that they know something about how the system works, that they keep an eye on their leaders, that they be jealous of their rights and conscious of their obligations—that they be, in short, good citizens. Political philosopher Benjamin Barber notes that "the price of liberty is citizenship," and that "free societies are sustained only by hard work."[1]

A Civic Crisis?

And yet, at least until recently, many observers of American politics have argued that we are in a crisis of citizenship—a civic crisis manifested by vast public ignorance about the political system and by something worse, an indifference and cynicism that leave citizens cold, untouched, and uninterested in learning who their leaders are and how they lead. In an important book about this problem, *Why Americans Hate Politics*, *Washington Post* columnist E. J. Dionne warns that "[a] nation that hates politics will not long survive as a democracy."[2]

Political apathy and low levels of political knowledge are not spread equally throughout the population—there are decided generational effects. Those raised during the Great Depression and World War II are far more likely to see government in a positive light and are far more likely to vote for the things they want. Baby boomers raised in the fifties, sixties, and seventies may have lived through the disillusionment of the Watergate scandal, but they also had the positive political experiences of working for civil rights, protesting the Vietnam War, and supporting early environmental efforts in this country. They too vote in fairly large numbers. As they get ready to retire, they are lobbying government to protect Social Security, to build up Medicare, and to look after the interests of an aging but politically active cohort.

It is the generation of young Americans who scholars and pundits have worried about being most truly lost politically. Generation X, Generation Y, Generation

Next—poll after poll of people from their teens to their thirties tell us that most young people have not seen government as relevant to their lives, responsive to their concerns, or worth their time and trouble. Although these same generations volunteer in churches, neighborhoods, and schools in record numbers, their interest in community life has not extended to government life. And in a giant self-fulfilling prophecy, most politicians continue to respond to the issues of the middle-aged and elderly people who vote, and not the young people who have become ever more cynical about the process.

The Readings in This Chapter

The first two readings in this chapter suggest that the presidential election in 2008 gave observers reason to hope that younger generations of Americans might be reengaging in the political system. In the first, the *Washington Post*'s Ezra Klein, only 24 himself in 2008, discusses the policy changes that occurred in the country in the four years following Barack Obama's first election. In the second reading, political scientist Robert Putnam, writing in the *Boston Globe*, suggests that younger voters are members of a generation shaped by 9/11 and captured by the idea of national service. Finally, President John F. Kennedy presents a classic American view of patriotism and national service. As he notes, his election represented the passing of the torch to a new political generation, much as would President Obama's election nearly fifty years later. What views of national service and political engagement are likely to hold sway with the newest generation of citizens?

Notes

1. Benjamin R. Barber, "Foreword." In *Education for Citizenship*, edited by Grant Reeher and Joseph Cammarano, ix. Lanham, MD.: Rowman & Littlefield, 1997.
2. E. J. Dionne Jr., *Why Americans Hate Politics*, 355. New York: Touchstone Books, 1991.

● ●

1.1   A Remarkable, Historic Period of Change
Ezra Klein, *Washington Post*

Why We Chose This Piece

Cynics like to argue that democratic politics in the United States doesn't matter, that people coming together collectively cannot effect change because the corridors of power in Washington are filled with rich lobbyists and corrupt politicians. This piece, by Ezra Klein, suggests otherwise—that at some periods in our history, democratic politics can be a powerful tool indeed. We thought it was a fitting (and hopeful) start to a critical thinking reader about American government.

Five days isn't a long time to digest a presidential election, all that came before it, and all that's likely to come after. But it's long enough to get a bit of perspective.

Selection published: November 11, 2012

Max Weber wrote that "politics is the strong and slow boring of hard boards." It is not a vocation that rewards impatience. Progress is slow. It's tough. It requires compromises and is marked by disappointments. It's incremental even when it needs to be transformational. At least, that's how it usually is.

But step back and take an accounting of these last few years: The United States of America, a land where slaves were kept 150 years ago and bathrooms were segregated as recently as 50 years ago, elected and reelected our first black president. We passed and ratified a universal health-care system. We saw the first female Speaker of the House, the first Hispanic Supreme Court Justice, and the first openly gay member of the Senate. We stopped a Great Depression, rewrote the nation's financial regulations, and nearly defaulted on our debt for the first time in our history. Connecticut, Iowa, Massachusetts, New Hampshire, New York, Vermont, Maine, Maryland, Washington and the District of Columbia legalized gay marriage, and the president and the vice president both proclaimed their support. Colorado and Washington legalized marijuana. We killed the most dangerous terrorist in the world and managed two wars. We've seen inequality and debt skyrocket to some of the highest levels in American history. We passed a stimulus and investment bill that will transform everything from medical records to education and began a drone campaign that will likely be seen as an epochal shift in the way the United States conducts war.

Americans of good faith disagree over the worth of these initiatives and the nature of these milestones. None of us know the verdict that history will render. But we can say with certainty that the pace of change has been breathlessly fast. We have toppled so many barriers, passed so many reforms, completed so many long quests, begun so many experiments, that even those of us who've been paying attention have become inured to how much has happened.

It is common, for instance, to hear pundits wonder why the president didn't invest in long-term infrastructure after the financial crisis or move Medicare beyond fee-for-service as a way to cut the debt, either forgetting or never knowing the stimulus was one of the largest one-time infrastructure investments in the nation's history and that the Affordable Care Act is the most ambitious effort to move American health care towards a pay-for-quality paradigm ever mounted.

The even more frequent complaint is that the pace and scale of change has been, if anything, insufficient. The stimulus should've been bigger, the health reforms more ambitious, the largest banks broken apart, the wars either finished more swiftly or expanded more decisively. All that may be true, but it doesn't obviate the remarkable pace and scale of the changes that have come.

More troublesome is that even once change has happened, it takes time for it to be felt. The health-care law, for instance, won't go into effect until 2014. And in some cases, the extraordinary efforts were meant to keep something from happening. Our success in stopping another Great Depression will be studied by economists for years to come, but in real people's lives, that work meant less change, not more, though we should be thankful for that.

Political journalism, meanwhile, is built to obscure change once it's happened. The demands of reporting the news require us to focus on what's being done, rather than what's been done (notice how, less than a week after the presidential election, we have already moved on to the Petraeus affair). The focus on conflict elevates voices that argue that we haven't done nearly enough, or that what we've done wasn't worth doing. The internal culture of the media encourages a kind of jaded cynicism—you're always safer pretending to have seen it all before than admitting to never have seen anything like it.

There is a theory in evolutionary biology called "punctuated equilibrium." It holds that most species don't change much for long periods of time, but then they change dramatically, in rapid bursts, over geologically short periods of time.

Political scientists Frank Baumgartner and Bryan Jones have argued that "punctuated equilibrium" describes the path of political systems, too. Typically, politics is held in stasis, with little progress being made in the slow boring of those hard boards. But when change does come, it's not a steady process of incremental advances but a breathless flurry in which the boards give all at once.

Whether we intended to or not, whether it was sufficient or not, whether we liked it or not, we have been living through a remarkable period of political change in these last few years. We have bored through so many hard boards that we're no longer surprised when we reach the other side, and we mainly wonder why we haven't gotten through more of them, or why we didn't choose different ones. But viewed against most other eras in American life, the pace of policy change in these last few years has been incredibly fast. Historians, looking back from more quiescent periods, will marvel at all that we have lived through. Activists, frustrated at their inability to shake their countrymen out of their tranquility, will wish they'd been born in a moment when things were actually getting done, a moment like this one.

Consider the source and the audience

- Ezra Klein is a relatively young (born in 1984) writer who has a blog called *Wonkblog* at the *Washington Post* website. His work appears in the *Post* and other political outlets, and he frequently appears on MSNBC, a liberal cable station. While his politics are clearly left of center, his passion, and the passion of his blog, is for the nitty-gritty details of policy. Knowing all that about him, how would you expect him to think about the question of political change?
- For whom is he writing? Who would be likely to read a blog called *Wonkblog*, anyway?

Lay out the argument, the values, and the assumptions

- Writing right after Obama's reelection in 2012, Klein notes a number of policy changes that took place during his first administration. How does Klein think political change normally takes place, and what is different about the period he discusses?
- What is the theory of punctuated equilibrium, and how does it apply to policy?
- Does Klein suggest that the policy changes he writes about are good or bad things? What forces work to obscure the pace of change?

Uncover the evidence

- Klein provides lots of examples to support his claim that the four years he is discussing have been a time of unusual policy change. Is that enough for you to evaluate his argument that this change is unusual?
- What else would it be helpful for you to know?

Evaluate the conclusion

- Klein suggests that the first Obama administration was a time of great and good change, but he acknowledges that there are those who think it was a time of great and bad change as well. Is it possible to disagree with the conclusion that it was a time of great change?

Sort out the political significance

- Klein says that future activists will wish they had lived during the times he discusses because so many things got done. Does he help you to think about what those future activists could do to replicate the success of activists from 2008–2012?
- What kinds of political change would you like to see, and what could you do to bring them about?

1.2   The Rebirth of American Civic Life

Robert D. Putnam, *Boston Globe*

Why We Chose This Piece

In 1995 political scientist Robert Putnam wrote a book called Bowling Alone *about declining civic life and community in America. In this 2008 article he changes his tune, talking about a "rebirth of American civic life," prompted by the effect of the national tragedy of 9/11 on young people. He is happy to see the excitement as this generation of Americans comes of political age, but he is worried that their enthusiasm for politics will wane if the rules of the game appear to be rigged. His specific concern is with some pretty arcane rules in the Democratic Party that have the potential to overrule the results of the primaries and caucuses by choosing a nominee other than the winner of the most delegates in those contests. Note that his concern here is with the Democrats because (1) Obama had generated unusual levels of enthusiastic support from younger voters and (2) Republicans have different primary rules than the Democrats. John McCain, the winner of the Republican primaries and caucuses, was never in danger of not being selected by his party.*

Selection published: March 2, 2008

As you read the article, don't worry too much about the details of the Florida and Michigan primaries or the Democratic "superdelegates"—you will learn more about those topics as you get further into the study of American politics. For now, concentrate on what Putnam has to say about civic engagement and young people—what he calls the "new Greatest Generation"—and the importance of "the simple playground rules of fairness" to keeping people engaged in the system. If you are between eighteen and twenty-four years old, do you think he has accurately described your generation's political experience? If you were a Democratic voter, how would you have felt if party officials had chosen Clinton over Obama?

In the mushrooming procedural debate about Democratic superdelegates and the uncontested Florida and Michigan primaries, more is at stake than the identity of the presidential nominee or even the Democrats' chances of victory in November. Primaries and caucuses coast to coast in the last two months have evinced the sharpest increase in civic engagement among American youth in at least a half-century, portending a remarkable revitalization of American democracy. But that rebirth of American civic life would be aborted if the decision rendered by millions of ordinary Americans could be overturned by a backroom deal among political insiders. The issue is not public jurisprudence or obscure party regulations or the alleged "wisdom" of party elders, but simple playground notions of fairness.

Throughout the last four decades of the 20th century, young people's engagement in American civic life declined year after year with depressing regularity. In fall 1966, well before the full flowering of Vietnam War protests, a UCLA poll of college freshmen nationwide found that "keeping up with politics" was a "very important" goal in their lives for fully 60 percent.

Thirty-four years later that figure had plummeted to 28 percent. In 1972, when the vote was first extended to 18-year-olds, turnout in the presidential election among 18- to 24-year-olds was a disappointing 52 percent. But even beginning at that modest level, rates of voting in presidential elections by young people steadily fell throughout the '70s, '80s, and '90s, reaching barely 36 percent in 2000. National commissions bemoaned the seemingly inexorable increase in youthful apathy and incivism. The National Commission on Civic Renewal said, "When we assess our country's civic and moral condition, we are deeply troubled. . . . We are in danger of becoming a nation of spectators."

Then came the attacks of Sept. 11, 2001, a national tragedy, but also a vivid reminder that we are all in this together. Civic seismometers across the land showed a sharp spike in virtually every measure of community-mindedness. It was, I wrote at the time, not only a tragedy, but also the sort of opportunity for civic revival that comes along once or twice a century. Just as Pearl Harbor had spawned the civic-minded "Greatest Generation," so too Sept. 11 might turn out to produce a more civically engaged generation of young people.

For most Americans the half-life of the civic boomlet after the attacks was barely six months. Within a year measures of civic engagement had returned to the previous levels, from which they have barely budged since. Except among young people.

Among the cohort of Americans caught by 9/11 in their formative years, the effects of the attacks on their civic consciousness were more enduring. The annual UCLA chart of interest in politics jumped upward in 2001 for the first time in decades and has kept rising every year since.

Last month the UCLA researchers reported that "For today's freshmen, discussing politics is more prevalent now than at any point in the past 41 years." This and other evidence led us and other observers to speak hopefully of a 9/11 generation, perhaps even a "new Greatest Generation." In the 2004 and 2006 elections, turnout among young people began at last to climb after decades of decline, reaching the highest point in 20 years in 2006. As we approached the presidential season of 2008, young Americans were, in effect, coiled for civic action, not because of their stage of life, but because of the lingering effects of the unifying national crisis they had experienced in their formative years.

The exceptionally lively presidential nominating contests of this year—and, it must be said, the extraordinary candidacy of Barack Obama—have sparked into white hot flame a pile of youthful kindling that had been stacked and ready to flare for more than six years. The 18-year-olds first eligible to vote in 2008 were in sixth grade when the twin towers fell, and their older sisters and brothers who were college seniors in September 2001 are now 28 or 29. It is precisely this group, above all others in America, that has pushed participation rates in this spring's caucuses and primaries to record levels. Turnout in this spring's electoral contests so far has generally been higher than in previous presidential nominating contests, but for twentysomethings the rise has been truly phenomenal—turnout often three or four times greater than ever before measured.

The 2008 elections are thus the coming-out party of this new Greatest Generation. Their grandparents of the original Greatest Generation were the civic pillars of American democracy for more than a half-century, and at long last, just as that generation is leaving the scene, reinforcements are arriving. Americans of every political persuasion should rejoice at this epochal swing of the generational pendulum, for it portends precisely the sort of civic renaissance for which Jeremiahs have been calling for many years.

This, then, is what is at stake in the otherwise inside-baseball controversies about superdelegates and pledged delegates and the uncontested Florida and Michigan primaries—controversies now roiling Democratic party leaders. If the results of the caucuses and primaries are, despite record-breaking rates of popular participation, overturned by unelected (though officially legitimate) superdelegates or by delegates from states that all candidates had previously agreed not to contest, the lesson for the young civic stalwarts would be unmistakable—democratic politics is a sham. Politics is actually controlled by party bosses behind the scenes. Civic engagement is for suckers.

From Little League to student council races, we all learn to accept defeats we have lost fair and square. But losing in a contest in which the rules can be rigged teaches that the game is not worth the candle. Who can honestly doubt that if the Democratic presidential candidate preferred by a majority of the delegates elected in this spring's competitive contests (and by the overwhelming majority of young voters) were to be rejected solely by the power of unelected delegates (or those "elected" without any serious competition), the unmistakable civics lesson would be catastrophic for this incipient cadre of super citizens?

So as the superdelegates, the two campaigns, and Democratic Party leaders contemplate how to resolve the procedural issues before them—what to do about Michigan and Florida, and how superdelegates should vote—let's hope that they weigh the consequences not merely for their own candidates this year, and not merely for the Democratic prospects in the fall, but for the future vitality of American democracy.

Consider the source and the audience

- This article appeared in the *Boston Globe* in March 2008, just as it began to sink in that Barack Obama was going to do better than anyone had guessed in the Democratic nominating contest, but at a time when Hillary Clinton still had a lead in the unelected superdelegate count as well as "victories" in the uncontested and uncounted primaries in Florida and Michigan. Who is Putnam speaking to here—the young people excited about Obama's candidacy or the Democratic Party officials he feared would "throw" the election to Clinton?

Lay out the argument, the values, and the assumptions

- What does Putnam mean by referring to the "Greatest Generation?" Why does he value civic participation? How does he define "fairness?"
- What is the link between civic engagement and fairness, in his mind?

Uncover the evidence

- What evidence does Putman provide that today's young people are a "new Greatest Generation?"
- Does he have empirical evidence to back up his claim that if Democratic officials overrule the result of the Democratic primary process, then "the rebirth of American civic life would be aborted?" Does he need evidence for that claim?

Evaluate the conclusion

- Was Putnam right? Do you think that 18–24-year-olds have been shaped to be more politically active by growing up in the shadow of 9/11?
- What impact would it have had on young Democratic voters you know if Clinton had been made the nominee despite Obama's primary and caucus victories? How important is it in securing your own investment in a system that the rules be perceived to be "fair"?

Sort out the political implications

- The Democrats eventually decided not to count the Michigan and Florida primary results at full strength, and the superdelegates ended up moving overwhelmingly to Obama. Do you think they and the Democratic officials might have been persuaded by arguments about the probability of disillusioning and alienating a generation of new voters?

• •

1.3 Inaugural Address
John F. Kennedy

Why We Chose This Piece

John F. Kennedy's inaugural address, now more than forty years old, calls on Americans facing a long battle to preserve their ideals and their way of life to exhibit a selfless citizenship and devotion to country. His words to a nation challenged by the Cold War are poignant today, when the same nation is struggling with war of a different but equally destructive kind. One definition of an effective leader may be that a leader holds up a mirror before a nation's citizens and helps them see themselves as a people bound by values and heritage, willing to sacrifice for worthy common goals. How does Kennedy take the opportunity presented by this speech to establish himself as a national leader?

We observe today not a victory of party, but a celebration of freedom—symbolizing an end, as well as a beginning—signifying renewal, as well as change. For I have sworn before you and Almighty God the same solemn oath our forebears prescribed nearly a century and three-quarters ago.

The world is very different now. For man holds in his mortal hands the power to abolish all forms of human poverty and all forms of human life. And yet the same revolutionary beliefs for which our forebears fought are still at issue around the globe—the belief that the rights of man come not from the generosity of the state, but from the hand of God.

We dare not forget today that we are the heirs of that first revolution. Let the word go forth from this time and place, to friend and foe alike, that the torch has been passed to a new generation of Americans—born in this century, tempered by war, disciplined by a hard and bitter peace, proud of our ancient heritage, and unwilling to witness or permit the slow undoing of those human rights to which this nation has always been committed, and to which we are committed today at home and around the world.

Let every nation know, whether it wishes us well or ill, that we shall pay any price, bear any burden, meet any hardship, support any friend, oppose any foe, to assure the survival and the success of liberty.

This much we pledge—and more.

To those old allies whose cultural and spiritual origins we share, we pledge the loyalty of faithful friends. United there is little we cannot do in a host of cooperative ventures. Divided there is little we can do—for we dare not meet a powerful challenge at odds and split asunder.

To those new states whom we welcome to the ranks of the free, we pledge our word that one form of colonial control shall not have passed away merely to be replaced by a far more iron tyranny. We shall not always expect to find them supporting our view. But we shall always hope to find them strongly supporting their own freedom—and to remember that, in the past, those who foolishly sought power by riding the back of the tiger ended up inside.

Selection delivered: January 20, 1961

To those people in the huts and villages of half the globe struggling to break the bonds of mass misery, we pledge our best efforts to help them help themselves, for whatever period is required—not because the Communists may be doing it, not because we seek their votes, but because it is right. If a free society cannot help the many who are poor, it cannot save the few who are rich.

To our sister republics south of our border, we offer a special pledge: to convert our good words into good deeds, in a new alliance for progress, to assist free men and free governments in casting off the chains of poverty. But this peaceful revolution of hope cannot become the prey of hostile powers. Let all our neighbors know that we shall join with them to oppose aggression or subversion anywhere in the Americas. And let every other power know that this hemisphere intends to remain the master of its own house.

To that world assembly of sovereign states, the United Nations, our last best hope in an age where the instruments of war have far outpaced the instruments of peace, we renew our pledge of support—to prevent it from becoming merely a forum for invective, to strengthen its shield of the new and the weak, and to enlarge the area in which its writ may run.

Finally, to those nations who would make themselves our adversary, we offer not a pledge but a request: that both sides begin anew the quest for peace, before the dark powers of destruction unleashed by science engulf all humanity in planned or accidental self-destruction.

We dare not tempt them with weakness. For only when our arms are sufficient beyond doubt can we be certain beyond doubt that they will never be employed.

But neither can two great and powerful groups of nations take comfort from our present course—both sides overburdened by the cost of modern weapons, both rightly alarmed by the steady spread of the deadly atom, yet both racing to alter that uncertain balance of terror that stays the hand of mankind's final war.

So let us begin anew—remembering on both sides that civility is not a sign of weakness, and sincerity is always subject to proof. Let us never negotiate out of fear, but let us never fear to negotiate.

Let both sides explore what problems unite us instead of belaboring those problems which divide us.

Let both sides, for the first time, formulate serious and precise proposals for the inspection and control of arms, and bring the absolute power to destroy other nations under the absolute control of all nations.

Let both sides seek to invoke the wonders of science instead of its terrors. Together let us explore the stars, conquer the deserts, eradicate disease, tap the ocean depths, and encourage the arts and commerce.

Let both sides unite to heed, in all corners of the earth, the command of Isaiah—to "undo the heavy burdens, and [to] let the oppressed go free."

And, if a beachhead of cooperation may push back the jungle of suspicion, let both sides join in creating a new endeavor—not a new balance of power, but a new world of law—where the strong are just, and the weak secure, and the peace preserved.

All this will not be finished in the first one hundred days. Nor will it be finished in the first one thousand days; nor in the life of this Administration; nor even perhaps in our lifetime on this planet. But let us begin.

In your hands, my fellow citizens, more than mine, will rest the final success or failure of our course. Since this country was founded, each generation of Americans has been summoned to give testimony to its national loyalty. The graves of young Americans who answered the call to service surround the globe.

Now the trumpet summons us again—not as a call to bear arms, though arms we need—not as a call to battle, though embattled we are—but a call to bear the burden of a long twilight struggle, year in and year out, "rejoicing in hope; patient in tribulation," a struggle against the common enemies of man: tyranny, poverty, disease, and war itself.

Can we forge against these enemies a grand and global alliance, North and South, East and West, that can assure a more fruitful life for all mankind? Will you join in that historic effort?

In the long history of the world, only a few generations have been granted the role of defending freedom in its hour of maximum danger. I do not shrink from this responsibility—I welcome it. I do not believe that any of us would exchange places with any other people or any other generation. The energy, the faith, the devotion which we bring to this endeavor will light our country and all who serve it. And the glow from that fire can truly light the world.

And so, my fellow Americans, ask not what your country can do for you; ask what you can do for your country.

My fellow citizens of the world, ask not what America will do for you, but what together we can do for the freedom of man.

Finally, whether you are citizens of America or citizens of the world, ask of us here the same high standards of strength and sacrifice which we ask of you. With a good conscience our only sure reward, with history the final judge of our deeds, let us go forth to lead the land we love, asking His blessing and His help, but knowing that here on earth God's work must truly be our own.

Consider the source and the audience

- Here you are reading a president's inaugural address. What are the goals of such a speech? Is it addressed only to Americans?

Lay out the argument, the values, and the assumptions

- Is Kennedy making an argument in this speech? How might the claims made in an inaugural address differ from those in a more traditional argument?
- What is Kennedy's major point? Who are the new generation of Americans to which the torch is being passed? How does their political experience make them different?
- What is Kennedy's view of a good government? What is his view of how the world should be ordered? What values are worth fighting for? What is his view of national service?

Uncover the evidence

- What kind of evidence is Kennedy obliged to provide in support of the claims he makes here?
- When can ideals, convictions, and historical tradition substitute for factual evidence?

Evaluate the conclusion

- What does Kennedy see as the fundamental tasks to be done?
- Were there other visions of America and its role in the world that he might have offered then? What values might this role have been based on?

Sort out the political implications

- How effective do you imagine this speech was as a political call to arms and a call "to bear the burden?" How might it have shaped the generations to whom it was addressed?
- How might such a speech be received today?

2

Political Culture and Ideology

How do we recognize "people like us"—the people we grow up with, go to school with, attend church with, hang out with? The people who live in our neighborhoods, our towns, our cities, and our states? How do we identify Americans from all the other people in the world? That odd, intangible thing that separates "us" from "them," that answers the question "who are we?" is called political culture—the set of ideas, beliefs, and values about who we are as a nation, what we believe in, what kind of government we should have, and what our relationship to that government should be.

Political culture can be a hard concept to grasp because it is abstract. We can't see it or touch it; in fact, it is very difficult to be aware of our own political culture when we are immersed in it. Like kids looking through play glasses with tinted lenses, we see everything colored by the lens of our culture. We think we are seeing the truth—the way things really are—but really we see just our version of reality, shaped by our cultural preferences and values. Other people observing us from other cultures can often see more easily what our own familiarity with our values and beliefs hides from us. Sometimes we see the differences most clearly when we are traveling in another country among people who are not "like us."

Understanding political culture is important because the way we think about ourselves politically and the values we share help to shape our political systems and the way politics takes place within them. Today, our political culture is based on a commitment to individual freedom from extensive government action; on the value of equality, defined as equal opportunity rather than equality of results; and on the principle that decisions should be made through a representative democracy, heeding the voices of individuals and organized interests in the formation of public policy. All these values together go into the ideal of the "American dream"—the idea that all citizens have the opportunity to live prosperous lives, that they are entitled to "life, liberty and the pursuit of happiness."

Within these values, of course, there is plenty of room for disagreement about what sorts of political, economic, and cultural choices we as a nation should make. Sometimes these days it seems the ideas that divide us, called ideologies, are much stronger than the culture that unites us, but that is mostly because the arguments about what kind of country we want to live in are loud and the consensus about the things that are not contested is quiet. Ideologies in the United States pretty much fall under two labels—liberal, which corresponds with the Democratic Party, and conservative, which corresponds with the Republican Party. Within each ideology there is lots of room for disagreement as well, so Americans frequently hear debates about what ideas are truly liberal or progressive, and who counts as a "real" conservative. One of the joys of living in a free society where the culture puts a premium on free speech is that we get to hear a lot of these debates.

We have chosen the selections in this chapter to showcase different interpretations of the ideas that unite us as Americans and of the ideas that divide us. The first article, by David Brooks of the *New York Times*, compares our political culture and the individualism on which it is based with the collectivism of China—the new powerhouse on the international stage. Will the "Chinese dream" someday be as compelling an idea around the world as the American dream? The second draws out what it claims is a "culture war" about the foundations of our system, with the author, Arthur C. Brooks (no relation to David), arguing that some liberal Americans reject the free enterprise system in favor of state control of the economy. Brooks's argument notwithstanding, however, what is striking is how much consensus there is in the United States on the value of a capitalist economic system, with both liberals and conservatives committed to the free market. What they differ on is how much to regulate that market, but that is an ideological difference, not one that shakes the very foundations. The third article in this chapter, by Katie Glueck of *Politico*, looks at whether there might not be biological reasons that predispose some to be liberal and others to be conservative. The next two pieces, by Ronald Brownstein of *National Journal* and Thomas Edsall of the *New York Times*, look at the changing ideological terrain in the United States. Finally, in the last selection, we look at President Abraham Lincoln's very famous, and very short, Gettysburg Address, where he lays out a vision of our common American culture that is still used today as a symbol of who we are.

● ●

2.1 Harmony and the Dream
David Brooks, *New York Times*

Why We Chose This Piece

Contemplating the opening ceremonies of the Beijing Olympics, David Brooks, a conservative columnist at the New York Times, *nails one of the central elements of American political culture—our tendency to see the whole as no more than a*

Selection published: August 11, 2008

collection of individual parts. In contrast with collectivist cultures like China's, we credit individuals with their successes and blame them for their failures, generally without looking to see what aspects of society might have boosted the chances of some, or damaged those of others. Even American liberals, who tend to be slightly more willing to look at society in a collectivist way than conservatives, come down firmly in the individualist camp. Although as a conservative American he clearly finds individualism more attractive, Brooks sees certain advantages in China's culture.

When you read this article, you will not only get an appreciation for a part of American culture you probably share, but may never have articulated, but you will also get a comparative sense of how our approach measures up with that of another country. Such comparisons can be valuable when you are looking at as pervasive and all-encompassing a phenomenon as political culture because it gives us an external standpoint from which to consider our own cultural assumptions. Why would such an external standpoint be helpful?

The world can be divided in many ways—rich and poor, democratic and authoritarian—but one of the most striking is the divide between the societies with an individualist mentality and the ones with a collectivist mentality.

This is a divide that goes deeper than economics into the way people perceive the world. If you show an American an image of a fish tank, the American will usually describe the biggest fish in the tank and what it is doing. If you ask a Chinese person to describe a fish tank, the Chinese will usually describe the context in which the fish swim.

These sorts of experiments have been done over and over again, and the results reveal the same underlying pattern. Americans usually see individuals; Chinese and other Asians see contexts.

When the psychologist Richard Nisbett showed Americans individual pictures of a chicken, a cow and hay and asked the subjects to pick out the two that go together, the Americans would usually pick out the chicken and the cow. They're both animals. Most Asian people, on the other hand, would pick out the cow and the hay, since cows depend on hay. Americans are more likely to see categories. Asians are more likely to see relationships.

You can create a global continuum with the most individualistic societies—like the United States or Britain—on one end, and the most collectivist societies—like China or Japan—on the other.

The individualistic countries tend to put rights and privacy first. People in these societies tend to overvalue their own skills and overestimate their own importance to any group effort. People in collective societies tend to value harmony and duty. They tend to underestimate their own skills and are more self-effacing when describing their contributions to group efforts.

Researchers argue about why certain cultures have become more individualistic than others. Some say that Western cultures draw their values from ancient Greece, with its emphasis on individual heroism, while other cultures draw more on tribal philosophies. Recently, some scientists have theorized that it all goes back to microbes. Collectivist societies tend to pop up in parts of the world, especially around the equator, with plenty of disease-causing microbes. In such an environment, you'd want to shun outsiders, who might bring strange diseases, and enforce a certain conformity over eating rituals and social behavior.

Either way, individualistic societies have tended to do better economically. We in the West have a narrative that involves the development of individual reason and conscience during the Renaissance and the Enlightenment, and then the subsequent flourishing of capitalism. According to this narrative, societies get more individualistic as they develop.

But what happens if collectivist societies snap out of their economic stagnation? What happens if collectivist societies, especially those in Asia, rise economically and come to rival the West? A new sort of global conversation develops.

The opening ceremony in Beijing was a statement in that conversation. It was part of China's assertion that development doesn't come only through Western, liberal means, but also through Eastern and collective ones.

The ceremony drew from China's long history, but surely the most striking features were the images of thousands of Chinese moving as one—drumming as one, dancing as one, sprinting on precise formations without ever stumbling or colliding. We've seen displays of mass conformity before, but this was collectivism of the present—a high-tech vision of the harmonious society performed in the context of China's miraculous growth.

If Asia's success reopens the debate between individualism and collectivism (which seemed closed after the cold war), then it's unlikely that the forces of individualism will sweep the field or even gain an edge.

For one thing, there are relatively few individualistic societies on earth. For another, the essence of a lot of the latest scientific research is that the Western idea of individual choice is an illusion and the Chinese are right to put first emphasis on social contexts.

Scientists have delighted to show that so-called rational choice is shaped by a whole range of subconscious influences, like emotional contagions and priming effects (people who think of a professor before taking a test do better than people who think of a criminal). Meanwhile, human brains turn out to be extremely permeable (they naturally mimic the neural firings of people around them). Relationships are the key to happiness. People who live in the densest social networks tend to flourish, while people who live with few social bonds are much more prone to depression and suicide.

The rise of China isn't only an economic event. It's a cultural one. The ideal of a harmonious collective may turn out to be as attractive as the ideal of the American Dream.

It's certainly a useful ideology for aspiring autocrats.

Consider the source and the audience

- The *New York Times* is a mainstream print media outlet, with a slightly left-of-center orientation and an educated readership. How might that affect the way Brooks couches his argument?

Lay out the argument, the values, and the assumptions

- What are the basic principles of the individualism Brooks describes? Of collectivism?
- What does he indicate might be the advantages of each?
- Why does he think collectivism might have an edge? What is its attraction for autocrats—that is, rulers who have unlimited power?

Uncover the evidence

- Brooks uses a variety of kinds of evidence to support his case. Who are his experts and what kinds of evidence does he provide? Is such an eclectic collection of sources more or less persuasive than a single source?

Evaluate the conclusion

- Brooks thinks that China's cultural identity might end up being as persuasive as the American dream. How would you describe the "Chinese dream" he is thinking of?

Sort out the political implications

- Must collectivism go hand in hand with autocracy? Is there such a thing as democratic collectivism?
- Are individualistic cultures necessarily at a disadvantage when confronting collectivist cultures?

2.2 America's New Culture War: Free Enterprise vs. Government Control

Arthur C. Brooks, *Washington Post*

Why We Chose This Piece

The 2012 election presented voters with a stark choice. On the one hand: a vision of an America divided between those who produce and those who freeload on the producers' efforts, helped along by "big government" programs that redistribute wealth (food stamps, welfare, Social Security, and Medicare)—the makers and takers, in the Romney campaign's words. On the other hand: a vision that was based on a more egalitarian view that government should play an essential role in supporting private enterprise and ensuring the well-being of all its citizens. This Washington Post *opinion piece, written in 2010 as the Tea Party movement was*

Selection published: May 23, 2010

taking off in American politics, comes down strongly on behalf of the first vision of American culture. How would Ezra Klein, from Chapter 1, respond to Brooks?

A merica faces a new culture war.

This is not the culture war of the 1990s. It is not a fight over guns, gays or abortion. Those old battles have been eclipsed by a new struggle between two competing visions of the country's future. In one, America will continue to be an exceptional nation organized around the principles of free enterprise—limited government, a reliance on entrepreneurship and rewards determined by market forces. In the other, America will move toward European-style statism grounded in expanding bureaucracies, a managed economy and large-scale income redistribution. These visions are not reconcilable. We must choose.

It is not at all clear which side will prevail. The forces of big government are entrenched and enjoy the full arsenal of the administration's money and influence. Our leaders in Washington, aided by the unprecedented economic crisis of recent years and the panic it induced, have seized the moment to introduce breathtaking expansions of state power in huge swaths of the economy, from the health-care takeover to the financial regulatory bill that the Senate approved Thursday. If these forces continue to prevail, America will cease to be a free enterprise nation.

I call this a culture war because free enterprise has been integral to American culture from the beginning, and it still lies at the core of our history and character. "A wise and frugal government," Thomas Jefferson declared in his first inaugural address in 1801, "which shall restrain men from injuring one another, shall leave them otherwise free to regulate their own pursuits of industry and improvement, and shall not take from the mouth of labor the bread it has earned. This is the sum of good government." He later warned: "To take from one, because it is thought that his own industry and that of his fathers has acquired too much, in order to spare to others, who, or whose fathers, have not exercised equal industry and skill, is to violate arbitrarily the first principle of association, the guarantee to every one of a free exercise of his industry and the fruits acquired by it." In other words, beware government's economic control, and woe betide the redistributors.

Now, as then, entrepreneurship can flourish only in a culture where individuals are willing to innovate and exert leadership; where people enjoy the rewards and face the consequences of their decisions; and where we can gamble the security of the status quo for a chance of future success.

Yet, in his commencement address at Arizona State University on May 13, 2009, President Obama warned against precisely such impulses: "You're taught to chase after all the usual brass rings; you try to be on this "who's who" list or that Top 100 list; you chase after the big money and you figure out how big your corner office is; you worry about whether you have a fancy enough title or a fancy enough car. That's the message that's sent each and every day, or has been in our culture for far too long— that through material possessions, through a ruthless competition pursued only on your own behalf—that's how you will measure success." Such ambition, he cautioned, "may lead you to compromise your values and your principles."

I appreciate the sentiment that money does not buy happiness. But for the president of the United States to actively warn young adults away from economic ambition is remarkable. And he makes clear that he seeks to change our culture.

The irony is that, by wide margins, Americans support free enterprise. A Gallup poll in January found that 86 percent of Americans have a positive image of "free enterprise," with only 10 percent viewing it negatively. Similarly, in March 2009, the Pew Research Center asked individuals from a broad range of demographic groups: "Generally, do you think people are better off in a free-market economy, even though there may be severe ups and downs from time to time, or don't you think so?" Almost 70 percent of respondents agreed that they are better off in a free-market economy, while only 20 percent disagreed.

In fact, no matter how the issue is posed, not more than 30 percent of Americans say they believe we would fare better without free markets at the core of our system. When it comes to support for free enterprise, we are essentially a 70–30 nation.

So here's a puzzle: If we love free enterprise so much, why are the 30 percent who want to change that culture in charge?

It's not simply because of the election of Obama. As much as Republicans may dislike hearing it, statism had effectively taken hold in Washington long before that.

The George W. Bush administration began the huge Wall Street and Detroit bailouts, and for years before the economic crisis, the GOP talked about free enterprise while simultaneously expanding the government with borrowed money and increasing the percentage of citizens with no income tax liability. The 30 percent coalition did not start governing this country with the advent of Obama, Nancy Pelosi and Harry Reid. It has been in charge for years.

But the real tipping point was the financial crisis, which began in 2008. The meltdown presented a golden opportunity for the 30 percent coalition to attack free enterprise openly and remake America in its own image.

And it seized that opportunity. While Republicans had no convincing explanation for the crisis, seemed responsible for it and had no obvious plans to fix it, the statists offered a full and compelling narrative. Ordinary Americans were not to blame for the financial collapse, nor was government. The real culprits were Wall Street and the Bush administration, which had gutted the regulatory system that was supposed to keep banks in line.

The solution was obvious: Vote for a new order to expand the powers of government to rein in the dangerous excesses of capitalism.

It was a convincing story. For a lot of panicky Americans, the prospect of a paternalistic government rescuing the nation from crisis seemed appealing as stock markets and home prices spiraled downward. According to this narrative, government was at fault in just one way: It wasn't big enough. If only there had been more regulators watching the banks more closely, the case went, the economy wouldn't have collapsed.

Yet in truth, it was government housing policy that was at the root of the crisis. Moreover, the financial sector—where the crisis began and where it has had the most serious impact—is already one of the most regulated parts of our economy. The chaos happened despite an extensive, intrusive regulatory framework, not because such a framework didn't exist.

More government—including a super-empowered Federal Reserve, a consumer protection watchdog and greater state powers to wind down financial firms and police market risks—does not mean we will be safe. On the contrary, such changes would give us a false sense of security, especially when Washington, a primary culprit in the crisis, is creating and implementing the new rules.

The statist narrative also held that only massive deficit spending could restore economic growth. "If nothing is done, this recession could linger for years," Obama warned a few days before taking office. "Only government can provide the short-term boost necessary to lift us from a recession this deep and severe. Only government can break the cycle that is crippling our economy."

This proposition is as expensive as it is false. Recessions can and do end without the kind of stimulus we experienced, and attempts to shore up the economy with huge public spending often do little to improve matters and instead chain future generations with debt. In fact, all the evidence so far tells us that the current $787 billion stimulus package has overpromised and underdelivered, especially when it comes to creating jobs.

If we reject the administration's narrative, the 70–30 nation will remain strong. If we accept it, and base our nation's policies on it, we will be well on our way to a European-style social democracy. Punitive taxes and regulations will make it harder to be an entrepreneur, and the rewards of success will be expropriated for the sake of greater income equality.

The new statism in America, made possible by years of drift and accelerated by the panic over the economic crisis, threatens to make us permanently poorer. But that is not the greatest danger. The real risk is that in the new culture war, we will forsake the third unalienable right set out in our Declaration of Independence: the pursuit of happiness.

Free enterprise brings happiness; redistribution does not. The reason is that only free enterprise brings earned success.

Earned success involves the ability to create value honestly—not by inheriting a fortune, not by picking up a welfare check. It doesn't mean making money in and of itself. Earned success is the creation of value in our lives or in the lives of others. Earned success is the stuff of entrepreneurs who seek value through innovation, hard work and passion. Earned success is what parents feel when their children do wonderful things, what social innovators feel when they change lives, what artists feel when they create something of beauty.

Money is not the same as earned success but is rather a symbol, important not for what it can buy but for what it says about how people are contributing and what kind of difference they are making. Money corresponds to happiness only through earned success.

Not surprisingly, unearned money—while it may help alleviate suffering—carries with it no personal satisfaction. Studies of lottery winners, for instance, show that after a brief period of increased happiness, their moods darken as they no longer derive the same enjoyment from the simple pleasures in life, and as the glow of buying things wears off.

The same results emerge with other kinds of unearned income—welfare payments, for example. According to the University of Michigan's 2001 Panel Study of Income Dynamics, going on the welfare rolls increases by 16 percent the likelihood of a person saying that she or he has felt inconsolably sad over the past month. Of course, the misery of welfare recipients probably goes well beyond the check itself. Nonetheless, studies show that recipients are far unhappier than equally poor people who do not receive such government benefits.

Benjamin Franklin (a pretty rich man for his time) grasped the truth about money's inability by itself to deliver satisfaction. "Money never made a man happy yet, nor will it," he declared. "The more a man has, the more he wants. Instead of filling a vacuum, it makes one."

If unearned money does not bring happiness, redistributing money by force won't make for a happier America—and the redistributionists' theory of a better society through income equality falls apart.

The goal of our system should be to give all Americans the greatest opportunities possible to succeed based on their work and merit. And that's exactly what the free enterprise system does: It makes earned success possible for the most people. This is the liberty that enables the true pursuit of happiness.

To win the culture war, those of us in the 70 percent majority must reclaim—and proclaim—the morality of our worldview.

Unfortunately, we often fail to do this. Instead, we sound unabashedly materialistic. We talk about growth rates, inflation and investment, while the 30 percent coalition walks off with the claims to happiness and fairness. (According to Obama, for example, we need to restore "fairness" to our tax code by increasing taxes on the wealthy and exempting more people at the bottom from paying anything.)

The irony is that it is the 30 percent coalition, not the 70 percent majority, that is fundamentally materialistic. What do they consider the greatest problem of poor people in America? Insufficient income. What would be evidence of a fairer society? Greater income equality. For the leaders of the 30 percent coalition, money does buy happiness—as long as it is spread evenly. That is why redistribution of income is a fundamental goal and why free enterprise, which rewards some people and penalizes others, cannot be trusted.

The 70 percent majority, meanwhile, believes that ingenuity and hard work should be rewarded. We admire creative entrepreneurs and disdain rule-making bureaucrats. We know that income inequality by itself is not what makes people unhappy, and that only earned success can make them happy.

We must do more to show that while we use the language of commerce and business, we believe in human flourishing and contentment. We must articulate moral principles that set forth our fundamental values, and we must be prepared to defend them.

This defense is already underway, in a disorganized, grass-roots, American kind of way. Protests against the new statism have flared around the nation for more than a year. And while some have tried to dismiss the "tea party" demonstrations and the town hall protests of last summer as the work of extremists, ignorant backwoodsmen or agents of the health-care industry, these movements reveal much about the culture war that is underway.

Just compare the protests in America with those in Europe. Here, we see tea partiers demonstrating against the government's encroachment on the free enterprise system and protesting the fact that the state is spending too much money bailing out too many people. Why are people protesting in Greece? Because they want the government to give them even more. They are angry because their government—in the face of its worst economic and perhaps existential crisis in decades—won't pay the lavish pensions to which they feel entitled. There's no better example of the cultural difference between America and Europe today, yet it is toward European-style social democracy that the 30 percent coalition wants to move us.

Fortunately, it is hard to dismiss the voice of the voters in some of our most recent electoral contests. Scott Brown won the late Ted Kennedy's Senate seat from Massachusetts in January by declaring himself not an apparatchik Republican but a moral enthusiast for markets. "What made America great?" he asked. "Free markets, free enterprise, manufacturing, job creation. That's how we're gonna do it, not by enlarging government." His cultural pitch for free enterprise hit just the right chord, even in liberal Massachusetts. It struck at the heart of the 30 percent coalition's agenda for America.

Brown's victory—and Rand Paul's triumph in Kentucky's Republican Senate primary last week, for that matter—are but warning shots in the burgeoning culture war. The most intense battles are still ahead.

To win, the 70 percent majority must come together around core principles: that the purpose of free enterprise is human flourishing, not materialism; that we stand for equality of opportunity, not equality of income; that we seek to stimulate true prosperity rather than simply treat poverty; and that we believe in principle over power.

This final idea is particularly challenging. In Washington, a lot of people think they know how to win. They say what is needed are telegenic candidates, dirty tricks and lots of campaign money. To them, thinking long-term means thinking all the way to 2012. In other words, they talk only of tactics, parties and power.

They are wrong. What matters most to Americans is the commitment to principle, not the exercise of power. The electorate did not repudiate free enterprise in 2008; it simply punished an unprincipled Republican Party.

But political turmoil can lead to renewal, and the challenges of this new culture war can help us mobilize and reassert our principles. The 2008 election was perhaps exactly what America needed. Today there is a very real threat that the 30 percent coalition may transform our great nation forever. I hope this threat will clear our thinking enough to bring forth leaders—regardless of political party—with our principles at heart and the ideas to match. If free enterprise triumphs over the quest for political power, America will be the stronger for it.

Consider the source and the audience

- Arthur C. Brooks is the president of the American Enterprise Institute, a conservative Washington think tank. He is writing this piece in the *Washington Post*, where it will get maximum exposure to the movers and shakers in American politics. What is his goal in writing this piece for the *Post*?

Lay out the argument, the values, and the assumptions

- Brooks is articulating a classic argument for free enterprise—that producing value is the source of happiness, and that a system based on the free exchange of goods produces the most value (and thus happiness) for the most people. Brooks, however, claims a more extreme version of that credo—that *only* producing value can bring happiness. Why does he claim that?

- What is the vision of European-style "statism" that he fears?
- Does the threat he sees (embodied by Presidents George W. Bush and Barack Obama and 30 percent of Americans who supposedly reject the free enterprise system) really exist, or is it a "straw man" (a simplified version of an argument set up because it is easier to shoot down than a more complex reality)? Why would he frame it that way if it does not?

Uncover the evidence

- Brooks moves from polling data that show that people receiving government assistance are not happy to the conclusion that it is being on government assistance that actually causes them to be unhappy. Can he make this causal leap?
- Insofar as most of his argument is a moral rather than an empirical or factual case, what kinds of evidence does he need to provide to be persuasive?

Evaluate the conclusion

- Brooks concludes that 70 percent of Americans who embody economic success are under siege by 30 percent who have nothing but handouts from the wealthy. Is this likely or, given the rules of American politics, possible?

Sort out the political significance

- Writing in 2010, right before the summer that saw Tea Party rallies across the country and the huge Tea Party success in the 2010 midterm elections, Brooks's optimism that the Tea Party would renew the vision of American culture that he values does not seem misplaced. How might events since then, especially the 2012 election (in which Republican senator Scott Brown of Massachusetts was defeated), have changed his mind?

2.3 Left, Right: The Brain Science of Politics
Katie Glueck, *Politico*

Why We Chose This Piece

These days in American politics it seems like political ideology—the ideas that divide us into liberals and conservatives—is more potent than ever. While as Americans we share a political culture, we are polarized into opposing political camps in a way that sometimes makes our differences more apparent than our similarities. This article from Politico recounts the work of some social scientists who say the differences between us may be more intractable, but more understandable, than we once thought.

Selection published: March 10, 2013

25

Sick of partisanship in Washington? Blame science.

A growing body of experimental research is finding evidence suggesting that, to some degree, political inclinations and ideological leanings may be tied to innate factors like a person's biology, physiology and genetics.

In fact, Al Gore recently raised the thorny issue when he spoke about political differences in "human nature."

"I think, first of all, scientists now know that there is, in human nature, a divide between what we sometimes call 'liberals' and 'conservatives,'" the former vice president said on MSNBC earlier this year. "And it gives an advantage, you can speculate, to the human species to have some people who are temperamentally inclined to try to change the future, experiment with new things, and others who are temperamentally inclined to say, 'Wait a minute, not too fast, let's make sure we don't do anything rash here.'"

The area of research is relatively new, but researchers say they have already made some startling findings, leaving them with no doubt that they are on the right track. But the nascent field is still struggling to win acceptance in many corners of academia, said Prof. George Marcus of Williams College, an expert in political psychology and the author of the 2012 book "Political Psychology: Neuroscience, Genetics, and Politics."

Even the terms that different groups of researchers use to describe their own work illustrate the debate over how strong a connection to make between biology and belief: Some use names like "biopolitics" or "genopolitics," while others don't go so far, relying instead on broader titles, like "political psychology," that suggest less of a cause-and-effect.

"Those interested in new work find it exciting," Marcus told POLITICO. "Those committed to established ways of thinking are pretty much wedded to rejecting it so far . . . kind of like climate science."

Marcus, whose book explores the notion that factors like genes and brain make-up help shape ideology, predicted that view will eventually become "the dominant way of thinking about how things go," though he noted that many questions in the burgeoning area remain unanswered.

Another leading scholar on the subject, Professor John Hibbing of the University of Nebraska, added, "It's not surprising that there are significant chunks of my colleagues that think it's not a good way to go . . . but they're coming around to it. . . . We're hoping that Mick Jagger was right: That time is on our side."

While researchers are discovering possible physiological and genetic connections that could help account for differences in how liberals and conservatives experience fear or even how those on the left and right think about the issue of immigration, to take one policy example, the academics also say their work has real-world implications and could mark the beginning of important understandings of what's really behind our seemingly intractable ideological divisions.

Hibbing trained as a political scientist and described himself as a "normal kind of guy" who studied Congress and public opinion—until about 13 years ago, when he decided that "maybe the things going on, surveys, weren't able to get to a lot of things we bring into our heads, things we're not aware of."

Since then, he and other colleagues—in Lincoln, Neb., and around the country—have emerged as pioneers in the field of what he calls "biology and politics." Hibbing and members of his lab are currently working on a book titled "Predisposed: Liberals, Conservatives and the Biology of Political Difference" that's slated for publication this fall. The work will summarize research examining subjects like the physiological and neurological differences between liberals and conservatives, as well as differences in taste—liberals, for instance, tend to enjoy spicy foods and be open to new eating experiences while conservatives would rather eat their go-to favorites.

One key finding that "Predisposed" will highlight: conservatives and liberals respond differently when presented with extremely pleasant images—like people skiing, fruit baskets and sunsets—and disturbing pictures, like fires, vomit and rodents.

Study participants, after answering an extensive battery of questions about their political beliefs, were hooked up to sensors that test skin conductance—the measure of how quickly electricity moves through the body, which sometimes manifests itself in outward signs like sweaty palms. When conservatives viewed the negative images, researchers measured a greater increase in skin conductance when compared with liberals, indicating those on the right were responding more strongly.

"If you're responding [strongly] to those things, you want to protect yourself, your family, your country," Hibbing said of conservatives reacting intensely to the negative images.

Conservatives also spent more time focused on the unpleasant images than liberals did.

"If you focus on the negative, perhaps it makes more sense to you to believe in strong defense or be reluctant about immigration," Hibbing said.

In another experiment, subjects looked at a computer screen featuring a cartoon face, with instructions to hit the space bar when they saw a black dot appear on the screen. When the cartoon's eyes were looking away from the dot, liberals were much slower to hit the space bar than when the eyes were turned to the same side of the screen on which the dot was located. Conservatives weren't affected [by] the cartoon's gaze and tapped the space bar just as quickly, whether the cartoon was looking at the dot or away from it.

Hibbing says that's because liberals were much more focused on the gaze of the cartoon character.

So what's the political takeaway from the study? Hibbing says, "Liberals will say it's a good thing, you should be influenced by eyes on a screen. Conservatives say we should be strong individuals, we shouldn't be influenced by people around us. It's whether you're empathetic and in touch, or strong and independent."

Hibbing acknowledged that to some in the political world and beyond, such work "sounds mushy and sloppy." But taken together, he said, clear trends are emerging.

"The pattern is that conservatives are somewhat more attuned and responsive to negative features of the environment, negative situations, negative stimuli," he said.

He stressed that the research doesn't mean conservatives are "scared" or liberals are "selfish and hedonistic," as some of his critics have charged.

"We're just saying, no, they just pay attention to different things," Hibbing said. "It probably makes quite a bit of sense to pay attention to bad things. Maybe it's a positive thing for society to have a combination, a mixture of people who are pretty acutely attuned to dangerous, negative things, and [those] who are maybe more carefree."

His latest research also finds that people with higher levels of cortisol, the stress hormone, are less likely to vote and participate in the political process. Cortisol, which can be measured through blood or saliva samples, was found in higher levels among people whose voting records indicated that they didn't go to the polls often, and vice versa.

"Consistent voters tend to have low cortisol levels," Hibbing said, noting that the findings were statistically significant. "Politics is pretty stressful, you could argue . . . going to the polls could make you nervous, and people with high cortisol tend to avoid that."

As for any genetic component of current research, Professor Rose McDermott of Brown University stressed to POLITICO that there's no such thing as a "liberal" gene or a "conservative" gene. But McDermott, who has conducted extensive research focused on the relationship between political behavior and genetics, is part of a group of researchers who are studying how genetics—"broadly construed," she says—can influence political preferences and ideology.

"It's not that anyone thinks there's a gene for liberalism, but to think there are aspects of social and the political world influenced by our genetic and biological tendencies," McDermott said.

She recently co-authored a long paper summing up where the study of politics and genetics stands today—much of the work has relied on studies of twins, a method that has long been the "gold standard" for exploring genetic links to politics. That process allows researchers to see "what part of the outcome is related to genetics, and what is related to common experience, for example the family you grow up in." Those studies have found that between 40 and 60 percent of differences in political ideology, across a population, can be explained by genetics.

Even decades ago there were tantalizing signs of the link between biology and politics that researchers are putting more focus on exploring today. One early study from the 1970's, for instance, found that identical twins correlated more highly than did fraternal twins "on measures of ideology constructed from a scale of attitudes, including the death penalty, ethnocentrism, morality, unions, unemployment, and abortion, among others," her report said.

McDermott acknowledged that while the study of politics and genetics is growing, it's not yet "mainstream." But she sees significant policy implications in the research she has conducted. One study, published earlier this year in the American Journal of Political Science, found that people who she says are genetically inclined to be more fearful—who possess stronger social phobias and feel less comfortable in settings with unfamiliar people—tend to be conservative on issues like immigration.

"So the best way to think about it is, there's individual difference in how much underlying fear individuals have as they enter the world," she said. "Some are more prepared to be afraid of things than other people, that's just individual difference based in part on genetic backgrounds . . . and so you can show that people who have higher levels of social fear . . . those people tend to have more anti-immigration attitudes."

That doesn't mean that conservatives are inherently more prone to uneasiness in the face of new experiences or people—but according to this study, it does mean that naturally nervous people tend to lean right.

"What we find is, it's not the case that conservatives are more fearful, but fearful people are more conservative," she said. "We were able to make that association because we were able to look in our data at parents and children. What you find is really fearful people have more conservative children, as opposed to conservative people having more fearful children. What's really driving it is, people who have higher baselines of social phobia are much more likely to be conservative."

Washington could learn a thing or two from the study of the intersection between politics and science, experts in the field say.

McDermott she said that the findings of the fear study, along with other work related to genetics and politics, should shape how people think about hot-topic political issues.

"I think the immigration thing is the best example [of real-world implications]," she said. "It's a debate going on in Congress right now, and there's no recognition of the fact that people start with very different fundamental proclivities toward issues such as 'segregation'"—a term that she uses to encompass issues ranging from immigration to same-sex marriage.

"There's this underlying notion in Western democratic culture that we all start off on an equal playing field . . . that it's just a matter of discourse, if we all sit down and talk about it, we can compromise," she continued. "But if we understand things differently, we actually don't have the common ground we think we do. . . . I think that genetics influences differences in our emotional realities, and we may not always fully recognize that."

Hibbing, who has presented his findings to a number of people in the political world—including Rep. Adrian Smith (R-Neb.) and to attendees at a conference organized by the Department of Defense—told POLITICO that he sees ways to reduce partisanship in his research findings.

"In terms of identity, and correlating who's on the left and who's on the right, it might make people a little more understanding of their political opponents," he said. "Instead of saying they are stupid, uninformed—all of these things may be true—but [there are people who] are really perceiving the world in a different fashion than you do."

If partisans understood that some of their differences with the other side could be rooted in science, rather than perceived intransigence, that could take some rancor out of policy debates, he said.

"You sit side by side, but really you're worlds apart because you're just absorbing things in a different way," Hibbing said. "It may be naive, but I'm kind of hopeful that if people take seriously that people can't assume [other] people are seeing the same things I am, even though I still think he's wrong, maybe it will help . . . understand what can be done in order to come together."

Consider the source and the audience

- *Politico* is a mainstream Washington newspaper and online journal widely read by people in politics. This is a straight news story (not an opinion piece or analysis) on political science research. Why did the editors think this research would be of interest to their readers?

Lay out the argument, the values, and the assumptions

- The argument made by political scientists like John Hibbing is that we may be genetically or biologically predisposed to hold certain political views. What kinds of people might be attracted to this kind of argument? Why does one researcher compare it to the debate over climate science?
- The working definition that the article uses for what distinguishes liberals and conservatives is their attitude toward change—liberals favor it while conservatives favor the status quo. Is that the essential difference between them?

Uncover the evidence

- The researchers find a number of differences in how liberals and conservatives react to various visual stimuli and even differences in their physical chemistry. Do their findings persuade you that there are biological differences between them?
- If you were designing an experiment intended to capture biological differences between liberals and conservatives, what might you look for?

Evaluate the conclusion

- Most of these researchers note that conservatives focus more on negative things in their environment and appear to be more fearful, or to have more social phobia, than do liberals. They conclude from their data that this is what causes conservatives to be wary of change, while liberals' more "carefree" predisposition leads them to be more willing to explore change. Do you buy this?
- Would these data correspond with other ideological differences between liberals and conservatives, like attitudes toward government action or social issues, or do they just apply to attitudes toward change?

Sort out the political significance

- The researchers suggest (as does the former vice president quoted early in the article) that having people with biological predispositions to change might be very functional for society. What practical lessons might we take from this on how to settle political disputes among warring factions in American politics?

● ●

2.4 Today's Politics: Coalition of Transformation vs. Coalition of Restoration

Ronald Brownstein, *National Journal*

Why We Chose This Piece

Angry at what they saw as President Obama's "give-aways" to "taker groups," people like Arthur C. Brooks put their faith in the electorate to vote Obama out in 2012—"taking our country back," as some Tea Party members phrased it. We picked this article because it couches the outcome of the election as a response to that view. Ronald Brownstein has written before about what he calls the Coalition of the Ascendant—the growing numbers of minorities, young people, women, and college-educated whites who see the role of government in a more positive light than do the older, working-class whites who tended to form the backbone of the Tea Party movement. Here he is writing about them again, this time calling them the Coalition of Transformation. In this short article, Brownstein suggests that their 2012 victory over the Coalition of Restoration says more about how the country is changing than it does about Obama, and that those changes have clear implications for the political culture of the country and the way it views government.

This long march of a presidential election, after all its expense and duration, proved far more memorable for what it said about the country than what it revealed about the two men vying to lead it.

Neither President Obama nor Mitt Romney ran a particularly inspiring campaign. Each delivered a dud of a convention speech. (Quick: Can you remember a single thing either one said?)

Except for one golden night in Denver, Romney was gaffe-prone, distant, and, as it turned out, possessed of insular, elitist views that radiated contempt for just about anyone who didn't vote for him. Obama offered a forthright defense of activist government in principle; yet, in practice, he presented an agenda with few, and mostly modest, specifics.

In each case, the candidate's own performance lagged behind the effort that sprouted around him. Romney's actual campaign apparatus sputtered (failing to match both Obama's early ad assault and the closing kick of his turnout operation). But the independent-expenditure campaign that coalesced on his behalf was breathtaking in its scale (if not its results). Obama benefited from a digital-age marvel of a campaign that hit its marks with stunning efficiency—in the negative-ad barrage that stamped Romney's image as an indifferent plutocrat and in the precisely targeted voter-mobilization system that overwhelmed the GOP efforts. Campaign strategists will profitably study that juggernaut for years.

Selection published: November 21, 2012

And yet, what historians are likely to most remember about this campaign is what it revealed about the evolving nature of the country itself and how the parties are positioning themselves against those dynamics. Above all, this was a year when it became clear that, in a time of hurtling change, the two parties now represent a Coalition of Transformation and a Coalition of Restoration.

In terms of shaping the Democrats' long-term trajectory, by far the most important decisions Obama made this year were to dive into the powerful cultural and demographic currents transforming the American landscape. Previously, many party leaders have qualified (or entirely withheld) their support from causes such as gay marriage or legalizing undocumented immigrants, for fear of alienating culturally conservative whites. Obama this year embraced both without qualification; then, for good measure, he accepted a collision with the GOP and the Catholic Church (over the availability of free contraception under health care reform) that crystallized contrasting attitudes about the role of women. Obama, beginning an overdue rebalancing in federal spending, even shifted resources from seniors to the much more racially diverse working-age population by funding health coverage for the uninsured partly through savings in Medicare.

Romney, in his sulfurous postelection remarks, interpreted Obama's moves as providing voters "gifts" to buy their support. But these decisions represented nothing more malevolent or unusual than a party responding to the needs of its emerging constituencies.

Obama's choices undoubtedly contributed to his historically weak showing among older and blue-collar whites. Yet, with those voters stampeding toward the GOP, Obama won reelection behind a much more ideologically unified coalition than Democrats usually assemble; according to exit polls, four-fifths of his voters, for instance, said they supported a pathway to citizenship for illegal immigrants. Notably, in the exit polls, most Hispanics and African-Americans also said they supported gay marriage. All this means that, compared to even President Clinton's era, the Democrats are now operating with a largely coherent Coalition of Transformation that will allow (and even pressure) them to align more unreservedly with the big cultural and demographic forces remaking America.

For better or worse, this election more clearly stamped the Republicans as a Coalition of Restoration, overwhelmingly dependent on the votes of whites unsettled by those changes. After Obama's victory, conservative grandees such as Rush Limbaugh and Bill O'Reilly portrayed the election as something like the Alamo, with true Americans overrun by hordes of benefit-grubbing minorities and young people. "We are outnumbered," Limbaugh despaired. Romney capped this keening last week with his postelection diatribe to donors about Obama's "gifts"—possibly the bitterest screed from a loser since Richard Nixon declared, "You won't have Dick Nixon to kick around anymore" after he lost California's 1962 governor's race.

Romney's remarks weren't just sour grapes; they reflect a widespread fear among the Right that a heavily nonwhite class of "takers" will vote itself ever-expanding benefits at the expense of mostly white "makers." Romney earlier expressed that conviction in his broadside against the "47 percent," and running mate Rep. Paul Ryan has made similar arguments for years. Yuval Levin (identified this week by David Brooks as one of the Right's "two or three most influential young writers") recently described Democrats as "an incoherent amalgam of interest groups . . . vying for benefits . . . at the expense of other Americans."

These comments reveal a profound sense of demographic retreat on the Right that makes explicit the sub rosa implications of the tea party's 2010 cry to "take back our country." To the extent that longing means restoring the political dominance of married, churchgoing white families, the most important message of 2012 is that those days are gone. As if with a cannon burst, this election announced the arrival of a reconfigured America. Led by Romney, many in the GOP have responded by raging against it. It's just a guess, but responding to the needs of this emerging Next America might prove a more profitable long-term strategy.

Consider the source and the audience

- Ronald Brownstein is a veteran political reporter and analyst, writing in the *National Journal*, a weekly Washington journal with a primary audience of politicians, bureaucrats, and political junkies. Would he be making a partisan argument here, or an analytic (more objective) one?

Lay out the argument, the values, and the assumptions

- Writing without a political axe to grind, Brownstein is focused not on who deserves to win in American politics, but who *is* winning. What does he see as the role of demographics here in changing political culture?
- Why does the Coalition of Transformation have a more positive view of government action than the Coalition of Restoration? What is it the latter really wants to restore?

Uncover the evidence

- Brownstein thinks the outcome of the election demonstrates that his argument is correct, and he assumes that his readers know the demographic turnout data that would support his conclusions. Are there other explanations for the election's outcome?
- Would there be other evidence that would persuade you to accept his conclusions?

Evaluate the conclusion

- Brownstein goes bold here. The country is transfigured—the Coalition of Transformation has changed it, and it isn't going back. The new culture is characterized by a majority view that sees a positive role of government action, not the European statism that Arthur C. Brooks warns about in the earlier selection, but a role for government in expanding rights and opportunities for previously excluded groups. Is he correct that this is the direction in which the country is moving?

Sort out the political significance

- In the immediate aftermath of the 2012 election, Republicans' own analysis seemed to agree that they needed to reach out to women, Hispanics, and other minorities, and embrace some of the issues (like marriage equality) that younger voters endorse. Within six months, however, they were reconsidering, trying to stop passage of a comprehensive immigration bill, passing restrictive voting regulations in the wake of the Supreme Court's overturning of part of the Voting Rights Act, and tightening abortion laws across the country. What do you think is the correct response for conservatives, given the demographic changes in the country?

2.5 Is Rush Limbaugh's Country Gone?

Thomas Edsall, *New York Times*

Why We Chose This Piece

We chose to include this article because it puts some data teeth in the argument we have seen in the United States over the proper role of government. Although it is doubtful that those who say they favor socialism in the survey cited here really mean socialism (government ownership of factories and industry), it is clear that they do favor more regulation of the capitalist economy, and a more proactive role of government in investing in education, infrastructure, and other social efforts. Still, the folks on the other side get plenty of government benefits—from tax breaks to Social Security. Might there be something else behind this debate about the role of government? What is at stake here for the side that fears it is losing?

The morning after the re-election of President Obama, Rush Limbaugh told his listeners:

I went to bed last night thinking we're outnumbered. I went to bed last night thinking all this discussion we'd had about this election being the election that will tell us whether or not we've lost the country. I went to bed last night thinking we've lost the country. I don't know how else you look at this.

The conservative talk show host, who had been an upbeat, if initially doubtful, Romney supporter throughout the campaign, was on a post-election downer:

In a country of children where the option is Santa Claus or work, what wins? And say what you want, but Romney did offer a vision of traditional America. In his way, he put forth a great

---

Selection published: November 18, 2012

vision of traditional America, and it was rejected. It was rejected in favor of a guy who thinks that those who are working aren't doing enough to help those who aren't. And that resonated.

Limbaugh echoed a Republican theme that was voiced before and after the election: Barack Obama has unleashed a coalition of Americans "who are dependent upon government, who believe that they are victims, who believe the government has a responsibility to care for them, who believe that they are entitled to health care, to food, to housing, to you-name-it—that that's an entitlement. And the government should give it to them"—as Mitt Romney put it in his notorious commentary on the 47 percent.

You can find this message almost everywhere on the right side of the spectrum. The Heritage Foundation, for example, annually calculates an "Index of Dependence on Government," which grows every year:

> Today, more people than ever before depend on the federal government for housing, food, income, student aid, or other assistance once considered to be the responsibility of individuals, families, neighborhoods, churches, and other civil society institutions. The United States reached another milestone in 2010: For the first time in history, half the population pays no federal income taxes. It is the conjunction of these two trends—higher spending on dependence-creating programs, and an ever-shrinking number of taxpayers who pay for these programs—that concerns those interested in the fate of the American form of government.

William Bennett, conservative stalwart, television commentator and secretary of education under President Reagan, complained on the CNN Web site that Democrats have been successful in setting

> the parameters and focus of the national and political dialogue as predominantly about gender, race, ethnicity and class. This is the paradigm, the template through which many Americans, probably a majority, more or less view the world, our country, and the election. It is a divisive strategy and Democrats have targeted and exploited those divides. How else can we explain that more young people now favor socialism to capitalism?

In fact, the 2011 Pew Research Center poll Bennett cites demonstrates that in many respects conservatives are right to be worried:

Not only does a plurality (49–43) of young people hold a favorable view of socialism— and, by a tiny margin (47–46), a negative view of capitalism—so do liberal Democrats, who view socialism positively by a solid 59–33; and African Americans, 55–36. Hispanics are modestly opposed, 49–44, to socialism, but they hold decisively negative attitudes toward capitalism, 55–32.

Much of the focus in the media in recent years has been on the growing hard-line stance of the Republican Party. At the same time, there are significant developments taking place as a new left alliance forms to underpin the Democratic Party. John Judis and Ruy Teixeira originally described this alliance in 2002 as the emerging Democratic majority in a pioneering book of the same name. More recently, the pollster Stan Greenberg and a group of liberal activists have described it as the "rising American electorate."

Celinda Lake, a Democratic pollster who has devoted much of her work to analyzing the changing shape of the liberal and conservative coalitions, said in an e-mail that the rising American electorate

Table 2.5.1   Views of "Capitalism" and "Socialism"

Reaction to . . .	Capitalism		Socialism		
	Pos %	Neg %	Pos %	Neg %	Diff in % positive
Total	50	40	31	60	+19
White	55	35	24	68	+31
Black	41	51	55	36	−14
Hispanic	32	55	44	49	−12
18–29	46	47	49	43	−3
30–49	50	40	34	58	+16
50–64	53	39	25	68	+28
65+	52	32	13	72	+39
Family income					
$75,000+	68	28	22	71	+46
$30,000–$74,999	52	43	27	68	+25
Less than $30,000	39	47	43	46	−4
Party and ideology					
Conserv Republican	66	29	6	90	+60
Mod/Lib Republican	54	40	25	66	+29
Independent	52	39	32	60	+20
Cons/Mod Democrat	42	49	37	51	+5
Liberal Democrat	46	47	59	33	−13
Occupy Wall Street					
Support (44%)	45	47	39	52	+6
Oppose (35%)	67	28	18	76	+49
Tea party movement					
Agree (19%)	71	26	12	85	+59
Disagree (19%)	53	39	37	53	+16
No opinion (50%)	42	46	35	55	+7

PEW RESEARCH CENTER Dec. 7-11, 2011. Whites and Blacks are non-Hispanic only; Hispanics are of any race.

will have profound implications because the R.A.E. has a very different approach to the role for government, very different views on race and tolerance, different views on gender roles, and very different views on economic opportunity and security. These are some of the biggest divides in our culture.

Robert Borosage, co-director of the liberal-left Campaign for America's Future, put it more bluntly in a blog post:

> In our Gilded Age of extreme inequality, with a middle class that increasingly understands the rules are rigged against them, this was the first election in what is likely to be an era of growing class warfare.

Two post-election polls—one released Nov. 14 by the Democracy Corps (founded by Stan Greenberg and James Carville), the other released Nov. 16 by the Public Religion Research Institute—reveal the decisively liberal views of the core constituencies within the rising American electorate and its support for government activism, especially measures to help the disadvantaged.

The findings from the P.R.R.I. survey are very illuminating:

> When voters were asked whether cutting taxes or investing in education and infrastructure is the better policy to promote economic growth, the constituencies of the new liberal electorate consistently chose education and infrastructure by margins ranging from 2–1 to 3–2—African Americans by 62–33, Hispanics by 61–37, never-married men by 56–38, never-married women by 64–30, voters under 30 by 63–34, and those with post-graduate education by 60–33.

Conservative constituencies generally chose lowering taxes by strong margins— whites by 52–42, married men by 59–34, married women by 51–44, all men by 52–41; older voters between the ages of 50 and 65 by 54–42.

> The constituencies that make up the rising American electorate are firmly in favor of government action to reduce the gap between rich and poor, by 85–15 among blacks, 74–26 for Hispanics; 70–30 never-married men; 83–15 never-married women; and 76–24 among voters under 30. Conservative groups range from lukewarm to opposed: 53–47 for men; 53–47 among voters 50–65; 46–54 among married men; 52–47 among all whites.
>
> One of the clearest divides between the rising American electorate and the rest of the country is in responses to the statement "Government is providing too many social services that should be left to religious groups and private charities. Blacks disagree 67–32; Hispanics disagree 57–40; never-married women 70–27; never-married men, 59–41; young voters, 66–34; and post-grad, 65–34. Conversely, whites agree with the statement 54–45; married men agree, 60–39; married women, 55–44; all men, 55–43.

The Democracy Corps survey specifically broke out the collective views of the liberal alliance and contrasted them with the views of those on the right. Some findings:

> By a margin of 60–13, voters on the left side of the spectrum favor raising taxes on incomes above $1 million, while voters outside of the left are much less supportive, 39–25. In the case of raising the minimum wage, the left backs a hike by an overwhelming 64–6 margin, while those on the right are far less supportive, 32–18. The rising American electorate backs raising the minimum wage by 64–6, while the people outside it back a hike by just 32–18. The left coalition supports a carbon tax or fee by 43–14 while right-leaning voters are opposed, 37–24.

Policies supported by the rising American electorate—which closely overlaps with the Obama coalition—provoke intense opposition from the right. In the aftermath of the election, Romney blamed his defeat on the "gifts" Obama handed out to "the African-American community, the Hispanic community and young people."

In fact, the rising American electorate represents a direct threat to the striking array of government benefits for the affluent that the conservative movement has won over the past 40 years. These include the reduction of the top income tax rate from 50 percent in 1986 to 35 percent; the 15 percent tax rate on dividend and capital gains income, which was 39.9 percent in 1977; the lowering of the top estate tax rate from 70 percent in 1981, with just $175,000 exempted from taxation, to a top rate of 35 percent this year with $5.1 million exempted from taxation.

At the same time, the Pew survey cited above shows the high levels of skepticism and hostility toward capitalism on the part of the emerging Democratic majority. Insofar as the liberal coalition succeeds in electing senators and representatives who share those views, the business community will have increasing difficulty in winning approval of its deregulated market and free trade agenda.

As Obama negotiates with Republican House and Senate leaders to prevent a dive over the "fiscal cliff," he will be under strong pressure from his reinvigorated liberal supporters to take a tough stand in support of tax hikes on the well-to-do and to more firmly limit spending cuts.

"Looking ahead to their post-election agenda, this is not a group looking for 'austerity,' " the Democracy Corps wrote in a report accompanying its post-election survey. "Indeed, their issues are explicitly progressive and investment-oriented," in terms of human capital. The report went on:

> The rising American electorate's most important priority for the president and the Congress is "investing in education," followed by "protecting Social Security and Medicare."

In effect, the 21st century version of class conflict sets the stage for an exceptionally bitter face-off between the left and the right in Congress. The national government is facing the prospect of forced austerity, weighing such zero-sum choices as raising capital gains taxes or cutting food stamps, slashing defense spending or restricting unemployment benefits, establishing a 15 cents-a-gallon gasoline tax or pushing citizens off the Medicaid rolls, pushing central bank policy favorable to the financial services industry or curtailing Medicare eligibility.

In broader terms, the political confrontation pits taxpayers, who now form the core of the center-right coalition, against tax consumers who form the core of the center-left. According to the Tax Policy Center, 46.4 percent of all tax filers had no federal income tax liability in 2011 (although most people pay a combination of state, sales, excise, property and other levies). There are clear exceptions to this dichotomy, as many Social Security and Medicare beneficiaries (tax recipients) vote Republican, and many college-educated upper-income citizens of all races and ethnicities (tax payers) vote Democratic. Nonetheless, the overarching division remains, and the battle lines are drawn over how to distribute the costs of the looming fiscal crisis. The outcome of this policy fight will determine whether Limbaugh is correct to fear that his side has "lost the country."

Consider the source and the audience

- Thomas Edsall is a veteran journalist who teaches at Columbia University, writing an analysis as part of the *New York Times'* 2012 election coverage. The *Times* is the paper of record in the United States, widely read by educated urban professionals. Which side of this debate about the role of government are they likely to fall on?

Lay out the argument, the values, and the assumptions

- Edsall examines the claim made by Rush Limbaugh and other conservatives that they have "lost" the country and finds that that might be true insofar as the groups who voted for President Obama (the Coalition of Transformation, in Ronald Brownstein's words in the previous selection) favor a more activist government and less inequality. He frames this as a debate between "tax-payers" and "tax consumers." Is that necessarily correct?

Uncover the evidence

- There are two kinds of evidence presented in this article: Edsall cites conservatives to show the worry they feel and uses data to look at whether that worry is warranted. Is there anything else you would like to know before accepting his conclusions?

Evaluate the conclusion

- Although he cites exceptions, Edsall suggests that the data back up his conclusion—that taxpayers are on one side of the debate and tax consumers are on the other. Is that the correct way to look at the data he presents?

Sort out the political significance

- Edsall says that the outcome of the fiscal cliff crisis will show whether Limbaugh and his ilk have "lost the country." In that crisis the president prevailed and George W. Bush–era tax cuts for the wealthy were allowed to lapse. In subsequent run-ins, however, House Republicans held their ground, forcing the austerity cuts of the sequester. Have conservatives really lost?
- If you think about the argument Ronald Brownstein made in the previous article, what would you predict will happen in the future?

2.6 Gettysburg Address
Abraham Lincoln

Why We Chose This Piece

Given the fact that most of the other entries in this chapter deal with real tensions and rifts in American culture, it is perhaps useful to remember that our roots as a nation divided go way back. In the midst of the Civil War, President Abraham Lincoln spoke the following few words that still today remind us of what we have in common, even as our political differences continue to tear us apart.

Four score and seven years ago our fathers brought forth on this continent a new nation, conceived in liberty, and dedicated to the proposition that all men are created equal.

Now we are engaged in a great civil war, testing whether that nation, or any nation so conceived and so dedicated, can long endure. We are met on a great battlefield of that war. We have come to dedicate a portion of that field, as a final resting place for those who here gave their lives that that nation might live. It is altogether fitting and proper that we should do this.

But, in a larger sense, we cannot dedicate, we cannot consecrate, we cannot hallow this ground. The brave men, living and dead, who struggled here, have consecrated it, far above our poor power to add or detract. The world will little note, nor long remember what we say here, but it can never forget what they did here. It is for us the living, rather, to be dedicated here to the unfinished work which they who fought here have thus far so nobly advanced. It is rather for us to be here dedicated to the great task remaining before us—that from these honored dead we take increased devotion to that cause for which they gave the last full measure of devotion—that we here highly resolve that these dead shall not have died in vain—that this nation, under God, shall have a new birth of freedom—and that government of the people, by the people, for the people, shall not perish from the earth.

Consider the source and the audience

- In the Gettysburg Address Lincoln is speaking at the consecration of a graveyard for Union soldiers killed in the Battle of Gettysburg, midway through the Civil War. While he says "the world will little note, nor long remember what we say here," clearly the world has remembered these words for a very long time and Lincoln seems to know that it will. How is he directing his thoughts to a wider audience?

Selection delivered: November 19, 1863

Lay out the argument, the values, and the assumptions

- The argument here is simple—that the sacrifice of the soldiers who died should not be in vain but should herald a recommitment to the values underlying the nation. What are those values?

Uncover the evidence

- There are no data offered here, and no persuasive evidence. What does Lincoln use to make his case?

Evaluate the conclusion

- History allows us to evaluate Lincoln's conclusion, at least so far. Has "that government of the people, by the people, for the people" perished?
- What might Lincoln say if he could see the issues dividing us today?

Sort out the political significance

- Lincoln emphasizes the values of freedom, equality, and democracy as underpinning the American ideal. How does a commitment to those cultural values allow us to disagree politically?
- Are democratic systems strengthened or weakened by disagreement?

3

Immigration and American Demographics

While political culture can be thought of as the ideas that bring us together, that unite us as a people, we are also a nation of immigrants, whose culture is continually being added to and enhanced by the values and beliefs of the new people who come here. The way that immigrants are absorbed into our culture becomes a central element of who we are.

From the time we are schoolchildren, we are taught two competing views of ourselves as a people. One view holds that we are a melting pot, where our identities merge together into a kind of homogeneous American soup. The other holds that we are a crazy salad, with each of us keeping our unique identities, even as we share the same bowl. The question of which of these views should hold sway has itself become a defining issue in American culture.

In the not very distant future, white Americans of European extraction will become a minority in the United States. Populations that we currently think of as "minorities"—African Americans, Latinos, and Asian Americans, as well as smaller demographic groups—will soon, together, be the majority. As the article by Ronald Brownstein in the previous chapter suggests, this prospect has caused no end of turmoil in American politics.

Partly because of Richard Nixon's so-called "southern strategy" in the 1970s, when the Republican Party used race as a wedge issue to recruit conservative southern Democrats, that party has not been seen as a hospitable home by many African Americans. As the Republican Party has simultaneously gotten more conservative it has rejected liberal policies on immigration, on dealing with the estimated twelve million immigrants who entered this country illegally, and on social programs important to immigrant communities finding their footing in the United States. In the 2012 election, Barack Obama—himself, of course, African American—received 93 percent of the African American vote, 71 percent of the Latino vote, and 73 percent of the Asian American vote; Mitt Romney got 59 percent of the white vote. In the aftermath of the election, Republicans concluded that demographic trends were working against them and that they needed to be more inclusive. Many Republicans in the Senate joined with Democrats in the summer of 2013 to pass a bipartisan immigration bill that combined tougher border security with a path to citizenship for the undocumented immigrants, but when the bill got to the House of Representatives, the more conservative members balked. As of this writing, the bill is in legislative limbo, its fact uncertain.

The way the country deals with its changing demographics will have important cultural consequences, and the way the parties handle them will have enormous political implications. To get you thinking about some of the issues involved, the first selection in this chapter is by an undocumented immigrant, a professional journalist who arrived here, without papers, as a child. His story is a compelling personal take on a situation most Americans have no direct experience of. The second article is a look at where immigrants are settling in the United States and what parts of the country have the most to gain from immigration reform. The third piece, written by an academic in the *Christian Science Monitor*, argues that the crazy salad model of multiculturalism can be threatening to democratic stability. In the fourth, a Pulitzer Prize–winning journalist for the *Washington Post* examines the political, cultural, and ideological challenges facing the country given its changing demographics. Finally, a selection that touches on concerns in all these pieces is Martin Luther King Jr.'s classic "I Have a Dream" speech. Here, King looks at the whole culture that ties Americans together, especially its commitment to freedom and equality, and demands access to that culture for African Americans and, by implication, other excluded groups.

● ●

3.1 Not Legal Not Leaving

Jose Antonio Vargas, *Time* magazine

Why We Chose This Piece

Many people have strong feelings one way or another about immigration and the presence of undocumented immigrants in the United States, but fewer of us have the opportunity to get the perspective of an undocumented worker on his experience. Unlike most people in his situation, journalist Jose Antonio Vargas discusses his status publicly. Does his story influence your understanding of the immigration issue?

UPDATE: Shortly after Jose Antonio Vargas' story on the issue of the undocumented was published in *Time*, the U.S. Department of Homeland Security announced that it would no longer deport young undocumented residents who qualify for the DREAM Act. Those eligible will receive work permits.

Selection published: June 25, 2012

"**W**hy haven't you gotten deported?"

That's usually the first thing people ask me when they learn I'm an undocumented immigrant or, put more rudely, an "illegal." Some ask it with anger or frustration, others with genuine bafflement. At a restaurant in Birmingham, not far from the University of Alabama, an inebriated young white man challenged me: "You got your papers?" I told him I didn't. "Well, you should get your ass home, then." In California, a middle-aged white woman threw up her arms and wanted to know: "Why hasn't Obama dealt with you?" At least once a day, I get that question, or a variation of it, via e-mail, tweet or Facebook message. Why, indeed, am I still here?

It's a fair question, and it's been hanging over me every day for the past year, ever since I publicly revealed my undocumented status. There are an estimated 11.5 million people like me in this country, human beings with stories as varied as America itself yet lacking a legal claim to exist here. Like many others, I kept my status a secret, passing myself off as a U.S. citizen—right down to cultivating a homegrown accent. I went to college and became a journalist, earning a staff job at the *Washington Post*. But the deception weighed on me. When I eventually decided to admit the truth, I chose to come out publicly—very publicly—in the form of an essay for the *New York Times* last June. Several immigration lawyers counseled against doing this. ("It's legal suicide," warned one.) Broadcasting my status to millions seemed tantamount to an invitation to the immigration cops: Here I am. Come pick me up.

So I waited. And waited some more. As the months passed, there were no knocks on my door, no papers served, no calls or letters from U.S. Immigration and Customs Enforcement (ICE), which deported a record 396,906 people in fiscal 2011. Before I came out, the question always at the top of my mind was, What will happen if people find out? Afterward, the question changed to What happens now? It seemed I had traded a largely hidden undocumented life in limbo for an openly undocumented life that's still in limbo.

But as I've crisscrossed the U.S.—participating in more than 60 events in nearly 20 states and learning all I can about this debate that divides our country (yes, it's my country too)—I've realized that the most important questions are the ones other people ask me. I am now a walking conversation that most people are uncomfortable having. And once that conversation starts, it's clear why a consensus on solving our immigration dilemma is so elusive. The questions I hear indicate the things people don't know, the things they think they know but have been misinformed about and the views they hold but do not ordinarily voice.

I've also been witness to a shift I believe will be a game changer for the debate: more people coming out. While closely associated with the modern gay-rights movement, in recent years the term coming out and the act itself have been embraced by the country's young undocumented population. At least 2,000 undocumented immigrants—most of them under 30—have contacted me and outed themselves in the past year. Others are coming out over social media or in person to their friends, their fellow students, their colleagues. It's true, these individuals—many brought to the U.S. by family when they were too young to understand what it means to be "illegal"—are a fraction of the millions living hidden lives. But each becomes another walking conversation. We love this country. We contribute to it. This is our home. What happens when even more of us step forward? How will the U.S. government and American citizens react then?

The contradictions of our immigration debate are inescapable. Polls show substantial support for creating a path to citizenship for some undocumenteds—yet 52% of Americans support allowing police to stop and question anyone they suspect of being "illegal." Democrats are viewed as being more welcoming to immigrants, but the Obama Administration has sharply ramped up deportations. The probusiness GOP waves a KEEP OUT flag at the Mexican border and a HELP WANTED sign 100 yards in, since so many industries depend on cheap labor.

Election-year politics is further confusing things, as both parties scramble to attract Latinos without scaring off other constituencies. President Obama has as much as a 3-to-1 lead over Mitt Romney among Latino voters, but his deportation push is dampening their enthusiasm. Romney has a crucial ally in Florida Senator Marco Rubio, a Cuban American, but is burdened by the sharp anti-immigrant rhetoric he unleashed in the primary-election battle. This month, the Supreme Court is expected to rule on Arizona's controversial anti-immigrant law. A decision either way could galvanize reform supporters and opponents alike.

But the real political flash point is the proposed Dream Act, a decade-old immigration bill that would provide a path to citizenship for young people educated in this country. The bill never passed, but it focused attention on these youths, who call themselves the Dreamers. Both the President and Rubio have placed Dreamers at the center of their reform efforts—but with sharply differing views on how to address them.

ICE, the division of the Department of Homeland Security (DHS) charged with enforcing immigration laws, is its own contradiction, a tangled bureaucracy saddled with conflicting goals. As the weeks passed after my public confession, the fears of my lawyers and friends began to seem faintly ridiculous. Coming out didn't endanger me; it had protected me. A Philippine-born, college-educated, outspoken mainstream journalist is not the face the government wants to put on its deportation program. Even so, who flies under the radar, and who becomes one of those unfortunate 396,906? Who stays, who goes, and who decides? Eventually I confronted ICE about its plans for me, and I came away with even more questions.

I am not without contradictions either. I am 31 and have been a working journalist for a decade. I know I can no longer claim to be a detached, objective reporter, at least in the traditional sense. I am part of this evolving story and growing movement. It is personal. Though I have worked hard to approach this issue like any other, I've also found myself drawn to the activists, driven to help tell their story.

This is the time to tell it.

"Why don't you become legal?" asked 79-year-old William Oglesby of Iowa City, Iowa. It was early December, a few weeks before the Iowa caucuses, and I was attending a Mitt Romney town hall at an animal-feed maker. Romney had just fielded questions from a group of voters, including Oglesby and his wife Sharon, both Republicans. Addressing immigration, Romney said, "For those who have come here illegally, they might have a transition time to allow them to set their affairs in order and then go back home and get in line with everybody else."

"I haven't become legal," I told William, "because there's no way for me to become legal, sir."

Sharon jumped in. "You can't get a green card?"

"No, ma'am," I said. "There's no process for me." Of all the questions I've been asked in the past year, "Why don't you become legal?" is probably the most exasperating. But it speaks to how unfamiliar most Americans are with how the immigration process works.

As Angela M. Kelley, an immigration advocate in Washington, told me, "If you think the American tax code is outdated and complicated, try understanding America's immigration code." The easiest way to become a U.S. citizen is to be born here—doesn't matter who your parents are; you're in. (The main exception is for children of foreign diplomatic officials.) If you were born outside the U.S. and want to come here, the golden ticket is the so-called green card, a document signifying that the U.S. government has granted you permanent-resident status, meaning you're able to live and, more important, work here. Once you have a green card, you're on your way to eventual citizenship—in as little as three years if you marry a U.S. citizen—as long as you don't break the law and you meet other requirements such as paying a fee and passing a civics test.

Obtaining a green card means navigating one of the two principal ways of getting permanent legal status in the U.S.: family or specialized work. To apply for a green card on the basis of family, you need to be a spouse, parent, child or sibling of a citizen. (Green-card holders can petition only for their spouses or unmarried children.) Then it's time to get in line. For green-card seekers, the U.S. has a quota of about 25,000 green cards per country each year. That means Moldova (population: 3.5 million) gets the same number of green cards as Mexico (population: 112 million). The wait time depends on demand. If you're in Mexico, India, the Philippines or another nation with many applicants, expect a wait of years or even decades. (Right now, for example, the U.S. is considering Filipino siblings who applied in January 1989.)

Taking the employment route to a green card means clearing a pretty high bar if you have an employer who's willing to hire you. There are different levels of priority, with preference given to people with job skills considered crucial, such as specialized medical professionals, advanced-degree holders and executives of multinational companies. There's no waiting list for those. If you don't qualify for a green card, you may be able to secure one of the few kinds of temporary work visas—including the now famous H1-B visas that are common in Silicon Valley. For those already in the U.S. without documentation—those who have sneaked across a border or overstayed a temporary visa—it's even more complicated. Options are extremely limited. One route is to marry a U.S. citizen, but it's not as easy as the movies would have you think. The process can take years, especially if a sham marriage is suspected. I couldn't marry my way into citizenship even if I wanted to. I'm gay. Same-sex marriage is not recognized by the federal government—explicitly so, ever since Congress passed the Defense of Marriage Act. From the government's perspective, for me to pursue a path to legalization now, I would have to leave the U.S., return to the Philippines and hope to qualify via employment, since I don't have any qualifying family members here. But because I have admitted to being in the U.S. illegally, I would be subject to a 10-year bar before any application would be considered.

47

The long-stalled Dream Act is the best hope for many young people. The original 2001 version would have created a path to legal status—effectively a green card—for undocumented people age 21 and under who had graduated from high school and resided in the U.S. for five years. As the bill stalled in Congress and Dreamers got older, the age requirement went up, getting as high as 35. Rubio is expected to introduce his own variation, granting nonimmigrant visas so Dreamers could legally stay in the U.S., go to school and work. Its prospects are dim in a gridlocked Congress. Obama, meanwhile, is said to be weighing an Executive Order that would halt deportation of Dream Act—eligible youth and provide them with work permits. Under both Rubio's bill (details of which are not yet confirmed) and Obama's Executive Order (which is being studied), Dreamers could become legal residents. However, both proposals are only the first steps of a longer journey to citizenship.

"Why did you get your driver's license when you knew it wasn't legal? Do you think you belong to a special class of people who can break any laws they please?"

These were the questions of a polite, mild-mannered man named Konrad Sosnow, who I later learned was a lawyer. In late March, Sosnow and I participated in what was billed as a "civility roundtable" on immigration in my adopted hometown of Mountain View, Calif. About 120 people attended. Sosnow had read my coming-out story and wanted to know why I had such disregard for laws.

"I don't think I belong to a special class of people—not at all," I remember telling Sosnow. "I didn't get the license to spite you or disrespect you or because I think I'm better than you. I got the license because, like you, I needed to go to work. People like me get licenses because we need to drop kids off at school and because we need to pick up groceries. I am sorry for what I did, but I did it because I had to live and survive." Sosnow nodded, not exactly in agreement but at least with some understanding. We shook hands as the evening drew to a close. Months later, Sosnow told me he's written e-mails to the President and other elected officials, asking for immigration reform.

Everyday life for an undocumented American means a constant search for loopholes and back doors. Take air travel, for instance. Everyone knows that in the post-9/11 era, you can't fly without a government-issued ID. The easiest option for most people is their driver's license. Most states will not issue a license without proof of legal residency or citizenship. But a few grant licenses to undocumented immigrants, New Mexico and Washington State among them. Like many others, I had falsely posed as a Washington State resident in order to get a license. Weeks after my coming-out essay was published last year, Washington revoked the license—not because I'm undocumented but because I don't actually live in Washington.

For those who don't have a driver's license—that includes me now—a passport from our native country can serve as ID. But it makes every flight a gamble. My passport, which I got through the Philippine embassy, lacks a visa. If airport security agents turn the pages and discover this, they can contact Customs and Border Protection, which in turn can detain me. But for domestic flights, security usually checks just the name, photo and expiration date, not for the visa.

We may be nonpeople to the TSA but not to the IRS. Undocumented workers pay taxes. I've paid income taxes, state and federal, since I started working at 18. The IRS doesn't care if I'm here legally; it cares about its money. Some undocumented people, of course, circumvent the system, just like some citizens. But according to the nonpartisan Institute on Taxation and Economic Policy, households headed by undocumented workers collectively paid $11.2 billion in state and local taxes in 2010—$1.2 billion in income taxes, $1.6 billion in property taxes (because undocumented immigrants do own property) and $8.4 billion in consumption taxes. We also pay into Social Security. Even as many of us contribute, we cannot avail ourselves of a great deal of the services those tax dollars pay for.

When you lack legal status, the threat of deportation is a constant concern. In three years, Obama has deported 1.2 million; it took President George W. Bush eight years to deport 1.6 million. "Under both the Bush and Obama administrations, we have reversed ourselves as a nation of immigrants," Bill Ong Hing, a veteran immigration lawyer, told me. (Indeed, nations like Canada now have higher percentages of immigrants than the "melting pot" of the U.S.)

A big driver of the deportation numbers is ICE's Secure Communities program, which was meant to target terrorists and serious criminals but also winds up snaring those whose only crimes are civil violations connected to being undocumented (like driving without a license). Students and mothers have been detained and deported alongside murderers and rapists.

Depending on how the politics plays to the local electorate, many states wind up writing their own immigration laws. Two years ago, Arizona passed SB 1070—its "Show me your papers" bill—then the strictest immigration law in the country. It embodies an attrition-through-enforcement doctrine: the state will so threaten the livelihood of its undocumented population that they will just give up and self-deport. Among the bill's most controversial provisions, currently being reviewed by the Supreme Court, is one giving law-enforcement officials the power to stop anyone whom they suspect to be "illegal." Arizona's law inspired copycat bills across the country.

For all the roadblocks, though, many of us get by thanks to our fellow Americans. We rely on a growing network of citizens—Good Samaritans, our pastors, our co-workers, our teachers who protect and look after us. As I've traveled the country, I've seen how members of this underground railroad are coming out about their support for us too.

"So you're not Mexican?" an elderly white woman named Ann (she declined to give her last name) asked me when I told her about my undocumented status last October. We stood in front of a Kohl's department store in Alabama, which last year outdid Arizona by passing HB 56, the country's most draconian immigration law. HB 56 requires public schools to collect the immigration status of new students and their parents and makes it a felony for anyone to transport or house an undocumented immigrant. Both provisions are currently blocked by federal courts pending a ruling.

Ann, a registered Republican, was born and raised in the South, where immigration is introducing a new variable into the old racial divide. Alabama's immigrant population, though still relatively small, has nearly doubled in the past decade. The state's Latino population alone grew from 1.7% of the overall population in 2000 to nearly 4% in 2010—about 180,000 people, according to Census figures. But when I told Ann I am Filipino, she scrunched her forehead. "My border," I explained, "was the Pacific Ocean."

Though roughly 59% of the estimated 11.5 million undocumented immigrants in the U.S. are from Mexico, the rest are not. About 1 million come from Asia and the Pacific

Islands, about 800,000 from South America and about 300,000 from Europe. Others come from Nigeria, Israel, pretty much everywhere. In the case of countries that don't share a border with the U.S., these are almost always people who entered the country legally—as vacationers or on temporary visas—and overstayed the time permitted.

But perception has become reality. What's cemented in people's consciousness is the television reel of Mexicans jumping a fence. Reality check: illegal border crossings are at their lowest level since the Nixon era, in part because of the continued economic slump and stepped-up enforcement. According to the Office of Immigration Statistics at DHS, 86% of undocumented immigrants have been living in the U.S. for seven years or longer.

Still, for many, immigration is synonymous with Mexicans and the border. In several instances, white conservatives I spoke to moved from discussing "illegals" in particular to talking about Mexicans in general—about Spanish being overheard at Walmart, about the onslaught of new kids at schools and new neighbors at churches, about the "other" people. The immigration debate, at its core, is impossible to separate from America's unprecedented and culture-shifting demographic makeover. Whites represent a shrinking share of the total U.S. population. Recently the U.S. Census reported that for the first time, children born to racial- and ethnic-minority parents represent a majority of all new births.

According to the Pew Hispanic Center, there are also at least 17 million people who are legally living in the U.S. but whose families have at least one undocumented immigrant. About 4.5 million U.S.-citizen kids have at least one undocumented parent. Immigration experts call these mixed-status families, and I grew up in one. I come from a large Filipino clan in which, among dozens of cousins and uncles and aunties and many American-born nieces and nephews, I'm the only one who doesn't have papers. My mother sent me to live with my grandparents in the U.S. when I was 12. When I was 16 and applied for a driver's permit, I found out that my green card—my main form of legal identification—was fake. My grandparents, both naturalized citizens, hadn't told me. It was disorienting, first discovering my precarious status, then realizing that when I had been pledging allegiance to the flag, the republic for which it stands didn't have room for me.

"Why did you come out?" asked 20-year-old Gustavo Madrigal, who attended a talk I gave at the University of Georgia in late April. Like many Dreamers I've met, Madrigal is active in his community. Since he grew up in Georgia, he's needed to be. A series of measures have made it increasingly tough for undocumented students there to attend state universities.

"Why did you come out?" I asked him in turn.

"I didn't have a choice," Madrigal replied.

"I also reached a point," I told him, "when there was no other choice but to come out." And it is true for so many others. We are living in the golden age of coming out. There are no overall numbers on this, but each day I encounter at least five more openly undocumented people. As a group and as individuals, we are putting faces and names and stories on an issue that is often treated as an abstraction.

Technology, especially social media, has played a big role. Online, people are telling their stories and coming out, asking others to consider life from their perspective and testing everyone's empathy quotient. Some realize the risks of being so public; others, like me, think publicity offers protection. Most see the value of connecting with others and sharing experiences—by liking the page of United We Dream on Facebook, for example, or watching the Undocumented and Awkward video series on YouTube.

This movement has its roots in the massive immigrant-rights rallies of 2006, which were held in protest of HR 4437, a Republican-backed House bill that would have classified undocumented immigrants and anyone who helped them enter and remain in the U.S. as felons. Though the bill died, it awakened activism in this young generation. Through Facebook, Twitter and YouTube, I encountered youths who were bravely facing their truths.

"For many people, coming out is a way of saying you're not alone," says Gaby Pacheco of United We Dream. Her parents came from Ecuador and brought her to the U.S. in 1993, when she was 7. Immigration officials raided her home in 2006, and her family has been fighting deportation since. Now 27, she has three education degrees and wants to be a special-education teacher. But her life remains on hold while she watches documented friends land jobs and plan their futures. Says Pacheco: "In our movement, you come out for yourself, and you come out for other people."

The movement, as its young members call it, does not have a single leader. News travels by tweet and Facebook update, as it did when we heard that Joaquin Luna, an undocumented 18-year-old from Texas, killed himself the night after Thanksgiving and, though this is unproved, we instantly connected his death to the stresses of living as a Dreamer. Some Dreamers, contemplating coming out, ask me whether they should pretend to be legal to get by. "Should I just do what you did? You know, check the citizenship box [on a government form] and try to get the job?" a few have asked me. Often I don't know how to respond. I'd like to tell them to be open and honest, but I know I owe my career to my silence for all those years. Sometimes all I can manage to say is "You have to say yes to yourself when the world says no."

"What next?" is the question I ask myself now. It's a question that haunts every undocumented person in the U.S. The problem is, immigration has become a third-rail issue in Washington, D.C.—more controversial even than health care because it deals with issues of race and class, of entitlement and privilege, that America has struggled with since its founding. As much as we talk about the problem, we rarely focus on coming up with an actual solution—an equitable process to fix the system.

Maybe Obama will evolve on immigrant rights, just as he's evolved on gay rights, and use his executive powers to stop the deportations of undocumented youths and allow us to stay, go to school and work, if only with a temporary reprieve. The Republican Party can go one of two ways. It will either make room for its moderate voices to craft a compromise; after all, John McCain, to name just one, was a supporter of the Dream Act. Or the party will pursue a hard-line approach, further isolating not just Latinos, the largest minority group in the U.S., but also a growing multiethnic America that's adapting to the inevitable demographic and cultural shifts. In 21st century politics, diversity is destiny.

As for me, what happens next isn't just a philosophical question. I spend every day wondering what, if anything, the government plans to do with me. After months of waiting for something to happen, I decided that I would confront immigration officials myself. Since I live in New York City, I called the local ICE office. The phone operators I first reached were taken aback when I explained the reason for my call. Finally I was connected to an ICE officer.

"Are you planning on deporting me?" I asked.

I quickly found out that even though I publicly came out about my undocumented status, I still do not exist in the eyes of ICE. Like most undocumented immigrants, I've never been arrested. Therefore, I've never been in contact with ICE.

"After checking the appropriate ICE databases, the agency has no records of ever encountering Mr. Vargas," Luis Martinez, a spokesman for the ICE office in New York, wrote me in an e-mail.

I then contacted the ICE headquarters in Washington. I hoped to get some insight into my status and that of all the others who are coming out. How does ICE view these cases? Can publicly revealing undocumented status trigger deportation proceedings, and if so, how is that decided? Is ICE planning to seek my deportation?

"We do not comment on specific cases," is all I was told.

I am still here. Still in limbo. So are nearly 12 million others like me—enough to populate Ohio. We are working with you, going to school with you, paying taxes with you, worrying about our bills with you. What exactly do you want to do with us? More important, when will you realize that we are one of you?

Consider the source and the audience

- Vargas is himself an undocumented immigrant, writing for *Time* magazine. He "came out" as undocumented in the *New York Times*. Why would he pick these popular outlets with mass circulations to tell his story?
- What is his motivation for coming out of the shadows?

Lay out the argument, the values, and the assumptions

- Is Vargas making an argument here amidst the autobiographical detail?
- What does he think about U.S. immigration law and the way politicians handle the issue?

Uncover the evidence

- Vargas is relying on his own story and experience as the sources for his essay. In a first-person account, is anything else needed to back up the author's conclusions? If so, what would enhance his case?

Evaluate the conclusion

- How does Vargas characterize his experience and those of people like him? When he says, "We are one of you," what does he mean?

Sort out the political significance

- By the time you read this, Congress will either have acted on immigration reform or chosen not to. At this writing the Senate has passed a bill with a path to citizenship for people in Vargas's position, but conservatives in the House have refused to entertain the citizenship component. How does this political situation tie into the Coalition of Transformation that Ronald Brownstein discusses in Selection 2.4?

3.2 Why the Red States Will Benefit Most from Immigration

Joel Kotkin, newgeography

Why We Chose This Piece

Some of the strongest opponents of immigration (and the strongest supporters of the Tea Party movement with its anti-immigration overtones) live in the so-called "red states"—the states that reliably vote Republican on Election Day. Here, journalist Joel Kotkin points out that the red states are more and more often the destinations of immigrants seeking jobs, business opportunities, and affordable housing. Think about the political consequences of that trend.

In recent years, the debate over immigration has been portrayed in large part as a battle between immigrant-tolerant blue states and regions and their less welcoming red counterparts. Yet increasingly, it appears that red states in the interior and the south may actually have more to gain from liberalized immigration than many blue state bastions.

Indeed an analysis of foreign born population by demographer Wendell Cox reveals that the fastest growth in the numbers of newcomers are actually in cities (metropolitan areas) not usually seen as immigrant hubs. The fastest growth in population of foreign born residents--more than doubling over the decade was #1 Nashville, a place more traditionally linked to country music than ethnic diversity. Today besides the Grand Old Opry, the city also boasts the nation's largest Kurdish population, and a thriving "Little Kurdistan," as well as growing Mexican, Somali and other immigrant enclaves.

Other cities are equally surprising, including #2 Birmingham, AL; #3 Indianapolis, IN; #4 Louisville, KY and #5 Charlotte, NC, all of which doubled their foreign born population between 2000 and 2011. Right behind them are #6 Richmond, VA, #7 Raleigh, NC, #8

Selection published: February 22, 2013

Orlando, FL, #9 Jacksonville, FL and #10 Columbus, OH. All these states either voted for Mitt Romney last year or have state governments under Republican control. None easily fit the impression of liberally minded immigrant attracting bastions from only a decade ago.

Although the New York metropolitan area still has the greatest numeric growth in immigrants since 2000, a net gain of more than 600,000, there's no question that the momentum lies with these fast growing immigrant hubs. The reasons are not too difficult to fathom. In the modern global economy, migrants represent the veritable "canaries in the coalmine". They go to economic opportunities that are often the greatest, which often means thriving places like Nashville, Raleigh, Charlotte, Columbus or #11 Austin, TX. Housing prices and business climate also seem to be a factor here; all these areas have lower home prices relative to income than many traditional immigrant hubs.

As a result, many immigrants are moving from their traditional "comfort zone" cities with historical larger immigrant populations—New York, Los Angeles, San Francisco and Chicago—to generally faster growing, more affordable cities.

This is drastically reshaping the demographic future of the country. Over the past decade the increase in foreign born residents accounted for 44% of the nation's overall population growth rate. With the U.S. birthrate heading downwards, at least for now, immigration represents perhaps the one way regions can boost their populations and energize their economies. It may be America's biggest hope as well in keeping Social Security and Medicare from collapse.

Ironically, even as they migrate elsewhere, immigrants also may prove particularly critical in some of our older cities. Newcomers have been vital to maintaining population growth or at least fending off stagnation. Los Angeles, Miami, New York, Chicago and San Francisco metros have maintained enough growth among the foreign born to keep [from] going negative due to significant losses in net domestic migration. Yet even among the biggest metros the biggest growth has been among lower-cost, until fairly recently largely native-born, regions such as Houston, Dallas-Fort Worth and Atlanta.

The impact on these areas is likely to be profound over time. Urbanists like to speak about the "great inversion" of upper-class professionals to cities, but it's really the immigrants who provide the demographic and economic momentum for our largest metros. This point may be missed because many times immigrants—unlike the much cherished (and much publicized) hip, cool, largely white professionals—often do not choose to live in the overpriced, crowded urban core (although some may have businesses there).

Instead immigrants tend to cluster in the less dense, more affordable and spacious periphery, where their "American dream" of a single family house is often far more achievable. In Southern California, for example, decidedly exurban #25 San Bernardino Riverside added three times as many foreign born than long-time immigrant hub Los Angeles, despite having only one-third the total population. Los Angeles actually recorded the smallest percentage growth in foreign born of any major U.S. metro.

Over time, the immigrant impact may prove greatest in terms of economics. Immigrants, in a word, tend to be resilient, and opportunistic by nature. Although many immigrants and their offspring still lag behind economically, over time they appear to be integrating. Overall their rate of home ownership still lags that of native born Americans, but appears to have held up better since the recession.

Nowhere is the impact greater than in the entrepreneurial sector. Between 1982 and 2007, the number of businesses owned by the primary immigrant groups, Asian Americans and Hispanics grew by 545% and 696% respectfully. In contrast businesses owned by whites grew by only 81%.

Perhaps more important still, even in the midst of the recession, newcomers continued to form businesses at a record rate, even as those by native-born entrepreneurs declined. The immigrant share of all new businesses, notes Kauffman, more than doubled from 13.4% in 1996 to 29.5% in 2010.

Some emerging tech centers are particularly dependent on foreign born migration as evidenced by rapid growth in Raleigh, Austin and Columbus. Established tech centers like San Jose, San Francisco and Seattle also all have large foreign born populations. Overall immigrants are responsible for roughly a quarter of all high-tech start ups.

Much of this can be attributed to Asians, who constitute over 40% of all newcomers and now stand as the fastest growing immigrant group. They now account for roughly twenty percent of all tech workers, four times their percentage of the population.

Yet these impacts will be felt well beyond the tech community. Professionals of all kinds are moving in record numbers from the riskier political environment and pollution of China, seeking places where they can use their skills most effectively. Immigrants also play an increasingly important role in such less tech oriented industries, from the garment, carpet and furniture industries as well as small scale retail enterprise.

Newcomers also are playing a major role in the reviving housing market, particularly in places such as New York, Los Angeles, Miami, Phoenix and the Bay Area. A house that might seem outrageously overpriced to the average American family might seem rather a bargain if you are coming from Hong Kong, Beijing or Shanghai.

It is likely that, if sensible reform is passed, these impacts will begin to extend to other parts of country—such as Cleveland, Milwaukee and Memphis—that still get very little new foreign immigration. Like Houston in the 1990s, these areas have affordable housing to attract newcomers and, with any resurgence of economic growth, could provide opportunities for up and coming immigrants. A decade ago, after all, who would have seen Nashville, the ultimate symbol of our country heritage, as a rising immigrant hub?

Consider the source and the audience

- Kotkin is a journalist who covers demographic trends both for his own online journal, newgeography, and for *Forbes* magazine, among other outlets. This article appeared on websites for both. *Forbes* is a business magazine; why would Kotkin's perspective be useful to the business community?

Lay out the argument, the values, and the assumptions

- Kotkin implies that the increased immigration to red-state cities is a good thing. What benefits does he see immigration conferring on those places?
- Why might immigrants be more entrepreneurial than native residents?

Uncover the evidence

- There is a lot of demographic and economic data here. Is it sufficient for you to determine if immigration is an asset to these communities that other cities would be glad to share?
- What else might you like to see?

Evaluate the conclusion

- Kotkin concludes that the economic growth that would accompany waves of immigration would make the immigrants welcome across the country. Are economic concerns the only ones that red-state opponents of immigration might have?

Sort out the political significance

- If the ideological/demographic trends we discussed in Chapter 2 continue, new immigrants might also hold more positive ideas about the role of government than do the older, white populations in red states. If these new red-state citizens are more liberal, how might that change the political future of red states?

3.3 The End of Multiculturalism

The US Must Be a Melting Pot
Lawrence E. Harrison, *Christian Science Monitor*

Why We Chose This Piece

Lawrence E. Harrison, a professor at Tufts University, is interested in the role of culture in shaping human progress. We chose this version of his argument, which appeared in the Christian Science Monitor, because it presents a view not heard all that often these days. Multiculturalism and assimilation (or the crazy salad and the melting pot) have been the two competing paradigms for understanding American political culture. One view has us highlighting our diversity, and the other has us downplaying our differences in favor of our similarities.

Where many see multiculturalism as a tool that allows us to celebrate and include parts of the population that previously were excluded, Harrison clearly thinks multiculturalism can carry a heavy cost, especially in the United States, where we have long had a political culture that supports democracy. According to Harrison, the influx of new cultures, especially when they are not conducive to democracy, can threaten political stability.

Selection published: February 26, 2008

Is his argument an all-or-nothing argument? If you buy part of it (that some cultures are more supportive of democracy than others), do you have to buy the rest (that the addition of other cultures must do damage to democracy)?

Future generations may look back on Iraq and immigration as the two great disasters of the Bush presidency. Ironically, for a conservative administration, both of these policy initiatives were rooted in a multicultural view of the world.

Since the 1960s, multiculturalism has become a dominant feature of the political and intellectual landscape of the West. But multiculturalism rests on a frail foundation: cultural relativism, the notion that no culture is better or worse than any other—it is merely different.

When it comes to democratic continuity, social justice, and prosperity, some cultures do far better than others. Research at Tufts University's Fletcher School of Law and Diplomacy, summarized in my recent book, "The Central Liberal Truth: How Politics Can Change a Culture and Save It From Itself," makes this clear.

Extensive data suggest that the champions of progress are the Nordic countries—Denmark, Finland, Iceland, Norway, and Sweden—where, for example, universal literacy was a substantial reality in the 19th century. By contrast, no Arab country today is democratic, and female illiteracy in some Arab countries exceeds 50 percent.

Culture isn't about genes or race; it's about values, beliefs, and attitudes. Culture matters because it influences a society's receptivity to democracy, justice, entrepreneurship, and free-market institutions.

What, then, are the implications for a foreign policy based on the doctrine that "These values of freedom are right and true for every person, in every society"? The Bush administration has staked huge human, financial, diplomatic, and prestige resources on this doctrine's applicability in Iraq. It is now apparent that the doctrine is fallacious.

A key component of a successful democratic transition is trust, a particularly important cultural factor for social justice and prosperity. Trust in others reduces the cost of economic transactions, and democratic stability depends on it.

Trust is periodically measured in 80-odd countries by the World Values Survey. The Nordic countries enjoy very high levels of trust: 58 to 67 percent of respondents in four of these countries believe that most people can be trusted, compared with 11 percent of Algerians and 3 percent of Brazilians.

The high levels of identification and trust in Nordic societies reflect their homogeneity; common Lutheran antecedents, including a rigorous ethical code and heavy emphasis on education; and a consequent sense of the nation as one big family imbued with the golden rule.

Again, culture matters—race doesn't. The ethnic roots of both Haiti and Barbados lie in the Dahomey region of West Africa. The history of Haiti, independent in 1804 in the wake of a slave uprising against the French colonists, is one of corrupt, incompetent leadership; illiteracy; and poverty. Barbados, which gained its independence from the British in 1966, is today a prosperous democracy of "Afro-Saxons."

Immigration

Hispanics now form the largest US minority, approaching 15 percent—about 45 million—of a total population of about 300 million. They're projected by the Pew Research Center to swell to 127 million in 2050—29 percent of a total population of 438 million. Their experience in the United States recapitulates Latin America's culturally shaped underdevelopment. For example, the Hispanic high school dropout rate in the US is alarmingly high and persistent—about 20 percent in second and subsequent generations. It's vastly higher in Latin America.

Samuel Huntington was on the mark when he wrote in his latest book "Who Are We? The Challenges to America's National Identity": "Would America be the America it is today if it had been settled not by British Protestants but by French, Spanish, or Portuguese Catholics? The answer is no. It would not be America; it would be Quebec, Mexico, or Brazil."

In "The Americano Dream," Mexican-American Lionel Sosa argues that the value system that has retarded progress in Latin America is an impediment to upward mobility of Latino immigrants. So does former US Rep. Herman Badillo, a Puerto Rican whose book, "One Nation, One Standard," indicts Latino undervaluing of education and calls for cultural change.

The progress of Hispanic immigrants, not to mention harmony in the broader society, depends on their acculturation to mainstream US values. Efforts—for example, long-term bilingual education—to perpetuate "old country" values in a multicultural salad bowl undermine acculturation to the mainstream and are likely to result in continuing underachievement, poverty, resentment, and divisiveness. So, too, does the willy-nilly emergence of bilingualism in the US. No language in American history has ever before competed with English to the point where one daily hears, on the telephone, "If you want to speak English, press one; *Si quiere hablar en español, oprima el botón número dos.*"

Although border security and environmental concerns are also in play, the immigration debate has been framed largely in economic terms, producing some odd pro-immigration bedfellows, for example the editorial pages of *The New York Times* and *The Wall Street Journal*. Among the issues: whether the US economy needs more unskilled immigrants; whether immigrants take jobs away from US citizens; to what extent illegal immigrants drain resources away from education, healthcare, and welfare; and whether population growth, largely driven by immigration, is necessary for a healthy economy.

But immigration looks very different when viewed in cultural terms, particularly with respect to the vast legal and illegal Latino immigration, a million or more people a year, most of them with few skills and little education. To be sure, the US has absorbed large numbers of unskilled and uneducated immigrants in the past, and today the large majority of their descendants are in the cultural mainstream. But the numbers of Latino immigrants and their geographic concentration today leave real doubts about the prospects for acculturation: 70 percent of children in the Los Angeles public schools and 60 percent in the Denver schools are Latino.

In a letter to me in 1991, the late Mexican-American columnist Richard Estrada captured the essence of the problem:

"The problem in which the current immigration is suffused is, at heart, one of numbers; for when the numbers begin to favor not only the maintenance and replenishment of the immigrants' source culture, but also its overall growth, and in particular growth so large that the numbers not only impede assimilation but go beyond to pose a challenge to the traditional culture of the American nation, then there is a great deal about which to be concerned."

Some recommendations

If multiculturalism is a myth, how do we avoid the woes that inevitably attend the creation of an enduring and vast underclass alienated from the upwardly mobile cultural mainstream? Some policy implications, one for Latin America, the others for the US and Canada, are apparent.

We must calibrate the flow of immigrants into the US to the needs of the economy, mindful that immigration has adversely affected low-income American citizens, disproportionately African-American and Hispanic, as Barbara Jordan stressed as chair of the 1990s Immigration Reform Commission. But the flow must also be calibrated to the country's capacity to assure acculturation of the immigrants.

We must be a melting pot, not a salad bowl. The melting pot, the essence of which is the Anglo-Protestant cultural tradition, is our way of creating the homogeneity that has contributed so much to the trust and mutual identification—and progress—of the Nordic societies.

As with immigration flows of the late 19th and early 20th centuries, an extensive program of activities designed to facilitate acculturation, including mastery of English, should be mounted. A law declaring English to be the national language would be helpful.

The costs of multiculturalism—in terms of disunity, the clash of classes, and declining trust—are likely to be huge in the long run. All cultures are not equal when it comes to promoting progress, and very few can match Anglo-Protestantism in this respect. We should be promoting acculturation to the national mainstream, not a mythical, utopian multiculturalism. And we should take care that the Anglo-Protestant virtues that have brought us so far do not fall into disrepair, let alone disrepute.

Consider the source and the audience

- The *Christian Science Monitor* is a well-respected, independently owned newspaper, with no clear ideological slant. Is this article more compelling appearing here than it would be if it appeared in a conservative source?

Lay out the argument, the values, and the assumptions

- What is the connection, according to Harrison, between culture and democracy? What is the danger threatened by multiculturalism?
- How does immigration figure in Harrison's argument? What new cultures is he particularly worried about in the United States and why?

Uncover the evidence

- What kind of evidence does Harrison provide to support his claim about the connections between culture, democracy, and immigration? Is this evidence adequate?

Evaluate the conclusion

- Is it enough to show that those in thriving democracies hold certain values to conclude that those who hold different values are a threat to democracy?
- Are there ways to assimilate cultures in terms of their democratic values while still celebrating the languages, foods, and traditions that mark different cultures?

Sort out the political implications

- If we buy Harrison's conclusions, what kind of immigration policy should we enact? Are there other policies we could put in place to offset the effects he is worried about?

3.4 What America Will We Pick?

Eugene Robinson, *Washington Post*

Why We Chose This Piece

We selected this Washington Post *article, by Pulitzer Prize–winning journalist Eugene Robinson, because it ties together the ideological arguments we read in Chapter 2 with the demographic patterns noted in this one. Robinson is writing in the weeks right before the 2012 presidential election, a contest he says was really about national identity. Is he right?*

This election is only tangentially a fight over policy. It is also a fight about meaning and identity—and that's one reason voters are so polarized. It's about who we are and who we aspire to be.

President Obama enters the final days of the campaign with a substantial lead among women—about 11 points, according to the latest *Washington Post*/ABC News poll—and enormous leads among Latinos and African Americans, the nation's two largest minority groups. Mitt Romney leads among white voters, with an incredible 2-to-1 advantage among white men.

Selection published: October 25, 2012

It is too simplistic to conclude that demography equals destiny. Both men are being sincere when they vow to serve the interests of all Americans. But it would be disingenuous to pretend not to notice the obvious cleavage between those who have long held power in this society and those who are beginning to attain it.

When Republicans vow to "take back our country," they never say from whom. But we can guess.

Issues of race, power and privilege are less explicit this year than they were in 2008, but in some ways they are even stronger.

Four years ago, we asked ourselves whether the nation would ever elect a black president. The question was front and center. Every time we see the president and his family walk across the White House lawn to board Marine One, we're reminded of the answer.

The intensity of the opposition to Obama has less to do with who he is than with the changes in U.S. society he not only represents but incarnates. Citing his race as a factor in the way some of his opponents have bitterly resisted his policies immediately draws an outraged cry: "You're saying that just because I oppose Obama, I'm a racist." No, I'm not saying that at all.

What I'm saying is that Obama's racial identity is a constant reminder of how much the nation has changed in a relatively short time. In my lifetime, we've experienced the civil rights movement, the countercultural explosion of the 1960s, the sexual revolution, the women's movement and an unprecedented wave of Latino immigration. Within a few decades, there will be no white majority in this country—no majority of any kind, in fact. We will be a nation of racial and ethnic minorities, and we will only prosper if everyone learns to give and take.

Our place in the world has changed as well. The United States remains the dominant economic and military power; our ideals remain a beacon for those around the globe still yearning to breathe free. But our capacity for unilateral action is diminished; we can assert but not dictate, and we must learn to persuade.

Obama's great sin, for some who oppose him, is to make it impossible to ignore these domestic and international megatrends. Take one look at Obama and the phenomenon of demographic change is inescapable. Observe his approach to international crises in places such as Libya or Syria and the reality of America's place in the world is unavoidable.

I'm deliberately leaving aside what should be the biggest factor in the election: Obama's policies. It happens that I have supported most of them, but of course there are legitimate reasons to favor Romney's proposals, insofar as we know what they really are—and the extent to which they really differ from Obama's.

In foreign affairs, judging by Monday's debate, the differences are too small to discern; Romney promises to speak in a louder voice and perhaps deploy more battleships, but that's about it. Domestically, however, I see a clear choice. I consider the Affordable Care Act a great achievement, and Romney's promise to repeal it would alone be reason enough for me to oppose him. Add in the tax cuts for the wealthy, the plan to "voucherize" Medicare and the appointments Romney would likely make to the Supreme Court, and the implications of this election become even weightier.

Issues may explain our sharp political divisions, but they can't be the cause of our demographic polarization. White men need medical care, too. African Americans and Latinos understand the need to get our fiscal house in order. The recession and the slow recovery have taken a toll across the board.

Some of Obama's opponents have tried to delegitimize his presidency because he doesn't embody the America they once knew. He embodies the America of now.

Consider the source and the audience

- Robinson's column is published by the *Washington Post*, but it is syndicated in newspapers around the country. He is an opinion writer who doesn't claim to be objective, as he makes clear in this piece. To whom is he addressing this column?

Lay out the argument, the values, and the assumptions

- Robinson is an African American journalist who got teary on television the night that Obama won the presidency in 2008. He has been frank about the changes he thinks Obama's election signaled, and he does not think that economics is the only thing dividing right and left in this country. In what way does he think we are fighting for our national identity?
- What does he think is behind the conservative demand to "take our country back"?

Uncover the evidence

- Does Robinson give any evidence for his arguments about demography and power? Does he need to?
- How could you find evidence to support or disprove his claims?

Evaluate the conclusion

- Robinson argues that some critics of Obama have tried to delegitimize his presidency because they fear that his ascendance means that they and people like them will no longer hold power. Is that a plausible conclusion?
- Was the election about who we want the face of America to be?

Sort out the political significance

- Obama won the election, as we saw in Chapter 2, with outsized portions of the black, Hispanic, Asian, women, and youth vote. What does this growing coalition say about American national identity?

● ●

3.5 I Have a Dream
Martin Luther King Jr.

Why We Chose This Piece

Several of the pieces in this chapter have attempted to define the "American dream," and some have looked specifically at the place of race in that dream. We will deal with the civil rights movement in a later chapter, but for now we cannot separate the pervasive issue of race from fundamental questions about American political culture, particularly when we attempt to understand the central American ideal of equality.

This famous speech by Martin Luther King Jr., given at a Washington, D.C., civil rights rally in August 1963, is a classic statement about the meaning of equality in the American dream. In this speech, King outlines the many ways that the United States had failed African Americans in the middle of the twentieth century, and he describes his hopes for an America in which the equality promised in the Declaration of Independence becomes a reality for all Americans, black and white. How does King define equality? How does his definition compare with others we have seen in this chapter? Has the election of President Obama realized King's dream, or moved us closer to it?

I am happy to join with you today in what will go down in history as the greatest demonstration for freedom in the history of our nation.

Five score years ago, a great American, in whose symbolic shadow we stand today, signed the Emancipation Proclamation. This momentous decree came as a great beacon light of hope to millions of Negro slaves who had been seared in the flames of withering injustice. It came as a joyous daybreak to end the long night of their captivity.

But 100 years later, the Negro still is not free. One hundred years later, the life of the Negro is still sadly crippled by the manacles of segregation and the chains of discrimination. One hundred years later, the Negro lives on a lonely island of poverty in the midst of a vast ocean of material prosperity. One hundred years later, the Negro is still languishing in the corners of American society and finds himself an exile in his own land. And so we've come here today to dramatize a shameful condition.

In a sense we've come to our nation's capital to cash a check. When the architects of our republic wrote the magnificent words of the Constitution and the Declaration of Independence, they were signing a promissory note to which every American was to fall heir. This note was a promise that all men—yes, black men as well as white men—would be guaranteed the unalienable rights of life, liberty, and the pursuit of happiness.

Selection delivered: August 28, 1963

It is obvious today that America has defaulted on this promissory note insofar as her citizens of color are concerned. Instead of honoring this sacred obligation, America has given the Negro people a bad check, a check that has come back marked "insufficient funds."

But we refuse to believe that the bank of justice is bankrupt. We refuse to believe that there are insufficient funds in the great vaults of opportunity of this nation. And so we've come to cash this check, a check that will give us upon demand the riches of freedom and security of justice. We have also come to his hallowed spot to remind America of the fierce urgency of now. This is no time to engage in the luxury of cooling off or to take the tranquilizing drug of gradualism. Now is the time to make real the promises of democracy. Now is the time to rise from the dark and desolate valley of segregation to the sunlit path of racial justice. Now is the time to lift our nation from the quicksands of racial injustice to the solid rock of brotherhood. Now is the time to make justice a reality for all of God's children.

It would be fatal for the nation to overlook the urgency of the moment. This sweltering summer of the Negro's legitimate discontent will not pass until there is an invigorating autumn of freedom and equality. Nineteen sixty-three is not an end but a beginning. Those who hoped that the Negro needed to blow off steam and will now be content will have a rude awakening if the nation returns to business as usual. There will be neither rest nor tranquility in America until the Negro is granted his citizenship rights. The whirlwinds of revolt will continue to shake the foundations of our nation until the bright day of justice emerges.

But there is something that I must say to my people who stand on the warm threshold which leads into the palace of justice. In the process of gaining our rightful place we must not be guilty of wrongful deeds. Let us not seek to satisfy our thirst for freedom by drinking from the cup of bitterness and hatred. We must forever conduct our struggle on the high plane of dignity and discipline. We must not allow our creative protest to degenerate into physical violence. Again and again we must rise to the majestic heights of meeting physical force with soul force. The marvelous new militancy which has engulfed the Negro community must not lead us to a distrust of all white people, for many of our white brothers, as evidenced by their presence here today, have come to realize that their destiny is tied up with our destiny. And they have come to realize that their freedom is inextricably bound to our freedom. We cannot walk alone.

And as we walk, we must make the pledge that we shall always march ahead. We cannot turn back. There are those who are asking the devotees of civil rights, "When will you be satisfied?" We can never be satisfied as long as the Negro is the victim of the unspeakable horrors of police brutality. We can never be satisfied as long as our bodies, heavy with the fatigue of travel, cannot gain lodging in the motels of the highways and the hotels of the cities. We cannot be satisfied as long as the Negro's basic mobility is from a smaller ghetto to a larger one. We can never be satisfied as long as our children are stripped of their selfhood and robbed of their dignity by signs stating "for whites only." We cannot be satisfied as long as a Negro in Mississippi cannot vote and a Negro in New York believes he has nothing for which to vote. No, no we are not satisfied and we will not be satisfied until justice rolls down like waters and righteousness like a mighty stream.

I am not unmindful that some of you have come here out of great trials and tribulations. Some of you have come fresh from narrow jail cells. Some of you have come from areas where your quest for freedom left you battered by storms of persecution and staggered by the winds of police brutality. You have been the veterans of creative suffering. Continue to work with the faith that unearned suffering is redemptive.

Go back to Mississippi, go back to Alabama, go back to South Carolina, go back to Georgia, go back to Louisiana, go back to the slums and ghettos of our northern cities, knowing that somehow this situation can and will be changed.

Let us not wallow in the valley of despair. I say to you today my friends—so even though we face the difficulties of today and tomorrow, I still have a dream. It is a dream deeply rooted in the American dream.

I have a dream that one day this nation will rise up and live out the true meaning of its creed: "We hold these truths to be self-evident, that all men are created equal."

I have a dream that one day on the red hills of Georgia the sons of former slaves and the sons of former slave owners will be able to sit down together at the table of brotherhood.

I have a dream that one day even the state of Mississippi, a state sweltering with the heat of injustice, sweltering with the heat of oppression, will be transformed into an oasis of freedom and justice.

I have a dream that my four little children will one day live in a nation where they will not be judged by the color of their skin but by the content of their character.

I have a dream today.

I have a dream that one day down in Alabama, with its vicious racists, with its governor having his lips dripping with the words of interposition and nullification—one day right there in Alabama little black boys and black girls will be able to join hands with little white boys and white girls as sisters and brothers.

I have a dream today.

I have a dream that one day every valley shall be exalted, and every hill and mountain shall be made low, the rough places will be made plain, and the crooked places will be made straight, and the glory of the Lord shall be revealed and all flesh shall see it together.

This is our hope. This is the faith that I go back to the South with. With this faith we will be able to hew out of the mountain of despair a stone of hope. With this faith we will be able to transform the jangling discords of our nation into a beautiful symphony of brotherhood. With this faith we will be able to work together, to pray together, to struggle together, to go to jail together, to stand up for freedom together, knowing that we will be free one day.

This will be the day, this will be the day when all of God's children will be able to sing with new meaning "My country 'tis of thee, sweet land of liberty, of thee I sing. Land where my fathers died, land of the Pilgrim's pride, from every mountainside, let freedom ring!"

And if America is to be a great nation, this must become true. And so let freedom ring from the prodigious hilltops of New Hampshire. Let freedom ring from the mighty mountains of New York. Let freedom ring from the heightening Alleghenies of Pennsylvania.

Let freedom ring from the snow-capped Rockies of Colorado. Let freedom ring from the curvaceous slopes of California.

But not only that; let freedom ring from Stone Mountain of Georgia.

Let freedom ring from Lookout Mountain of Tennessee.

Let freedom ring from every hill and molehill of Mississippi—from every mountainside.

Let freedom ring. And when this happens, and when we allow freedom to ring—when we let it ring from every village and every hamlet, from every state and every city, we will be able to speed up that day when all of God's children— black men and white men, Jews and Gentiles, Protestants and Catholics—will be able to join hands and sing in the words of the old Negro spiritual: "Free at last! Free at last! Thank God Almighty, we are free at last!"

Consider the source and the audience

- King is gaining access to a real national audience for the first time in this speech. How does he use symbols, language, and history to appeal to that audience?

Lay out the argument, the values, and the assumptions

- How would King define the basic values of equality and freedom he talks about? What is his dream?
- What political tactics does he think will make his dream reality?

Uncover the evidence

- Does King offer evidence to make his case? What kind?
- What rhetorical tactics does he use to support his case? What is the purpose of laying claim to important symbols like the Declaration of Independence, the American dream, and "My Country 'Tis of Thee"?

Evaluate the conclusion

- Is King successful in claiming for black Americans the fundamental American rights and dreams that white people take for granted?
- What kind of case would his opponents have to make to argue against him?

Sort out the political implications

- What strategies does King use to make his declaration and his intentions nonthreatening to whites? How did his strategy advance the civil rights movement in the 1960s?
- What might King have said if he could have witnessed the presidential election of 2008?
- What groups today might want to give their own "I Have a Dream" speech?

4

Federalism and the Constitution

By most estimations, the U.S. Constitution is a marvel. It provides a stable yet flexible political structure that guarantees us unprecedented individual freedom, although most of the time we are barely aware it is there. In normal times we take it for granted, but when things turn tough—when a president is impeached, an election is contested, the nation is attacked, or the country launches a war—we are sharply aware of the value of what the founders wrought. Since September 11, 2001, Americans have had more cause than usual to appreciate the brilliance of James Madison and his colleagues, as events that might have blown another nation off its course have ultimately been no more than choppy seas for the American ship of state. In this chapter we explore three of the central principles that make our Constitution work: federalism, separation of powers, and checks and balances.

Federalism is the concept of dividing power between the national government and its regional governments (in our case, the states). With the Articles of Confederation the founders had tried a system in which the power was grounded in the states, but most of them rejected it because the absence of a strong center led to political and economic instability. The alternative, a unitary system in which all the power was centralized, was unacceptable to men who feared a strong government on the English model. A federal system, in which states possessed some constitutional power but the national government was supreme, was a compromise that has proved flexible enough to weather many constitutional storms. Indeed, the balance of power has shifted back and forth between nation and states throughout our history, driven by historical events and judicial interpretation.

The principles of separation of powers and checks and balances hold that liberty is best preserved and power limited when it is divided among three branches of government that are mostly separate but with each given a little power over the others to keep an eye on them. The founders believed that by dividing power between the two federal levels, and then among three branches at each level, they were providing the best security for the new republic.

The readings in this chapter give you a variety of perspectives on the Constitution and the principles on which it is based. The opening piece, by Keith Olbermann on his now-defunct show on MSNBC, uses humor to mock the notion that Texas should secede from the United States. The second piece looks at an Iowa congressman's efforts to derail a California law regarding the proper way to raise chickens. In a *New York Times* column, Sanford Levinson writes that the Constitution is rife with outmoded mechanisms that don't work. This piece raises arguments made in that classic work on checks and balances, Madison's *Federalist* No. 51, our final selection.

4.1 "Countdown with Keith Olbermann" for Friday, May 15, 2009

Keith Olbermann, MSNBC

Why We Chose This Piece

You might be surprised to run in to Keith Olbermann in these pages, but even liberal figures like MSNBC's Olbermann (or Bill O'Reilly, his conservative nemesis on Fox News) can raise interesting issues—the trick is to recognize their ideology and be careful to process what they have to say accordingly.

In this transcript, Olbermann is on a rant about the issue of Texas secession, a possibility Texas governor Rick Perry had raised earlier. While Olbermann's goal is to be funny (a goal you might think he has met if you are a liberal, or failed dismally at if you are conservative), he makes a point often overlooked in the debate that followed Perry's pronouncement.

Perry had hinted that secession might be on the agenda because President Barack Obama's stimulus package was forcing states to adopt spending programs, possibly in violation of the Tenth Amendment, which says that all powers not given to the national government by the Constitution are reserved to the states. What Olbermann focuses on is not the federal programs that Texas would be forced to adopt by the stimulus plan, but the ones Texas would be forced to give up if it seceded. By Olbermann's reckoning, secession would be very costly to Texas, indeed.

As you read this piece, remember that Olbermann is (1) pretty liberal and (2) an entertainer. (He made the leap to political commentary from sports commentary and sometimes treats the two activities like halves of the same whole.) So strip out the drama and rhetoric and just look at the contrast Olbermann draws between Texas as part of the United States and Texas as its own country. What are the political and economic advantages of belonging to a greater union? What would Texas give up if it decided to go it alone? What does this tell us about the strengths and weaknesses of federalism from a states' rights point of view?

Selection aired: May 15, 2009

OLBERMANN: Finally, as promised, tonight's number one story, our new regular feature, the WTF moment. An elected governor of an American state continues to flirt with treason. Rick Perry of Texas, who probably would advocate stoning the heathen in Valverde if it would win him 37 extra votes, has once again refused the opportunity to step back from the stupidity that is secession.

(BEGIN VIDEO CLIP)

GOV. RICK PERRY, TEXAS: We live in a great country. America is -

Texas is a very unique state inside that great country. And there's no reason for us to be even talking at seceding.

But if Washington continues to force these programs on the states, if Washington continues to disregard the Tenth Amendment, you know, who knows what happens. There may be people standing up all the country in tea parties saying, enough. All right.

(END VIDEO CLIP)

OLBERMANN: How about them standing up in Texas and saying enough, all right, governor ass hat. Recent polling suggests more than a third of all Texans believe the place would be better off independent of the United States. It is a split among Republicans. But when you reduce it to just the bully's threat to take his ball and go home, 51 percent of all Texas Republicans approve of the suggestion that Texas may need to leave the United States.

You know what the South Carolina politician James Lewis Pettigrew said of his state, just before the Civil War, too small for a republic and too big for an insane asylum.

Governor, have you or your separatist friends considered what would happen if you actually seceded? Assuming the rest of the country did not decide it was a rebellion, and didn't send in federal troops, and didn't try to capture you and hang you, and, in a bitter irony, did not suspend habeas corpus in the rebellious territory, so that former President George W. Bush could be detained without charge and without access to attorneys?

I'm talking about what would happen if we all just sat back and said, bye, have fun storming the castle.

Let's start internally. Your taxes would shoot through the roof. Just FEMA has sent $3,449,000,000 to Texas since 2001. Other agencies sent you another billion just for Hurricane Ike last year.

When NASA pulls out of Houston, that's 26,000 jobs, another 2.5 billion you just lost from your economy. We'd obviously move everybody out of Ft. Hood, Texas, whose financial impact on your new kingdom is another six billion.

Your own country? Get your own damn forts, and you're own damn Air Force, Army, Navy. What is that, 10 billion a year, 100, a trillion? You'll need some form of welfare, Social Security. You'll have to get your own FDA, CDC, FDC, FEC, FBI, CIA, NSA, Post Office. You'll need a lot of new investments after the Americans—I'm sorry, the Gringos pull out. You've got four nuclear power plants there. Good for you. Where were you going to put all the nuclear waste? The Alamo?

Remember, these are all the startup costs. I lost track at about 500 billion and we haven't even gotten to annual maintenance or expansion or improvements. Pell Grants, I forgot Pell Grants. The U.S. gave Texas students a billion dollars in Pell Grants for the academic year 2006–2007. Good luck with that.

What are you going do about your sports franchises? The Cowboys just spent a billion on that new stadium. "America's team." That's funny, the Cowboys, "North Texas' team."

Now, no American network is going to want to televise their games, because the ratings in Texas will no longer count in America. You'll be Canada with something of a twang. Do you think it's a coincidence that half the Canadian baseball teams went out of business because of TV revenues and other reasons, and half of the Canadian basketball teams?

So take your choice, Astros or Rangers. One of them is going to move to Charlotte. Who exactly do you think your University of Texas football team is going to play now? USC? Oklahoma? Try Sul Ross or San Jacinto JC or the new big rivalry with Tom Delay Exterminator University.

Now, security. You'll need your own Gitmo. Starting wars is optional, of course. See your Mr. Bush about that. And since you'll be surrounded by the United States and Mexico, presumably the U.S. will continue this knuckle headed border fence you guys started, only it won't be on your southern border anymore. Now it will be on your northern one, because the rest of us here, we can't risk the economic impact of hordes of illegal aliens fleeing the chaos of the United State of Texas, or the Texican nation, or Texaco, or whatever you're going to call yourselves.

So you'll have to put up your own fence at your own expense.

We'll talk politics for a second too. Let's look at what your departure will mean back here in the northern 49. Congratulations to the Democrats and their filibuster proof 60 seats in the 98 seat, Texas-free Senate. And thanks from the Dems in California, New York, Florida, Illinois and Michigan, which will take the lion's portions of those Texas electoral college seats, 13. Eleven more would go to other blue states. The other red states would, of course, get the leftovers, ten.

Per Nate Silver's calculation, if Texas had left last year, Obama would have won the electoral college by 242 votes, not by 192. And also speaking of politics, remember sovereign republic of Texas, you've got your big political nightmare coming up 11 years from now. The big political nightmare, the big political nightmare, you know, when the Mexican Texans get the ballot initiative passed on whether or not Texas should become part of Mexico.

Right now, Texas is 48 percent Anglo, 36 percent Hispanic. With no major change in population, just progressing things outward, by 2020, every projection has Anglos being outnumbered by Hispanics in Texas. That's in 2020. By 2040, the Anglos will comprise barely a fourth of the population of Texas.

I'm sorry, of Tejas. Texas state in Mexico. Hasta la vista, baby.

Don't let Oklahoma hit you on the backside on the way out.

Secession; what the——

That's COUNTDOWN for this the 2,206th day since the previous president declared mission accomplished in Iraq. I'm Keith Olbermann, good night and good luck.

Consider the source and the audience

- "Countdown with Keith Olbermann" is an unabashedly liberal source, and Olbermann is clearly mocking the Republican governor of Texas in this piece. Does his bias render everything he says suspect? How can you sort the worthwhile from the purely ideological?
- There is no doubt that Olbermann is "preaching to the choir" on his show—that is, he is speaking to people who already agree with him. Would this piece be likely to sway any stray conservative watchers who happened to tune in? Why or why not?

Lay out the argument, the values, and the assumptions

- What is Olbermann's point about federalism? Is there much to be gained by states in the relationship? If so, why would a state threaten to withdraw from the union?

Uncover the evidence

- What kinds of evidence does Olbermann use to make the case that states benefit from federalism and big states like Texas benefit greatly?
- Besides data on the monetary value of the programs that Texas receives, Olbermann raises cultural issues such as sports, language, and identity. Does that strengthen or weaken his case?

Evaluate the conclusion

- Olbermann clearly thinks that Governor Perry is foolish for talking about secession, given what his state gains by being part of the Union. How effectively does he make that point in this segment?
- Olbermann uses humor as a tool to drive home his point. Does humor make a serious conclusion easier or harder to absorb?

Sort out the political implications

- What political motivation might Perry have had for talking about secession? Who would be attracted by such talk, and who repelled?
- How important is the federal relationship to our identities as citizens of states and of the United States?

• •

4.2 An Iowa Fox in California's Hen House

Editorial, *Press Democrat*

Why We Chose This Piece

Should states be allowed to decide how the food sold within their limits is produced? California has passed a law specifying that hens that lay eggs sold in California must be treated humanely. A congressman from Iowa is working (so far unsuccessfully, but that may change by the time you read this) to pass a national law that would override state laws on this practice. Who should get to decide issues about food sold within a state? We chose this editorial because it illustrates just how complex the federal relationship can get.

Rep. Steve King is a small-government conservative, a tea-party darling who will enthusiastically tell you that Washington meddles too much in state and local affairs.

Until he disagrees with local voters and their elected representatives.

Then he's all for Washington laying down the law.

King, R-Iowa, doesn't like a California law that sets standards for humane treatment of hens on egg-producing farms.

You may not be surprised to learn that there are 42 million hens in King's district—about 80 birds for every human—making it the Big Roost in the nation's top egg-producing state.

But this isn't a simple tale of a congressman sticking up for a local industry—at least not the industry in question. Contrary to King's stance, the Iowa Poultry Association, the egg lobby in King's home state, has endorsed national standards for humane treatment based on California's law.

Legislation to set such standards is stalled in the Senate. In the House, meanwhile, King is working on behalf of beef and pork producers, who fear that they too could be yoked to humane treatment standards, to undermine California's law.

Five years ago, Golden State voters overwhelmingly approved Proposition 2, which requires that cages on California farms be large enough for chickens to stand up, turn around and spread their wings. How much space is that? About as much as an 8½-by-11-inch sheet of paper.

The initiative takes effect in 2015, and so does a statute adopted by the Legislature to apply the same standard for any eggs sold in California.

King cried foul. He says states are free to set standards for their own farms, but those standards shouldn't apply to food produced in other states.

Iowa's egg farmers aren't the only ones asking for a national standard. Legislation modeled on Proposition 2 was endorsed by the United Egg Producers, an industry group representing the owners of 95 percent of the nation's egg-laying hens, and the Humane Society of the United States.

Selection published: June 13, 2013

It was offered in the Senate by Democrat Dianne Feinstein of California. Despite industry support, Feinstein's amendment was left out of the Senate version of the Farm Bill, which was passed this week. King's amendment was inserted in the House version, which is expected to come to the floor in the coming weeks.

There's a lot to dislike about both versions of the Farm Bill. They're packed with subsidies and sweetheart deals benefitting, among others, dairy farmers and sugar producers. They create a new crop insurance program that costs taxpayers too much money and creates perverse incentives to farm marginal land. They cut the food stamp program and generally favor Big Ag over small farmers.

The two bills will eventually land in a conference committee where there will be a chance to undo some of the worst provisions, including, we hope, King's effort to thwart the will of California voters.

California isn't the only state that stands to lose if King's amendment becomes law. Scores of state laws, including those protecting New Hampshire maple syrup and sweet Vidalia onions from Georgia, are at stake.

Congress should let the states—like hens on California farms—spread their wings, leaving King's amendment to line cages.

Consider the source and the audience

- This is an editorial—clearly designed to convey the opinion of the editors— from a California newspaper. Since the issue is about the validity of a California state law, whose interests would you expect them to support?

Lay out the argument, the values, and the assumptions

- The editors are upfront about where they stand. Why do they reject the efforts of the U.S. Congress to replace state standards for food sold in California with national standards?
- What motives do they assign to Rep. Steve King?
- They are not very happy with the Farm Bill in general. Why not?

Uncover the evidence

- How do the editors know that King's motivation is to protect the interests of beef and pork producers? Is there any way to find out this information?
- How do they know there is widespread support for making California's standards national?

Evaluate the conclusion

- The paper's editors argue that states should be allowed to set their own standards. How would they feel if the national Farm Bill enforced California's standards on all the other states?

Sort out the political significance

- The paper accuses Representative King of hypocrisy for favoring state control until it conflicts with the interests of his corporate agriculture supporters, but many people are inconsistent in their support of state or national problem solving when it hits close to home. Is there a fair and consistent way to handle the problem of state standards of production in a national market?

● ●

4.3 Our Imbecilic Constitution

Sanford Levinson, *New York Times*

Why We Chose This Piece

Most Americans have a pretty reverential attitude to the Constitution, no matter how cynical they may be about the way politics plays out within its rules. In this piece, Professor Sanford Levinson takes a refreshingly contrarian view—that the Constitution itself is dysfunctional. We chose this article to remind you that the provisions of the Constitution were political choices made by long-gone politicians. Are those choices still relevant today?

Advocating the adoption of the new Constitution drafted in Philadelphia, the authors of "The Federalist Papers" mocked the "imbecility" of the weak central government created by the Articles of Confederation.

Nearly 225 years later, critics across the spectrum call the American political system dysfunctional, even pathological. What they don't mention, though, is the role of the Constitution itself in generating the pathology.

Ignore, for discussion's sake, the clauses that helped to entrench chattel slavery until it was eliminated by a brutal Civil War. Begin with the Senate and its assignment of equal voting power to California and Wyoming; Vermont and Texas; New York and North Dakota. Consider that, although a majority of Americans since World War II have registered opposition to the Electoral College, we will participate this year in yet another election that "battleground states" will dominate while the three largest states will be largely ignored.

Our vaunted system of "separation of powers" and "checks and balances"—a legacy of the founders' mistrust of "factions"—means that we rarely have anything that can truly be described as a "government." Save for those rare instances when one party has hefty control over four branches—the House of Representatives, the Senate, the White House and the Supreme Court—gridlock threatens. Elections are increasingly meaningless, at least in terms of producing results commensurate with the challenges facing the country.

Selection published: May 28, 2012

But if one must choose the worst single part of the Constitution, it is surely Article V, which has made our Constitution among the most difficult to amend of any in the world. The last truly significant constitutional change was the 22nd Amendment, added in 1951, to limit presidents to two terms. The near impossibility of amending the national Constitution not only prevents needed reforms; it also makes discussion seem futile and generates a complacent denial that there is anything to be concerned about.

It was not always so. In the election of 1912, two presidents—past and future—seriously questioned the adequacy of the Constitution. Theodore Roosevelt would have allowed Congress to override Supreme Court decisions invalidating federal laws, while Woodrow Wilson basically supported a parliamentary system and, as president, tried to act more as a prime minister than as an agent of Congress. The next few years saw the enactment of amendments establishing the legitimacy of the federal income tax, direct election of senators, Prohibition and women's right to vote.

No such debate is likely to take place between Barack Obama and Mitt Romney. They, like most contemporary Americans, have seemingly lost their capacity for thinking seriously about the extent to which the Constitution serves us well. Instead, the Constitution is enveloped in near religious veneration. (Indeed, Mormon theology treats it as God-given.)

What might radical reform mean?

We might look to the 50 state constitutions, most of which are considerably easier to amend. There have been more than 230 state constitutional conventions; each state has had an average of almost three constitutions. (New York, for example, is on its fifth Constitution, adopted in 1938.) This year Ohioans will be voting on whether to call a new constitutional convention; its Constitution, like 13 others, including New York's, gives voters the chance to do so at regular intervals, typically 20 years.

Another reform would aim to fix Congressional gridlock. We could permit each newly elected president to appoint 50 members of the House and 10 members of the Senate, all to serve four-year terms until the next presidential election. Presidents would be judged on actual programs, instead of hollow rhetoric.

If enhanced presidential power seems too scary, then the solution might lie in reducing, if not eliminating, the president's power to veto legislation and to return to true bicameralism, instead of the tricameralism we effectively operate under. We might allow deadlocks between the two branches of Congress to be broken by, say, a supermajority of the House or of Congress voting as a whole.

One might also be inspired by the states to allow at least some aspects of direct democracy. California—the only state with a constitution more dysfunctional than that of the United States—allows constitutional amendment at the ballot box. Maine, more sensibly, allows its citizenry to override legislation they deem objectionable. Might we not be far better off to have a national referendum on "Obamacare" instead of letting nine politically unaccountable judges decide?

Even if we want to preserve judicial review of national legislation, something Justice Oliver Wendell Holmes Jr. believed could be dispensed with, perhaps we should emulate North Dakota or Nebraska, which require supermajorities of their court to invalidate state legislation. Why shouldn't the votes of, say, seven of the nine Supreme Court justices be required to overturn national legislation?

Or consider the fact that almost all states have rejected the model of judges nominated by the president and then confirmed by the Senate. Most state judges are electorally accountable in some way, and almost all must retire at a given age. Many states have adopted commissions to limit the politicization of the appointment process.

What was truly admirable about the framers was their willingness to critique, indeed junk, the Articles of Confederation. One need not believe that the Constitution of 1787 should be discarded in quite the same way to accept that we are long overdue for a serious discussion about its own role in creating the depressed (and depressing) state of American politics.

Consider the source and the audience

- The author of this opinion article is a law and politics professor at the University of Texas, and he is writing in the *New York Times*, just months before the 2012 election. While this is a theme he has written on before, why does he think it was relevant at the time he wrote this piece?
- How is his national audience in the *Times* likely to react?

Lay out the argument, the values, and the assumptions

- Levinson argues that the founders were not afraid to junk their first constitutional draft (the Articles of Confederation). How does he suggest they might perceive the way the current Constitution plays out in American politics?
- He lists a number of rule changes that would alter the way the Constitution works. What problems are they designed to fix?

Uncover the evidence

- Levinson suggests that the current constitutional order is dysfunctional. Does he provide evidence, or does he assume that his audience naturally agrees with him? Why?

Evaluate the conclusion

- Levinson believes the founders would have been willing to change the Constitution to make it work better. If this is the case, why didn't they make it easier to amend?

Sort out the political significance

- Is the inability of politicians today to get anything done a problem of the system or a choice of today's lawmakers? If it is the latter, should they be allowed to make that choice?
- Levinson is willing to break a lot of eggs to make a new constitutional omelet. What would the system look like if some of these changes were enacted?

●●●

4.4 *Federalist* No. 51

James Madison, *The Federalist Papers*

Why We Chose This Piece

Here speaks the main author of the U.S. Constitution, many of whose provisions have been debated, critiqued, and revered in this chapter's previous selections. Federalist No. 51 is James Madison's famous justification of the principles of federalism, separation of powers, and checks and balances. It is based on his notion that if people are too ambitious and self-interested to produce good government, then government will have to be adapted to the realities of human nature. A mechanism must be created by which the product of government will be good, even if the nature of the human beings participating in it cannot be counted on to be so. The solution, according to Madison, is to create a government that prevents one person or one group from obtaining too much power. How does he make human nature, warts and all, work for the public interest in the Constitution? [We present Madison's Federalist No. 51, slightly abridged in order to throw into sharper relief his argument about the constitutional protections of liberty.]

In order to lay a due foundation for that separate and distinct exercise of the different powers of government, which to a certain extent is admitted on all hands to be essential to the preservation of liberty, it is evident that each department should have a will of its own; and consequently should be so constituted, that the members of each should have as little agency as possible in the appointment of the members of the others. Were this principle rigorously adhered to, it would require that all the appointments for the supreme executive, legislative, and judiciary magistracies should be drawn from the same fountain of authority, the people, through channels having no communication whatever with one another. Perhaps such a plan of constructing the several departments would be less difficult in practice than it may in contemplation appear. Some difficulties, however, and some additional expense would attend the execution of it. Some deviations, therefore, from the principle must be admitted. In the constitution of the judiciary department in particular, it might be inexpedient to insist rigorously on the principle; first, because peculiar qualifications being essential in the members, the primary consideration ought to be to select that mode of choice which best secures these qualifications; secondly, because the permanent tenure by which the appointments are held in that department, must soon destroy all sense of dependence on the authority conferring them.

It is equally evident that the members of each department should be as little dependent as possible on those of the others, for the emoluments annexed to their offices. Were the executive magistrate, or the judges, not independent of the legislature in this particular, their independence in every other would be merely nominal.

But the great security against a gradual concentration of the several powers in the same department, consists in giving to those who administer each department the necessary constitutional means and personal motives to resist encroachments of the others. The provision for defense must in this, as in all other cases, be made commensurate to the danger of attack. Ambition must be made to counteract ambition. The interest of the man must be connected with the constitutional right of the place. It may be a reflection on human nature, that such devices should be necessary to control the abuses of government. But what is government itself, but the greatest of all reflections on human nature? If men were angels, no government would be necessary. If angels were to govern men, neither external nor internal controls on government would be necessary. In framing a government which is to be administered by men over men, the great difficulty lies in this: You must first enable the government to control the governed; and in the next place, oblige it to control itself. A dependence on the people is, no doubt, the primary control on the government; but experience has taught mankind the necessity of auxiliary precautions.

This policy of supplying, by opposite and rival interests, the defect of better motives, might be traced through the whole system of human affairs, private as well as public. We see it particularly displayed in all the subordinate distributions of power, where the constant aim is to divide and arrange the several offices in such a manner as that each may be a check on the other that the private interest of every individual, may be a sentinel over the public rights. These inventions of prudence cannot be less requisite in the distribution of the supreme powers of the state.

But it is not possible to give each department an equal power of self defense. In republican government, the legislative authority necessarily predominates. The remedy for this inconvenience is to divide the legislative into different branches; and to render them, by different modes of election and different principles of action, as little connected with each other as the nature of their common functions and their common dependence on the society will admit. It may even be necessary to guard against dangerous encroachments by still further precautions. As the weight of the legislative authority requires that it should be thus divided, the weakness of the executive may require, on the other hand, that it should be fortified. An absolute negative on the legislature appears, at first view, to be the natural defense with which the executive magistrate should be armed. But perhaps it would be neither altogether safe nor alone sufficient. On ordinary occasions it might not be exerted with the requisite firmness, and on extraordinary occasions it might be perfidiously abused. May not this defect of an absolute negative be supplied by some qualified connection between this weaker department and the weaker branch of the stronger department, by which the latter may be led to support the constitutional rights of the former, without being too much detached from the rights of its own department?

If the principles on which these observations are founded be just, as I persuade myself they are, and they be applied as a criterion to the several State constitutions, and to the federal Constitution, it will be found that if the latter does not perfectly correspond with them, the former are infinitely less able to bear such a test.

There are, moreover, two considerations particularly applicable to the federal system of America, which place the system in a very interesting point of view.

First. In a single republic, all the power surrendered by the people is submitted to the administration of a single government; and usurpations are guarded against by a division of the government into distinct and separate departments. In the compound republic of America, the power surrendered by the people is first divided between distinct governments, and then the portion allotted to each subdivided among distinct and separate departments. Hence a double security arises to the rights of the people. The different governments will control each other; at the same time that each will be controlled by itself.

Second. It is of great importance in a republic not only to guard the society against the oppression of its rulers, but to guard one part of the society against the injustice of the other part. Different interests necessarily exist in different classes of citizens. If a majority be united by a common interest, the rights of the minority will be insecure. There are but two methods of providing against this evil: The one by creating a will in the community independent of the majority that is, of the society itself; the other, by comprehending in the society so many separate descriptions of citizens as will render an unjust combination of a majority of the whole very improbable, if not impracticable. The first method prevails in all governments possessing an hereditary or self-appointed authority. This, at best, is but a precarious security; because a power independent of the society may as well espouse the unjust views of the major, as the rightful interests of the minor party, and may possibly be turned against both parties. The second method will be exemplified in the federal republic of the United States. While all authority in it will be derived from and dependent on the society, the society itself will be broken into so many parts, interests, and classes of citizens, that the rights of individuals, or of the minority, will be in little danger from interested combinations of the majority. . . . In the extended republic of the United States, and among the great variety of interests, parties, and sects which it embraces, a coalition of a majority of the whole society could seldom take place on any other principles than those of justice and the general good; whilst there being thus less danger to a minor from the will of the major party, there must be less pretext, also, to provide for the security of the former, by introducing into the government a will not dependent on the latter, or, in other words, a will independent of the society itself. It is no less certain than it is important, notwithstanding the contrary opinions which have been entertained, that the larger the society, provided it lie within a practicable sphere, the more duly capable it will be of self-government. And happily for the *republican cause*, the practicable sphere may be carried to a very great extent, by a judicious modification and mixture of the *federal principle*.

Consider the source and the audience

- This piece was originally published in a New York newspaper in 1788, at a time when New Yorkers were debating whether to ratify the new Constitution. What was its political purpose? Who was Madison arguing against?

Lay out the argument, the values, and the assumptions

- What two ways did Madison think the Constitution would undertake to preserve liberty?
- What assumptions did he make about the purpose of government?

Uncover the evidence

- What sort of evidence did Madison rely on to make his case? Was any other evidence available to him at that time?

Evaluate the conclusion

- Was Madison right about the best way to preserve liberty in a republic? How would the other authors we've read in this chapter answer this question?

Sort out the political implications

- What will the political process be like in a political system that is divided between national and state levels, and at each level among executive, legislative, and judicial branches? Will policymaking be quick and efficient, gradual and judicious, or slow and sluggish? Why?
- How much power do everyday citizens end up having in such a system? Why didn't Madison give us more power?

5

Civil Liberties

It's awfully easy to take our freedoms for granted when no one is trying to take them away. For many Americans, as the twenty-first century dawned, our civil liberties—things like freedom of speech, freedom of religion, due process of law—almost seemed like part of the landscape. Certain rights for certain people may have seemed controversial, and there were perennial, irresolvable debates such as where the line between church and state should be drawn, or whether women had a right to an abortion, but as far as the fundamentals went, Americans knew they lived in the freest country in history.

They still do; but since September 11, 2001, the premises and the stakes have changed, and with them some of the unalterable freedoms to which we have become accustomed. Indeed, it was our very openness and freedom that made us vulnerable to terrorist attack, and many observers argued that to become less defenseless we had to be a little less open, a little less free. Individual freedoms often conflict with the common good, and an inevitable tension exists between freedom and security—we could be completely secure if we gave up all of our liberty to a caretaker state, but very few of us are willing to make that deal.

Our civil liberties are the individual freedoms we possess that government cannot take away. Although they exist to empower us, they also exist to limit government. Because they deal with power, both individual and governmental, civil liberties will always be controversial. Since everyone wants power, since there is not enough power to go around, and since some people's power gain will always be other people's loss, our civil liberties can be controversial, to say the least.

In fact, one of the great debates at our Constitution's founding concerned civil liberties—whether that document established a government that was powerful enough to need limiting through the addition of the first ten amendments, or whether it was so weak as it stood that it would not try to infringe on our lives. Those making the first of those arguments won, of course, and the Bill of Rights is an established part of our constitutional law. But we continue to debate the centrality of civil liberties in this country—many argue that the election of Barack Obama as president in 2008 was a reassertion of the idea that the United States is a nation of laws, and in the protection of our freedoms we can also find security.

In the United States we rarely have to resort to violence to solve our conflicts over rights and freedom (although people do occasionally try to take the law into their own hands). Generally, however, there is a consensus that we should look to politics to resolve clashes of rights—specifically to the Supreme Court, with some assistance from Congress and the president and even the American public, organized into interest groups like the American Civil Liberties Union or the National Rifle Association.

In this chapter we look at readings that examine several contemporary civil liberties issues and the inherent tensions within them. The first looks at President Obama's efforts to reframe the right to bear arms as a right to life. The second examines the tension between religious liberty and the government's effort to ensure equitable health care for all. The third focuses on the rights of the accused and the limits of procedural due process rights. Finally, we look at an excerpt from Alexander Hamilton's *Federalist* No. 84, in which he objects to the addition of the Bill of Rights to our Constitution.

● ●

5.1 Obama's New Frame
Gun Rights vs. the Right to Life
Jill Lawrence, *National Journal*

Why We Chose This Piece

President Obama has regarded his inability to get legislation passed that enforces gun safety as one of the failures of his time in office, but he is up against a powerful gun lobby in the National Rifle Association (which represents many gun owners but also gun manufacturers), and a majority of Americans who, despite their desire to see safer gun laws, have a positive view of the NRA. In an effort to get the public to see the issue differently, the president tried to emphasize the variety of civil liberties that are encompassed by the gun issue. We chose this article because it nicely showcases the fact that most civil liberties and rights are complex political issues— for one person's rights to be protected, another's may be endangered.

I can't remember a time when "gun rights"—the rights of people to buy, own, and carry pretty much any gun and in many cases any number of guns they want—did not dominate debates about gun policy. The phrase has been part of the political lexicon for what seems like decades.

Selection published: January 16, 2013

President Obama turned that argument in an interesting direction, away from the Second Amendment and toward rights and themes at the core of other foundational documents, as he unveiled his package of gun proposals. The Declaration of Independence, the First Amendment, and the Gettysburg Address all made appearances in a speech that cast a new and different meaning on another familiar political phrase, the right to life.

"The right to worship freely and safely, that right was denied to Sikhs in Oak Creek, Wisconsin. The right to assemble peaceably, that right was denied shoppers in Clackamas, Oregon, and moviegoers in Aurora, Colorado," Obama said in an explicit reference to the First Amendment in the Bill of Rights.

"That most fundamental set of rights to life and liberty and the pursuit of happiness—fundamental rights that were denied to college students at Virginia Tech, and high school students at Columbine, and elementary school students in Newtown, and kids on street corners in Chicago on too frequent a basis to tolerate, and all the families who've never imagined that they'd lose a loved one to a bullet—those rights are at stake," the president continued, paraphrasing the Declaration of Independence.

Obama did not leave out the part of the Declaration about Americans being "endowed by our Creator with certain inalienable rights that no man or government can take away from us," as he put it. But he added: "As we've also long recognized, as our founders recognized, that with rights come responsibilities. Along with our freedom to live our lives as we will comes an obligation to allow others to do the same. We don't live in isolation. We live in a society, a government of, and by, and for the people." That final phrase comes from Abraham Lincoln's impassioned Gettysburg Address.

Speaking in Newtown, Conn., on Dec. 16, two days after a gunman mowed down 20 first-graders and six adults trying to protect them, Obama hinted briefly at these ideas. "Can we say that we're truly doing enough to give all the children of this country the chance they deserve to live out their lives in happiness and with purpose?" he asked then.

Most of that speech, however, alternated between consolation and attempts to douse the nation with cold water, to rip the cobwebs from our eyes. The unstated subtext was clearly along the lines of "What on Earth have we been thinking? Our background-check system is a sieve, we have no way to track guns used by criminals, we don't even have research on guns, and why do civilians need assault weapons, anyway?"

Obama, of course, has been part of the inertia, a point underscored sadly by the speech he gave in Tucson, Ariz., almost exactly two years ago, after a gunman shot then-Rep. Gabrielle Giffords in the head, wounded a dozen others, and killed six people, including 9-year-old Christina Taylor Green. He implored the country back then to meet the expectations of a child who had come to meet her congressional representative. "I want our democracy to be as good as Christina imagined it. I want America to be as good as she imagined it," he said.

It took a singularly horrific incident, first-graders massacred with a semiautomatic weapon in their classroom, to jolt Obama and perhaps America into action.

On Wednesday, Christina was succeeded by 7-year-old Grace McDonnell, killed in Newtown, an aspiring painter whose work now hangs in Obama's private study off the Oval Office. "Every time I look at that painting, I think about Grace. And I think about the life that she lived and the life that lay ahead of her, and most of all, I think about how, when it comes to protecting the most vulnerable among us, we must act now—for Grace," Obama said.

The difference is that instead of skirting cold, hard policy decisions, as he did in an emotional but non-substantive speech two years ago, this time Obama signed 23 executive orders on the spot and sent a package of proposals to Congress, even as he acknowledged the difficulty of passing them in an overheated political environment.

"There will be pundits and politicians and special-interest lobbyists publicly warning of a tyrannical, all-out assault on liberty," he said. In fact that strain of thinking and rhetoric is already full-throated. How effectively Obama can defuse all the "don't tread on me" bombast with the words of Jefferson, Madison, and Lincoln is unclear, but it can't hurt to remind people that gun rights were not the only rights the founders had in mind way back when.

Consider the source and the audience

- The author of this piece is writing in the *National Journal*, which we have already seen is a nonpartisan outlet for Washington insider news and analysis. Is the author trying to make her own argument here, or is she just conveying the argument made by President Obama?

Lay out the argument, the values, and the assumptions

- Why is Obama trying to broaden the terms of the gun debate? Why does he want to regulate gun ownership?
- What civil liberties does he think are involved in addition to the Second Amendment?
- Are the rights of gun owners consistent with the protection of our other rights? How so?

Uncover the evidence

- How does Obama go about making his argument?
- Where does he get the evidence that civil liberties have been lost because guns were not regulated? Is other evidence needed?

Evaluate the conclusion

- President Obama uses the authority of the founders to remind Americans that the Constitution protects multiple rights. He clearly doesn't think that the Second Amendment should take priority over the others. Do you buy this?

Sort out the political significance

- Gun regulation didn't pass in Congress, despite a bipartisan effort to get some very limited rules through (background checks on gun purchasers and limits on guns that can fire multiple rounds without reloading, for instance). Was there any argument that Obama could have made that would have convinced the leaders of the NRA that selling fewer guns was an acceptable trade-off for safer communities?

• •

5.2 The Courts, Birth Control, and Phony Claims of "Religious Liberty"

Barry W. Lynn, *Washington Post*

Why We Chose This Piece

One provision of the Affordable Care Act mandates that health insurance plans cover birth control prescriptions without charge for those who want them. This law has generated tremendous debate about the meaning of religious freedom in the United States. We include this article here to give you a sense of how many seemingly unrelated issues can be subject to religious freedom claims. Why is birth control a religious freedom issue?

Should your boss be able to determine which prescription medications you take at home? Should your boss have a say in how many children you have?

Most Americans would answer a resounding "No!" to these questions. Yet if current political and legal trends continue, more and more Americans may find that their health care hinges not on what their doctors think is best for them but what their bosses believe about religion.

This curious state of affairs stems from a deliberate attempt to redefine religious freedom in America. You read that right—religious liberty. A freedom that has historically been interpreted as an individual right of self-determination is being twisted into a means of controlling others and meddling in their most personal affairs. For the sake of true freedom, this must be stopped.

The Affordable Care Act mandates that certain basic services and features must be offered in employee health-care plans. Birth control is among these. Houses of worship and similar ministries are exempt from the mandate, and religiously affiliated entities (hospitals, colleges and social service groups) have been accommodated in other ways.

This is not enough for some ultra-conservative religious leaders who oppose birth control. They are insisting that any business owner should be able to deny his or her employees access to birth control no matter what the nature of the business.

At the behest of the Catholic bishops and their fundamentalist Christian allies, far-right legal groups have filed a slew of cases insisting that secular corporations and other employers have a right according to the principle of religious freedom to deny contraceptive coverage to the men and women who work for them. Among those waging this crusade are the Becket Fund for Religious Liberty, TV evangelist Pat Robertson's American Center for Law and Justice and the Alliance Defending Freedom, an organization founded by radio and TV preachers.

Selection published: May 23, 2013

Several of these cases have bubbled up to the federal appeals courts. The U.S. Court of Appeals for the 7th Circuit heard arguments in one case on Wednesday involving two firms, K&L Contractors and Grote Industries, and the following day the appeals court for the 10th Circuit heard a challenge brought by Hobby Lobby, a chain of craft stores.

These are all secular firms. K&L is a construction company, Grote makes auto-related products, and Hobby Lobby is in the retail business, hawking items such as pink flamingo wind chimes and 3-D garden gnome stickers. In each case, their owners personally oppose some forms of birth control.

Since these firms concede that they're not religious institutions, the only question is whether the evangelical Christian and Catholic owners of the companies have the right to ignore a federal law that they disagree with on religious grounds—in this case, a law mandating birth control coverage in health-insurance plans.

They do not. The principle of religious liberty protects your right to make moral decisions for yourself, not others. Obviously, a law that required Hobby Lobby's owners to use birth control would be a gross violation of their religious liberty. But the mandate doesn't do that. It merely requires that the 22,000 employees of Hobby Lobby be given the right, if they choose, to access birth control through a health-insurance plan.

Nor can Hobby Lobby's owners plausibly argue that their rights are violated because they must pay for these health-care plans. The fact is, if we allowed everyone to opt out of paying for everything they object to on moral grounds, society would quickly grind to a halt.

Fundamentalist Christians might refuse to pay for a public school system that teaches evolution. Conservative Muslims might refuse to pay for public museums that may contain art that offends them. More to the point, a boss who believes in spiritual healing might refuse to provide medical coverage at all, arguing that only God, not a doctor, can make you well.

In fact, if a company can refuse to cover your insurance costs for what it considers an "immoral" practice, what's to stop it from simply refusing to hire anyone who might buy contraceptives with cash from a paycheck?

Under the First Amendment, you are shielded from being forced to pay for someone else's religion. But nothing in the Constitution protects you from paying for things you just happen to object to on moral grounds. In a country as politically splintered as ours, such a la carte taxation would make it virtually impossible to get anything done.

This issue is also important from a medical perspective. Americans use birth control for many reasons—not just to limit births. Some women need birth control pills to manage serious issues such as endometriosis. Americans value their medical privacy. No one should be forced to go to their boss begging for medication they need to treat a serious condition. Religious freedom is not a license to meddle in someone else's health issues.

The appeals court rulings in these cases are unlikely to be the last word. This issue is so important there's a good chance it will land before the Supreme Court. If it does, the court should take the opportunity to make one thing very clear: As precious as it may be, religious freedom gives you no right to make moral or medical decisions for others.

Consider the source and the audience

- Barry Lynn is the executive director of a group called Americans United for Separation of Church and State. What would you expect such a group's position to be on the issue of religious freedom?
- Why would he want to publish his views in a widely read publication like the *Washington Post?*

Lay out the argument, the values, and the assumptions

- How does Lynn define "religious freedom"? Who is it freedom for, and what is it freedom from?
- How does he say the opponents of birth control define religious freedom?
- What is the central difference in the way the two sides see the issue?

Uncover the evidence

- Lynn makes his argument based on his analysis of the concept of religious freedom and on logical inference about the consequences of adopting his opponent's view. Is this kind of evidence persuasive? Is there any that would be conclusive in an issue like this?

Evaluate the conclusion

- Lynn's view is that religious freedom is the ability to make your own religious choices, not to make someone else's. Do you buy that, or the counterclaim that real freedom means not having to engage in an activity of which you disapprove?

Sort out the political significance

- After trying to accommodate religious groups and institutions, the Obama administration has continued to carry out the provisions of the Affordable Care Act, including the birth control mandate. If it were to come before the Supreme Court, how do you think the justices should rule on the mandate? Think about the constitutional issues involved, not just your own personal position.

• •

5.3   Dead Letter Office

The Case That Has Even Antonin Scalia Wondering What to Do About Incompetent Lawyers in Death Penalty Cases

Dahlia Lithwick, *Slate*

Why We Chose This Piece

> *The Bill of Rights provides for considerable due process protections for those accused of federal crimes—not because the founders loved criminals but because they wanted to hold the government in check. That means our criminal justice system has a heavy emphasis on procedural considerations—making sure the rules are followed by those in power. We chose this article because it demonstrates the limitations of a strict adherence to the rules. When does justice require abandoning the rules as opposed to enforcing them?*

Cory R. Maples is facing execution because his lawyers got lost in the mail. At oral argument in his case this morning, Justice Antonin Scalia found himself all alone in thinking that was OK. Yet it is Scalia who notes, toward the end of the hourlong session, that there are never any consequences when defense lawyers screw up a capital case. "Does anything happen to the counsel who have been inadequate in a capital case?" Scalia asks Alabama Solicitor General John Neiman. "Other than getting *another* capital case?"

Hard to imagine a more damning indictment of the American capital justice system than that.

Maples was convicted in 1997 of killing two friends after a night of heavy drinking, driving, and pool-playing. (The pool playing was significant to the appellate court for some reason.) At his trial, Maples' lawyers warned the jury that their inexperience might look like they were "stumbling around in the dark." They also failed to present evidence of Maples' mental health history, which includes suicide attempts; the fact that he drank heavily that night; and information about his history of alcohol and drug use.

Alabama is the only state that doesn't grant taxpayer-funded legal assistance to death-row inmates seeking to challenge what happened at trial. So for his appeal, Maples had local counsel acting in name only, while he was represented for free by a pair of second-year associates at the fabulous New York law firm of Sullivan and Cromwell. For 18 months nothing happened with his appeal, during which period his young lawyers left their firm without notifying Maples or the court. They did tell the mailroom. So when the Alabama court sent a ruling to his two lawyers indicating that his appeal had been denied, the mailroom stamped it "Return to Sender" and sent it back to Alabama. The county clerk stuck it in a file and Maples—who knew nothing of any of this—missed the 42-day deadline for filing

---

Selection published: October 4, 2011

another appeal. Maples' local counsel, John Butler Jr., also received a copy of the ruling, but because he believed he was Maples' lawyer in name only, he did nothing with it.

So Maples thought he had three lawyers when in fact he had none. He missed his filing deadline.

Reviewing courts all rejected Maples' request for an extension in the filing deadline. The 11th Circuit Court of Appeals wrote that "any and all fault here lies with Maples for not filing a timely notice of appeal." The Supreme Court itself has not had a lot of patience for missed deadlines of late.

But the question before the court today is whether Maples' missed filing deadline can be excused if he himself was blameless, and the government's actions were a contributing factor. The majority of the court is flummoxed at Alabama's decision to deny a man the right to appeal when he missed a deadline—quoting Justice Samuel Alito—"through no fault of his own, through a series of very unusual and unfortunate circumstances."

George W. Bush's former solicitor general, Gregory G. Garre, represents Maples, and immediately Scalia attacks him for claiming that local counsel wasn't the attorney of record in this case: "You want us to believe the local attorney had *no* responsibility for the case at all? . . . Even if local counsel was just a functionary, surely his functions would include forwarding a notice?"

Justice Ruth Bader Ginsburg points out that the state prosecutor sent a notice directly to Maples in prison telling him he'd lost his appeal, presumably because he knew that local counsel wasn't acting on his behalf. Scalia retorts that there is nothing in the Constitution or the federal rules of procedure that says the accused has a right to judicial notice. Garre replies that death penalty cases might be different. Scalia asks why. "Once you are in court and you have a lawyer, it's up to your lawyer to follow what goes on in the court."

Justice Anthony Kennedy is bothered by the fact that the Alabama trial judge sat on the case for 18 months, and by the assumption that Maples would naturally just fail to appeal. Even the solicitor general of Alabama is willing to concede that most capital defendants do appeal.

When Neiman stands to represent Alabama, he discovers that most of the court's conservatives are just not willing to be *that guy*—by which I mean, the guy who sends another guy to the chair because of a mailroom error. Only Scalia battles on, arguing first that "Return to Sender" stamped on the Sullivan and Cromwell envelopes doesn't necessarily mean his attorneys had abandoned him; it could just mean that the court had the "wrong address." When the prosecutor mailed a letter directly to Maples in prison indicating that he had lost his appeal, Scalia asks, that wasn't so much a recognition that his lawyers had abandoned him as an "extraneous volunteer statement to Maples."

Chief Justice John Roberts looks puzzled. "Why did he do it, then? Just gloating that the fellow had lost? He must have thought there was a problem, right?"

Justice Elena Kagan puts it this way: "The question that we are supposed to ask ourselves is: Is this what somebody would do if they actually wanted the person to get that letter. So I'm just going to ask you, general, if you were a lawyer in an important litigation and you send off an important letter to two lawyers, your principal adversaries, as well as to a local counsel who you think may not be involved in the substance of the litigation. . . . So you send off this letter and you get it back from the principal attorneys, and you ask yourself: Huh, should I do anything now? What would *you* say?"

Neiman grudgingly replies, "I suspect that in those circumstances I might well personally do something else."

Alito has had enough. "Mr. Maples has lost his right to appeal through no fault of his own, through a series of very unusual and unfortunate circumstances. Now, when his attorneys moved to file an out-of-time appeal, why wouldn't you just consent to that? If he did not receive effective assistance of counsel at trial, why not give a decision on the merits of that?"

Roberts questions Neiman on what it is that Maples' local counsel, Butler, ostensibly did in the case to suggest he was actively involved. When Neiman can't produce an answer, Roberts retorts: "You still haven't told me one thing he did more than move the admission of the out-of-town attorneys." Neiman looks distressed.

Garre concludes his rebuttal by explaining the stakes: "Mr. Maples is not asking to be released from prison. He is asking for an opportunity to present a serious constitutional claim of ineffective assistance of counsel. . . . Allowing those claims to be adjudicated on the merits will go a long way to preserve the legitimacy of the system of criminal justice in a case in which a man's life is at stake."

It says an awful lot about the Alabama capital justice system that it is willing to put to death a man who—for all intents and purposes—had no legal representation. Today the court is clearly more horrified by Alabama's willingness to press forward on that technicality than by any of the foul-ups that comprise these facts. That's too bad because those screw-ups are depressingly common in death penalty cases. Not even Scalia denies that fact.

Consider the source and the audience

- Dahlia Lithwick is *Slate*'s court reporter. She has legal training and her political views tend to be liberal. Does that affect the argument she is making in her piece?

Lay out the argument, the values, and the assumptions

- What does Lithwick think would constitute just treatment for Cory Maples? Is this piece about his innocence or guilt, or just about how he is treated by Alabama law?
- What would justice look like in his case?

Uncover the evidence

- What kind of evidence does Lithwick need to provide about what happened to Maples? Are you satisfied? Does she provide enough dialog from the Supreme Court for you to understand the main lines of questions and answers?

Evaluate the conclusion

- Lithwick thinks that Maples deserves a second chance at an appeal, and it is clear that at least some of the Supreme Court justices agree. Do you?

Sort out the political significance

- As it happens, the Supreme Court decided, 7–2, that Alabama had deprived Maples of his rights when it refused his petition to extend the deadline to appeal when he missed it the first time through no fault of his own. The two dissenters were Justices Antonin Scalia and Clarence Thomas, both conservatives. Two other conservatives, Chief Justice John Roberts and Justice Samuel Alito, voted with the majority. Why did the conservatives split on this one?

5.4 *Federalist* No. 84

Alexander Hamilton, *The Federalist Papers*

Why We Chose This Piece

The original text of the Constitution contained no Bill of Rights, and that would almost be its undoing. Fearful of a strong central government, the Anti-Federalists insisted that they would not vote to ratify the Constitution unless it contained some built-in limitations to its own power. In Federalist *No. 84, the second-to-last of The Federalist Papers, Alexander Hamilton was busy tying up loose ends that had not been dealt with in previous essays. It was here that he chose to rebut the Anti-Federalist claim that a Bill of Rights was needed. It was not necessary, he argued, because many of the state constitutions admired by the Anti-Federalists did not have bills of rights, and in any case the text of the Constitution had many rights built in, among them the protection against the suspension of habeas corpus, the prohibition against bills of attainder and ex post facto laws, and the entitlement to trial by jury.*

Hamilton went further than arguing that a Bill of Rights was unnecessary, however. In the excerpt reprinted here, he claimed that it was actually dangerous to liberty. Are we freer or less free than we were at the time of the founding?

I t has been several times truly remarked that bills of rights are, in their origin, stipulations between kings and their subjects, abridgements of prerogative in favor of privilege, reservations of rights not surrendered to the prince. Such was

Selection published: May 28, 1788

MAGNA CHARTA, obtained by the barons, sword in hand, from King John. Such were the subsequent confirmations of that charter by succeeding princes. Such was the PETITION OF RIGHT assented to by Charles I, in the beginning of his reign. Such, also, was the Declaration of Right presented by the Lords and Commons to the Prince of Orange in 1688, and afterwards thrown into the form of an act of parliament called the Bill of Rights. It is evident, therefore, that, according to their primitive signification, they have no application to constitutions professedly founded upon the power of the people, and executed by their immediate representatives and servants. Here, in strictness, the people surrender nothing; and as they retain every thing they have no need of particular reservations. "WE, THE PEOPLE of the United States, to secure the blessings of liberty to ourselves and our posterity, do ORDAIN and ESTABLISH this Constitution for the United States of America." Here is a better recognition of popular rights, than volumes of those aphorisms which make the principal figure in several of our State bills of rights, and which would sound much better in a treatise of ethics than in a constitution of government.

But a minute detail of particular rights is certainly far less applicable to a Constitution like that under consideration, which is merely intended to regulate the general political interests of the nation, than to a constitution which has the regulation of every species of personal and private concerns. If, therefore, the loud clamors against the plan of the convention, on this score, are well founded, no epithets of reprobation will be too strong for the constitution of this State. But the truth is, that both of them contain all which, in relation to their objects, is reasonably to be desired.

I go further, and affirm that bills of rights, in the sense and to the extent in which they are contended for, are not only unnecessary in the proposed Constitution, but would even be dangerous. They would contain various exceptions to powers not granted; and, on this very account, would afford a colorable pretext to claim more than were granted. For why declare that things shall not be done which there is no power to do? Why, for instance, should it be said that the liberty of the press shall not be restrained, when no power is given by which restrictions may be imposed? I will not contend that such a provision would confer a regulating power; but it is evident that it would furnish, to men disposed to usurp, a plausible pretense for claiming that power. They might urge with a semblance of reason, that the Constitution ought not to be charged with the absurdity of providing against the abuse of an authority which was not given, and that the provision against restraining the liberty of the press afforded a clear implication, that a power to prescribe proper regulations concerning it was intended to be vested in the national government. This may serve as a specimen of the numerous handles which would be given to the doctrine of constructive powers, by the indulgence of an injudicious zeal for bills of rights.

On the subject of the liberty of the press, as much as has been said, I cannot forbear adding a remark or two: in the first place, I observe, that there is not a syllable concerning it in the constitution of this State; in the next, I contend, that whatever has been said about it in that of any other State, amounts to nothing. What signifies a declaration, that "the liberty of the press shall be inviolably preserved?" What is the liberty of the press? Who can give it any definition which would not leave the utmost latitude for evasion? I hold it to be impracticable; and from this I infer, that its security, whatever fine declarations may be inserted in any constitution respecting it, must altogether depend on public opinion, and on the general spirit of the people and of the government. And here, after all, as is intimated upon another occasion, must we seek for the only solid basis of all our rights.

There remains but one other view of this matter to conclude the point. The truth is, after all the declamations we have heard, that the Constitution is itself, in every rational sense, and to every useful purpose, A BILL OF RIGHTS. The several bills of rights in Great Britain form its Constitution, and conversely the constitution of each State is its bill of rights. And the proposed Constitution, if adopted, will be the bill of rights of the Union. Is it one object of a bill of rights to declare and specify the political privileges of the citizens in the structure and administration of the government? This is done in the most ample and precise manner in the plan of the convention; comprehending various precautions for the public security, which are not to be found in any of the State constitutions. Is another object of a bill of rights to define certain immunities and modes of proceeding, which are relative to personal and private concerns? This we have seen has also been attended to, in a variety of cases, in the same plan. Adverting therefore to the substantial meaning of a bill of rights, it is absurd to allege that it is not to be found in the work of the convention. It may be said that it does not go far enough, though it will not be easy to make this appear; but it can with no propriety be contended that there is no such thing. It certainly must be immaterial what mode is observed as to the order of declaring the rights of the citizens, if they are to be found in any part of the instrument which establishes the government. And hence it must be apparent, that much of what has been said on this subject rests merely on verbal and nominal distinctions, entirely foreign from the substance of the thing.

Consider the source and the audience

- Hamilton was directing this essay to staunch opponents of the Constitution, and on this point, at least, they were winning. He was also speaking to citizens of New York who admired their own state constitution. How did these considerations shape the way he framed his argument?

Lay out the argument, the values, and the assumptions

- How powerful a government did Hamilton believe was established by the Constitution?
- Why did he think a Bill of Rights would be unnecessary?
- Why did he think it would be dangerous? What mischief would be done if the government were told it was not allowed to do things it didn't have the power to do anyway?

Uncover the evidence

- Hamilton used historical evidence to discuss why bills of rights had existed in the past. Did that evidence have anything to do with the case he was discussing?
- How did he use logic to make the case that a Bill of Rights was dangerous?

Evaluate the conclusion

- Did Hamilton persuade you that a Bill of Rights would empower government officials to argue that government had all the powers not specifically listed in a written Bill of Rights? Would the burden be on us to prove that we had any rights other than those listed?

Sort out the political implications

- Today many Americans argue that we have a right to privacy. People who interpret the Constitution strictly, as did many members of the Bush administration, believe that we have only the rights that are written down in the Constitution. How does this debate relate to Hamilton's argument here?

6

Civil Rights

For all the lip service we pay to the principle that "all men are created equal," American history has been a story of exclusion from the very beginning. The early colonies excluded people from political power who were not members of the right church, or who did not have the right amount of land or the right sum of money in their pockets. At various times we have excluded people from the rights of American citizenship because of the color of their skin, their gender, the country in which they were born, or the language they spoke. Today, groups like the disabled, gays and lesbians, and noncitizens still find themselves excluded from access to some of the basic rights that others in America enjoy. The search for equality in the United States has been a perennial theme of those who stand outside the charmed circle of the privileged and the free, fighting hard to get their share of the American dream.

We call the battle for equality in this country a battle for civil rights—citizenship rights guaranteed by the Constitution or, when the Constitution has not been specific enough to protect some groups, its provisions in the Thirteenth, Fourteenth, Fifteenth, Nineteenth, and Twenty-sixth Amendments. The struggle for civil rights that produced those amendments and the laws that enforce them has been harrowing and long because so much is at stake. Rights are more than words on paper—they are political power. To deny people the right to do something is to have power over them and make them conform to your will. If they gain rights despite your efforts, they have acquired power to stop you from doing what you want. People fight furiously to restrict and to gain rights because they care so deeply about who shall have the power to decide what kind of society we live in—whose will counts and whose does not.

Groups that fight for civil rights—for recognition of their will and inclusion in the system—are handicapped from the start by the fact that, by definition, they are outside the system in significant ways. The initial challenge these groups face is finding an arena in which they can begin their fight. Consider the plight of African Americans after the Civil War, which officially ended slavery. The Southern states had shut blacks out of political power; the justices on the Supreme Court had previously refused to consider them as potential citizens, and within several decades would declare that segregation was legal; Congress refused to pass legislation enforcing the newly passed Thirteenth, Fourteenth, and Fifteenth Amendments; and the president, himself a Southerner, had no interest in protecting blacks' newfound rights. It took nearly a hundred years—until the composition of the Supreme Court changed sufficiently to be receptive to a brilliant legal strategy mapped out by the National Association for the Advancement of Colored People—for African Americans to get a toehold in the courts, and into the political arena where the fight for enforcement of their civil rights could eventually be won. Civil rights struggles are very much about politics, about using the rules of the system to change public opinion, to change the laws, and to change the way the laws are enforced.

In this chapter we look at the civil rights battles still being fought by various groups in the political, legal, and cultural arenas. The first selection looks at the continued segregation of some high school proms in the South. It raises the difficult question of how private discrimination should be handled. The second piece examines the issue of marriage equality, and one man's journey to understanding his gay son. The third article is a mocking look at the gender issues that have divided the parties. Finally, for our classic statement about civil rights, we look at the speech given by then-candidate Barack Obama during his campaign for the Democratic nomination for president. He argues that we need to break our stalemate when it comes to discussing race. Have we done that? What does Obama's election say about race in America today?

• •

6.1 Segregated Prom Tradition Yields to Unity

Jamie Gumbrecht, CNN

Why We Chose This Piece

In the 1950s the Supreme Court declared that the doctrine of "separate but equal" was unconstitutional. When it came to education, the Court ruled in Brown v. Board of Education *that the very act of separation created inequality, so that separate was unequal by definition. Black students, forced to go to separate schools, felt inferior, and consequently the education they received was inferior.*

A half-century later, most of us think that the issue of legal segregation of public facilities is dead. As this CNN article reveals, however, some unsettled, gray areas remain that look like a throwback to a more racist past. At some southern high schools, separate junior–senior proms are held for white students and black students, despite black students' requests to merge them. We chose this article because it shows that in some very real ways, the struggle for racial equality continues. What are the students here fighting—deep-seated "habit," or enduring racism?

Selection published: April 30, 2013

Wilcox County, Georgia (CNN)—It's a springtime tradition in this stretch of the magnolia midlands for crowds to gather at high school students' proms. They'll cheer for teens in tuxedos and gowns while an announcer reads what the students will do once they leave this pecan grove skyline.

Earlier this month, Wilcox County High School senior Mareshia Rucker rode to a historic theater in the nearby town of Fitzgerald to see her own classmates' prom celebration. She never left the car, even to catch up with her friends. She'd recently helped to invite the critical gaze of the world to her county; few would be happy to see her there, she said. Besides, she's black and wasn't invited to this prom reserved for white students anyway.

For as long as most remember, Wilcox County High School hasn't sponsored a prom for its 400 students. Instead, parents and their children organize their own private, off-site parties, known casually as white prom and black prom—a vestige of racial segregation that still lives on.

"When people say that seeing is believing, it truly is," Mareshia says a few days later from the comfortable bustle of her family's kitchen, central command for the three generations that share it.

"Just talking about it, it didn't hurt my feelings. I didn't care," she says. "When I saw it, I felt really crappy. I didn't understand what was so different about me and them."

She apologizes as her eyes grow shiny and tears dribble down her face. Toni Rucker swoops in to fold her arms around her oldest daughter.

"What is the difference," she murmurs, Mareshia's head resting on her chest. "There is no difference."

Mareshia and her friends bucked 40 years of local customs this month by organizing their own integrated prom, a formal dance open to Wilcox County's white, black, Latino and Asian high school students. Organizers, both black and white, said they lost friends in the process—a grim experience in the waning weeks of the school year. It's been hard on the rest of their hometown, too.

When the story erupted on TV and social media, Wilcox County became a symbol of race relations stuck in the past. People around the world heard about the sneers from some classmates, the silence from some adults, the school board that says it supports them but didn't sponsor its own prom. Thousands lashed out at the old tradition or offered up kind words, cash, dresses, a DJ. Stunned, they wanted to know, could this be true? In 2013?

Segregated proms are a longstanding reality in this farming community 160 miles south of Atlanta, and until recently, at several schools nearby. Some in Wilcox County say it's just an old habit that's hard to break. A few argue the proms are private because of cost and liability or because parents won't cede control. They say people "self-segregate," and kids can't agree on country or hip-hop, "white music" or "black music."

Some say some preachers and some parents implicitly encourage segregation, but there's no point to arguing: People are entitled to their opinions, even if they're racist.

Plenty here shrug off the debate entirely and say a high school dance is nothing to make a fuss about.

Mareshia is 17, a good student, a cheerleader who's active in the Junior Reserve Officer Training Corps. She knew long ago that proms were segregated, but she didn't think much about it till last year, when she and three friends first realized they'd be split up.

"How do you want your last moments of high school to be," Mareshia asked herself then. "What do you want your memories to encompass?"

More than 40 years after these South Georgia schools desegregated, students are still separated on what they see as the brightest nights of their lives. Some from all the county's small towns—Abbeville, Pineview, Pitts, Rochelle—say nobody ever questioned the segregation till this year. But keep asking, and high school graduates will say they wondered about it, questioned it or even asked to make a change. Until this year, the plans always fell through.

"We were different because we always have been together throughout school," Mareshia said. "We've cheered together at football games. We've gone to each other's houses and spent the night. . . . There was no need in us having two separate [proms]."

High school is brief, though, and memories are short. Decades earlier, Wilcox County alumni remembered, there was no prom at all.

"A prom I never had"

In 1970, Barbara King's mom made a trip to the city for a ruffled peach gown for her daughter's junior prom, a formal dance in the school gym. King attended Excelsior, a school for all of Wilcox County's black students. White students went to a school down the road in Rochelle, the county's largest city.

The Supreme Court's *Brown v. Board of Education* decision had struck down the legal basis for "separate but equal" schools in 1954, but state politics had stalled integration so long, King never thought it would happen. Excelsior had loving teachers, a new football team, a competitive a cappella choir and, naturally, its own prom.

But before school let out for the summer, they learned Excelsior would close. The black students would integrate into the all-white Wilcox County schools. They cried, she says, out of sadness and fear.

"The black kids, we'd heard horror stories about the white school and the white kids," she says. "We did not want to go."

That fall, tension between black and white students sizzled in the hallways, King says. In that volatile atmosphere, students learned there would be no homecoming dance. Before long, they understood there would be no prom either.

It was a blow to everyone, King says. She doesn't remember any proms or private, formal parties happening—it never occurred to them to plan a dance outside the gym. Integration was painful, but it would get easier.

"I always felt that we were robbed," says King, who now lives in Arizona. "It was just devastating."

She didn't realize that tumultuous year might have been the kernel of the county's long tradition of segregated proms. She graduated, left Wilcox County and assumed the big dances were revived a few years later.

King only learned the proms remained segregated when her niece, a Wilcox County student, told her about the plan for an integrated prom. Forty years after the struggle to integrate schools, she was shocked to realize kids still fought to integrate their social lives. On the Excelsior Facebook page, which she runs from her home in Arizona, she posted dozens of news stories about the integrated prom and put out calls to donate money.

"I think, deep down, it was my way of having a prom I never had," she says.

When she thinks back to 1971 now, she believes they could've had a nice prom if they'd been given the chance. It might have meant white students on one side of the gym and black students on another, but they would have danced.

Why, she wonders, should today's students fight the same ugly battles they did? Maybe, it's just been too long to remember.

"If there's something that you're born into," she says, "you think it's normal."

"Picking up the pieces"

"Normal" for Rochelle is the quiet strip of hair salons and flower shops. It's murals in blue and gold, the colors for the Wilcox County High School Patriots. It's generations that stick close to home, even when jobs are sparse.

The unemployment rate is 12.3%, far higher than the nation's 7.6%, and the median income is $31,712. Workers farm, process peanuts, teach kids at school or cook for them in the cafeteria. Some of the county's 9,000 residents commute about 20 miles to Cordele or even 45 miles to Tifton just to keep a paycheck coming.

People here will talk about jobs and the economy—they know that's a problem. Race? Not so much.

"Nobody wants to be called a racist," says lifelong Wilcox County resident Melissa Davis, 39.

She and her husband run Skin Deep Tattoos and Piercings in Rochelle. Christian imagery is popular among their clients—Jesus' face, crosses—and American Indian symbols.

The county is about 62% white, 35% black, 3% Latino. On the 2010 Census, Asians and American Indians hardly register. Diverse customers come to every shop in Rochelle, Davis says, but if the town has a reputation for racism, how would that hurt business?

After all the coverage about the prom, it stings to overhear insults at the store, or read them online and know who they're about. Outsiders don't see how people rally in hard times, she said. Her neighbors give generously and buy endless plates of barbecue and beans to support each other's causes.

Personally, she supports an integrated prom. She had a great time at her own segregated prom about 20 years ago, but it didn't make much sense to her then, she said. Someday, she hopes her 15-year-old son attends a school-sponsored prom that's open to everybody. But she can understand why so few people want to talk about it.

"These young girls, I applaud them in one sense because they were willing to do something, but then I look at them and think to myself, there is such a better way of doing this than going to the media," Davis says. "They're going to graduate. They're going to be leaving this little town . . . we're not. We're going to be sitting here picking up the pieces for years."

Harriet Hollis, the racial healing coordinator for the nonprofit Southwest Georgia Project for Community Education, says media attention was necessary to start the conversation about the prom, and disparities in schools and the workforce.

"I can't go in talking about 'racial healing,'" Hollis says. "People won't call me back."

She helped the teens coordinate the integrated prom and hates that people feel they were portrayed incorrectly. But it's difficult to raise awareness when people are afraid to lose customers, offend neighbors or be ostracized at church. Talking about race in a small town is a quick way to risk everything.

"You realize it takes courage to do this kind of stuff," she remembers telling the teens planning the integrated prom. "You're going to get pushback. You're going to get teachers who are not going to be happy, and classmates who don't want you to do it."

They told her, "'This can happen. We can do this.'"

"It could have been us"

Just last spring, Ashley Saylor didn't even try to buy a prom ticket. She approached the committee planning the white prom with a question: "Are you going to let us go together?"

Ashley and her boyfriend, Antonio Gibson, were seniors. As freshmen, they sat across from each other in JROTC. They talked, texted and dated ever since.

Ashley is white; Antonio is black. They hid their relationship at first. Ashley's mom "wasn't raised that way," and even strangers shot nasty looks. But people grew to love them as a couple, including their parents, teachers and friends.

They'd gone together to the school's annual JROTC ball for years; it has always been integrated. She swears she remembers every second of their first dance—her turquoise dress with the low back and not-too-high slit, his dress green uniform, the words to the GinuWine song, "Differences."

> My whole life has changed
>
> Since you came in, I knew back then
>
> You were that special one
>
> I'm so in love, so deep in love

With their years in high school ending and Antonio heading to basic training, she wanted another dance. They weren't the first ones to float the idea of an integrated prom, she said, so she posed the question to the white students.

"I was told that I should just bring someone else," Ashley says. "Bring someone who is white."

Ashley cried in her mom's arms. It stressed her relationship with Antonio. So many things were changing; they couldn't stomach a fight with 40-year-old prom rituals, or the people who kept them going.

"It's hard to grow up in that town and not be racist," she says.

Her name is Ashley Gibson now. She and Antonio married, and have a daughter, 5-month-old Riley Jean. They live near San Diego, where Antonio is stationed with the Navy.

She still keeps their last JROTC ball photo on their dresser. When she heard about Wilcox County's new integrated prom, she wished she'd fought harder for it—for another chance to mark the end of high school, to dress up with her oldest friends, to dance with the man she'd marry.

It might have been different if she'd known that one year later some of her old Wilcox County classmates would pull it off.

"It could've been us. We could've done it," Ashley said. "It was all about taking the first step."

"The timing was just right"

Why this year? How could they carry out an integrated prom now, but not 1971, 2012, or the decades between?

Part of it might be Facebook, students suggested. They're all friends, and that's where evidence of limousine rides and slow dances tick across the screen.

Some said it was the outside help, the media attention, the voice of the NAACP. The neighbors who paid for car washes, doughnuts of barbecue plates were key, the students agree. So, too, were the parents.

"When you have people in your county stand with you . . . it makes everything easier," said Brandon Davis, a white Wilcox County senior who helped to plan the integrated prom. "When my parents told me, 'We will stand beside you and support you,' that was just amazing."

Barbara King, who graduated with the first integrated class, says she could already see some change in Wilcox County when she returned for a reunion last year. Black and white people sat together in the stands during the Patriots' homecoming football game. Some white classmates—the same folks she hardly spoke to in high school—came to the class celebration.

Ashley Gibson said she and Antonio could move back someday. She loves how, in the last couple years, people stopped her on the street or in the bank just to ask about her husband and baby.

"For people who don't live in a situation like this, it's so normal. Where we came from, that's a huge deal," she says. "Regardless of what happened, and what we've been through, and how much it forced us to grow, I love my town."

By this time next year, prom in Wilcox County could be entirely different. The high school's leadership will consider hosting a prom in 2014, Superintendent Steve Smith says. It might not eliminate private, segregated proms, but if it happens, it could promise a dance open to everybody.

"Maybe the timing was just right," Smith says. "I'm proud of 'em. It's a shame, I guess, that it takes four teenage girls to open our eyes."

On Saturday night, at the community clubhouse in Cordele, a finger-food dinner of chicken wings, red velvet cupcakes and peach lemonade awaited. A DJ drove 14 hours from Houston with strobe lights and speakers to blare Flo Rida, Justin Timberlake and Rihanna. A basket of feathered masks—a complement to their theme, "Masquerade Ball in Paris"—waited by the door.

About 100 people came to the integrated prom, most of them from Wilcox County. Even more came for that other old tradition—watching. There were fathers, grandmothers, curious onlookers, reporters, a gaggle of students from Atlanta, a local NAACP rep and Shirley Sherrod, the former U.S. Department of Agriculture official in Georgia who was smeared by a misleading video that showed her discussing race.

Students wobbled in rhinestone-studded heels, traded tuxes for T-shirts, stole away to dark corners, shared a toast of sparkling grape juice, crowned a king and queen, Harlem shook, cha-cha slid.

In the last minutes of the prom, a few soft piano chords melted out of the speakers—the slowest song of the night so far. Girls clasped their hands around their date's necks. A few friends made sloppy waltzes around the dance floor.

In one corner, a pair swayed back and forth, at first just holding hands. Then two more joined in, then a few more and more still. The circle unfurled, and grew hand by hand to include almost every person in the room.

It seemed like what Mareshia hoped for when they started: "If we're all together and we love each other the way we say we do, then there are no issues," she said. "This is something that should have happened a long time ago."

Consider the source and the audience

- This is a CNN story, and CNN is a cable station with a wide, nonpartisan reach. Is this the kind of story you would expect it to cover? Why?

Lay out the argument, the values, and the assumptions

- The students who started the integrated prom in 2013 did so for what reason?
- What strategy did they use to make the integrated prom a reality?
- What kinds of reactions have they gotten from town members? Why do some people support them and some not?

Uncover the evidence

- Do the students arguing for an integrated prom need any evidence to support them? Do their opponents have any evidence to support them?
- On whose side would the Constitution be?

Evaluate the conclusion

- Despite the pushback from some in their community, these students went ahead and held a prom that was attended by one hundred of their classmates. They believe they did the right thing; indeed, some school officials thanked them for "opening their eyes." Do you think the students were right to take their case to the media and start their own prom?

Sort out the political significance

- What do you think will happen in the years following this first integrated prom? Will the new prom get institutionalized, or will the private proms continue to compete?
- What can government do to change discrimination in private activities like this? Anything?

● ●

6.2 A Father's Journey
Frank Bruni, *New York Times*

Why We Chose This Piece

This is a first-person essay, written by the former food critic for the New York Times *who now writes an opinion column for that paper. We chose this piece because one of the reasons why public opinion has changed so dramatically so quickly on issues of gay rights is that more and more Americans are coming to realize that they know someone who is gay. This is the story of one father's evolution to understanding his son.*

For a long while, my father's way of coping was to walk quietly from the room. He doesn't remember this. I do. I can still see it, still feel the pinch in my chest when the word "gay" came up—perhaps in reference to some event in the news, or perhaps in reference to me—and he'd wordlessly take his leave of whatever conversation my mother and my siblings and I were having. He'd drift away, not in disgust but in discomfort, not in a huff but in a whisper. I saw a lot of his back.

And I was grateful. Discomfort beat rejection. So long as he wasn't pushing me away, I didn't need him to pull me in. Heart-to-hearts weren't his style, anyway. With Dad you didn't discuss longings, anxieties, hurts. You watched football. You played cards. You went to dinner, you picking the place, him picking up the check. He always commandeered the check. It was the gesture with which he communicated everything he had trouble expressing in other ways.

But at some point Dad, like America, changed. I don't mean he grew weepy, huggy. I mean he traveled from what seemed to me a pained acquiescence to a different, happier, better place. He found peace enough with who I am to insist on introducing my partner, Tom, to his friends at the golf club. Peace enough to compliment me on articles of mine that use the same three-letter word that once chased him off. Peace enough to sit down with me over lunch last week and chart his journey, which I'd never summoned the courage to ask him about before.

It's been an extraordinary year, probably the most extraordinary yet in this country's expanding, deepening embrace of gays and lesbians as citizens of equal stature, equal worth. For the first time, an American president still in office stated his belief that two men or two women should be able to marry. For the first time, voters themselves—not lawmakers, not courts—made same-sex marriage legal. This happened on Election Day in three states all at once: Maine, Maryland and Washington. A corner was turned.

And over the quarter-century leading up to it, at a succession of newspapers in a succession of cities, I interviewed scores of people about the progress we were making and why. But until last week, I couldn't bring myself to examine that subject with the person whose progress has meant the most to me: my dad.

Selection published: December 22, 2012

He's 77. Closing in fast on 78. Hasn't voted for a Democrat in a presidential election since Kennedy. Pledged a fraternity in college. Served as an officer in the Navy. Chose accounting as his profession. Remained married to his high school sweetheart, my mother, until she died in 1996, just shy of their 40th anniversary. He still mentions her daily.

She was the freer spirit, and I told her I was gay back in 1981, when I was 17. She implored me not to tell him—too risky, she said—and to let her handle it. A few years later, she informed me that she'd done so, and that was that. Dad said nothing to me. I said nothing to him. When I would come home to Connecticut from college in North Carolina, he would give me the same kind of hug he'd always given me: manly, swift, sincere. When I was in graduate school in New York City, he would swoop into town to take me to the Four Seasons for duck.

I was sure that he'd resolved simply to put what he'd learned about me out of his mind and pretend it didn't exist. I was wrong. He was mulling it over, trying to figure it out.

"It was just so *unusual* to me," he recalled, groping for the right word.

He'd heard it said that gay people were somehow stunted, maybe even ill. But that made no sense to him, because he was confident that I was neither of those things.

He'd heard it said that peculiar upbringings turned children gay. "I thought about it a lot," he said, "and I came to the conclusion that it had to be in your genes, in you, because I couldn't think how the environment for you was any different than it was for your two brothers."

He said he worried that I was in for a more difficult, less complete life than they and my sister were. I asked him why he'd never broached that with me. He said that it would have been an insult—that I was obviously smart enough to have assessed the terrain and figured out for myself how I was going to navigate it.

In the years before Mom died, I had my first long-term relationship, and I could tell that seeing me coupled, just like my brothers and my sister were, gave him a new, less abstract way to understand me. I just wanted what they wanted. Someone special.

He welcomed the man I was with effusively. Took the two of us out to eat.

Then Mom was gone, and all the parenting fell to Dad. He tapped reserves I'd never imagined in him. When I broke up with the man he'd been so effusive toward, he must have told me six times how sorry he was about that. It was a message—that he was rooting for my happiness, no matter how that happiness came to me.

What he struggled most with, he admitted to me over our lunch, was his worry about what others would think of me, of him, of our family. His Italian-immigrant parents had been fanatics about the face a person presented to the world—the "bella figura," as Italians say—and when I would write candidly about my life, as I did on occasion, he'd flinch a bit. Still does.

But he has decided that such writing is necessary. "There's prejudice out there, and it's good to fight that," he said, adding that visibility and openness are obviously integral to that battle. "I'm convinced that people who don't accept gays just don't really know any of them."

He's increasingly irked at his political party, which he thinks is signing its own death warrant with its attitude toward gays, toward guns, toward immigrants. You have to bend to reality. Evolve with the times. Be open-minded. Be fair.

His evolution continues. Same-sex marriage is a tough one for him, as it is, still, for no small number of Americans. It's as exotic a proposition as my being gay once was, a challenge to the way he understood the world and its traditions for so very long.

But he's not prepared to say that what two committed men or two committed women share is anything less than what a man and a woman do. In any case, he noted, society is moving in only one direction on this front. And he's O.K. with that.

As our meal ended he asked me—first time ever—if I wanted or planned on kids. I don't. He said he was sad that I'd never be a father, because it was an experience with such deep satisfactions and so much joy.

Grabbing the check for once, I confessed that I'd long felt a measure of guilt about the extra burden I'd confronted him with, the added struggle.

He shook his head: "I almost think I love you more for it—for being what you are rather than what was expected of you."

Consider the source and the audience

- Bruni is on familiar terrain here—he has written at the *Times* for years. Still, this is a deeply personal article. Why did he write it?

Lay out the argument, the values, and the assumptions

- This essay is not so much the construction of an argument as it is a recounting of a journey. What point is Bruni making here about the nation's evolution on the issue of gay rights, and how is his father a proxy for that evolution?
- What values does his conservative father rely on to come to his stance on gay rights?

Uncover the evidence

- In this piece the story is its own evidence; the evidence is anecdotal on purpose. Could the story be told any other way?
- Would figures and data be more persuasive than feelings and emotions?

Evaluate the conclusion

- There are two conclusions here—Bruni's, that the tides are turning on gay rights in this country as evidenced by his father's progress; and his father's, that building the character necessary to realize one's real self is a lovable and honorable thing. One is an empirical claim, the other normative. Where do you stand on these issues?

Sort out the political significance

- In the months after Bruni wrote this essay the Supreme Court struck down the Defense of Marriage Act that defined marriage for federal purposes (like filing taxes jointly or receiving a spouse's Social Security benefits) as between a man and a woman. Where do you think the nation goes from here on the issue of marriage equality?

• •

6.3 Trent Franks's Abortion Claim and the Manly Republican Party

Dana Milbank, *Washington Post*

Why We Chose This Piece

Restrictions on abortion and birth control proved to be toxic issues for the Republicans in the 2012 election. When they tried to discuss why they could not tolerate exceptions to abortion limits even for victims of rape, the (invariably) men tended to end up with both feet in their mouths, trying to explain what they meant by talking about "legitimate rape" (Todd Akin from Missouri) or about a pregnancy caused by a rape being God's will (Richard Mourdock from Indiana). The Democrats billed it as the "Republican war on women" to good effect; President Obama ended up winning the women's vote by 18 percentage points, and both Akin and Mourdock lost races they should easily have won. In this article, Washington Post columnist Dana Milbank, known for mocking members of both parties when called for, turns his sights on the Republican House members in 2013 who hadn't seemed to have learned the lessons from 2012.

Ladies and gentlemen, Republicans are again voting on new abortion restrictions. Cue their theme song:

"Men men men men, manly men men men!"

 "Men men men men, manly men men men!"

The House Judiciary Committee gathered Wednesday to pass another anti-abortion bill, and the nameplates on the majority side told the story:

Mr. Goodlatte.

Mr. Sensenbrenner.

Mr. Coble.

Mr. Smith.

Mr. Chabot.

Mr. Bachus.

Mr. Issa.

Mr. Forbes.

Mr. King.

Mr. Franks.

Selection published: June 12, 2013

In all, the nameplates of 23 misters lined both rows on the GOP side; there isn't one Republican woman on the panel. The guys muscled through a bill that would upend *Roe v. Wade* by effectively banning all abortions after 20 weeks.

The manly men voted down a Democratic effort to add enhanced protections for the life and health of the mother. They voted down a Democratic amendment that would allow exceptions for women with heart or lung disease or diabetes. They even voted down an amendment that would have made exceptions for victims of rape or incest. If that weren't enough, the chief sponsor of the legislation, Rep. Trent Franks, R-Ariz., had a Todd Akin moment as he attempted to argue that women aren't likely to become pregnant from rape. Franks provided his variation of "legitimate rape" theory when he argued against the rape-and-incest exception because the amendment didn't require women to report the crime.

"What difference does that make?" asked Rep. Jerrold Nadler, D-N.Y. "The point I was trying to make, Mr. Nadler, is that, you know, before when my friends on the left side of the aisle here tried to make rape and incest the subject, because, you know, the incidents of rape resulting in pregnancy are very low," he said. "But when you make that exception, there's usually a requirement to report the rape within 48 hours."

Hold on. The incidents of rape resulting in pregnancy are very low? "I just find it astonishing to hear a phrase repeated that the incidence of pregnancy from rape is low," said Rep. Zoe Lofgren of California, one of five Democratic women on the panel. "There's no scientific basis for that. The idea that the Republican men on this committee think they can tell the women of America that they have to carry to term the product of a rape is outrageous."

Even before the hearing, Democrats were talking about the legislation as evidence that the GOP had returned to its "war on women," a favorite Democratic theme to widen the party's advantage among female voters. But if this really is a war, women have nothing to worry about: These Republicans can't shoot straight.

"Too immoral or too stupid"

The legislation, even if it clears the House, has no chance in the Senate and would face a certain veto. And yet House Republicans pressed ahead. "This looks like just another battle in the Republican war on women," Nadler observed, saying the majority thinks women are "too immoral or too stupid" to make their own choices.

To counter this argument, Franks invoked Kermit Gosnell, a Philadelphia abortion doctor who was convicted last month of murdering babies. But Gosnell was convicted under existing law and therefore didn't help Franks rebut the war-on-women charges.

Lofgren told the story of a woman whose pregnancy was putting her life at risk. "The idea that we would force somebody like Vicki to endanger her own life—the Republican men on this committee think they have the right to do that," she said.

The men easily defeated the rape-and-incest exception. But when it came time to vote on an exception for a mother's health, there were 11 Democrats in the room and only 10 Republicans. "It is good for everybody to have lunch, so we will stand in recess," announced the chairman, Bob Goodlatte, R-Va. "Can we vote on this amendment, please?" asked Rep. Sheila Jackson Lee, D-Texas, the sponsor.

"We will vote on it when we return," Goodlatte said. The Republicans needed more manpower.

Consider the source and the audience

- Milbank writes for the ultimate Washington insider paper, and his audience is people well versed in Washington politics. Even though he uses humor to make his argument, his columns are pointed. Why does he think this column will resonate with his audience?

Lay out the argument, the values, and the assumptions

- The argument here is not about the morality of abortion; rather, it concerns the political strategy of a party that does poorly in elections among women, and yet continues to try to pass legislation that affects women's lives profoundly, without any input from women lawmakers. As this is legislation that had no actual chance to become law, why did the men insist on voting on it?
- What does Milbank think about the way they elevate principle over politics?

Uncover the evidence

- Milbank uses humor rather than data or empirical evidence to make his point. Does it work?

Evaluate the conclusion

- Do you agree that the Republicans are damaging themselves by focusing on legislation that is politically unpopular because they believe it is the right thing to do, or should they stick to their principles on this?
- Would they come to any different conclusions if they were working with women legislators?

Sort out the political significance

- The gender gap in American politics (the tendency for women to vote for Democrats more than they vote for Republicans) has been determinative in several presidential elections. What issues other than women's health policy do you think would lead to that gap?

6.4 A More Perfect Union
Barack Obama

Why We Chose This Piece

In March 2008, then-senator Barack Obama's promising campaign for the Democratic nomination for the presidency appeared to be hitting turbulent waters. Cable stations were playing video of his former pastor, the Reverend Jeremiah

Selection delivered: March 18, 2008

*Wright, shouting spiteful words about white America from his pulpit, and even some
Obama supporters were wondering if their candidate had spent his Sunday
mornings listening to the rantings of a disillusioned and angry man. Many African
Americans, more familiar with the proceedings of traditionally black churches than
their white compatriots, found Wright's shouting to be normal and his words to be
understandable, even if they did not agree with the message. Wright, a former
marine who had lived through segregation, could not help but note where the
promise of America fell short for black America. A glass that many Americans
wanted to view as half full still looked half empty to blacks from Wright's generation.*

*Obama, born of a white mother and an African father, and self-educated in the
culture of black America, had hoped to keep race off the front burner in his campaign,
but the old Wright videos made that impossible. He saw himself as facing not only a
critical moment in his campaign but also a "teachable moment." He could hunker
down and hope the scandal faded, or he could tackle it with a speech on race. He
chose to do the latter, a response viewed as risky at the time, though in hindsight it
may have been the very thing to set his campaign back on track. He says he wants his
speech to open a new conversation about race in this country. Does it do that? How?*

"We the people, in order to form a more perfect union. . ."—221 years
ago, in a hall that still stands across the street, a group of men gathered and, with these simple words, launched America's improbable
experiment in democracy. Farmers and scholars, statesmen and patriots who had
traveled across an ocean to escape tyranny and persecution finally made real their
declaration of independence at a Philadelphia convention that lasted through the
spring of 1787.

The document they produced was eventually signed but ultimately unfinished. It
was stained by this nation's original sin of slavery, a question that divided the colonies
and brought the convention to a stalemate until the founders chose to allow the slave
trade to continue for at least 20 more years, and to leave any final resolution to future
generations.

Of course, the answer to the slavery question was already embedded within our
Constitution—a Constitution that had at its very core the ideal of equal citizenship
under the law; a Constitution that promised its people liberty and justice and a union
that could be and should be perfected over time.

And yet words on a parchment would not be enough to deliver slaves from bondage,
or provide men and women of every color and creed their full rights and obligations as
citizens of the United States. What would be needed were Americans in successive generations who were willing to do their part—through protests and struggles, on the
streets and in the courts, through a civil war and civil disobedience, and always at great
risk—to narrow that gap between the promise of our ideals and the reality of their time.

This was one of the tasks we set forth at the beginning of this presidential campaign—to continue the long march of those who came before us, a march for a more
just, more equal, more free, more caring and more prosperous America. I chose to run
for president at this moment in history because I believe deeply that we cannot solve

the challenges of our time unless we solve them together, unless we perfect our union by understanding that we may have different stories, but we hold common hopes; that we may not look the same and we may not have come from the same place, but we all want to move in the same direction—toward a better future for our children and our grandchildren.

This belief comes from my unyielding faith in the decency and generosity of the American people. But it also comes from my own story.

I am the son of a black man from Kenya and a white woman from Kansas. I was raised with the help of a white grandfather who survived a Depression to serve in Patton's Army during World War II and a white grandmother who worked on a bomber assembly line at Fort Leavenworth while he was overseas. I've gone to some of the best schools in America and lived in one of the world's poorest nations. I am married to a black American who carries within her the blood of slaves and slaveowners—an inheritance we pass on to our two precious daughters. I have brothers, sisters, nieces, nephews, uncles and cousins of every race and every hue, scattered across three continents, and for as long as I live, I will never forget that in no other country on Earth is my story even possible.

It's a story that hasn't made me the most conventional of candidates. But it is a story that has seared into my genetic makeup the idea that this nation is more than the sum of its parts—that out of many, we are truly one.

Throughout the first year of this campaign, against all predictions to the contrary, we saw how hungry the American people were for this message of unity. Despite the temptation to view my candidacy through a purely racial lens, we won commanding victories in states with some of the whitest populations in the country. In South Carolina, where the Confederate flag still flies, we built a powerful coalition of African-Americans and white Americans.

This is not to say that race has not been an issue in this campaign. At various stages in the campaign, some commentators have deemed me either "too black" or "not black enough." We saw racial tensions bubble to the surface during the week before the South Carolina primary. The press has scoured every single exit poll for the latest evidence of racial polarization, not just in terms of white and black, but black and brown as well.

And yet, it has only been in the last couple of weeks that the discussion of race in this campaign has taken a particularly divisive turn.

On one end of the spectrum, we've heard the implication that my candidacy is somehow an exercise in affirmative action; that it's based solely on the desire of wide-eyed liberals to purchase racial reconciliation on the cheap. On the other end, we've heard my former pastor, Jeremiah Wright, use incendiary language to express views that have the potential not only to widen the racial divide, but views that denigrate both the greatness and the goodness of our nation, and that rightly offend white and black alike.

I have already condemned, in unequivocal terms, the statements of Reverend Wright that have caused such controversy and, in some cases, pain. For some, nagging questions remain. Did I know him to be an occasionally fierce critic of American domestic and foreign policy? Of course. Did I ever hear him make remarks that could be considered controversial while I sat in the church? Yes. Did I strongly disagree with many of his political views? Absolutely—just as I'm sure many of you have heard remarks from your pastors, priests, or rabbis with which you strongly disagreed.

But the remarks that have caused this recent firestorm weren't simply controversial. They weren't simply a religious leader's efforts to speak out against perceived injustice. Instead, they expressed a profoundly distorted view of this country—a view that sees white racism as endemic, and that elevates what is wrong with America above all that we know is right with America; a view that sees the conflicts in the Middle East as rooted primarily in the actions of stalwart allies like Israel, instead of emanating from the perverse and hateful ideologies of radical Islam.

As such, Reverend Wright's comments were not only wrong but divisive, divisive at a time when we need unity; racially charged at a time when we need to come together to solve a set of monumental problems—two wars, a terrorist threat, a falling economy, a chronic health care crisis and potentially devastating climate change— problems that are neither black or white or Latino or Asian, but rather problems that confront us all.

Given my background, my politics, and my professed values and ideals, there will no doubt be those for whom my statements of condemnation are not enough. Why associate myself with Reverend Wright in the first place, they may ask? Why not join another church? And I confess that if all that I knew of Reverend Wright were the snippets of those sermons that have run in an endless loop on the television sets and YouTube, or if Trinity United Church of Christ conformed to the caricatures being peddled by some commentators, there is no doubt that I would react in much the same way.

But the truth is, that isn't all that I know of the man. The man I met more than 20 years ago is a man who helped introduce me to my Christian faith, a man who spoke to me about our obligations to love one another, to care for the sick and lift up the poor. He is a man who served his country as a United States Marine; who has studied and lectured at some of the finest universities and seminaries in the country, and who for over 30 years has led a church that serves the community by doing God's work here on Earth—by housing the homeless, ministering to the needy, providing day care services and scholarships and prison ministries, and reaching out to those suffering from HIV/AIDS.

In my first book, *Dreams From My Father*, I describe the experience of my first service at Trinity:

"People began to shout, to rise from their seats and clap and cry out, a forceful wind carrying the reverend's voice up into the rafters. And in that single note—hope!—I heard something else: At the foot of that cross, inside the thousands of churches across the city, I imagined the stories of ordinary black people merging with the stories of David and Goliath, Moses and Pharaoh, the Christians in the lion's den, Ezekiel's field of dry bones. Those stories—of survival and freedom and hope—became our stories, my story. The blood that spilled was our blood, the tears our tears, until this black church, on this bright day, seemed once more a vessel carrying the story of a people into future generations and into a larger world. Our trials and triumphs became at once unique and universal, black and more than black. In chronicling our journey, the stories and songs gave us a meaning to reclaim memories that we didn't need to feel shame about—memories that all people might study and cherish, and with which we could start to rebuild."

That has been my experience at Trinity. Like other predominantly black churches across the country, Trinity embodies the black community in its entirety—the doctor and the welfare mom, the model student and the former gang-banger. Like other black churches, Trinity's services are full of raucous laughter and sometimes bawdy humor. They are full of dancing and clapping and screaming and shouting that may seem jarring to the untrained ear. The church contains in full the kindness and cruelty, the fierce intelligence and the shocking ignorance, the struggles and successes, the love and, yes, the bitterness and biases that make up the black experience in America.

And this helps explain, perhaps, my relationship with Reverend Wright. As imperfect as he may be, he has been like family to me. He strengthened my faith, officiated my wedding, and baptized my children. Not once in my conversations with him have I heard him talk about any ethnic group in derogatory terms, or treat whites with whom he interacted with anything but courtesy and respect. He contains within him the contradictions—the good and the bad—of the community that he has served diligently for so many years.

I can no more disown him than I can disown the black community. I can no more disown him than I can disown my white grandmother—a woman who helped raise me, a woman who sacrificed again and again for me, a woman who loves me as much as she loves anything in this world, but a woman who once confessed her fear of black men who passed her by on the street, and who on more than one occasion has uttered racial or ethnic stereotypes that made me cringe.

These people are a part of me. And they are part of America, this country that I love.

Some will see this as an attempt to justify or excuse comments that are simply inexcusable. I can assure you it is not. I suppose the politically safe thing to do would be to move on from this episode and just hope that it fades into the woodwork. We can dismiss Reverend Wright as a crank or a demagogue, just as some have dismissed Geraldine Ferraro, in the aftermath of her recent statements, as harboring some deep-seated bias.

But race is an issue that I believe this nation cannot afford to ignore right now. We would be making the same mistake that Reverend Wright made in his offending sermons about America—to simplify and stereotype and amplify the negative to the point that it distorts reality.

The fact is that the comments that have been made and the issues that have surfaced over the last few weeks reflect the complexities of race in this country that we've never really worked through—a part of our union that we have not yet made perfect. And if we walk away now, if we simply retreat into our respective corners, we will never be able to come together and solve challenges like health care or education or the need to find good jobs for every American.

Understanding this reality requires a reminder of how we arrived at this point. As William Faulkner once wrote, "The past isn't dead and buried. In fact, it isn't even past." We do not need to recite here the history of racial injustice in this country. But we do need to remind ourselves that so many of the disparities that exist between the African-American community and the larger American community today can be traced directly to inequalities passed on from an earlier generation that suffered under the brutal legacy of slavery and Jim Crow.

Segregated schools were and are inferior schools; we still haven't fixed them, 50 years after *Brown v. Board of Education*. And the inferior education they provided, then and now, helps explain the pervasive achievement gap between today's black and white students.

Legalized discrimination—where blacks were prevented, often through violence, from owning property, or loans were not granted to African-American business owners, or black homeowners could not access FHA mortgages, or blacks were excluded from unions or the police force or the fire department—meant that black families could not amass any meaningful wealth to bequeath to future generations. That history helps explain the wealth and income gap between blacks and whites, and the concentrated pockets of poverty that persist in so many of today's urban and rural communities.

A lack of economic opportunity among black men, and the shame and frustration that came from not being able to provide for one's family contributed to the erosion of black families—a problem that welfare policies for many years may have worsened. And the lack of basic services in so many urban black neighborhoods—parks for kids to play in, police walking the beat, regular garbage pickup, building code enforcement— all helped create a cycle of violence, blight and neglect that continues to haunt us.

This is the reality in which Reverend Wright and other African-Americans of his generation grew up. They came of age in the late '50s and early '60s, a time when segregation was still the law of the land and opportunity was systematically constricted. What's remarkable is not how many failed in the face of discrimination, but how many men and women overcame the odds; how many were able to make a way out of no way, for those like me who would come after them.

For all those who scratched and clawed their way to get a piece of the American Dream, there were many who didn't make it—those who were ultimately defeated, in one way or another, by discrimination. That legacy of defeat was passed on to future generations—those young men and, increasingly, young women who we see standing on street corners or languishing in our prisons, without hope or prospects for the future. Even for those blacks who did make it, questions of race and racism continue to define their worldview in fundamental ways. For the men and women of Reverend Wright's generation, the memories of humiliation and doubt and fear have not gone away; nor has the anger and the bitterness of those years. That anger may not get expressed in public, in front of white co-workers or white friends. But it does find voice in the barber-shop or the beauty shop or around the kitchen table. At times, that anger is exploited by politicians, to gin up votes along racial lines, or to make up for a politician's own failings.

And occasionally it finds voice in the church on Sunday morning, in the pulpit and in the pews. The fact that so many people are surprised to hear that anger in some of Reverend Wright's sermons simply reminds us of the old truism that the most segregated hour of American life occurs on Sunday morning. That anger is not always productive; indeed, all too often it distracts attention from solving real problems; it keeps us from squarely facing our own complicity within the African-American community in our condition, and prevents the African-American community from forging the alliances it needs to bring about real change. But the anger is real; it is powerful. And to simply wish it away, to condemn it without understanding its roots, only serves to widen the chasm of misunderstanding that exists between the races.

113

In fact, a similar anger exists within segments of the white community. Most working- and middle-class white Americans don't feel that they have been particularly privileged by their race. Their experience is the immigrant experience—as far as they're concerned, no one handed them anything. They built it from scratch. They've worked hard all their lives, many times only to see their jobs shipped overseas or their pensions dumped after a lifetime of labor. They are anxious about their futures, and they feel their dreams slipping away. And in an era of stagnant wages and global competition, opportunity comes to be seen as a zero sum game, in which your dreams come at my expense. So when they are told to bus their children to a school across town; when they hear an African-American is getting an advantage in landing a good job or a spot in a good college because of an injustice that they themselves never committed; when they're told that their fears about crime in urban neighborhoods are somehow prejudiced, resentment builds over time.

Like the anger within the black community, these resentments aren't always expressed in polite company. But they have helped shape the political landscape for at least a generation. Anger over welfare and affirmative action helped forge the Reagan Coalition. Politicians routinely exploited fears of crime for their own electoral ends. Talk show hosts and conservative commentators built entire careers unmasking bogus claims of racism while dismissing legitimate discussions of racial injustice and inequality as mere political correctness or reverse racism.

Just as black anger often proved counterproductive, so have these white resentments distracted attention from the real culprits of the middle class squeeze—a corporate culture rife with inside dealing, questionable accounting practices and short-term greed; a Washington dominated by lobbyists and special interests; economic policies that favor the few over the many. And yet, to wish away the resentments of white Americans, to label them as misguided or even racist, without recognizing they are grounded in legitimate concerns—this too widens the racial divide and blocks the path to understanding.

This is where we are right now. It's a racial stalemate we've been stuck in for years. Contrary to the claims of some of my critics, black and white, I have never been so naïve as to believe that we can get beyond our racial divisions in a single election cycle, or with a single candidacy—particularly a candidacy as imperfect as my own.

But I have asserted a firm conviction—a conviction rooted in my faith in God and my faith in the American people—that, working together, we can move beyond some of our old racial wounds, and that in fact we have no choice if we are to continue on the path of a more perfect union.

For the African-American community, that path means embracing the burdens of our past without becoming victims of our past. It means continuing to insist on a full measure of justice in every aspect of American life. But it also means binding our particular grievances—for better health care and better schools and better jobs—to the larger aspirations of all Americans: the white woman struggling to break the glass ceiling, the white man who has been laid off, the immigrant trying to feed his family. And it means taking full responsibility for our own lives—by demanding more from our fathers, and spending more time with our children, and reading to them, and teaching them that while they may face challenges and discrimination in their own lives, they must never succumb to despair or cynicism; they must always believe that they can write their own destiny.

Ironically, this quintessentially American—and yes, conservative—notion of self-help found frequent expression in Reverend Wright's sermons. But what my former pastor too often failed to understand is that embarking on a program of self-help also requires a belief that society can change.

The profound mistake of Reverend Wright's sermons is not that he spoke about racism in our society. It's that he spoke as if our society was static; as if no progress had been made; as if this country—a country that has made it possible for one of his own members to run for the highest office in the land and build a coalition of white and black, Latino and Asian, rich and poor, young and old—is still irrevocably bound to a tragic past. But what we know—what we have seen—is that America can change. That is the true genius of this nation. What we have already achieved gives us hope—the audacity to hope—for what we can and must achieve tomorrow.

In the white community, the path to a more perfect union means acknowledging that what ails the African-American community does not just exist in the minds of black people; that the legacy of discrimination—and current incidents of discrimination, while less overt than in the past—are real and must be addressed, not just with words, but with deeds, by investing in our schools and our communities; by enforcing our civil rights laws and ensuring fairness in our criminal justice system; by providing this generation with ladders of opportunity that were unavailable for previous generations. It requires all Americans to realize that your dreams do not have to come at the expense of my dreams; that investing in the health, welfare and education of black and brown and white children will ultimately help all of America prosper.

In the end, then, what is called for is nothing more and nothing less than what all the world's great religions demand—that we do unto others as we would have them do unto us. Let us be our brother's keeper, scripture tells us. Let us be our sister's keeper. Let us find that common stake we all have in one another, and let our politics reflect that spirit as well.

For we have a choice in this country. We can accept a politics that breeds division and conflict and cynicism. We can tackle race only as spectacle—as we did in the O.J. trial—or in the wake of tragedy—as we did in the aftermath of Katrina—or as fodder for the nightly news. We can play Reverend Wright's sermons on every channel, every day and talk about them from now until the election, and make the only question in this campaign whether or not the American people think that I somehow believe or sympathize with his most offensive words. We can pounce on some gaffe by a Hillary supporter as evidence that she's playing the race card, or we can speculate on whether white men will all flock to John McCain in the general election regardless of his policies.

We can do that.

But if we do, I can tell you that in the next election, we'll be talking about some other distraction. And then another one. And then another one. And nothing will change.

That is one option. Or, at this moment, in this election, we can come together and say, "Not this time." This time, we want to talk about the crumbling schools that are stealing the future of black children and white children and Asian children and Hispanic children and Native American children. This time, we want to reject the cynicism that tells us that these kids can't learn; that those kids who don't look like us are somebody else's problem. The children of America are not those kids, they are our kids, and we will not let them fall behind in a 21st century economy. Not this time.

This time we want to talk about how the lines in the emergency room are filled with whites and blacks and Hispanics who do not have health care, who don't have the power on their own to overcome the special interests in Washington, but who can take them on if we do it together.

This time, we want to talk about the shuttered mills that once provided a decent life for men and women of every race, and the homes for sale that once belonged to Americans from every religion, every region, every walk of life. This time, we want to talk about the fact that the real problem is not that someone who doesn't look like you might take your job; it's that the corporation you work for will ship it overseas for nothing more than a profit.

This time, we want to talk about the men and women of every color and creed who serve together and fight together and bleed together under the same proud flag. We want to talk about how to bring them home from a war that should have never been authorized and should have never been waged. And we want to talk about how we'll show our patriotism by caring for them and their families, and giving them the benefits that they have earned.

I would not be running for President if I didn't believe with all my heart that this is what the vast majority of Americans want for this country. This union may never be perfect, but generation after generation has shown that it can always be perfected. And today, whenever I find myself feeling doubtful or cynical about this possibility, what gives me the most hope is the next generation—the young people whose attitudes and beliefs and openness to change have already made history in this election.

There is one story in particularly that I'd like to leave you with today—a story I told when I had the great honor of speaking on Dr. King's birthday at his home church, Ebenezer Baptist, in Atlanta.

There is a young, 23-year-old white woman named Ashley Baia who organized for our campaign in Florence, S.C. She had been working to organize a mostly African-American community since the beginning of this campaign, and one day she was at a roundtable discussion where everyone went around telling their story and why they were there.

And Ashley said that when she was 9 years old, her mother got cancer. And because she had to miss days of work, she was let go and lost her health care. They had to file for bankruptcy, and that's when Ashley decided that she had to do something to help her mom.

She knew that food was one of their most expensive costs, and so Ashley convinced her mother that what she really liked and really wanted to eat more than anything else was mustard and relish sandwiches—because that was the cheapest way to eat. That's the mind of a 9-year-old.

She did this for a year until her mom got better. So she told everyone at the round-table that the reason she joined our campaign was so that she could help the millions of other children in the country who want and need to help their parents, too.

Now, Ashley might have made a different choice. Perhaps somebody told her along the way that the source of her mother's problems were blacks who were on welfare and too lazy to work, or Hispanics who were coming into the country illegally. But she didn't. She sought out allies in her fight against injustice.

Anyway, Ashley finishes her story and then goes around the room and asks everyone else why they're supporting the campaign. They all have different stories and different reasons. Many bring up a specific issue. And finally they come to this elderly black man who's been sitting there quietly the entire time. And Ashley asks him why he's there. And he does not bring up a specific issue. He does not say health care or the economy. He does not say education or the war. He does not say that he was there because of Barack Obama. He simply says to everyone in the room, "I am here because of Ashley."

"I'm here because of Ashley." By itself, that single moment of recognition between that young white girl and that old black man is not enough. It is not enough to give health care to the sick, or jobs to the jobless, or education to our children.

But it is where we start. It is where our union grows stronger. And as so many generations have come to realize over the course of the 221 years since a band of patriots signed that document right here in Philadelphia, that is where the perfection begins.

Consider the source and the audience

- Obama is speaking at once to white Americans who might have been offended by Reverend Wright's words and to black Americans who believe that many of Wright's words were justified. How does he navigate these two different audiences?
- How does his background enable him to straddle the two cultures to which he is speaking?

Lay out the argument, the values, and the assumptions

- Why does Obama call his speech "A More Perfect Union?" Why does he see our Constitution as "unfinished?" What are the values he sees underlying it that might be the means to finishing it?
- How does he explain Reverend Wright's words? What does Obama believe is wrong with those words? What is right about them?
- What makes race so difficult for Americans to talk about? What is the racial stalemate we have been stuck in for years, what has kept us stuck, and how might we get out of it?

Uncover the evidence

- Is any evidence required for Obama's argument? When a speaker or writer relies on historical evidence, how can he or she respond to others who believe that the historical record says something different?
- Besides history, what does Obama use to back up his case?

Evaluate the conclusion

- Obama essentially argues that we are at a crossroads with respect to race and if we don't move out of the stalemate we are in we will stay stuck. Is this conclusion reasonable? What is required of us to move beyond this racial stalemate?

Sort out the political implications

- Obviously, this speech did the trick in terms of keeping Obama's campaign alive. Did it also meet his goal of starting a new conversation about race? How would we know?

7

Congress

The founders' passion for checks and balances reached a high point in their design of the U.S. Congress. Not only is that institution checked by the executive and judicial branches of government, but it is checked and balanced internally as well, by the requirement that both chambers—the large, unwieldy House of Representatives and the smaller, more disciplined Senate—agree on all bills that become national law.

Though we citizens may fuss and fume over what seem like endless gridlock or legislative logjams, slow, painstaking lawmaking is just what our cautious founders wanted.

In some ways, though, the Congress of today does not look like the founders' ideal. Their hope was that the House of Representatives would be responsive to public opinion and that it would be balanced by the more mature Senate, which would be focused on longer-term issues of the public interest. In truth, members of both institutions are subject to a legislative dilemma. They are torn between two roles—representing the particular interests of their constituencies (either a legislative district or a state) or engaging in lawmaking that serves the national interest but might not serve their constituency's interests nearly as well. Since the former course is far more likely to lead to their reelection, and reelection is the primary concern of almost every member of Congress, they have every incentive to ignore critical national problems, particularly in the House, where members come up for reelection every two years. Additionally, as some of the readings in this chapter make clear, representatives are also influenced—and sometimes constrained—by their political parties, which also may not have the national interest in mind.

The readings in this chapter touch on some, but by no means all, of the many critical issues concerning legislative politics. The first article, written by a bipartisan team, blames the problem of legislative gridlock in Congress on the Republican Party. The second piece, posted on CNN.com, offers a very different view. The author, Ira Shapiro, sees positives changes, particularly in the U.S. Senate, regarding legislative gridlock. Third, an article from the *New York Times* covers the debate over equal representation in the Senate. In the fourth piece, of all things a molecular biologist/neuroscientist argues that the Republican Party used the most recent redistricting process to increase its representation in the House of Representatives. The final selection is a 1950 speech made by Sen. Margaret Chase Smith, decrying the incivility and damage to personal liberty that came with the attempt by her colleague Sen. Joseph McCarthy to root out what he saw as a communist threat in American government.

●●

7.1   Let's Just Say It: The Republicans Are the Problem

Thomas E. Mann and Norman J. Ornstein, *Washington Post*

Why We Chose This Piece

This selection is a piece from a much longer argument that Mann and Ornstein made in their book It's Even Worse Than It Looks: How the American Constitutional System Collided with the New Politics of Extremism. *The article (and the book) received substantial discussion among pundits and scholars because of Mann and Ornstein's controversial claim that the Republican Party is to blame for most of the gridlock in Washington, D.C., today. The piece is also included because it raises questions about more than just the inability of Congress to get anything done; it could just as easily fit in the political parties or media chapters because of the issues it raises. How do Mann and Ornstein view political parties? Why are they critical of the media?*

Rep. Allen West, a Florida Republican, was recently captured on video asserting that there are "78 to 81" Democrats in Congress who are members of the Communist Party. Of course, it's not unusual for some renegade lawmaker from either side of the aisle to say something outrageous. What made West's comment— right out of the McCarthyite playbook of the 1950s—so striking was the almost complete lack of condemnation from Republican congressional leaders or other major party figures, including the remaining presidential candidates.

It's not that the GOP leadership agrees with West; it is that such extreme remarks and views are now taken for granted.

We have been studying Washington politics and Congress for more than 40 years, and never have we seen them this dysfunctional. In our past writings, we have criticized both parties when we believed it was warranted. Today, however, we have no choice but to acknowledge that the core of the problem lies with the Republican Party.

Selection published: April 27, 2012

The GOP has become an insurgent outlier in American politics. It is ideologically extreme; scornful of compromise; unmoved by conventional understanding of facts, evidence and science; and dismissive of the legitimacy of its political opposition.

When one party moves this far from the mainstream, it makes it nearly impossible for the political system to deal constructively with the country's challenges.

"Both sides do it" or "There is plenty of blame to go around" are the traditional refuges for an American news media intent on proving its lack of bias, while political scientists prefer generality and neutrality when discussing partisan polarization. Many self-styled bipartisan groups, in their search for common ground, propose solutions that move both sides to the center, a strategy that is simply untenable when one side is so far out of reach.

It is clear that the center of gravity in the Republican Party has shifted sharply to the right. Its once-legendary moderate and center-right legislators in the House and the Senate—think Bob Michel, Mickey Edwards, John Danforth, Chuck Hagel—are virtually extinct.

The post-McGovern Democratic Party, by contrast, while losing the bulk of its conservative Dixiecrat contingent in the decades after the civil rights revolution, has retained a more diverse base. Since the Clinton presidency, it has hewed to the center-left on issues from welfare reform to fiscal policy. While the Democrats may have moved from their 40-yard line to their 25, the Republicans have gone from their 40 to somewhere behind their goal post.

What happened? Of course, there were larger forces at work beyond the realignment of the South. They included the mobilization of social conservatives after the 1973 *Roe v. Wade* decision, the anti-tax movement launched in 1978 by California's Proposition 13, the rise of conservative talk radio after a congressional pay raise in 1989, and the emergence of Fox News and right-wing blogs. But the real move to the bedrock right starts with two names: Newt Gingrich and Grover Norquist.

From the day he entered Congress in 1979, Gingrich had a strategy to create a Republican majority in the House: convincing voters that the institution was so corrupt that anyone would be better than the incumbents, especially those in the Democratic majority. It took him 16 years, but by bringing ethics charges against Democratic leaders; provoking them into overreactions that enraged Republicans and united them to vote against Democratic initiatives; exploiting scandals to create even more public disgust with politicians; and then recruiting GOP candidates around the country to run against Washington, Democrats and Congress, Gingrich accomplished his goal.

Ironically, after becoming speaker, Gingrich wanted to enhance Congress's reputation and was content to compromise with President Bill Clinton when it served his interests. But the forces Gingrich unleashed destroyed whatever comity existed across party lines, activated an extreme and virulently anti-Washington base—most recently represented by tea party activists—and helped drive moderate Republicans out of Congress. (Some of his progeny, elected in the early 1990s, moved to the Senate and polarized its culture in the same way.)

Norquist, meanwhile, founded Americans for Tax Reform [ATR] in 1985 and rolled out his Taxpayer Protection Pledge the following year. The pledge, which binds its signers to never support a tax increase (that includes closing tax loopholes), had been signed as of last year by 238 of the 242 House Republicans and 41 of the 47 GOP senators, according to ATR. The Norquist tax pledge has led to other pledges, on issues such as climate change, that create additional litmus tests that box in moderates and make cross-party coalitions nearly impossible. For Republicans concerned about a primary challenge from the right, the failure to sign such pledges is simply too risky.

Today, thanks to the GOP, compromise has gone out the window in Washington. In the first two years of the Obama administration, nearly every presidential initiative met with vehement, rancorous and unanimous Republican opposition in the House and the Senate, followed by efforts to delegitimize the results and repeal the policies. The filibuster, once relegated to a handful of major national issues in a given Congress, became a routine weapon of obstruction, applied even to widely supported bills or presidential nominations. And Republicans in the Senate have abused the confirmation process to block any and every nominee to posts such as the head of the Consumer Financial Protection Bureau, solely to keep laws that were legitimately enacted from being implemented.

In the third and now fourth years of the Obama presidency, divided government has produced something closer to complete gridlock than we have ever seen in our time in Washington, with partisan divides even leading last year to America's first credit downgrade.

On financial stabilization and economic recovery, on deficits and debt, on climate change and health-care reform, Republicans have been the force behind the widening ideological gaps and the strategic use of partisanship. In the presidential campaign and in Congress, GOP leaders have embraced fanciful policies on taxes and spending, kowtowing to their party's most strident voices.

Republicans often dismiss nonpartisan analyses of the nature of problems and the impact of policies when those assessments don't fit their ideology. In the face of the deepest economic downturn since the Great Depression, the party's leaders and their outside acolytes insisted on obeisance to a supply-side view of economic growth—thus fulfilling Norquist's pledge—while ignoring contrary considerations.

The results can border on the absurd: In early 2009, several of the eight Republican co-sponsors of a bipartisan health-care reform plan dropped their support; by early 2010, the others had turned on their own proposal so that there would be zero GOP backing for any bill that came within a mile of Obama's reform initiative. As one co-sponsor, Sen. Lamar Alexander (R-Tenn.), told *The Washington Post*'s Ezra Klein: "I liked it because it was bipartisan. I wouldn't have voted for it."

And seven Republican co-sponsors of a Senate resolution to create a debt-reduction panel voted in January 2010 against their own resolution, solely to keep it from getting to the 60-vote threshold Republicans demanded and thus denying the president a seeming victory.

This attitude filters down far deeper than the party leadership. Rank-and-file GOP voters endorse the strategy that the party's elites have adopted, eschewing compromise to solve problems and insisting on principle, even if it leads to gridlock. Democratic voters, by contrast, along with self-identified independents, are more likely to favor deal-making over deadlock.

Democrats are hardly blameless, and they have their own extreme wing and their own predilection for hardball politics. But these tendencies do not routinely veer outside the normal bounds of robust politics. If anything, under the presidencies of Clinton and Obama, the Democrats have become more of a status-quo party. They are centrist protectors of government, reluctantly willing to revamp programs and trim retirement and health benefits to maintain its central commitments in the face of fiscal pressures.

No doubt, Democrats were not exactly warm and fuzzy toward George W. Bush during his presidency. But recall that they worked hand in glove with the Republican president on the No Child Left Behind Act, provided crucial votes in the Senate for his tax cuts, joined with Republicans for all the steps taken after the Sept. 11, 2001, attacks and supplied the key votes for the Bush administration's financial bailout at the height of the economic crisis in 2008. The difference is striking.

The GOP's evolution has become too much for some longtime Republicans. Former senator Chuck Hagel of Nebraska called his party "irresponsible" in an interview with the *Financial Times* in August, at the height of the debt-ceiling battle. "I think the Republican Party is captive to political movements that are very ideological, that are very narrow," he said. "I've never seen so much intolerance as I see today in American politics."

And Mike Lofgren, a veteran Republican congressional staffer, wrote an anguished diatribe last year about why he was ending his career on the Hill after nearly three decades. "The Republican Party is becoming less and less like a traditional political party in a representative democracy and becoming more like an apocalyptic cult, or one of the intensely ideological authoritarian parties of 20th century Europe," he wrote on the Truthout Web site.

Shortly before Rep. West went off the rails with his accusations of communism in the Democratic Party, political scientists Keith Poole and Howard Rosenthal, who have long tracked historical trends in political polarization, said their studies of congressional votes found that Republicans are now more conservative than they have been in more than a century. Their data show a dramatic uptick in polarization, mostly caused by the sharp rightward move of the GOP.

If our democracy is to regain its health and vitality, the culture and ideological center of the Republican Party must change. In the short run, without a massive (and unlikely) across-the-board rejection of the GOP at the polls, that will not happen. If anything, Washington's ideological divide will probably grow after the 2012 elections.

In the House, some of the remaining centrist and conservative "Blue Dog" Democrats have been targeted for extinction by redistricting, while even ardent tea party Republicans, such as freshman Rep. Alan Nunnelee (Miss.), have faced primary challenges from the right for being too accommodationist. And Mitt Romney's rhetoric and positions offer no indication that he would govern differently if his party captures the White House and both chambers of Congress.

We understand the values of mainstream journalists, including the effort to report both sides of a story. But a balanced treatment of an unbalanced phenomenon distorts reality. If the political dynamics of Washington are unlikely to change anytime soon, at least we should change the way that reality is portrayed to the public.

Our advice to the press: Don't seek professional safety through the even-handed, unfiltered presentation of opposing views. Which politician is telling the truth? Who is taking hostages, at what risks and to what ends?

Also, stop lending legitimacy to Senate filibusters by treating a 60-vote hurdle as routine. The framers certainly didn't intend it to be. Report individual senators' abusive use of holds and identify every time the minority party uses a filibuster to kill a bill or nomination with majority support.

Look ahead to the likely consequences of voters' choices in the November elections. How would the candidates govern? What could they accomplish? What differences can people expect from a unified Republican or Democratic government, or one divided between the parties?

In the end, while the press can make certain political choices understandable, it is up to voters to decide. If they can punish ideological extremism at the polls and look skeptically upon candidates who profess to reject all dialogue and bargaining with opponents, then an insurgent outlier party will have some impetus to return to the center. Otherwise, our politics will get worse before it gets better.

Consider the source and the audience

- This article has a bipartisan author team and appeared in the *Washington Post*, known for its mainstream coverage of national politics. They take to task not only national politicians but also the media that cover them, and all people who read the *Post*. Was that a gutsy move, astonishingly foolish, or just wrong-headed?

Lay out the argument, the values, and the assumptions

- Mann and Ornstein's primary concern seems to be that politics in Washington today resembles a game of dangerous brinksmanship. Why do they hold Gingrich and Norquist responsible? What do they see as the primary role of parties? And what is the role of media in a democracy? How would politics in the United States work if Mann and Ornstein had their way? What is the Republican case for not cooperating with Democrats?

Uncover the evidence

- Mann and Ornstein rely in part on historical events to make their case. Can those events be interpreted differently? They also use the words of disaffected Republicans to show how the party has changed. Does that help support their case? Are there any other kinds of evidence that you would like to see?

Evaluate the conclusion

- Do you agree with Mann and Ornstein that politics-as-brinkmanship is a problem? Are they correct to blame changes within the Republican Party for that conclusion? How would Republicans respond? Do you agree that in American politics the effort to be "neutral" means that sometimes analysts and reporters fail to tell the whole story?

Sort out the political implications

- The authors essentially say that it is up to the media and the voters to fix this situation if we want a government that can solve problems effectively. Are those two groups of people up to the task? How might Republicans be expected to react?

7.2 Say Goodbye to Gridlock in Washington
Ira Shapiro, CNN

Why We Chose This Piece

In the previous article, Thomas Mann and Norman Ornstein claim that Congress is broken. Here, Ira Shapiro paints a very different picture. We chose this article because it presents a nice contrast to the previous one, and students can evaluate the arguments against one another. We also included this selection because it takes a point of view that is counter to the conventional wisdom. Most people, including Mann and Ornstein, argue that gridlock is abundant and not on the wane; Shapiro strongly disagrees.

Cold weather has delayed spring in Washington, but we can detect a clear warming trend in our politics.

To be sure, the distance between the Obama administration and congressional Republicans remains vast, executive and judicial nominations remain blocked by an unprecedented number of filibusters and major legislative accomplishments are still months away. But the ice of gridlock is starting to thaw.

Evidence of a healthier, more normal politics is beginning to reappear, centered in the Senate, our political institution that has declined the longest and the furthest.

Congress has been in session only a few weeks, but the Senate has already passed its first budget in four years, after finding compromises to avoid the fiscal cliff and the "nuclear option." Across the range of tough issues, serious legislative work is moving forward, usually on a bipartisan basis. Eight senators, led by Democrat Chuck Schumer and Republicans John McCain, Lindsey Graham and Marco Rubio, have made significant progress toward an agreement on immigration.

The Judiciary Committee has reported the first major gun control legislation since 1994, though its fate is far from certain.

Democrat Carl Levin, joined by McCain, released a devastating report on the abusive trading practices of JPMorgan Chase.

Freshman Democrats Elizabeth Warren and Sherrod Brown have expressed similar views as have Republicans Bob Corker and Chuck Grassley on the dangers of "too big to fail" banks. Democrat Max Baucus, Senate Finance Committee chairman, and Republican Dave Camp, House Ways and Means chairman, have accelerated their effort, started two years ago, to enact the first major tax reform legislation since 1986.

The atmosphere is palpably better. President Barack Obama's "charm offensive" on Capitol Hill won approval from many Republicans.

Sen. Pat Roberts of Kansas, who after meeting with the president in 2010, called him "thin-skinned" and recommended that he "take valium," praised him generously this

Selection published: April 1, 2013

time around for the substantive meeting on the budget and related economic issues. Senate Minority Leader Mitch McConnell, who famously declared that defeating Obama was his highest priority, has this year shown much more graciousness, respect and even occasional humor.

Two factors are most responsible for the improvement.

First, it turns out that elections do have consequences.

Obama's decisive re-election, coupled with what amounted to a national landslide won by the Senate Democrats, has forced the Republicans into a period of reassessment and repositioning. Of course, some Republicans still believe that their party lost because its right wing views were did not come through clearly enough.

But most Republicans recognize that the party's combination of extremism and obstruction proved to be a losing strategy. They know the Republican brand is in deep trouble. The election results seemed to have convinced at least some of the Senate Republicans that finding areas in which to cooperate with the president is necessary.

But the second factor, less understood than the impact of election returns, is just as important. By the end of 2012, for many returning senators and those newly elected, dismay about the Senate has hardened into disgust and determination to change it.

Across the political spectrum, senators are fed up with lurching from crisis to crisis, leaders dictating straight party votes, endless filibusters and constant failure to address the nation's problems.

Sen. Jeff Sessions, R-Alabama, compared the Senate to "the Russian Duma . . . an endless series of secret conclaves . . . , with meetings everywhere but in the committee room or the open air of the Senate floor."

Sen. Barbara Mikulski, D-Maryland, took pride in the "zone of civility" created by the increasing number of women senators.

Sen. Schumer, D-New York, longingly "looked forward to the good old days when we had major legislation go through committees."

The shorthand for what the overwhelming number of senators want is "regular order"—legislation that results from committee consideration, vigorous debate, the opportunity to offer amendments and hard bargaining to reach principled compromise—and the Senate is changing as its leaders respond to the members' frustration and anger.

Legislating in our diverse, contentious country, with our system of separation of powers, has never been, and will never be, easy. Former Sen. Gary Hart once described the great Senate of the 1970s as "a kind of controlled madhouse."

The path to major legislative accomplishments is always treacherous and strewn with seemingly insurmountable obstacles.

Today, the partisan divide is much deeper and the political culture far more vitriolic than 20 or 30 years ago. Although senators cannot choose the era in which they serve, they can choose the way they approach their work and they can determine the way the Senate functions.

It doesn't take much time, or that many people, to change the Senate. Hopefully, day by day, that change is starting to happen.

Consider the source and the audience

- Ira Shapiro is a former Senate staffer. What kind of perspective does that give him?

Lay out the argument, the values, and the assumptions

- Why does Shapiro see a "clear warming trend in our politics"? According to him, what has led to that warming trend?

Uncover the evidence

- Shapiro provides several examples of the parties working together in the Senate. What are some of the examples? Are they persuasive?
- What evidence does he provide to support the reasons he believes gridlock is on the wane?

Evaluate the conclusion

- One of the interesting aspects of this argument is that it can be evaluated with time. Based on what you see in Congress today, does it appear that Shapiro's argument held true?
- Shapiro's argument is almost the exact opposite of that made by Mann and Ornstein in the previous article. Who is correct? What might have led them to come to different conclusions?

Sort out the political implications

- If Shapiro is correct, then what might that mean for legislative productivity during President Obama's second term? What role does the House of Representatives play in all of this?

7.3 Big State, Small State
Adam Liptak, *New York Times*

Why We Chose This Piece

The founders debated a number of issues at the Constitutional Convention. Central among them was the issue of representation. The founders wanted to balance the concerns of both heavily populated states and those that were more scarcely populated. The result was the compromise that made representation in the House of Representatives based on population and representation in the Senate equal among states. However, the debate did not end with this grand compromise, and it still exists today. The following article, by New York Times journalist Adam Liptak,

Selection published: March 10, 2013

makes that clear. We include this selection because it provides interesting perspectives on both sides regarding how representation should work in the United States.

RUTLAND, Vt.—In the four years after the financial crisis struck, a great wave of federal stimulus money washed over Rutland County. It helped pay for bridges, roads, preschool programs, a community health center, buses and fire trucks, water mains and tanks, even a project to make sure fish could still swim down the river while a bridge was being rebuilt.

Just down Route 4, at the New York border, the landscape abruptly turns from spiffy to scruffy. Washington County, N.Y., which is home to about 60,000 people—just as Rutland is—saw only a quarter as much money.

"We didn't receive a lot," said Peter Aust, the president of the local chamber of commerce on the New York side. "We never saw any of the positive impact of the stimulus funds."

Vermont's 625,000 residents have two United States senators, and so do New York's 19 million. That means that a Vermonter has 30 times the voting power in the Senate of a New Yorker just over the state line—the biggest inequality between two adjacent states. The nation's largest gap, between Wyoming and California, is more than double that.

The difference in the fortunes of Rutland and Washington Counties reflects the growing disparity in their citizens' voting power, and it is not an anomaly. The Constitution has always given residents of states with small populations a lift, but the size and importance of the gap has grown markedly in recent decades, in ways the framers probably never anticipated. It affects the political dynamic of issues as varied as gun control, immigration and campaign finance.

In response, lawmakers, lawyers and watchdog groups have begun pushing for change. A lawsuit to curb the small-state advantage in the Senate's rules is moving through the courts. The Senate has already made modest changes to rules concerning the filibuster, which has particularly benefited senators from small states. And eight states and the District of Columbia have endorsed a proposal to reduce the chances that the small-state advantage in the Electoral College will allow a loser of the popular vote to win the presidency.

To be sure, some scholars and members of Congress view the small-state advantage as a vital part of the constitutional structure and say the growth of that advantage is no cause for worry. Others say it is an authentic but insoluble problem.

What is certain is that the power of the smaller states is large and growing. Political scientists call it a striking exception to the democratic principle of "one person, one vote." Indeed, they say, the Senate may be the least democratic legislative chamber in any developed nation.

Behind the growth of the advantage is an increase in population gap between large and small states, with large states adding many more people than small ones in the last half-century. There is a widening demographic split, too, with the larger states becoming more urban and liberal, and the smaller ones remaining rural and conservative, which lends a new significance to the disparity in their political power.

128

The threat of the filibuster in the Senate, which has become far more common than in past decades, plays a role, too. Research by two political scientists, Lauren C. Bell and L. Marvin Overby, has found that small-state senators, often in leadership positions, have amplified their power by using the filibuster more often than their large-state counterparts.

Beyond influencing government spending, these shifts generally benefit conservative causes and hurt liberal ones. When small states block or shape legislation backed by senators representing a majority of Americans, most of the senators on the winning side tend to be Republicans, because Republicans disproportionately live in small states and Democrats, especially African-Americans and Latinos, are more likely to live in large states like California, New York, Florida and Illinois. Among the nation's five smallest states, only Vermont tilts liberal, while Alaska, Wyoming and the Dakotas have each voted Republican in every presidential election since 1968.

Recent bills to overhaul the immigration system and increase disclosure of campaign spending have won the support of senators representing a majority of the population but have not yet passed. A sweeping climate bill, meant to raise the cost of carbon emissions, passed the House, where seats are allocated by population, but not the Senate.

Each of those bills is a major Democratic Party priority. Throughout his second term, President Obama is likely to be lining up with a majority of large-state Congress members on his biggest goals and against a majority of small-state lawmakers.

It is easiest to measure the small-state advantage in dollars. Over the past few years, as the federal government has spent hundreds of billions to respond to the financial crisis, it has done much more to assist the residents of small states than large ones. The top five per capita recipients of federal stimulus grants were states so small that they have only a single House member.

"From highway bills to homeland security," said Sarah A. Binder, a political scientist at George Washington University, "small states make out like bandits."

Here in Rutland, the federal government has spent $2,500 per person since early 2009, compared with $600 per person across the state border in Washington County.

As the money started arriving, Senator Bernard Sanders, the Vermont independent, took credit for having delivered a "hefty share of the national funding." Senator Kirsten Gillibrand, a New York Democrat, vowed to fight for her state's "fair share."

As a matter of constitutional design, small states have punched above their weight politically for as long as the United States has existed. The founding of the country depended in part on the Great Compromise, which created a legislative chamber—the Senate—in which every state had the same political voice, regardless of population. The advantage small states enjoy in the Senate is echoed in the Electoral College, where each state is allocated votes not only for its House members (reflecting the state's population) but also for its senators (a two-vote bonus).

No one expects the small-state advantage to disappear, given its constitutional roots. But its growing importance has caused some large-state policy makers and advocates for giving all citizens an equal voice in democracy to begin exploring ways to counteract it. Those pushing for change tend to be Democrats.

One plan, enacted into law by eight states and the District of Columbia, would effectively cancel the small states' Electoral College edge. The nine jurisdictions have pledged to allocate their 132 electoral votes to the winner of the national popular vote—if they can persuade states with 138 more votes to make the same commitment. (That would represent the bare majority of the 538 electoral votes needed for a presidential candidate to prevail.)

The states that have agreed to the arrangement range in size from Vermont to California, and they are dominated by Democrats. But support for changing the Electoral College cuts across party lines. In a recent Gallup Poll, 61 percent of Republicans, 63 percent of independents and 66 percent of Democrats said they favored abolishing the system and awarding the presidency to the winner of the popular vote.

In 2000, had electoral votes been allocated by population, without the two-vote bonuses, Al Gore would have prevailed over George W. Bush. Alexander Keyssar, a historian of democracy at Harvard, said he would not be surprised if another Republican candidate won the presidency while losing the popular vote in coming decades, given the structure of the Electoral College.

Critics of the outsize power of small states have also turned to the courts. In December, four House members and the advocacy group Common Cause filed an appeal in a lawsuit challenging the Senate's filibuster rule on the ground that it "upsets the balance in the Great Compromise" that created the Senate.

The filibuster "has significantly increased the underrepresentation of people living in the most populous states," the suit said. But for the rule, it said, the Dream Act, which would have given some immigrants who arrived illegally as children a path to legalization, and the Disclose Act, requiring greater reporting of political spending, would be law.

A federal judge in Washington dismissed the suit, saying he was "powerless to address" what he acknowledged was an "important and controversial issue." The judge instead sided with lawyers for the Senate, who said that the challengers lacked standing to sue and that the courts lacked power to rule on the internal workings of another branch of the government.

However these individual efforts fare, the basic disparity between large and small states is wired into the constitutional framework. Some scholars say that this is as it should be and that the advantages enjoyed by small states are necessary to prevent them from becoming a voiceless minority.

"Without it, wealth and power would tend to flow to the prosperous coasts and cities and away from less-populated rural areas," said Stephen Macedo, a political scientist at Princeton.

Gary L. Gregg II, a political scientist who holds the Mitch McConnell Chair in Leadership at the University of Louisville, similarly argued that urban areas already have enough power, as the home of most major government agencies, news media organizations, companies and universities. "A simple, direct democracy will centralize all power," he wrote recently, "in urban areas to the detriment of the rest of the nation."

Others say the country needs to make changes to preserve its democratic vitality. They have called for an overhaul of the Constitution, as far-fetched an idea as that may be.

"The Senate constitutes a threat to the vitality of the American political system in the 21st century," said Sanford Levinson, a law professor at the University of Texas, "and it warrants a constitutional convention to rectify it."

Frances E. Lee, a political scientist at the University of Maryland, said the problem was as real as the solution elusive, adding that she and other scholars have tried without success to find a contemporary reason to exempt the Senate from the usual rules of granting citizens an equal voice in their government. "I can't think of any way to justify it based on democratic principles," Professor Lee said.

Consider the source and the audience

- Why would an article on representation in the Senate be of interest to *New York Times* readers?
- The *Times'* editorial board is known to lean to the left. Would a newspaper with a more conservative editorial board likely publish such an article?

Lay out the argument, the values, and the assumptions

- Why do some argue that the Senate may be "the least democratic legislative chamber in any developed nation"? Why, according to the article, is the disparity in representation becoming worse? What is being proposed to "fix" the problem that supporters of more heavily populated states describe? Why are Democrats generally the people pushing for a change?
- What do supporters of the less populated states have to say? Why do they believe that less populated states need to be protected?

Uncover the evidence

- Liptak is not so much making an argument in this article as he is relying on other people's perceptions. He mentions several different political scientists. What kinds of evidence do they cite to support their positions?

Evaluate the conclusion

- Why might the proposal offered by those concerned about representation in more populated states fix the problem? Why might it not?
- Which side is correct? How should the Constitution balance the interests of individuals and the interests of states? Can this debate be decided based on empirical data, or is it a normative debate over what a person values?

Sort out the political implications

- Why is what on its face is a debate over representation really an issue about partisan power?
- If some of the reforms pushed by those concerned about the power of the less populated states are passed, then how might policy outcomes be affected?

● ●

7.4 The Great Gerrymander of 2012

Sam Wang, *New York Times*

Why We Chose This Piece

Every ten years state legislatures (or nonpartisan commissions in some states) must redraw congressional districts to respond to population shifts in the most recent census. The process, known as redistricting, is often contentious. Because of the importance of drawing district lines on representation, redistricting is an extremely political, partisan process.

In many states, legislators might engage in partisan gerrymandering—the drawing of district lines to increase the odds that candidates from a particular party will win elections. How effective these partisan gerrymanders are is often debated intensely by social scientists. In this article, Sam Wang (the same Sam Wang referred to in Chapter 11) argues that the most recent round of redistricting unfairly benefitted the Republican Party. Is there a way to take the partisanship out of the redistricting process? Or is partisan gerrymandering a good thing?

Having the first modern democracy comes with bugs. Normally we would expect more seats in Congress to go to the political party that receives more votes, but the last election confounded expectations. Democrats received 1.4 million more votes for the House of Representatives, yet Republicans won control of the House by a 234 to 201 margin. This is only the second such reversal since World War II.

Using statistical tools that are common in fields like my own, neuroscience, I have found strong evidence that this historic aberration arises from partisan disenfranchisement. Although gerrymandering is usually thought of as a bipartisan offense, the rather asymmetrical results may surprise you.

Through artful drawing of district boundaries, it is possible to put large groups of voters on the losing side of every election. The Republican State Leadership Committee, a Washington-based political group dedicated to electing state officeholders, recently issued a progress report on Redmap, its multiyear plan to influence redistricting. The $30 million strategy consists of two steps for tilting the playing field: take over state legislatures before the decennial Census, then redraw state and Congressional districts to lock in partisan advantages. The plan was highly successful.

I have developed approaches to detect such shenanigans by looking only at election returns. To see how the sleuthing works, start with the naïve standard that the party that wins more than half the votes should get at least half the seats. In November, five states failed to clear even this low bar: Arizona, Michigan, North Carolina, Pennsylvania and Wisconsin.

Now let's do something more subtle. We can calculate each state's appropriate seat breakdown—in other words, how a Congressional delegation would be constituted if its districts were not contorted to protect a political party or an incumbent. We do this

Selection published: February 2, 2013

by randomly picking combinations of districts from around the United States that add up to the same statewide vote total. Like a fantasy baseball team, a delegation put together this way is not constrained by the limits of geography. On a computer, it is possible to create millions of such unbiased delegations in short order. In this way, we can ask what would happen if a state had districts that were typical of the rest of the nation.

In North Carolina, where the two-party House vote was 51 percent Democratic, 49 percent Republican, the average simulated delegation was seven Democrats and six Republicans. The actual outcome? Four Democrats, nine Republicans—a split that occurred in less than 1 percent of simulations. If districts were drawn fairly, this lopsided discrepancy would hardly ever occur.

Confounding conventional wisdom, partisan redistricting is not symmetrical between the political parties. By my seat-discrepancy criterion, 10 states are out of whack: the five I have mentioned, plus Virginia, Ohio, Florida, Illinois and Texas. Arizona was redistricted by an independent commission, Texas was a combination of Republican and federal court efforts, and Illinois was controlled by Democrats. Republicans designed the other seven maps. Both sides may do it, but one side does it more often.

Surprisingly absent from the guilty list is California, where 62 percent of the two-party vote went to Democrats and the average mock delegation of 38 Democrats and 15 Republicans exactly matched the newly elected delegation. Notably, California voters took redistricting out of legislators' hands by creating the California Citizens Redistricting Commission.

Gerrymandering is not hard. The core technique is to jam voters likely to favor your opponents into a few throwaway districts where the other side will win lopsided victories, a strategy known as "packing." Arrange other boundaries to win close victories, "cracking" opposition groups into many districts. Professionals use proprietary software to draw districts, but free software like Dave's Redistricting App lets you do it from your couch.

Political scientists have identified other factors that have influenced the relationship between votes and seats in the past. Concentration of voters in urban areas can, for example, limit how districts are drawn, creating a natural packing effect. But in 2012 the net effect of intentional gerrymandering was far larger than any one factor.

We can quantify this effect using three different methods. First, Democrats would have had to win the popular vote by 7 percentage points to take control of the House the way that districts are now (assuming that votes shifted by a similar percentage across all districts). That's an 8-point increase over what they would have had to do in 2010, and a margin that happens in only about one-third of Congressional elections.

Second, if we replace the eight partisan gerrymanders with the mock delegations from my simulations, this would lead to a seat count of 215 Democrats, 220 Republicans, give or take a few.

Third, gerrymandering is a major form of disenfranchisement. In the seven states where Republicans redrew the districts, 16.7 million votes were cast for Republicans and 16.4 million votes were cast for Democrats. This elected 73 Republicans and 34 Democrats. Given the average percentage of the vote it takes to elect representatives elsewhere in the country, that combination would normally require only 14.7 million Democratic votes. Or put another way, 1.7 million votes (16.4 minus 14.7) were effectively packed into Democratic districts and wasted.

Compared with a national total House vote of 121 million, this number is considerable. In Illinois, Democrats did the converse, wasting about 70,000 Republican votes. In both cases, the number of wasted votes dwarfs the likely effect of voter-ID laws, a Democratic concern, or of voter fraud, a Republican concern.

Some legislators have flirted with the idea of gerrymandering the presidency itself under the guise of Electoral College reform. In one short-lived plan, Virginia State Senator Charles Carrico sponsored legislation to allocate electoral votes by Congressional district. In contrast to the current winner-take-all system, which usually elects the popular vote winner, Mr. Carrico's proposal applied nationwide would have elected Mitt Romney, despite the fact that he won five million fewer votes than Mr. Obama. This is basically an admission of defeat by Republicans in swing states. Mr. Carrico's constituents might well ask whether these changes serve their interests or those of the Republican National Committee.

To preserve majority rule and minority representation, redistricting must be brought into fairer balance. I propose two plans. First, let's establish nonpartisan redistricting commissions in all 50 states. In Ohio, one such ballot measure failed in November, in part because of a poorly financed campaign. Maybe those who prodded voters to turn out could support future initiatives.

Second, we need to adopt a statistically robust judicial standard for partisan gerrymandering. In the Supreme Court's *Vieth v. Jubelirer* case, in 2004, Justice Anthony M. Kennedy voted against intervention in chicanery in Pennsylvania, but left the door open for future remedies elsewhere if a clear standard could be established.

The great gerrymander of 2012 came 200 years after the first use of this curious word, which comes from the salamander-shaped districts signed into law by Governor Elbridge Gerry of Massachusetts. Gov. Gerry's party engineered its electoral coup using paper maps and ink. But the advent of inexpensive computing and free software has placed the tools for fighting politicians who draw absurd districts into the hands of citizens like you and me.

Politicians, especially Republicans facing demographic and ideological changes in the electorate, use redistricting to cling to power. It's up to us to take control of the process, slay the gerrymander, and put the people back in charge of what is, after all, our House.

Consider the source and the audience

- Wang is a neuroscientist. Why might he be interested in redistricting? How, if at all, does his background make him qualified to make an argument about the effects of partisan gerrymandering?

Lay out the argument, the values, and the assumptions

- In Wang's view, what is a fair election outcome?
- Why does he believe that the Republican gerrymanders in the last round of redistricting have undermined representation?
- What does Wang propose to eliminate partisan gerrymandering?

Uncover the evidence

- Wang uses simulations to support his argument. What are the advantages of simulations? What limitations might exist? Do you know enough about Wang's simulations to judge their accuracy?
- What evidence does Wang provide that nonpartisan redistricting commissions will make election outcomes more representative of the state's population?

Evaluate the conclusion

- Are you convinced that partisan gerrymandering allowed Republicans to win a majority of the House seats even though Democratic congressional candidates won a majority of the House vote? What other explanations might account for this result?

Sort out the political implications

- One of the concerns about partisan gerrymandering is that it may lead to a lack of competitive elections. If elections are not competitive, how might that affect the quality of representation constituents receive from their members of Congress? If elections were more competitive, what problems might emerge as a result?

7.5 Declaration of Conscience

Margaret Chase Smith, Speech on the Senate Floor

Why We Chose This Piece

Many commentators and scholars have noted an increasingly polarized atmosphere in Congress, whose members are more extreme in their views than the majority of the population (see Reading 7.1). Democrats accuse Republicans of being racists and elitist warmongers; Republicans accuse Democrats of being big spenders and un-American peaceniks.

It's hard to imagine, however, a time as rancorous in U.S. legislative history as the 1950s; it was also a time of national fear and unease, when Republican senator Joe McCarthy used the Senate as a platform for rooting out anyone he thought had communist sympathies. As a result of his frequently unsubstantiated accusations and innuendo, many people lost reputations, jobs, and security. Democrats and Republicans accused one another of being too soft on communism or too restrictive of civil liberties.

Selection delivered: June 1, 1950

Congressional politics may seem partisan and nasty in the early years of the twenty-first century, but clearly it is not a new phenomenon. On the flip side, but also not new, is the kind of integrity and concern for the national good that led Republican senator Margaret Chase Smith (the first woman to have been elected to both the House and the Senate) to break with her party and make this speech on the Senate floor, condemning the politics of personal destruction. Following Smith's speech, others gathered to condemn McCarthy, including journalists such as Edward R. Murrow, and McCarthy was officially censured by the Senate in 1954. How could one go about building such a bridge between acrimonious partisans in Congress today?

I would like to speak briefly and simply about a serious national condition. It is a national feeling of fear and frustration that could result in national suicide and the end of everything that we Americans hold dear. It is a condition that comes from the lack of effective leadership in either the Legislative Branch or the Executive Branch of our Government.

That leadership is so lacking that serious and responsible proposals are being made that national advisory commissions be appointed to provide such critically needed leadership.

I speak as briefly as possible because too much harm has already been done with irresponsible words of bitterness and selfish political opportunism. I speak as simply as possible because the issue is too great to be obscured by eloquence. I speak simply and briefly in the hope that my words will be taken to heart.

I speak as a Republican. I speak as a woman. I speak as a United States Senator. I speak as an American.

The United States Senate has long enjoyed worldwide respect as the greatest deliberative body in the world. But recently that deliberative character has too often been debased to the level of a forum of hate and character assassination sheltered by the shield of congressional immunity.

It is ironical that we Senators can in debate in the Senate directly or indirectly, by any form of words, impute to any American who is not a Senator any conduct or motive unworthy or unbecoming an American—and without that non-Senator American having any legal redress against us—yet if we say the same thing in the Senate about our colleagues we can be stopped on the grounds of being out of order.

It is strange that we can verbally attack anyone else without restraint and with full protection and yet we hold ourselves above the same type of criticism here on the Senate Floor. Surely the United States Senate is big enough to take self-criticism and self-appraisal. Surely we should be able to take the same kind of character attacks that we "dish out" to outsiders.

I think that it is high time for the United States Senate and its members to do some soul-searching—for us to weigh our consciences—on the manner in which we are performing our duty to the people of America—on the manner in which we are using or abusing our individual powers and privileges.

I think that it is high time that we remembered that we have sworn to uphold and defend the Constitution. I think that it is high time that we remembered that the

Constitution, as amended, speaks not only of the freedom of speech but also of trial by jury instead of trial by accusation.

Whether it be a criminal prosecution in court or a character prosecution in the Senate, there is little practical distinction when the life of a person has been ruined.

Those of us who shout the loudest about Americanism in making character assassinations are all too frequently those who, by our own words and acts, ignore some of the basic principles of Americanism:

The right to criticize;
The right to hold unpopular beliefs;
The right to protest;
The right of independent thought.

The exercise of these rights should not cost one single American citizen his reputation or his right to a livelihood nor should he be in danger of losing his reputation or livelihood merely because he happens to know someone who holds unpopular beliefs. Who of us doesn't? Otherwise none of us could call our souls our own. Otherwise thought control would have set in.

The American people are sick and tired of being afraid to speak their minds lest they be politically smeared as "Communists" or "Fascists" by their opponents. Freedom of speech is not what it used to be in America. It has been so abused by some that it is not exercised by others.

The American people are sick and tired of seeing innocent people smeared and guilty people whitewashed. But there have been enough proved cases such as the Amerasia case, the Hiss case, the Coplon case, the Gold case, to cause nationwide distrust and suspicion that there may be something to the unproved, sensational accusations.

As a Republican, I say to my colleagues on this side of the aisle that the Republican Party faces a challenge today that is not unlike the challenge that it faced back in Lincoln's day. The Republican Party so successfully met that challenge that it emerged from the Civil War as the champion of a united nation—in addition to being a Party that unrelentingly fought loose spending and loose programs.

Today our country is being psychologically divided by the confusion and the suspicions that are bred in the United States Senate to spread like cancerous tentacles of "know nothing, suspect everything" attitudes. Today we have a Democratic Administration that has developed a mania for loose spending and loose programs. History is repeating itself—and the Republican Party again has the opportunity to emerge as the champion of unity and prudence.

The record of the present Democratic Administration has provided us with sufficient campaign issues without the necessity to resorting to political smears. America is rapidly losing its position as leader of the world simply because the Democratic Administration has pitifully failed to provide effective leadership.

The Democratic Administration has completely confused the American people by its daily contradictory grave warnings and optimistic assurances—that show the people that our Democratic Administration has no idea of where it is going.

The Democratic Administration has greatly lost the confidence of the American people by its complacency to the threat of communism here at home and the leak of vital secrets to Russia through key officials of the Democratic Administration. There are enough proved cases to make this point without diluting our criticism with unproved charges.

Surely these are sufficient reasons to make it clear to the American people that it is time for a change and that a Republican victory is necessary to the security of this country. Surely it is clear that this nation will continue to suffer as long as it is governed by the present ineffective Democratic Administration.

Yet to displace it with a Republican regime embracing a philosophy that lacks political integrity or intellectual honesty would prove equally disastrous to this nation. The nation sorely needs a Republican victory. But I don't want to see the Republican Party ride to political victory on the Four Horsemen of Calumny—Fear, Ignorance, Bigotry, and Smear.

I doubt if the Republican Party could—simply because I don't believe the American people will uphold any political party that puts political exploitation above national interest. Surely we Republicans aren't that desperate for victory.

I don't want to see the Republican Party win that way. While it might be a fleeting victory for the Republican Party, it would be a more lasting defeat for the American people. Surely it would ultimately be suicide for the Republican Party, and the two-party system that has protected our American liberties from the dictatorship of a one-party system.

As members of the Minority Party, we do not have the primary authority to formulate the policy of our Government. But we do have the responsibility of rendering constructive criticism, of clarifying issues, of allaying fears by acting as responsible citizens.

As a woman, I wonder how the mothers, wives, sisters, and daughters feel about the way in which members of their families have been politically mangled in Senate debate—and I use the word "debate" advisedly.

As a United States Senator, I am not proud of the way in which the Senate has been made a publicity platform for irresponsible sensationalism. I am not proud of the reckless abandon in which unproved charges have been hurled from this side of the aisle. I am not proud of the obviously staged, undignified countercharges that have been attempted in retaliation from the other side of the aisle.

I don't like the way the Senate has been made a rendezvous for vilification, for selfish political gain at the sacrifice of individual reputations and national unity. I am not proud of the way we smear outsiders from the Floor of the Senate and hide behind the cloak of congressional immunity and still place ourselves beyond criticism on the Floor of the Senate.

As an American, I am shocked at the way Republicans and Democrats alike are playing directly into the Communist design of "confuse, divide, and conquer." As an American, I don't want a Democratic Administration "whitewash" or "coverup" any more than I want a Republican smear or witch hunt.

As an American, I condemn a Republican "Fascist" just as much as I condemn a Democrat "Communist." I condemn a Democrat "Fascist" just as much as I condemn a Republican "Communist." They are equally dangerous to you and me and to our country.

As an American, I want to see our nation recapture the strength and unity it once had when we fought the enemy instead of ourselves.

It is with these thoughts that I have drafted what I call a "Declaration of Conscience." I am gratified that Senator Tobey, Senator Aiken, Senator Morse, Senator Ives, Senator Thye, and Senator Hendrickson have concurred in that declaration and have authorized me to announce their concurrence.

Consider the source and the audience

- This is a speech on the Senate floor made by a female junior senator (the only woman in the Senate at the time), criticizing a colleague from her own party (whom she never mentions by name). How might these circumstances have affected her credibility with her other colleagues and the way the speech was perceived?

Lay out the argument, the values, and the assumptions

- Why does Smith call this speech a "Declaration of Conscience"? What does she reveal explicitly about her basic values here—for instance, in terms of what it means to be an American? what is her view of the public interest and what values are more important than winning? What does she reveal about her values by her willingness to take McCarthy on when her other colleagues remained silent?
- How does Smith think the Senate should conduct itself? Why?
- What does Smith think are proper grounds for criticizing the Democrats, and how does she think that criticism is undermined by the Senate's behavior?

Uncover the evidence

- What kinds of evidence does Smith use to support her claims? Why were her claims about what Americans want persuasive even in the days before there was extensive polling evidence to back her up?
- How does she use historical evidence to support her views?

Evaluate the conclusion

- What does Smith imply are the proper limits of partisanship? Should the effort to advance one's own party's fortunes stop? How can partisanship be balanced against the public interest?

Sort out the political implications

- What would this speech sound like coming from a Democrat or a Republican today? What vision of the public interest could be offered to offset partisan views?

8

The Presidency

Since the New Deal in the 1930s, we have developed increasingly unrealistic expectations of our presidents—to solve our problems and ensure us the good life—while giving them limited constitutional power to do the things we demand. In addition, we expect them to be both head of government—sort of the politician in chief, passing legislation and leading their party—at the same time that we require them to take the more lofty role of head of state, guiding the government through difficult times and symbolizing all that is good and unifying in America.

Different presidents respond to these conflicting demands in different ways, but all of them are forced to confront a tough truth: If they do not have sufficient popularity with the public to convince Congress not to cross them, they will not have the leverage needed to get their laws passed and their appointments approved. In many ways, the chief resource of the American president, on which he depends to shape the country and its institutions in the direction he desires, is his power to persuade, and to control the way the media portray him (which, in turn, affects his standing with the public).

Many commentators believed that the presidency of George W. Bush, which began so ignominiously with the contested election of 2000, would last only one term—that his tentative electoral victory had denied him the mandate that would persuade the public to endorse his policies and enable him to govern effectively. Almost from the start, however, Bush confounded his critics.

The events of 2001, particularly the terror attacks on September 11, convinced the public that President Bush did have what it would take to lead during difficult times. With the support of his soaring approval ratings, Bush began to craft a presidency along lines stronger than those seen since the days of Richard Nixon. Arguing that, since the Watergate scandal of 1972, the power of the office had been nibbled away by Congress (and its stature diminished by White House occupants of whom it did not approve), the Bush administration set out to create an executive branch arguably more powerful than any we had seen before.

Barack Obama ran for the presidency, in part, on a platform of restoring checks and balances. Himself a constitutional law professor, Obama argued that the executive is a coequal branch of government with the legislature and the judiciary. Still, as his second administration unfolds, Obama faces some of the same issues that Bush faced about the creation of a strong security state that seems to ride roughshod over individual liberties.

In this chapter we look at several dimensions of the executive office. We begin with an editorial that is strong in its condemnation of what its authors see as an unconstitutional accrual of executive power on the part of the Bush administration. Second is an analysis of what it takes to be a successful president in the modern era. Third, we take a look at a blog post by writer Andrew Sullivan, comparing the leadership styles of Bush and Obama. Our fourth article argues that the president really doesn't have the power to get much done by himself. Finally, we turn to Abraham Lincoln, who also makes an "ends justify the means" argument about presidential power. In this speech excerpt he explains to Congress why he defied a ruling from a Supreme Court justice that his suspension of habeas corpus during wartime was unconstitutional.

· ·

8.1   The Real Agenda

Editorial, *New York Times*

Why We Chose This Piece

Written two years before the end of President George W. Bush's second term, this piece is concerned with the expanding reach of executive power under Bush's administration. This editorial looks at two instances of growing executive power: the administration's claims of authority over the detention camps at Guantánamo Bay and over the practice of domestic spying by the National Security Agency. How do these critiques of the growth of executive power compare with the founders' concerns about a limited executive?

It is only now, nearly five years after Sept. 11, that the full picture of the Bush administration's response to the terror attacks is becoming clear. Much of it, we can see now, had far less to do with fighting Osama bin Laden than with expanding presidential power.

Over and over again, the same pattern emerges: Given a choice between following the rules or carving out some unprecedented executive power, the White House always shrugged off the legal constraints. Even when the only challenge was to get required approval from an ever-cooperative Congress, the president and his staff preferred to go it alone. While no one questions the determination of the White House to fight terrorism, the methods this administration has used to do it have been shaped by another, perverse determination: never to consult, never to ask and always to fight against any constraint on the executive branch.

Selection published: July 16, 2006

One result has been a frayed democratic fabric in a country founded on a constitutional system of checks and balances. Another has been a less effective war on terror.

The Guantánamo Bay Prison

This whole sorry story has been on vivid display since the Supreme Court ruled that the Geneva Conventions and United States law both applied to the Guantánamo Bay detention camp. For one brief, shining moment, it appeared that the administration realized it had met a check that it could not simply ignore. The White House sent out signals that the president was ready to work with Congress in creating a proper procedure for trying the hundreds of men who have spent years now locked up as suspected terrorists without any hope of due process.

But by week's end it was clear that the president's idea of cooperation was purely cosmetic. At hearings last week, the administration made it clear that it merely wanted Congress to legalize President Bush's illegal actions—to amend the law to negate the court's ruling instead of creating a system of justice within the law. As for the Geneva Conventions, administration witnesses and some of their more ideologically blinkered supporters in Congress want to scrap the international consensus that no prisoner may be robbed of basic human dignity.

The hearings were a bizarre spectacle in which the top military lawyers—who had been elbowed aside when the procedures at Guantánamo were established—endorsed the idea that the prisoners were covered by the Geneva Convention protections. Meanwhile, administration officials and obedient Republican lawmakers offered a lot of silly talk about not coddling the masterminds of terror.

The divide made it clear how little this all has to do with fighting terrorism. Undoing the Geneva Conventions would further endanger the life of every member of the American military who might ever be taken captive in the future. And if the prisoners scooped up in Afghanistan and sent to Guantánamo had been properly processed first—as military lawyers wanted to do—many would never have been kept in custody, a continuing reproach to the country that is holding them. Others would actually have been able to be tried under a fair system that would give the world a less perverse vision of American justice. The recent disbanding of the C.I.A. unit charged with finding Osama bin Laden is a reminder that the American people may never see anyone brought to trial for the terrible crimes of 9/11.

The hearings were supposed to produce a hopeful vision of a newly humbled and cooperative administration working with Congress to undo the mess it had created in stashing away hundreds of people, many with limited connections to terrorism at the most, without any plan for what to do with them over the long run. Instead, we saw an administration whose political core was still intent on hunkering down. The most embarrassing moment came when Bush loyalists argued that the United States could not follow the Geneva Conventions because Common Article Three, which has governed the treatment of wartime prisoners for more than half a century, was too vague. Which part of "civilized peoples," "judicial guarantees" or "humiliating and degrading treatment" do they find confusing?

Eavesdropping on Americans

The administration's intent to use the war on terror to buttress presidential power was never clearer than in the case of its wiretapping program. The president had legal

143

means of listening in on the phone calls of suspected terrorists and checking their e-mail messages. A special court was established through a 1978 law to give the executive branch warrants for just this purpose, efficiently and in secrecy. And Republicans in Congress were all but begging for a chance to change the process in any way the president requested. Instead, of course, the administration did what it wanted without asking anyone. When the program became public, the administration ignored calls for it to comply with the rules. As usual, the president's most loyal supporters simply urged that Congress pass a law allowing him to go on doing whatever he wanted to do.

Senator Arlen Specter, chairman of the Senate Judiciary Committee, announced on Thursday that he had obtained a concession from Mr. Bush on how to handle this problem. Once again, the early perception that the president was going to bend to the rules turned out to be premature.

The bill the president has agreed to accept would allow him to go on ignoring the eavesdropping law. It does not require the president to obtain warrants for the one domestic spying program we know about—or for any other program—from the special intelligence surveillance court. It makes that an option and sets the precedent of giving blanket approval to programs, rather than insisting on the individual warrants required by the Constitution. Once again, the president has refused to acknowledge that there are rules he is required to follow.

And while the bill would establish new rules that Mr. Bush could voluntarily follow, it strips the federal courts of the right to hear legal challenges to the president's wiretapping authority. The Supreme Court made it clear in the Guantánamo Bay case that this sort of meddling is unconstitutional.

If Congress accepts this deal, Mr. Specter said, the president will promise to ask the surveillance court to assess the constitutionality of the domestic spying program he has acknowledged. Even if Mr. Bush had a record of keeping such bargains, that is not the right court to make the determination. In addition, Mr. Bush could appeal if the court ruled against him, but the measure provides no avenue of appeal if the surveillance court decides the spying program is constitutional.

The Cost of Executive Arrogance

The president's constant efforts to assert his power to act without consent or consultation has warped the war on terror. The unity and sense of national purpose that followed 9/11 is gone, replaced by suspicion and divisiveness that never needed to emerge. The president had no need to go it alone—everyone wanted to go with him. Both parties in Congress were eager to show they were tough on terrorism. But the obsession with presidential prerogatives created fights where no fights needed to occur and made huge messes out of programs that could have functioned more efficiently within the rules.

Jane Mayer provided a close look at this effort to undermine the constitutional separation of powers in a chilling article in the July 3 issue of the New Yorker. She showed how it grew out of Vice President Dick Cheney's long and deeply held conviction that the real lesson of Watergate and the later Iran-contra debacle was that the president needed more power and that Congress and the courts should get out of the way.

To a disturbing degree, the horror of 9/11 became an excuse to take up this cause behind the shield of Americans' deep insecurity. The results have been devastating.

Americans' civil liberties have been trampled. The nation's image as a champion of human rights has been gravely harmed. Prisoners have been abused, tortured and even killed at the prisons we know about, while other prisons operate in secret. American agents "disappear" people, some entirely innocent, and send them off to torture chambers in distant lands. Hundreds of innocent men have been jailed at Guantánamo Bay without charges or rudimentary rights. And Congress has shirked its duty to correct this out of fear of being painted as pro-terrorist at election time.

We still hope Congress will respond to the Supreme Court's powerful and unequivocal ruling on Guantánamo Bay and also hold Mr. Bush to account for ignoring the law on wiretapping. Certainly, the president has made it clear that he is not giving an inch of ground.

Consider the source and the audience

- Here we have an editorial from a liberal-leaning city paper, but one that echoes concerns from across the spectrum about increased executive power. Why does this issue unite liberals and conservatives? Where might conservatives break with the *Times* on this issue?

Lay out the argument, the values, and the assumptions

- Is the *Times* editorial board out to criticize only the Bush administration in particular, or does it have general concerns about the precedents that are set with expanded executive power? What are the board's concerns?
- What does the editorial board see as the results of Bush's preoccupation with "going it alone" and accruing power to the executive?

Uncover the evidence

- The *Times* editorial board claims the Bush administration has taken certain actions. What evidence is offered in support of these claims?
- What evidence does the *Times* present that the consequences it dislikes follow from those actions? Could these consequences have resulted from anything else?

Evaluate the conclusion

- The editorial ends with a list of the "costs" of the Bush administration's actions (trampled civil liberties, damaged national image, prisoner abuse, and the like). Is the *Times* right that these things have come to pass?
- Did the Bush administration weaken checks and balances and wage a less effective war on terror as a result of acting without the support of Congress and the courts?

Sort out the political implications

- Could the Bush administration have exercised its power in a way that would have protected Americans without the negative consequences the *Times* feared had come to pass? Is a stronger executive necessary to win the war against terrorists?

• •

8.2 How to Measure for a President

John Dickerson, *Slate*

Why We Chose This Piece

In the months before the 2012 election, John Dickerson wrote a multipart series about presidential power. In this piece he is discussing the qualities it takes to make a good president, and analyzing the two candidates, Barack Obama and Mitt Romney, as well as previous incumbents to see how they measure up. People, especially critics, are always quick to debate presidential leadership, but it is not always clear what that leadership entails. We chose this selection because Dickerson makes an effort to break down the concept of leadership and examines the qualities a leader requires. How would you define presidential leadership?

Ann Romney says that she and her husband call the rope line the "advice line." Every time the candidate works the crowd, well-meaning supporters lean across the rope to offer tips about how he can improve his campaign. At fundraisers, donors give him advice on everything from sovereign debt to his speaking style (slow down!). Conservative pundits have been offering critiques by the wagonful for months.

Ignore or adapt? That is the question for the Romney campaign, which finds itself down in the polls, under siege, and with 40 days before the election. If Romney has a clear vision for righting the ship, then he must smile and ignore the chatter. This is a laudable attribute. Who wants a weathervane as president? When Hillary Clinton was ahead in the polls, Barack Obama resisted calls to panic. It was one of the first signs he might be ready to be president.

On the other hand, if circumstances have changed, Romney should take a gamble, scrap his plan, and adapt. Otherwise he's going to blow his best chance to beat a weak incumbent.

Romney faces a management decision of presidential proportions right now. The decision over the direction of his campaign mirrors the constant tension a president faces—do I stick to my strategy or stop compounding the same mistakes? In the middle of a day swirling with other choices, a president must decide: ignore or adapt?

The way a presidential candidate manages his campaign tells us something about how he will govern. Vision, perseverance, risk-taking, and adaptation. These are all words from the corporate world where Mitt Romney made his fortune. Surely they've all been the subject of *Harvard Business Review* cover stories. But it's much more than management-speak. A president can be the most gifted politician of his generation, but if he bungles this part of the equation his administration isn't going anywhere. Just ask Jimmy Carter.

Selection published: September 27, 2012

What is the most important management quality?

It can get very loud in the Oval Office. Congressional enemies and allies, the press, and the public all want to tell you what you are doing wrong. If there is one management quality for a president above all others, it's the ability to ignore the noise. Make a decision and move on.

Nearly every chief of staff, top-level aide, and senior military officer I've asked says that decisiveness is a president's most crucial attribute. Clarity from the top trickles down, which removes the possibility that the president will later get mired in some smaller skirmish to enforce his will.

In interviews with military officials intimately involved in the operation to kill Osama Bin Laden, this decisiveness is the single quality they cite when asked open-ended questions about President Obama's role: His ability to convey clarity both in the questions he asked and in his final decision. "Anyone who says that any other person could have made those calls doesn't know what they're talking about," says one who was involved.

"The essence of the ultimate decision remains impenetrable to the observer," John Kennedy said of presidential decisions. This means a president, like a candidate, must be highly skeptical of the kibitzer. Lack of information does not, however, slow the critics. The critic is booked on all three cable networks and must say something.

Never mind the many ways the critic can be wrong. Sometimes they are blind to context. (The president isn't criticizing Saudi Arabia because the country's ruling family is helping him with a covert action against Iran.) Or, the critic is blind to the political reality. (The public option doesn't have the votes to pass and nothing will change that.) Or, the critic doesn't realize that the president hears the complaints but is arranging things to make it look like he came to the idea on his own so he doesn't appear weak.

Can you lead by doing nothing?

Usually the advice a president gets amounts to this: Do something. But there are times when leading means not acting. No matter what your reputation, critics will complain if you don't immediately start barking emergency orders into the telephone. "He will be remembered, I fear, as the unadventurous president who held on one term too long in the new age of adventure," presidential historian Clinton Rossiter wrote of Eisenhower. Apparently, you can lead Allied Forces to victory and people are still going to question whether you're too timid.

These critiques are often unjust. Mitt Romney was an enormous success in business, turned around the Winter Olympics, and won his party's nomination, but is still called a wimp for being risk-averse—in an age when excessive risk-taking arguably led to the financial collapse and some of the worst decisions in 11 years of war. Obama sent a surge of troops to Afghanistan, passed once-in-a-generation health care reform, and ordered the operation that killed Bin Laden, and yet the call goes up that, "We need a leader not a reader!"

Eisenhower should serve as a cautionary tale to presidential critics. While in office, he was derided as a distracted fellow whose biggest mark was the divots his golf shoes left in the Oval Office floor. But his presidential papers revealed that Ike was deeply involved behind the scenes. He was criticized, for example, for allowing a "missile gap" to grow between the United States and the Soviet Union. He knew from U-2 spy planes that no such gap existed, but he chose not to answer his critics for fear of inciting an even greater arms race. (To resist laying your critics low is an act of presidential temperament that we'll discuss in the final piece in this series.)

Conservatives criticize Barack Obama for "leading from behind." That's a term used by an anonymous staffer in a *New Yorker* profile about Obama's strategy in Libya, but it has grown into a laugh line at Republican rallies. It is supposed to show just how clueless the incumbent is about leadership. Leaders are supposed to clatter to the front, sword in hand, and lungs full of hot breath.

No.

"Leading from behind" shares similarities with the "hidden hand" that Eisenhower used so effectively. Eisenhower recognized that sometimes it was preferable for the president to work through others, as he did during the McCarthy episode of 1954. Publicly, Eisenhower said it was up to the Senate to discipline the reckless Wisconsin senator, but privately he guided the campaign that led to his censure. The task then, for those of us trying to evaluate leadership is not to immediately dismiss the style used, but to determine whether it is effective.

Whether a president chooses to act or not, strong leadership requires conviction and clarity. No presidential decision is easy, so all of them come with critics that must be ignored to keep an administration focused. Inside the administration, conviction and constancy (backed up by operational attentiveness) keep the bureaucracy from spinning out of control. In a possibly apocryphal story about Abraham Lincoln, the 16th president once called his advisers together to offer their opinions. When all disagreed with him, he said: "There are 12 against and one for and the ayes have it." Lincoln's team knew where he stood because he made it clear.

Lincoln didn't direct his administration by force alone. His famous appointment of a "team of rivals" thrived because Lincoln tended to them. He clashed with his secretary of state, William Seward, a former political rival who thought he knew better than the president. But as Donald Phillips points out in *Lincoln on Leadership*, the president's constant and regular attention to Seward eventually turned him into an ally. "Executive force and vigor are rare qualities," Seward wrote to his wife in 1861. "The President is the best of us."

Jimmy Carter presents the opposite case. Surrounded by a group of Georgia loyalists, he lost control of his Cabinet and the vast array of bureaucrats that make up the executive branch. This was in part by design. The notion of a "Cabinet government" was in vogue in the late 1970s. So Carter declared a hands-off organization, where each Cabinet head had the autonomy to pursue his own goals. As James Fallows outlined in his essay "The Passionless Presidency," his famous deconstruction of Carter's failures, the delegation led to predictable clashes as Cabinet heads followed their own ambitions, not the president's.

If various factions in an administration believe they can game the president, they will never carry out his wishes. This was the downside of Bill Clinton's long, rambling all-night meetings, which one staffer described to Elizabeth Drew as a "floating crap game about who runs what around here."

Mitt Romney has a well-earned reputation for ideological malleability on issues from abortion to gun control, but he also has an accomplished manager's ability to stick with the game plan. On some issues, like the full release of his tax returns, he is immovable. Those who worked with him on the Olympic Committee in Utah say that the defining characteristic of his success was his tenacious discipline and focus. And those who have served with him in his church describe the same quality, going back to his days as a missionary in France. After a car accident there that killed the wife of the head of the mission and nearly Romney himself, the 21-year-old put his injuries and feelings aside and stepped in to lead the entire enterprise.

Name a time when you reversed course and why?

Fortitude can be a liability. Some of the greatest presidential mistakes—from the Bay of Pigs to the strategic failures of the 2003 Iraq war—were the result of holding fast to decisions long after the facts on the ground had changed. Writing about Kennedy's blindness during the Cuban invasion, James MacGregor Burns describes "CIA experts who played to JFK's bias for action and eagerness to project strength. The White House had no process for registering dissent, or for bringing in independent voices from the outside." Arthur Schlesinger described a "curious atmosphere of assumed consensus."

George W. Bush was known for his lack of flexibility, but even he knew how to adapt. After months of pursuing a losing strategy in Iraq, Bush adopted Gen. David Petraeus' counterinsurgency strategy to turn around the course of the war. After heavy election losses for his party in 1994, Bill Clinton embraced Republican plans for welfare reform. Barack Obama dropped his opposition to the individual mandate to pass health care reform.

How a president determines to adapt to new circumstances is crucial to his management success. But in campaigns, we penalize adaptation. If a candidate changes positions, it's called flip-flopping. The tolerance for mistakes and course-corrections is so low that the smallest verbal miscue becomes a "gaffe" that controls a news cycle. (Whenever you read this, I'm betting a "gaffe" story has either just broken or begun to die down.)

Campaigns not only obscure our efforts to measure a candidate's ability to adapt, they actively weaken it. A candidate who survives a campaign has an overdeveloped "ignore muscle," since he's had to weather so much bad advice and silly non-controversies. For months, they have been coaxing campaign donors for cash, which puts them under a steady shower of advice from wealthy non-experts who are free to express their ideas any way they like.

When a candidate becomes president, they have to break out of that mode, because the plans they make for the next four years are going to be upended almost as soon as they take possession of the Oval Office bathroom key. As David Sanger reports, Barack Obama learned when he took over from George Bush that the United States was engaged in a secret cyber war against Iran. That reshaped his plans to engage the Islamic Republic. Bill Clinton's early read of the economic conditions caused him to focus more on deficit reduction in his first term than the stimulus he had promised as a candidate. Obama also quickly learned that the financial crisis was much worse than he expected. If a president can't plot midcourse corrections, it's going to be a very long four years.

How do you think about failure?

As James Fallows writes, "The sobering realities of the modern White House are: All presidents are unsuited to the office, and therefore all presidents fail in crucial aspects of the job."

149

Given this truth, presidents would be wise to follow that maxim from Silicon Valley: fail fast. Otherwise, they'll be stuck late in their administration with inevitably low approval ratings, the punishing requirements of getting re-elected, and the regret that they no longer have the room to maneuver that they once did. If they accept failures, they can learn from them and chart a new course while their administration is still young enough to act.

If we were really serious about looking for the best possible president during campaign season, we'd treat the candidates' stumbles more intelligently. Rather than rushing to Twitter, we'd look to see how candidates recovered from their missteps and what they learned. Since we know that presidents will have to adapt to circumstances, sometimes fast (Reverend Wright! The 47 percent!), paying attention to these moments is one of our best opportunities to see if candidates can think on their feet. But by treating every slip-up like a hand-in-the-cookie-jar moment, we spook the candidates. There's no upside for them to be candid with us about their mistakes, so they deny that they ever happened.

We obviously don't want a chronic fumbler in office, but no one can be successful without having made some mistakes. If they've never made a mistake, it means they weren't taking risks. And every president must take risks. This was one of FDR's great skills. "Bold, persistent experimentation," he called it. He was willing to try lots of things. Some failed and when they did, he learned and moved on. "I experimented with gold and that was a flop," he once told a group of senators. "Why shouldn't I experiment a little with silver?" Roosevelt wasn't afraid of failure.

Mitt Romney and Barack Obama have shown us very little about how they handle mistakes and adapt. Obama says that his biggest mistake is that he didn't tell better stories to explain where he wanted to take the country. Mitt Romney copped to the fact that he didn't think Jet Blue was a good investment. These non-admissions are nearly useless for the purpose of evaluating whether either man has what's required for the job.

For starters, Mitt Romney could tell us about the internal decision making that led to the Paul Ryan pick. That was a risk, picking the man with a paper trail who Democrats had tried to turn into a lightning rod for two years. It was a big risk, especially for the risk-averse "wimp" Romney. But campaigns resist talking about the real process that led to a decision. The only thing they want to be detailed about is the way Ryan sneaked out the back of his house to secretly meet up with Romney on the big day. If there was a little more honest inquiry into Romney's thought process, voters may get a window into the inner workings of the man. With 40 days before the election, voters have no such window.

Newt Gingrich talked about the need for quick adaptation during his candidacy. He said he would create a public comment system to help him identify mistakes quickly and fix them. Newt proposed a networked "feedback mechanism" where supporters "can go online and say that say, 'That didn't work,' or a mechanism for you to say, 'Try this' if you find something smarter or if the world changes and there's a new problem, the sooner we talk to each other the better."

This may be too unwieldy or zany. (Imagine the White House comments section: spoonboy343 says, "Yr Fed pix suk!") But at least Gingrich had a theory about how he would run his White House. Most presidential candidates end up in Kennedy's dilemma: "I spent so much time getting to know people who could help me get elected president," he said, "that I didn't have any time to get to know people who could help me, after I was elected, to be a good president."

150

What's the most important quality in a staffer and why?

A president can build adaptation into his White House staff. President Obama's former chief of staff Rahm Emanuel says that the most important quality a staffer can have is candor. They've got to be able to tell the president he is wrong, because the president is entombed in flattery. The halls are filled with your picture. Movie stars blanch in your presence. People talk about you in whispers.

George W. Bush used to tell the story of what it was like to eavesdrop on staffers or members of Congress sitting outside the Oval Office. When they were on the outside, they'd talk about how they were going to give the president a piece of their mind, but once they crossed the threshold, they were only able to compliment the president on his tie and tennis game.

Knowing about the perils of sycophancy isn't sufficient to insulate your presidency from groupthink. (Otherwise, George W. Bush would have short-circuited a few problems.) When President Obama came into office, he said he was reading Doris Kearns Goodwin's book *Team of Rivals*, about Lincoln's Cabinet of tough competing personalities. It was meant to show that he understood there needed to be competing viewpoints in his administration to keep the thinking fresh. This is also what Michael Kranish and Scott Helman describe in *The Real Romney* as "the Bain way." According to the authors, Romney always wanted as many smart minds in his inner circle as possible to ensure a competition of ideas. When there wasn't sufficient argument, he would take up the role of devil's advocate himself. Or, as Romney put it to a small group of Iowa businessmen during the primaries: "I am a capable enough business guy to know when people are blowing smoke and when they're not."

But the rivals can get out of hand. Obama had never run anything beside his campaign team. He had no experience managing an unruly group of egos who had not been with him in the campaign trenches and who lacked the deep personal loyalty that created. By several accounts, his inexperience contributed to the messy and backwards economic policy process. One of those accounts came in a memo from one of Obama's top advisers, as reported in Ron Suskind's book *Confidence Men*:

> First there is deep dissatisfaction within the economic team with what is perceived to be [Larry Summers'] imperious and heavy-handed direction of the economic policy process. Second, when the economic team does not like a decision by the President, they have on occasion worked to re-litigate the overall policy. Third, when the policy direction is firmly decided, there can be consideration/reconsideration of the details until to [sic] the very last moments. Fourth, once a decision is made, implementation by the Department of the Treasury has at times been slow and uneven. These factors all adversely affect execution of the policy process.

The fact that this memo exists suggests Obama has someone on his staff who can give him bad news. Aides say that Joe Biden and David Plouffe play this role sometimes. It's not entirely clear who can talk Mitt Romney down from a position. "He doesn't listen very well," said one GOP wise man who has spoken extensively with the candidate.

How do you know what you don't know?

Mitt Romney may be the best-equipped candidate in history to enter the presidency. When a new president comes from the party out of power, it is always a turnaround operation. Romney has done that before. That was part of his job as a venture capitalist. He describes the analytical challenge of analyzing a new company, examining its component parts, and finding a solution to make it work better with the glee of a weekend tinkerer in a recent *Bloomberg Businessweek* interview. He put those skills to use in managing the Salt Lake Olympics, which he took on midstream. One ally likened his efforts to save the Winter Games to "putting together an airplane in midflight."

Choosing the right staff for the moment is crucial, and a president is hampered by the hangover from his campaign. To pick his staff, a president starts with a long list of donors, party regulars, and campaign staffers expecting to go to the show, but those may not be the right people for the job. Noam Scheiber argues persuasively that President Obama's initial staff choices for his economic team, picked in the crisis moments of his early presidency, circumscribed his ultimate policy options and led to a far more Wall Street-friendly economic policy. For an administration, your staff can be your destiny.

Mitt Romney has more experience than most other presidents in knowing how to pick and manage a team. He built management teams again and again with the companies in which Bain invested.

When he was a governor, Romney cast a wide net beyond his party. He turned to people like Robert Pozen, a former top executive at Fidelity Investments and Douglas Foy, the longtime president of the nonprofit Conservation Law Foundation. He gave them autonomy, but never too far beyond his reach. His first presidential campaign was different. Riven by factions, it lacked an overall strategy—Romney switched from being a competent Mr. Fix-It to a conservative ideologue and back again. Advisers clashed with no clear direction from the candidate.

Romney also has something Obama lacked: networks. People joke that he knows the owners of NFL and NASCAR teams, but his age and experience give him access and association with people from a variety of backgrounds. He knows more people than Obama did, people who bring valuable experience. When Obama came to the Senate, he had a tight-knit group of close associates, but he lacked a wide group of talented friends like Bill Clinton or George H. W. Bush.

Whether Romney listens to or seeks those outside voices is another matter. Neither Obama nor Romney are the most gregarious and approachable of politicians. They are, like many men of accomplishment, difficult to convince they are wrong.

The model again is Lincoln. Phillips describes how Lincoln managed to constantly fertilize his thinking by practicing the technique of "management by walking around." He dropped in on Cabinet officials without warning, visited the troops and his generals, or simply talked with his fellow citizens. In 1861, he spent more time out of the White House than in it, and Lincoln's personal secretaries reported that he spent 75 percent of his time meeting with people. When he relieved Gen. John Fremont of his command of the Department of the West, Lincoln wrote, "His cardinal mistake is that he isolates himself, and allows nobody to see him; and by which he does not know what is going on in the very matter he is dealing with."

It would be hard for the modern president to collect outside views the way Lincoln did because presidents just don't have much time. According to a senior Bush aide, when Barack Obama spoke to the outgoing president on the day of his inauguration, he asked if he could call on Bush for advice if needed. Bush said he would be happy to take the call, but that Obama would not lack for advice and probably wouldn't want or have time to hear yet another voice.

Jimmy Carter took this quality too far. In July 1979, his administration adrift, he spent two days at Camp David interviewing a host of invited guests about what he was doing wrong as president. He took notes on a legal pad. It became the basis for his "malaise" speech which, along with the mass firing of his Cabinet several days later, was a political disaster that sapped his power and made his presidency look rudderless.

Carter was trying to reinvigorate his administration in midstream. Romney would face a different challenge. Having promised so much, if Romney wins, he will need to get up to speed fast. Obama will need to find a way to keep up the pace. How will he create innovation in an administration where people, including the president, are set in their ways? How will he avoid the scandal that often drags down a president's second term? He'll have to turn around his administration immediately to face a new set of challenges. Perhaps he'll bring in fresh eyes to look at how he's running things and suggest a new course. After beating Mitt Romney, he'll need someone with his management experience.

Consider the source and the audience

- John Dickerson is a longtime political reporter whose mother, Nancy Dickerson, was one of the first female journalists to cover the White House. How does he bring that long political pedigree to bear in this article?
- Dickerson writes for *Slate*, an online journal now owned by the *Washington Post*, that covers a variety of topics, often in a provocative light. What might Dickerson's motive be in writing this series?

Lay out the argument, the values, and the assumptions

- Dickerson has a clear notion of the qualities required to be president. What are they?
- What is the role of mistake making in developing these qualities?
- Which presidents does Dickerson admire?

Uncover the evidence

- This is a theoretical argument backed with conceptual analysis and historical examples. Does knowing where President Carter went wrong or where President Lincoln succeeded help us to understand how successful current candidates for office might be?

Evaluate the conclusion

- Among other qualities, Dickerson says presidents need to be decisive, to have the courage of their convictions, to be able to tune out distraction, and to be flexible. Is this an all-or-nothing proposition? If one has only some of these qualities, is that president doomed to failure?

- Is Dickerson in any way limited by his historical focus? Are there models of presidential leadership that have not yet been tried that Dickerson does not consider? What might they look like?

Sort out the political significance

- Is there a way to operationalize Dickerson's definition of presidential leadership? How would you use Dickerson's criteria for presidential success to evaluate future candidates for the office?

● ●

8.3 The Presider

Andrew Sullivan, *The Daily Dish blog*

Why We Chose This Piece

Andrew Sullivan is a writer, British by birth but an American resident, whose Daily Dish *blog appears regularly at andrewsullivan.theatlantic.com and who writes for the* Atlantic *and the* London Times. *Although he considers himself a libertarian conservative and initially supported the Iraq war, he grew disillusioned with President Bush and was an early Obama supporter from 2007 on, though he became more skeptical about Obama after he took office. In this blog post, Sullivan compares Bush's and Obama's leadership styles (though in January 2009 Obama was in just the early days of his administration). His analysis takes off from Bush's frequently stated belief that he was "the Decider." How does Sullivan think those leadership styles follow from the two men's views of the executive office?*

One impression from Obama's interactions with the Republicans and Democrats in Congress: Obama clearly sees the presidency as a different institution than his immediate predecessor. This is a good thing, it seems to me. Bush had imbibed a monarchical sense of the office from his father and his godfather (Cheney). The monarch *decided*. If you were lucky, you'd get an explanation later, usually dolled up in propaganda. But the president had one accountability moment—the election of 2004—and the rest of the time he saw the presidency as a form of power that should be used with total boldness and declarative clarity.

At times, Bush's indifference to the system around him bordered on a kind of political autism. And so one of the oddest aspects of Bush's presidency was his tendency to declare things as if merely saying them as president could make them so. The model was clear and dramatically intensified by wartime: the president pronounced; Congress anemically responded; the base rallied. At the start, it felt like magic, but as reality slipped through the fast-eroding firewall of reckless spending and military misadventure, Bush's authority disappeared all the more quickly—because his

Selection published: January 28, 2009

so-certain predictions were so obviously wrong. The Decider had no response to this. He just had to keep deciding and asserting, to less and less effect, that he was right all along. Hence the excruciating final months. Within a democratic system, we had replicated all the comedy and tragedy of cocooned authoritarianism.

Now look at Obama. What the critics misread in his Inaugural was its classical structure. He was not running any more. He was presiding. His job was not to rally vast crowds, but to set the scene for the broader constitutional tableau to come to life. Hence the obvious shock of some Republican Congressman at debating with a president who seemed interested in actual conversation, as opposed to pure politics. Last Tuesday, there were none of the bold declarative predictions of the Second Bush Inaugural—and none of the slightly creepy Decider idolatry. Yes, Obama set some very clear directional goals, but the key difference is what came next: a window of invitation. The invitation is to the other co-equal branches of government to play their part; and for the citizenry to play its. This is an understanding of the president as one node in a constitutional order—not a near-dictator outside and superior to other branches of government. It is a return to traditional constitutional order. And it is rooted in a traditional, small-c conservative understanding of the presidency.

If Bush was about the presidency as power, Obama is about the presidency as *authority*. It's fascinating to watch this deep difference in understanding slowly but unmistakably realize itself in public actions. Somewhere the Founders are smiling. The system is correcting itself after one of the most unbalanced periods in American history. But it took the self-restraint of one man to do it.

Consider the source and the audience

- This is a blog post by a writer who admittedly does not like President Bush. Can we trust anything he says about Bush, or is such analysis inevitably flawed by Sullivan's biases?
- Is a blog post a more or less reliable source than the mainstream media? To what standards should we hold it?

Lay out the argument, the values, and the assumptions

- For Sullivan, what is the difference between being a Decider and a Presider? How does this difference relate to the difference between power and authority?
- Sullivan clearly believes that one of these roles is more appropriate than the other in American politics. Which role, and why? What is his constitutional claim?

Uncover the evidence

- Does Sullivan offer any kind of evidence here? What kind? Would you like to see other kinds of evidence?
- Would he have had to document his evidence differently if this argument were appearing in a more mainstream outlet than his own blog? Does the absence of sources and footnotes negate the value of his argument?

Evaluate the conclusion

- Sullivan obviously prefers Obama's leadership style to Bush's on constitutional grounds. After one week in office, had Obama given Sullivan enough grounds to come to that conclusion? What would you say now that more time has passed?

Sort out the political implications

- What do you think the founders would have made of Sullivan's argument if they were magically brought back today? Was the Constitution written with a Decider or a Presider in mind?
- If Sullivan is right about the difference between the two men, how will the Obama administration look different from the Bush administration?

8.4 The Powerless Presidency

Ryan Lizza, *New Yorker*

Why We Chose This Piece

Some bloggers have coined the phrase the Green Lantern theory of the presidency to refer to the idea, common among American journalists and much of the public, that a president's failure to accomplish a goal must be due to a failure of leadership on his part, a breakdown of will. The two previous articles you read, if not exactly Green Lantern pieces, do attribute a lot of presidential success to the president's character. We thought this selection was a good counterbalance to those articles— it reminds us that the biggest obstacle to presidential power is a Congress led by the opposite party. Why do you think that concept is so difficult for observers to accept?

Last Friday's press conference by Barack Obama marked the end of an era. It was March 1st, the day that the sequester was set to kick in, and the President had just come from a meeting with congressional leaders in the Oval Office. On the eve of previous fiscal deadlines, the White House and Congress often found a way to reach a deal, even if it was only a patchwork solution or a temporary fix. Not this time.

A deal on the sequester was never really possible. Back in January, in return for agreeing to raise the debt ceiling for a few months, conservative House Republicans demanded that their leaders, John Boehner and Eric Cantor, allow the trillion dollars of cuts in the sequester to take effect. The White House, which wanted additional revenue as part of the replacement for the sequester, saw the G.O.P.'s

Selection published: March 5, 2013

all-cuts approach as a nonstarter, which means that sequestration is likely here to stay. (I wrote about the House G.O.P.'s road to the sequester in an article about Cantor last week.) When one considers that the alternative scenario was for House Republicans to precipitate a government default and a potential global financial crisis, the sequester cuts and the estimated three-quarters of a million jobs that they will cost this year are not so bad.

At Obama's press conference, after he explained the negative effects of sequestration, he cast blame on the Republicans, and a reporter challenged his analysis. "It sounds like you're saying that this is a Republican problem and not one that you bear any responsibility for," she said to the President.

Obama seemed taken aback. "Well, Julie, give me an example of what I might do."

Obama's slightly testy response is worth considering. I don't remember a President ever publicly expressing a similar sentiment. All Presidents come to appreciate the limits of the power of their office, and there are reams of quotes from Presidents privately expressing disdain for Congress's unwillingness to bend to their will. But rarely do they ventilate such thoughts in public.

A little later, Obama, using a reference from "Star Wars" (with some "Star Trek" mixed in), went even further, giving a short lesson on the separation of powers:

> I know that this has been some of the conventional wisdom that's been floating around Washington, that somehow, even though most people agree that I'm being reasonable, that most people agree I'm presenting a fair deal, the fact that they don't take it means that I should somehow do a Jedi mind-meld with these folks and convince them to do what's right. Well, they're elected. We have a constitutional system of government. The Speaker of the House and the leader of the Senate and all those folks have responsibilities. . . .
>
> This idea that somehow there's a secret formula or secret sauce to get Speaker Boehner or Mitch McConnell to say, You know what, Mr. President, you're right, we should close some tax loopholes for the well-off and well-connected in exchange for some serious entitlement reform and spending cuts of programs we don't need. I think if there was a secret way to do that, I would have tried it. I would have done it.

The tendency of many Washington pundits, especially those who cover the White House, is to invest the Presidency with far more power that the Constitution gives it. The idea that the Presidency and Congress are co-equal branches of government is the most basic fact of our system, and yet it is often absent from political coverage of standoffs between the two branches. *If only Obama would lead, this fiscal mess would be solved! If only he would socialize more with legislators the way L.B.J. did, his agenda would pass!*

The pundits are not alone in assuming that the President is all-powerful. Indeed, the fact that Barack Obama now so appreciates the limits of his office and his lack of Jedi powers is rich with irony. As I've written about before, the premise of Obamaism— from his famous convention speech in 2004, through his primary challenge to Hillary Clinton, in 2008, right up until the later half of his first term—was that Obama was a politician uniquely suited to transform American politics by breaking through the polarization in Washington and bringing the two parties together.

Obama's theme of post-partisanship and unity as a substitute for political ideology has always had its critics. Sean Wilentz, writing in *The New Republic*, in 2011, noted that Obama had arrived on the national stage, after all, with his speech at the Democratic National Convention in 2004 proclaiming that there was "not a liberal America and a conservative America—there's the United States of America."

As president, Obama would not only reach across the aisle, listen to the Republicans, and credit their good ideas, but also demonstrate that the division between the parties was exaggerated if not false, as many Americans, younger voters above all, fervently believed. Divisive and hot-tempered partisanship would give way to healing and temperate leadership, not least by means of Obama's eloquence, rational policies, and good faith.

Needless to say, that didn't happen. In reviewing the history of the politics of post-partisanship, Wilentz argues that Presidents who have used post-partisanship as merely a rhetorical device have been more successful than those who truly believed in the idea.

That Obama, who started his Presidency as a true believer, has now given up on the idea that he has any special powers to change the minds of his fiercest critics is probably a good thing. His devotion to post-partisan governance has long fed two mistaken ideas: that the differences between the parties are minor, and that divided government is inherently good for the country.

A fundamental fact of modern political life is that the only way to advance a coherent agenda in Washington is through partisan dominance. When Obama had large Democratic majorities in Congress during his first two years in office, he led one of the most successful legislative periods in modern history. After he lost the House, his agenda froze and the current status quo of serial fiscal crises began. Like it or not, for many years, Washington has been most productive when one party controlled both Congress and the White House.

The boring fact of our system is that congressional math is the best predictor of a President's success. This idea is not nearly as sexy as the notion that great Presidents are great because they twist arms in backrooms and inspire the American people to rise up and force Congress to bend to their will. But even the Presidents who are remembered for their relentless congressional lobbying and socializing were more often than not successful for more mundane reasons—like arithmetic.

Lyndon Johnson's celebrated legislative achievements were in reality only a function of the congressional election results—not his powers of persuasion. In 1965 and 1966, after the enormous Democratic gains of the 1964 election, Johnson was a towering figure who passed sweeping legislation. In 1967 and 1968, after he lost forty-eight Democrats in the House, he was a midget.

Each President is conflicted about how much to advertise the limits of his power. On one hand, pretending the office is more powerful than it is can have some benefits; in politics, perception is often reality. But, as Obama seems to have learned, reminding the public of the limits of the office can also help keep expectations more realistic.

Given all this, it's depressing but not entirely surprising that there are already stories about the White House looking beyond the current Congress, and focusing on winning back the House in 2014, so that Obama's last two years in office can be spent working with a Democratic majority. At his press conference on Friday, Obama hinted as much. He told reporters that while *he* can't "force Congress to do the right thing," perhaps "the American people may have the capacity to do that."

Consider the source and the audience

- Ryan Lizza writes for the *New Yorker*, a magazine with an upscale, educated, urban, and probably mostly liberal audience. How might that shape what he is arguing in this piece?

Lay out the argument, the values, and the assumptions

- How powerful does Lizza think the American presidency is?
- How does the power of that office weigh against the power of Congress?
- Are there any personal characteristics that can make a president more powerful than the Constitution allows him to be?

Uncover the evidence

- To make his point, Lizza looks at some of the more successful presidents with whom Obama is often unfavorably compared and argues that their success is more a function of having a Congress controlled by their own party than of any personal abilities to schmooze, twist arms, etc. Does this historical evidence persuade you?

Evaluate the conclusion

- Lizza concludes that a disillusioned president who knows he cannot transform politics can be more effective than one who has faith in his own abilities to transcend partisan barriers. Is he right?
- If he is correct, are those of us who are optimistic about our abilities to resolve our differences bound to be disappointed?
- Are there any grounds for optimism in Lizza's article? How does he suggest we can get things done in Washington?

Sort out the political significance

- If Lizza is right about how power works in Washington, how should journalists cover political struggles like the one over the sequester?
- Would citizens be more or less disillusioned if their expectations were realistic in the first place?

● ●

8.5 Excerpt from Speech to Congress
Abraham Lincoln

Why We Chose This Piece

In a list of restrictions on the powers of Congress, Article I, Section 9 of the U.S. Constitution says, "The Privilege of the Writ of Habeas Corpus shall not be suspended, unless when in Cases of Rebellion or Invasion the public Safety may require it." Habeas corpus, meaning literally "to have the body," is a way of protecting someone from being arrested and held for political reasons. A judge can issue a writ of habeas corpus and have the prisoner delivered before him, to inquire into the legality of the charge. For some people this writ is so essential to our notion of due process of law that they call it the "writ of liberty."

As the Civil War began, President Abraham Lincoln struggled to suppress the rebellion in the Southern states and the activities of its Northern sympathizers in the Democratic Party. In April 1861 he was fearful that the state of Maryland, leaning toward secession, would act to prevent the federal army from passing through the state. To control what he believed to be the subversive speech and actions of Maryland politicians, he suspended the writ of habeas corpus.

John Merryman was arrested in May of the same year. U.S. Supreme Court justice Roger B. Taney issued a writ of habeas corpus to the military to show cause for Merryman's arrest. Under Lincoln's orders, the military refused. Taney issued a judgment saying that under the Constitution only Congress had the power to suspend the writ, and that by taking that power on himself, Lincoln was taking not only the legislative power, but also the judicial power, to arrest and imprison without due process of law. Taney granted that he could not enforce his judgment against the power of the military but said that if the military were allowed to take judicial power in that way, then the people of the United States had ceased to live under the rule of law.

On July 4, Lincoln appeared before Congress and, among other things, attempted to defend his assumption of the power to suspend habeas corpus and his defiance of the Supreme Court's ordering him to stop. The following is an excerpt from his speech.

Obviously we have survived what Taney saw as an overzealous power grab. Although Lincoln expanded the suspension of habeas corpus in 1862, Congress finally acted to approve it in 1863, and it remained suspended until a Supreme Court ruling in 1866 (Ex Parte Milligan) officially restored it. What did Lincoln risk in defying the Supreme Court? Was it worth it?

Soon after the first call for militia it was considered a duty to authorize the commanding general in proper cases according to his discretion, to suspend the privilege of the writ of habeas corpus, or in other words to arrest and detain, without resort to the

---

Selection delivered: September 15, 1863

ordinary processes and forms of law, such individuals as he might deem dangerous to the public safety. This authority has purposely been exercised but very sparingly. Nevertheless the legality and propriety of what has been done under it are questioned and the attention of the country has been called to the proposition that one who is sworn to "take care that the laws be faithfully executed" should not himself violate them. Of course some consideration was given to the questions of power and propriety before this matter was acted upon. The whole of the laws which were required to be faithfully executed were being resisted and failing of execution in nearly one-third of the States. Must they be allowed to finally fail of execution, even had it been perfectly clear that by the use of the means necessary to their execution some single law, made in such extreme tenderness of the citizen's liberty that practically it relieves more of the guilty than of the innocent, should to a very limited extent be violated? To state the question more directly, are all the laws but one to go unexecuted and the Government itself go to pieces lest that one be violated? Even in such a case would not the official oath be broken if the Government should be overthrown, when it was believed that disregarding the single law would tend to preserve it? But it was not believed that this question was presented. It was not believed that any law was violated. The provision of the Constitution that "the privilege of the writ of habeas corpus shall not be suspended unless when in cases of rebellion or invasion the public safety may require it," is equivalent to a provision—is a provision—that such privilege may be suspended when in cases of rebellion or invasion the public safety does require it. It was decided that we have a case of rebellion, and that the public safety does require the qualified suspension of the privilege of the writ which was authorized to be made. Now, it is insisted that Congress and not the Executive is vested with this power. But the Constitution itself is silent as to which, or who, is to exercise the power; and as the provision was plainly made for a dangerous emergency, it cannot be believed the framers of the instrument intended that in every case the danger should run its course until Congress could be called together, the very assembling of which might be prevented, as was intended in this case, by the rebellion.

Consider the source and the audience

- Lincoln is speaking to Congress under a state of emergency. How does that fact affect the terms in which he casts his argument? When does urgency become panic? How far should it be resisted?

Lay out the argument, the values, and the assumptions

- What is Lincoln's essential purpose here, which he believes justifies some reduction in due process? What does he see as the trade-off facing him as executor of the laws?
- Why doesn't he mention the name of the person who has challenged his actions?
- How does he reason that the founders must not have intended members of Congress to be the ones to decide whether habeas corpus should be suspended?

Uncover the evidence

- What does a reading of the Constitution tell us about this matter? Is the Constitution indeed silent?

Evaluate the conclusion

- How persuasive is the "ends justify the means" argument in this context? What are its limits? What means might not be justified by a worthy end?

Sort out the political implications

- Is Lincoln's argument relevant to the Bush administration's acquisition of additional power after 9/11? What are the similarities between the two situations? What are the differences?

9

Bureaucracy

Bureaucracy. We may love to hate it—but we can't live without it. No other part of American government is so often mocked and maligned yet touches our lives more frequently or more directly. The job of American government in the twenty-first century is vast, and the people who do that job—who deliver our mail, approve our student loan checks, examine our tax returns, register us to vote, issue our driver's licenses, direct airport security, buy fighter jets, determine what intersections should have stop-lights, even the people who decide how much arsenic can safely be in our drinking water—are all federal, state, or local government employees, also known as bureaucrats.

A bureaucracy is really no more than a hierarchical organization (meaning that power flows from the top down), governed by explicit rules, where workers specialize in particular tasks and advance by merit. It is decision making by experts and specialists, where those with less power defer to those with more, and everyone defers to the rules. What it especially is not is democratic. Democratic decisions are made when we want to take account of as many views as possible, or to serve the broadest possible interests. Democracy is often slow and cumbersome, and certainly not very efficient. We would never want to decide democratically about whether to approve a new cancer drug, for instance, because most of us don't know enough to make a very good job of it; and by the time we all finished making our views heard, several people would no doubt have died waiting for the drug's approval.

Although it's difficult for Americans to accept, democracy is not always an appropriate decision-making technique. Bureaucracy sometimes does a much better job. But the things that make bureaucracy good at what it does—the expert decisions made behind closed doors, the lack of accountability to the public, the huge number of rules and massive amounts of paperwork (known as red tape) that help to ensure that bureaucrats treat all people the same—also make it ripe for criticism by an impatient and suspicious public. And that, perhaps, is the best check of all on a bureaucracy that, although subject to executive approval and legislative oversight, still wields a great deal of power without having to answer directly to the American voters.

In this chapter we present four selections that raise different issues facing bureaucracies. The first article reports on an artist who, frustrated with the system of highways in Los Angeles that repeatedly confused him and sent him the wrong way, decided to ignore regular bureaucratic channels and take matters into his own hands. Next, we include a blog entry by Jeffrey Toobin, who argues that the person responsible for leaking information about the National Security Administration's surveillance program of Americans' phone and e-mail records is not a whistleblower, but a criminal. Third, we turn to an article from the *New York Times* that discusses a judge's decision to block New York City mayor Michael Bloomberg's attempt to limit the sale of sugary drinks. Although the decision to limit sugary drinks (and the decision blocking it) were not made by a bureaucrat, the issues regarding regulation that emerge from the article definitely apply to the bureaucracy—the institution typically in charge of enacting regulations at the federal level. Finally, we close with a speech by President Harry Truman in 1945 calling for the creation of a Department of Defense.

• •

9.1 In Artist's Freeway Prank, Form Followed Function

Hugo Martin, *Los Angeles Times*

Why We Chose This Piece

We all like to kvetch about rules and regulations—usually the most visible sign of government bureaucracy in our lives—but few of us decide to do something about it the way Richard Ankrom did in the article below. We like this article because it embodies that American willingness to "fight City Hall," but we also like to imagine the consequences if we all took on the system the way Ankrom did. As you read this article, ask yourself what the opportunities and costs of this kind of civil disobedience are.

W hat more could an artist want? An unusual medium. A chance to take a jab at the establishment. An almost endless audience, speeding to see the work.

Richard Ankrom created that enviable milieu above an unlikely canvas—the Harbor Freeway in downtown Los Angeles.

For two years, the rail-thin artist planned and prepared for his most ambitious project, a piece that would be seen by more than 150,000 motorists per day on the freeway, near 3rd Street.

With friends documenting his every move on camera, Ankrom clandestinely installed the finished product on a gray August morning. For nine months, no one noticed. It even failed to catch the eye of California Department of Transportation officials.

Selection published: May 9, 2002

And that is exactly what Ankrom hoped for.

The 46-year-old Los Angeles artist designed, built and installed an addition to an overhead freeway sign—to exact state specifications—to help guide motorists on the sometimes confusing transition to the northbound Golden State Freeway a couple miles farther north.

He installed his handiwork in broad daylight, dressed in a hard hat and orange reflective vest to avoid raising suspicion. He even chopped off his shoulder-length blond hair to fit the role of a blue-collar freeway worker.

The point of the project, said Ankrom, was to show that art has a place in modern society—even on a busy, impersonal freeway. He also wanted to prove that one highly disciplined individual can make a difference.

Embarrassed Caltrans officials, who learned of the bogus sign from a local newspaper column, concede that the sign could be a help. They will leave it in place, for now. The transportation agency doesn't plan to press charges, for trespassing or tampering with state property.

Why didn't the counterfeit sign get noticed?

"The experts are saying that Mr. Ankrom did a fantastic job," conceded Caltrans spokeswoman Jeanne Bonfilio. "They thought it was an internal job."

Ankrom's work has also won praise from some in the art world.

Mat Gleason, publisher of the Los Angeles art magazine *Coagula*, learned about the project a few months ago. He calls it "terrific" because it shows that art can "benefit people and at the same time the bureaucracy a little."

The idea for the sign came to Ankrom back in 1999, when he found himself repeatedly getting lost trying to find the ramp to the north Golden State after the Harbor becomes the Pasadena Freeway. (The sharp left-lane exit sneaks up on drivers at the end of a series of four tunnels.)

He thought about complaining to Caltrans. But he figured his suggestion would get lost in the huge state bureaucracy. Instead, Ankrom decided to take matters into his own hands by adding a simple "North 5" to an existing sign.

"It needed to be done," he said from his downtown loft. "It's not like it was something that was intentionally wrong."

It didn't hurt that his work is displayed before 150,000 people daily. On an average day, even the Louvre gets only one-tenth that many visitors. He also didn't mind that his "guerrilla public service" made Caltrans look a bit foolish. "They are left with egg on their faces," he said.

Ankrom had planned to wait until August—a year after the installation—to reveal his forgery via video at an art show. But a photographer friend leaked the story.

From his tiny Brewery Art Complex loft, Ankrom said he tries to use his work to comment on current trends. The Seattle native fabricates hatchets embedded with roses and produces neon-illuminated laser guns. To pay the bills, he is also a freelance sign maker.

The expertise he gained in both fields helped him pull off the perfect counterfeit job.

He closely studied existing freeway signs, matching color swatches and downloading specifications from the Federal Highway Administration's Web site.

His biggest challenge was finding reflective buttons resembling those on Interstate signs—a dilemma finally resolved when he discovered a replica sold by a company in Tacoma, Wash.

The video he made of the entire process shows Ankrom snapping digital photos of existing Golden State Freeway signs and projecting the images onto paper, before tracing them onto a sheet of aluminum. He cut and painted the aluminum sign and even "aged" it with a layer of gray.

Ankrom affixed a contractor-style logo on the side of his pickup truck to add authenticity during the project. But closer examination might have raised suspicions. It read: Aesthetic De Construction. He even printed up a bogus work order, just in case he was stopped by police. "I tried to make this airtight, because I didn't want anything to go wrong," he said.

In early August, Ankrom launched the final phase of his project. After friends were in place with video and still cameras, one gave the all-clear signal via walkie-talkie: "Move in rubber ducky."

He made short work of the final installation—climbing up the sign and hanging over speeding traffic to install his addition. The main challenge was avoiding the razor wire on the way up.

Ankrom said he's not surprised that Caltrans isn't pressing charges, adding, "It wasn't straight-out vandalism."

For now, department officials say they will merely inspect the elements of Ankrom's sign to make sure they are securely fastened. They may be replaced in a few months as part of a program to retrofit all freeway signs with new, highly reflective models.

Caltrans officials had discussed adding more directional signs, but the agency spokeswoman said she is not sure why the department never followed through.

Ankrom said he would like Caltrans to return the work. "If they want to keep it up there, that is fine too," he said. "Hopefully it will help people out, which was the whole point."

Consider the source and the audience

- What does it mean that the source is a major-circulation, western-city newspaper?

Lay out the argument, the values, and the assumptions

- What did Ankrom think he was doing? What were his political goals, and why did he think he was justified in pursuing them? (For our present purposes, we can set aside his artistic goals.)
- Can you put Ankrom's argument into general terms, so that it would apply to other people in other situations?
- What can you tell about Ankrom's worldview and the values that underlie his thinking about this issue?

Uncover the evidence

- Does Ankrom offer any evidence to support his claim that his actions are justified?

Evaluate the conclusion

- Are Ankrom's actions justified? Can you imagine coming to the opposite conclusion? Which is more persuasive? Why?

Sort out the political implications

- Did Ankrom's actions cause any harm? Could they have? What if everyone behaved this way?

9.2 Edward Snowden Is No Hero

Jeffrey Toobin, *New Yorker*

Why We Chose This Piece

In 2013, the media exploded with allegations that the National Security Agency's (NSA) program had monitored phone call and e-mails of millions of Americans. The NSA's actions raise all kinds of questions about our fundamental freedoms—how can a government balance a person's right to privacy with the need to protect citizens from a potential terrorist attack? But the NSA's program raises more than just civil liberties questions; aspects of the controversy relate to the bureaucracy as well.

As noted in this chapter's introduction, bureaucracies are not democratic. As a result, bureaucracies can become corrupt or implement laws in ways in which they were not intended. When this happens, people known as whistleblowers— individuals who publicize instances of fraud or corruption in the bureaucracy— often make the public (or the authorities) aware of the wrongdoing.

In the case of the NSA controversy, Edward Snowden, a former NSA employee, believed he performed a public good by exposing a program that he felt violated the privacy of many Americans. In other words, in Snowden's mind he was acting as a whistleblower who wanted to expose what he perceived to be a wrongdoing. Like Richard Ankrom, the subject of the previous reading, Snowden took the law into his own hands. However, Snowden, unlike Ankrom, then sought refuge in a foreign land—one that is not necessarily on the best terms with the American government.

We chose this piece because it raises questions about whistleblowing and the responsibilities of civil servants. How should civil servants who disagree with a government action react? In this case, the NSA appeared to be doing nothing illegal. It was simply enacting a law passed by Congress, an elected body. Does that matter? In what ways might Snowden's actions be consistent with being a whistleblower? Why might one, including Toobin, argue that he is not a whistleblower, but a criminal?

Selection published: June 10, 2013

Edward Snowden, a twenty-nine-year-old former C.I.A. employee and current government contractor, has leaked news of National Security Agency programs that collect vast amounts of information about the telephone calls made by millions of Americans, as well as e-mails and other files of foreign targets and their American connections. For this, some, including my colleague John Cassidy, are hailing him as a hero and a whistle-blower. He is neither. He is, rather, a grandiose narcissist who deserves to be in prison.

Snowden provided information to the *Washington Post* and the *Guardian*, which also posted a video interview with him. In it, he describes himself as appalled by the government he served:

> The N.S.A. has built an infrastructure that allows it to intercept almost everything. With this capability, the vast majority of human communications are automatically ingested without targeting. If I wanted to see your e-mails or your wife's phone, all I have to do is use intercepts. I can get your e-mails, passwords, phone records, credit cards.
>
> I don't want to live in a society that does these sort of things. . . . I do not want to live in a world where everything I do and say is recorded. That is not something I am willing to support or live under.

What, one wonders, did Snowden think the N.S.A. did? Any marginally attentive citizen, much less N.S.A. employee or contractor, knows that the entire mission of the agency is to intercept electronic communications. Perhaps he thought that the N.S.A. operated only outside the United States; in that case, he hadn't been paying very close attention. In any event, Snowden decided that he does not "want to live in a society" that intercepts private communications. His latter-day conversion is dubious.

And what of his decision to leak the documents? Doing so was, as he more or less acknowledges, a crime. Any government employee or contractor is warned repeatedly that the unauthorized disclosure of classified information is a crime. But Snowden, apparently, was answering to a higher calling. "When you see everything you realize that some of these things are abusive," he said. "The awareness of wrongdoing builds up. There was not one morning when I woke up. It was a natural process." These were legally authorized programs; in the case of Verizon Business's phone records, Snowden certainly knew this, because he leaked the very court order that approved the continuation of the project. So he wasn't blowing the whistle on anything illegal; he was exposing something that failed to meet his own standards of propriety. The question, of course, is whether the government can function when all of its employees (and contractors) can take it upon themselves to sabotage the programs they don't like. That's what Snowden has done.

What makes leak cases difficult is that some leaking—some interaction between reporters and sources who have access to classified information—is normal, even indispensable, in a society with a free press. It's not easy to draw the line between those kinds of healthy encounters and the wholesale, reckless dumping of classified information by the likes of Snowden or Bradley Manning. Indeed, Snowden was so irresponsible in what he gave the *Guardian* and the *Post* that even these institutions thought some of it should not be disseminated to the public. The *Post* decided to publish only four of the forty-one slides that Snowden provided. Its exercise of judgment suggests the absence of Snowden's.

Snowden fled to Hong Kong when he knew publication of his leaks was imminent. In his interview, he said he went there because "they have a spirited commitment to free speech and the right of political dissent." This may be true, in some limited way, but the overriding fact is that Hong Kong is part of China, which is, as Snowden knows, a stalwart adversary of the United States in intelligence matters. . . . Snowden is now at the mercy of the Chinese leaders who run Hong Kong. As a result, all of Snowden's secrets may wind up in the hands of the Chinese government—which has no commitment at all to free speech or the right to political dissent. And that makes Snowden a hero?

The American government, and its democracy, are flawed institutions. But our system offers legal options to disgruntled government employees and contractors. They can take advantage of federal whistle-blower laws; they can bring their complaints to Congress; they can try to protest within the institutions where they work. But Snowden did none of this. Instead, in an act that speaks more to his ego than his conscience, he threw the secrets he knew up in the air—and trusted, somehow, that good would come of it. We all now have to hope that he's right.

Consider the source and the audience

- Jeffrey Toobin writes for the *New Yorker* about legal affairs. Does his background provide him with some insight on this particular controversy, or does he seem to be writing more as an upset citizen?
- Who do you think is Toobin's intended audience? Other legal scholars? Liberals or conservatives? The general public?

Lay out the argument, the values, and the assumptions

- How does Toobin view the role of government?
- Why does he believe Snowden should be in prison?
- Why is Toobin unconvinced by Snowden's defense for leaking the information?

Uncover the evidence

- Unlike many of the claims made in this book, Toobin's argument cannot be supported by empirical evidence; instead, it is simply his opinion. How does he support that opinion?

Evaluate the conclusion

- Toobin argues that Snowden broke the law, and Snowden essentially agrees. Can he be a hero if he broke the law?

Sort out the political implications

- The negative consequences of Snowden's actions seem fairly evident. It is possible that government's ability to prevent terrorist attacks will be hindered. Are there any positives that come from Snowden's actions? Do the positives of his actions outweigh the negatives?

● ●

9.3 Judge Blocks New York City's Limits on Big, Sugary Drinks

Michael M. Grynbaum, *New York Times*

Why We Chose This Piece

Have you ever walked into a restaurant that is entirely nonsmoking and were upset that you couldn't enjoy a cigarette over dinner? Maybe you've wondered why you are required to wear a seat belt or have complained that laws mandating that you wear a helmet while riding a motorcycle infringe on your personal freedoms. These examples involve regulations usually created and enforced by the bureaucracy to protect citizens. Critics complain that they limit personal freedom and create too much "red tape."

The following article highlights the debate over government regulations for public safety versus a person's individual freedom. It examines an attempt by New York City mayor Michael Bloomberg to limit the sale of large, sugary drinks that people often buy at the movies or at fast-food chains and a decision by a judge to block the proposal. Although in this case it was an elected official, not a bureaucratic agency, who proposed the limit, the issues the article raises can be applied to bureaucratic decision making as well. How do we decide where to draw the line between protecting the public good and allowing citizens to enjoy the personal freedom for which democracy is famous?

A judge struck down New York's limits on large sugary drinks on Monday, one day before they were to take effect, in a significant blow to one of the most ambitious and divisive initiatives of Mayor Michael R. Bloomberg's tenure.

In an unusually critical opinion, Justice Milton A. Tingling of [the] State Supreme Court in Manhattan called the limits "arbitrary and capricious," echoing the complaints of city business owners and consumers who had deemed the rules unworkable and unenforceable, with confusing loopholes and voluminous exemptions.

The decision comes at a sensitive time for Mr. Bloomberg, who is determined to burnish his legacy as he enters the final months of his career in City Hall, and his administration seemed caught off guard by the decision. Before the judge ruled, the mayor had called for the soda limits to be adopted by cities around the globe; he now faces the possibility that one of his most cherished endeavors will not come to fruition before he leaves office, if ever.

The mayor's plan, which he pitched as a novel effort to combat obesity, aroused worldwide curiosity and debate—and the ire of the American soft-drink industry, which undertook a multimillion-dollar campaign to block it, flying banners from airplanes over Coney Island, plastering subway stations with advertisements and filing the lawsuit that led to the ruling.

Selection published: March 11, 2013

Mr. Bloomberg said he would immediately appeal, and at a quickly arranged news conference, he fiercely defended the rationale for the rules, which would have limited the size of sugary drinks to 16 ounces at restaurants, theaters and food carts.

"I've got to defend my children, and yours, and do what's right to save lives," the mayor said. "Obesity kills. There's no question it kills."

He added, "We believe that the judge's decision was clearly in error, and we believe we will win on appeal."

The plan, unveiled last May, was hailed by many public health officials as a breakthrough in the effort to combat the effects of high-calorie, sugary drinks on the public's health. Similar proposals have been put forward in Los Angeles and Cambridge, Mass., even as the idea of a "war on soda" has become regular fare for late-night comedians.

Coffee shops and restaurants around the city had already begun editing menus, retraining employees and warning customers of the coming changes in the sorts of drinks they could and could not buy. Dunkin' Donuts, for instance, told its employees they could no longer add sugar to large coffees.

The measure was already broadly unpopular: In a *New York Times* poll conducted last August, 60 percent of city residents said it was a bad idea for the Bloomberg administration to pass the limits, although Bronx and Queens residents were more likely than Manhattan residents to oppose it.

In his ruling, Justice Tingling concurred with much of the beverage industry's legal arguments. He said the Board of Health, which is appointed by the mayor, had overreached in approving the plan, and wrote that the City Council was the only legislative body with the power to approve such a far-reaching initiative.

The administration, Justice Tingling wrote, had interpreted the board's powers broadly enough to "create an administrative Leviathan," capable of enacting any rules and "limited only by its own imagination."

The judge also criticized the rules themselves, noting they would apply only to certain sugared drinks—dairy-based beverages like milkshakes, for instance, would be exempt—and be enforced only in certain establishments, like restaurants and delis, but not others, like convenience stores and bodegas. The rules, the judge wrote, would create "uneven enforcement, even within a particular city block, much less the city as a whole."

Lawyers for the Bloomberg administration said on Monday that it remained confident the Board of Health—which has been the conduit through which the mayor has pushed through his boldest public health initiatives, including limits on trans fats in restaurants—had "the legal authority and responsibility" to address obesity in the city.

Mr. Bloomberg has some experience in prevailing over legal challenges to his public health initiatives, including his requirement that fast food menus include calorie counts.

But there was no immediate consensus on Monday on the likelihood of a reversal of Justice Tingling's ruling.

Ross Sandler, a professor at New York Law School, said city laws deemed "arbitrary and capricious" had frequently been reinstated upon appeal. But Ronald John Warfield, a civil and criminal lawyer who sued the Bloomberg administration over its cigarette-taxing policy, said he expected the appeal to fail.

"Their intention may be good," Mr. Warfield said of the city. "They went about this with an imperial hand."

The soft drink industry had viewed the fate of the city's rules as a global bellwether on government regulation of sugary drinks.

In court, the industry's lawyers, from the high-powered corporate firm Latham & Watkins, presented their argument in high dudgeon, calling the rules "ludicrous" and dreamed up by "scientists in the room, working with the mayor, creating a regulation here that is going to cost people a ton of money." The industry also suggested that small businesses would be unfairly hurt by the rules.

Lawyers for the administration offered a more subdued, highly technical rebuttal that only occasionally addressed the broader public health reasons for the plan. At one point, a city lawyer who had mumbled his words was asked by the court reporter to repeat his points, because she could not hear him.

On Monday, a spokesman for the American Beverage Association said that the court decision "provides a sigh of relief."

"With this ruling behind us, we look forward to collaborating with city leaders on solutions that will have a meaningful and lasting impact on the people of New York City," the spokesman, Christopher Gindlesperger, said.

It is unclear if the appeal of the case will be resolved before Mr. Bloomberg leaves office at the end of this year. His would-be successors are mixed in their views of the measure and may not share his zeal on the issue.

The mayor appears increasingly preoccupied with his legacy, and recently hired two public relations advisers—a former *Times* editor, Arthur Pincus, and a former television reporter, Andrew Kirtzman—to shape the public perception of the Bloomberg era.

Asked on Monday if he was concerned that a drawn-out legal battle over the soda limits could spill into the administration of a successor who does not favor them, Mr. Bloomberg, sounding a bit irked, muttered, "All of our time is running out," before saying, "I don't know who is going to be my successor."

The mayor added: "People are dying every day. This is not a joke. This is about real lives."

Consider the source and the audience

- Unlike many of the readings in this book, this selection's author is not making an argument here. Instead, this is a straight piece of news reporting in which he relies on others to argue for and against the proposal. Is it clear where the author stands on the issue? Does it matter?
- The article is from the *New York Times* regarding a decision made by the city's mayor. Why might the audience for this article be much larger than just those who live in New York City?

Lay out the argument, the values, and the assumptions

- Why did Bloomberg push to limit the sale of sugary drinks?
- Why did the judge block the proposal? Was it out of opposition to the proposal or something else?

Uncover the evidence

- What kinds of data did Bloomberg use to justify his proposal? Can you accept the accuracy of the data and still oppose the proposal?

Evaluate the conclusion

- Do we need more evidence to reach a conclusion on the issue, or is the evidence given sufficient?
- From what you have read, on which side of the debate do you fall? Why?

Sort out the political implications

- Actions like smoking have externalities that affect others. Does consuming large, sugary drinks have social costs?

9.4 Special Message to the Congress Recommending the Establishment of a Department of National Defense

Harry S. Truman

Why We Chose This Piece

Bureaucracies can be notoriously slow and inefficient. They can also be extremely difficult to change. Presidents often come into office with ideas about how to reorganize the federal bureaucracy, but that can be exceedingly challenging. No one learned this better than President Harry S. Truman. Almost seventy years ago, Truman called for the different branches of the military, previously managed by the War Department and the Department of the Navy, to be combined under a single command in the form of a new Department of Defense. This move involved restructuring existing government departments, with all the associated turf battles and disputes. In this speech, Truman lays out the case for why such a move was necessary. (We reprint only the first part of his long speech here.) Why is it so difficult to restructure the federal bureaucracy?

To the Congress of the United States: In my message of September 6, 1945, I stated that I would communicate with the Congress from time to time during the current session with respect to a comprehensive and continuous program of national security. I pointed out the necessity of making timely preparation for the

---

Selection delivered: December 19, 1945

Nation's long-range security now—while we are still mindful of what it has cost us in this war to have been unprepared.

On October 23, 1945, as part of that program, there was for your consideration a proposal for universal military training. It was based upon the necessities of maintaining a well-trained citizenry which could be quickly mobilized in time of need in support of a small professional military establishment. Long and extensive hearings have now been held by the Congress on this recommendation. I think that the proposal, in principle, has met with the overwhelming approval of the people of the United States.

We are discharging our armed forces now at the rate of 1,500,000 a month. We can with fairness no longer look to the veterans of this war for any future military service. It is essential therefore that universal training be instituted at the earliest possible moment to provide a reserve upon which we can draw if, unhappily, it should become necessary. A grave responsibility will rest upon the Congress if it continues to delay this most important and urgent measure.

Today, again in the interest of national security and world peace, I make this further recommendation to you. I recommend that the Congress adopt legislation combining the War and Navy Departments into one single Department of National Defense. Such unification is another essential step—along with universal training—in the development of a comprehensive and continuous program for our future safety and for the peace and security of the world.

One of the lessons which have most clearly come from the costly and dangerous experience of this war is that there must be unified direction of land, sea and air forces at home as well as in all other parts of the world where our Armed Forces are serving.

We did not have that kind of direction when we were attacked four years ago—and we certainly paid a high price for not having it.

In 1941, we had two completely independent organizations with no well-established habits of collaboration and cooperation between them. If disputes arose, if there was failure to agree on a question of planning or a question of action, only the President of the United States could make a decision effective on both. Besides, in 1941, the air power of the United States was not organized on a par with the ground and sea forces.

Our expedient for meeting these defects was the creation of the Joint Chiefs of Staff. On this Committee sat the President's Chief of Staff and the chiefs of the land forces, the naval forces, and the air forces. Under the Joint Chiefs were organized a number of committees bringing together personnel of the three services for joint strategic planning and for coordination of operations. This kind of coordination was better than no coordination at all, but it was in no sense a unified command.

In the theaters of operation, meanwhile, we went further in the direction of unity by establishing unified commands. We came to the conclusion—soon confirmed by experience—that any extended military effort required overall coordinated control in order to get the most out of the three armed forces. Had we not early in the war adopted this principle of a unified command for operations, our efforts, no matter how heroic, might have failed.

But we never had comparable unified direction or command in Washington. And even in the field, our unity of operations was greatly impaired by the differences in training, in doctrine, in communication systems, and in supply and distribution systems, that stemmed from the division of leadership in Washington.

174

It is true, we were able to win in spite of these handicaps. But it is now time to take stock, to discard obsolete organizational forms and to provide for the future the soundest, the most effective and the most economical kind of structure for our armed forces of which this most powerful Nation is capable.

I urge this as the best means of keeping the peace.

No nation now doubts the good will of the United States for maintenance of a lasting peace in the world. Our purpose is shown by our efforts to establish an effective United Nations Organization. But all nations—and particularly those unfortunate nations which have felt the heel of the Nazis, the Fascists or the Japs—know that desire for peace is futile unless there is also enough strength ready and willing to enforce that desire in any emergency. Among the things that have encouraged aggression and the spread of war in the past have been the unwillingness of the United States realistically to face this fact, and her refusal to fortify her aims of peace before the forces of aggression could gather in strength.

Now that our enemies have surrendered it has again become all too apparent that a portion of the American people are anxious to forget all about the war, and particularly to forget all the unpleasant factors which are required to prevent future wars.

Whether we like it or not, we must all recognize that the victory which we have won has placed upon the American people the continuing burden of responsibility for world leadership. The future peace of the world will depend in large part upon whether or not the United States shows that it is really determined to continue in its role as a leader among nations. It will depend upon whether or not the United States is willing to maintain the physical strength necessary to act as a safeguard against any future aggressor. Together with the other United Nations, we must be willing to make the sacrifices necessary to protect the world from future aggressive warfare. In short, we must be prepared to maintain in constant and immediate readiness sufficient military strength to convince any future potential aggressor that this Nation, in its determination for a lasting peace, means business.

We would be taking a grave risk with the national security if we did not move now to overcome permanently the present imperfections in our defense organization. However great was the need for coordination and unified command in World War II, it is sure to be greater if there is any future aggression against world peace. Technological developments have made the Armed Services much more dependent upon each other than ever before. The boundaries that once separated the Army's battlefield from the Navy's battlefield have been virtually erased. If there is ever going to be another global conflict, it is sure to take place simultaneously on land and sea and in the air, with weapons of ever greater speed and range. Our combat forces must work together in one team as they have never been required to work together in the past.

We must assume, further, that another war would strike much more suddenly than the last, and that it would strike directly at the United States. We cannot expect to be given the opportunity again to experiment in organization and in ways of teamwork while the fighting proceeds. True preparedness now means preparedness not alone in armaments and numbers of men, but preparedness in organization also. It means establishing in peacetime the kind of military organization which will be able to meet the test of sudden attack quickly and without having to improvise radical readjustment in structure and habits.

The basic question is what organization will provide the most effective employment of our military resources in time of war and the most effective means for maintaining peace. The manner in which we make this transition in the size, composition, and organization of the armed forces will determine the efficiency and cost of our national defense for many years to come.

Improvements have been made since 1941 by the President in the organization of the War and Navy Departments, under the War Powers Act. Unless the Congress acts before these powers lapse, these Departments will revert to their prewar organizational status. This would be a grievous mistake.

The Joint Chiefs of Staff are not a unified command. It is a committee which must depend for its success upon the voluntary cooperation of its member agencies. During the war period of extreme national danger, there was, of course, a high degree of cooperation. In peacetime the situation will be different. It must not be taken for granted that the Joint Chiefs of Staff as now constituted will be as effective in the apportionment of peacetime resources as they have been in the determination of war plans and in their execution. As national defense appropriations grow tighter, and as conflicting interests make themselves felt in major issues of policy and strategy, unanimous agreements, will become more difficult to reach.

It was obviously impossible in the midst of conflict to reorganize the armed forces of the United States along the lines here suggested. Now that our enemies have surrendered, I urge the Congress to proceed to bring about a reorganization of the management of the Armed Forces. . . .

I recommend that the reorganization of the armed services be along the following broad lines:

(1)   There should be a single Department of National Defense. This Department should be charged with the full responsibility for armed national security. It should consist of the armed and civilian forces that are now included within the War and Navy Departments.

(2)   The head of this Department should be a civilian, a member of the President's cabinet, to be designated as the Secretary of National Defense. Under him there should be a civilian Under Secretary and several civilian Assistant Secretaries.

(3)   There should be three coordinated branches of the Department of National Defense: one for the land forces, one for the naval forces, and one for the air forces, each under an Assistant Secretary. The Navy should, of course, retain its own carrier, ship, and water-based aviation, which has proved so necessary for efficient fleet operation. And, of course, the Marine Corps should be continued as an integral part of the Navy.

(4)   The Under Secretary and the remaining Assistant Secretaries should be available for assignment to whatever duties the President and the Secretary may determine from time to time.

(5)   The President and the Secretary should be provided with ample authority to establish central coordinating and service organizations, both military and civilian, where these are found to be necessary. Some of these might be placed under Assistant Secretaries, some might be organized as central service organizations,

and some might be organized in a top military staff to integrate the military leadership of the department. I do not believe that we can specify at this time the exact nature of these organizations. They must be developed over a period of time by the President and the Secretary as a normal part of their executive responsibilities. Sufficient strength in these department-wide elements of the department, as opposed to the separate Service elements, will insure that real unification is ultimately obtained. The President and the Secretary should not be limited in their authority to establish department-wide coordinating and service organizations.

(6) There should be a Chief of Staff of the Department of National Defense. There should also be a commander for each of the three component branches—Army, Navy, and Air.

(7) The Chief of Staff and the commanders of the three coordinate branches of the Department should together constitute an advisory body to the Secretary of National Defense and to the President. There should be nothing to prevent the President, the Secretary, and other civilian authorities from communicating with the commanders of any of the components of the Department on such vital matters as basic military strategy and policy and the division of the budget. Furthermore, the key staff positions in the Department should be filled with officers drawn from all the services, so that the thinking of the Department would not be dominated by any one or two of the services.

As an additional precaution, it would be wise if the post of Chief of Staff were rotated among the several services, whenever practicable and advisable, at least during the period of evolution of the new unified Department. The tenure of the individual officer designated to serve as Chief of Staff should be relatively short—two or three years—and should not, except in time of a war emergency declared by the Congress, be extended beyond that period.

Unification of the services must be looked upon as a long-term job. We all recognize that there will be many complications and difficulties. Legislation of the character outlined will provide us with the objective, and with the initial means whereby forward-looking leadership in the Department, both military and civilian, can bring real unification into being. Unification is much more than a matter of organization. It will require new viewpoints, new doctrine, and new habits of thinking throughout the departmental structure. But in the comparative leisure of peacetime, and utilizing the skill and experience of our staff and field commanders who brought us victory, we should start at once to achieve the most efficient instrument of national safety.

Once a unified department has been established, other steps necessary to the formulation of a comprehensive national security program can be taken with greater ease. Much more than a beginning has already been made in achieving consistent political and military policy through the establishment of the State-War-Navy Coordinating Committee. With respect to military research, I have in a previous message to the Congress proposed the establishment of a federal research agency, among whose responsibilities should be the promotion and coordination of fundamental research pertaining to the defense and security of the Nation. The development of a coordinated, government-wide intelligence system is in process. As the advisability of additional action to insure a broad and coordinated program of national security becomes clear, I shall make appropriate recommendations or take the necessary action to that end.

The American people have all been enlightened and gratified by the free discussion which has taken place within the Services and before the committees of the Senate and the House of Representatives. The Congress, the people, and the President have benefited from a clarification of the issues that could have been provided in no other way. But however strong the opposition that has been expressed by some of our outstanding senior officers and civilians, I can assure the Congress that once unification has been determined upon as the policy of this nation, there is no officer or civilian in any Service who will not contribute his utmost to make the unification a success.

I make these recommendations in the full realization that we are undertaking a task of greatest difficulty. But I am certain that when the task is accomplished, we shall have a military establishment far better adapted to carrying out its share of our national program for achieving peace and security.

Consider the source and the audience

- Truman is speaking to Congress and also, indirectly, to the American public. How does that affect the way he frames the issue and the stakes he emphasizes?

Lay out the argument, the values, and the assumptions

- How does Truman view America's role in the world and the kinds of threats that are likely to be levied against it?
- Why does he feel that the United States could not count on another victory of the sort it won in World War II? What were the flaws in the existing military command structure?
- What would increase America's ability to provide security for its own citizens and its chances of continuing its leadership role in the world? Why?

Uncover the evidence

- Does Truman offer real examples of problems under the existing military structure to support his case?
- How does he use logic, examples of changes in the military, and the threat of possible future defeat as support for the kind of change he wants to bring about?

Evaluate the conclusion

- Was Truman right in saying that combining the two departments was sufficient to offset the kinds of problems he foresaw? Has our military history since World War II borne that out?

Sort out the political implications

- What would be the situation today if we were trying to conduct military action with two unlinked Departments of War and Navy?

10

The Courts

Trying to persuade New Yorkers that they had nothing to fear from the proposed Constitution, founder Alexander Hamilton wrote in *The Federalist Papers* that the judicial branch was not a threat to liberty since it possessed the power of neither the purse nor the sword. Unable to raise money or troops, insulated from political pressure and public opinion by lifetime tenure, it would be the "least dangerous branch" of the new government.

While the original Supreme Court was an institution of so little prestige that President George Washington had trouble finding qualified people who were willing to sit on it, today's Court is a monument of political power that has made decisions as central as whether someone has the right to die, to speak freely, to have an abortion, or to go to the public school of his or her choice. In 2000 it took on the ultimate political role of kingmaker, when a 5–4 conservative majority decided the closely contested presidential election in favor of George W. Bush.

In this chapter we deal with complicated and abstract issues that focus on the political power of the courts. The overarching theme in all these issues is that, contrary to Hamilton's expectations, the courts are powerful and political institutions. They are deeply involved in divvying up scarce resources, choosing who gets to have their way about the kind of society we live in, and ruling on the most fundamental issues: who lives, who dies, and who gets to decide.

The articles in this chapter were selected to help you see how these abstract concepts play out in the political world. The first selection examines the increasingly contentious process of Senate confirmation of presidential nominations for the federal bench. The second, from the *New Yorker*, takes a close look at the views of the current chief justice, John Roberts. The third focuses on the equality issues that underlie some of the most consequential cases the Court has decided in its recent history. The fourth questions the value of compromise on the Court. Finally, we turn to *The Federalist Papers* themselves, for Hamilton's original explanation of why the judiciary is the least danger-ous branch of government. Would he be surprised by judicial politics today?

● ●

10.1 Obstruction of Judges

Jeffrey Rosen, *New York Times Magazine*

Why We Chose This Piece

The Constitution gives the Senate the job of approving presidential nominees to the federal judiciary from the Supreme Court on down. This article is about the growing trend for senators to subject nominees to the federal appeals courts to the same stringent ideological tests that they have been applying to Supreme Court nominees since the 1970s. The result of this practice is that when the president and the majority party in the Senate are from different parties, many nominees can be blocked based on questions such as whether the Constitution should be read strictly or flexibly, and whether judges should take an active role in overturning the laws of legislatures and making policy.

This selection is as accurate today (if not more so) as it was when it was published in 2002. Although there are more recent articles on this phenomenon, we like this one because, interestingly, one of the judges on whom Rosen focuses is John Roberts, who has since become chief justice of the United States. If he had known that would happen, would Rosen have written this article differently?

Allen Snyder and John Roberts are two of the most respected appellate lawyers in Washington. They were at the top of their classes at Harvard Law School, and they went on to clerk for Justice William Rehnquist on the Supreme Court. Both ended up at the glamorous law firm Hogan & Hartson, where they became partners as well as friends, advising each other about ethical issues and preparing each other for arguments before the Supreme Court. In recognition of their exceptional talents, they were nominated by the president to sit on the U.S. Court of Appeals for the District of Columbia Circuit, widely viewed as the second most important court in the nation.

Roberts, a Republican, was nominated by the first President Bush; Snyder, a Democrat, was nominated by President Clinton. But neither nominee made it through the Senate, and together they stand as examples—call them exhibits A and B—of a crisis that has paralyzed the judicial nomination process for more than a decade. Roberts was nominated by Bush in January 1992. The Senate, controlled at the time by the Democrats, refused to give him a hearing, and his nomination lapsed with Bush's defeat that November. In September 1999, Clinton nominated Snyder; the Senate, back in the hands of Republicans, refused to bring his nomination to a vote. Last May, the second President Bush renominated Roberts to the seat he was denied a decade ago—but just when Senate Republicans were on the verge of scheduling a hearing, James

Selection published: August 11, 2002

Jeffords of Vermont renounced the G.O.P., and the Democrats took control once again. Now more than a year has passed since Roberts's second nomination, and the Judiciary Committee has still not scheduled a hearing and is in no rush to do so. "I can't tell you," Senator Charles Schumer said when I asked if Roberts would get a hearing. "I think it's the intention to have hearings on most of the nominees, although we're not going to be stampeded. What the ideologues want to do is stampede us."

The confirmation process for federal judges is in something of a meltdown. Appellate nominations are now provoking a level of partisan warfare that used to be reserved for the Supreme Court. In a fit of recriminations, Democrats and Republicans are blaming each other for changing the rules of the game. James Buckley, a former judge on the D.C. Circuit, recently wrote an op-ed column in *The Wall Street Journal* accusing Senate Democrats of "obstruction of justice" for refusing to grant hearings to President Bush's appellate nominees. "This extraordinary inaction is having a significant effect on the court's ability to handle its workload," he wrote. Democrats made identical charges against Republicans during the Clinton years.

Already this year the Democrats have rejected one Bush nominee, Charles Pickering, and are now trying to defeat another, Priscilla Owen, largely because of concerns about *Roe v. Wade*. And the recent decision by a federal appeals court in California striking down the Pledge of Allegiance has only fanned the partisan flames. "This highlights what the fight over federal judges is all about," said the Senate minority leader, Trent Lott.

Despite the suggestion of Republicans, the federal appeals courts are not yet paralyzed by the slowdown of the confirmation process, which began during the first Bush administration. The U.S. Court of Appeals for the D.C. Circuit, which had 12 judges at its peak, has been able to function with four standing vacancies. (Indeed, Republicans argued during the Clinton years that the court had too little work to occupy 10 judges.) And the Pledge of Allegiance decision—written by a Nixon appointee—will almost certainly be reversed.

Like the fight over abortion, however, the Pledge of Allegiance decision is a symptom of a broader dysfunction in American politics: the legalization of the culture wars. That phenomenon, which is at the heart of the breakdown of the confirmation process, has its roots in the 1980's, when an army of interest groups on the left and on the right were created to lobby the courts for victories over cultural disputes that each side was unable to win in the legislatures. Right-wing groups resolved to use the courts to restrict Congress's power to pass anti-discrimination laws, affirmative action and environmental regulations, while left-wing groups pledged to extend the logic of *Roe v. Wade* to protect gay rights, the right to die and other forms of personal autonomy.

These groups cut their teeth on Supreme Court nominations, especially the conflagrations over Robert Bork and Clarence Thomas. But now there hasn't been a Supreme Court vacancy for eight years—the longest period since the beginning of the 19th century. Biding their time until the next Supreme Court explosion, the interest groups have been working to justify their continued existence by turning their vast screening machinery on the lower federal courts. Both sides have urged sympathetic senators to treat each nominee to the federal appellate courts as a Supreme Court justice in miniature, and to ask the nominees not merely whether they would follow Supreme Court precedents like *Roe v. Wade* but also whether they personally agree with them.

181

This strategy makes no sense. Unlike Supreme Court justices, lower-court judges are required to apply Supreme Court precedents, rather than second-guess them. By treating every appellate-court nomination as a dress rehearsal for a Supreme Court battle to come, the Senate and the interest groups have created the misleading impression that lower-court judges are more polarized and less constrained than they actually are. In fact, on the best functioning appellate courts, there are clear right and wrong answers in most cases that judges, Democrats and Republicans alike, can identify after careful study of the complicated facts and relevant precedents. By subjecting lower-court nominees to brutalizing confirmation hearings in the Supreme Court style, the Senate is contributing to the Clarence Thomas syndrome, which occurs when a judge is so scarred and embittered by his confirmation ordeal that he becomes radicalized on the bench, castigating his opponents and rewarding his supporters. In short, by exaggerating the stakes in the lower-court nomination battles, interest groups on both sides may be encouraging the appointment of judges who will fulfill their worst fears.

As a case study in the way that nominees on both sides are being caricatured by the confirmation process, I arranged to meet with Allen Snyder and with John Roberts. Snyder, who is 56, is based at home these days; after his nomination died in the Senate in 2000, he resigned his partnership at Hogan and took early retirement.

Quiet and mild-mannered, Snyder exudes moderation and weighs his words carefully. But he is clearly still frustrated by the fact that the opposition to him was almost entirely masked. "As a nominee, you get virtually no information as to what's going on," he said in a conversation at Hogan & Hartson. "I got a call the afternoon before that I was getting a hearing the very next morning." Snyder's hearing in May 2000, eight months after he was nominated, was something of a lovefest. Though he was nominated by Clinton, he had the support of several influential conservatives, including his former boss, Chief Justice Rehnquist, and Robert Bork, who worked with him on behalf of Netscape in the Justice Department's suit against Microsoft. At the hearing, whose chairman was Senator Arlen Specter of Pennsylvania, Snyder proclaimed his devotion to judicial restraint. "Senator Specter congratulated me on how well things had gone and told me he was confident I would be confirmed and told me I would be a great judge," Snyder recalls. "And then the committee never took a vote."

A week after the hearing, *The Wall Street Journal* wrote a vicious editorial attacking Senator Orrin Hatch for having granted Snyder a hearing in the first place. Titled "A G.O.P. Judicial Debacle?" the editorial's only charge against Snyder was that he served as a lawyer for Bruce Lindsey, President Clinton's White House counsel. Calling the nomination Snyder's reward for "counseling the consigliere," the editorial pointed out that "conservatives still hold a 6-4 ideological edge on the D.C. Circuit on most issues" and that Snyder's confirmation might mean "a 5-5 split that could haunt the first year of a Bush Presidency." Blaming the Democrats for having "established a precedent for sitting on election-year nominees" by denying a hearing to John Roberts in 1992, the editorial concluded, "If Senator Hatch lacks the backbone, we suspect the nomination could still be stopped with the right phone call—to Senate Majority Leader Trent Lott from George W. Bush." Shortly after, Snyder was told that Lott had decided to kill his nomination.

"I think what happened to John Roberts and others caused there to be a sense of payback," Snyder says.

A few days after meeting Snyder, I returned to the 13th floor of Hogan & Hartson to meet Roberts. If Snyder is quiet and gently formal, Roberts, 47, is boyish and ebullient. Although he felt frustrated and out-of-sorts during the wait for a hearing during his first nomination, now, during his second, he is 10 years older and resolved to be more patient, fully aware of the uncertainties ahead. The Democrats have not yet decided whether they will give Roberts a hearing. And even if he does get a hearing, his candidacy has been thrown into further question by the Democrats' decision to make each confirmation a referendum on a single case: Roe v. Wade.

In 1990, when he was a deputy solicitor general, Roberts signed a brief in a case about abortion financing that included a footnote calling for Roe v. Wade to be overturned, the Bush administration's official position at the time. "I think that raises very serious questions about where he is on this issue," I was told by Kate Michelman, the head of the National Abortion and Reproductive Rights Action League. Was it really fair, I asked, to hold Roberts accountable for defending the Bush administration's position, which was after all his job? "I think Roberts is going to have to speak directly as to whether or not he believes that the Constitution protects the right to choose," Michelman replied, "and if not, then I think he should not sit on the bench."

Michelman's challenge—that all Bush's judicial nominees must swear a loyalty oath not merely to accept Roe but personally to embrace it—is one that several Democratic senators on the Judiciary Committee have taken up. Several of the Democrats say they are haunted by the example of Clarence Thomas, who swore at his confirmation hearing that he believed that the Constitution protects a right to privacy and then promptly voted to overturn Roe v. Wade. To avoid a repeat of this, Senate Democrats have decided to ask nominees not merely whether they would apply Roe v. Wade in the future but whether they have questioned it in the past.

In the case of Priscilla Owen, a nominee to the federal appeals court in Texas, the Democrats' concerns are arguably justified: even President Bush's White House counsel, Alberto Gonzales, called Owen's attempt to narrow a Texas law allowing minors to have abortions without their parents' consent "an unconscionable act of judicial activism" when he was a colleague of Owen's in Texas. But the Democrats have also opposed other nominees who had no clear judicial record on abortion. During the confirmation hearing earlier this year for Charles Pickering, whom the Judiciary Committee ultimately rejected, Senator Maria Cantwell of Washington State pressed Pickering to explain where, precisely, he found a right to privacy in the Constitution. "My personal view is immaterial and irrelevant," Pickering responded, adding that he would follow Roe v. Wade. (The exchange shook a conservative friend of mine. "She wanted to know what was in Pickering's soul," he marveled.)

Many lawyers and law professors—on both sides of the abortion issue, Democratic as well as Republican—view Roe as a loosely reasoned decision that failed to explain convincingly why the Constitution protects the right to choose during the first trimester of pregnancy. Nevertheless, after the Supreme Court reaffirmed Roe in 1992, not even the most conservative lower-court judge in the country has refused to apply it for a simple reason: lower-court judges are required to follow Supreme Court precedents whether they like them or not.

By putting abortion at the center of the lower-court nomination battles, the Democrats seem more interested in placating liberal interest groups than in examining the issues that the lower-court judges actually decide. "Kate Michelman is very helpful to us in identifying problems with nominees," says a Democratic Senate staff member, "and in deciding who is vulnerable."

But the Democrats' extremism on the abortion question is matched by the extremism of the right. The man who has been called the leading judicial attack dog on the right is Thomas Jipping. He recently moved from the Free Congress Foundation to a group called the Concerned Women for America, whose mission is to "bring Biblical principles into all levels of public policy." This means outlawing abortion, promoting school prayer and fighting all pornography and obscenity. Jipping defines a judicial activist as anyone who accepts three decades of Supreme Court precedent in abortion cases. "This entire abortion area is just an exercise in judicial invention," he told me. "I have not heard of a Clinton nominee who embraced judicial restraint."

Taking an even more combative view of the culture wars, Robert Bork, the rejected Supreme Court nominee, recently wrote a polemic in *The New Criterion* urging conservatives to relitigate the entire 20th century. Describing a pitched battle between the "traditionalists" and the "emancipationists," Bork wrote that the courts, and especially the Supreme Court, are "the enemy of traditional culture," in areas including "speech, religion, abortion, sexuality, welfare, public education and much else." "It is not too much to say," Bork argued, "that the suffocating vulgarity of popular culture is in large measure the work of the court."

Bork is living in a dystopian time warp. As sociologists like Alan Wolfe and Francis Fukuyama have demonstrated, social conservatives largely lost the culture wars in the 1990's not because of the Supreme Court but because of MTV, the Internet, the expansion of sexual equality and other democratizing forces of popular culture. Nevertheless, because a minority of extreme Republican and Democratic interest groups and judges refuse to accept the Supreme Court's relatively moderate compromises on abortion and religion, our confirmation battles continue to be fought over the most extreme positions in the culture wars, which the American people have already rejected.

This is particularly true on the court to which Roberts and Snyder were nominated. The U.S. Court of Appeals for the D.C. Circuit hasn't heard an important abortion-rights case in living memory. Instead, the D.C. Circuit focuses on the less sexy but no less important issues concerning the limitations of federal power and the boundaries of the regulatory state. There is a pitched battle among liberal and conservative judges, from the Supreme Court on down, about whether the Constitution imposes meaningful limits on Congress's ability to regulate the environment, the workplace and affirmative action. Here it is the Republicans who want to use the courts to strike down laws passed by legislatures and the Democrats who are defending judicial restraint. For this reason, Senator Schumer has vowed to ask all Bush nominees what they think of the Supreme Court's recent decisions limiting the scope of federal power. Schumer argues plausibly that since President Clinton, by and large, appointed moderate rather than extremist Democrats to the appellate courts, the Senate should ensure balance by screening out extremist Republicans.

Asking the nominees their views about federalism is a more appropriate way of smoking out extremists than grilling them about *Roe v. Wade*. But even when it comes to the debates over federalism, the D.C. Circuit today is far less polarized than the confirmation battles it has ignited might suggest. Eleven years ago, when I was a law clerk for Abner Mikva, then the chief judge of the D.C. Circuit, the liberal and conservative judges were at one another's throats. On the left and on the right, a few of the judges had strong ideological agendas and aggressive personalities, and this combination led them to fight constantly over internecine issues.

Over the past decade, however, the personalities on both the D.C. Circuit and the legal landscape in America have mellowed. Many of the most bruising legal battles in the culture wars have been settled by the Supreme Court: now that the justices have significantly restricted the discretion of lower courts in cases involving criminals' rights, for example, there is far less for lower-court judges to fight about. In fact, an alliance between libertarian Republicans and libertarian Democrats has produced important victories for privacy and free expression since Sept. 11.

Moreover, President Clinton's appointments to the D.C. Circuit have won the respect of their conservative colleagues for their personal as well as their judicial moderation. Because the judges now trust one another enough to reason together, fewer than 3 percent of the cases between 1995 and 2001 provoked any dissenting opinions at all. In an impressive sign of the court's bipartisanship and mutual trust, all seven judges joined together last June to find Microsoft liable for antitrust violations.

Federal courts, as it happens, are very much like university faculties: small groups of prima donnas, often with too much time on their hands, whose political dynamics can be shaped as much by personalities as by reasoned arguments. On a small court, the addition of one or two disruptive figures can change the dynamics of the entire group, causing Democrats and Republicans to gravitate toward increasingly extreme positions in order to signal their allegiance to one side or the other. Once a court has been polarized, moreover, it can easily deteriorate into a group of squabbling children. The U.S. Court of Appeals for the Sixth Circuit demonstrated this tendency in its recent opinion upholding the University of Michigan Law School's affirmative action program. One of the dissenting judges published a remarkable appendix accusing the chief judge of having cherry-picked the judges on an earlier panel to reach a predetermined result.

The D.C. Circuit at the moment is one of the best-functioning courts in the country. It would be bad for the law and bad for the future of the regulatory state if President Bush's successful nominees were so embittered by their confirmation ordeals that, like Clarence Thomas, they arrived on the court in the mood for pay back. Instead of flyspecking their views about *Roe v. Wade* therefore, it would make more sense for the Senate to explore whether nominees like John Roberts have the judicial temperament and personal humility to defer to Congress and to apply the Supreme Court's precedents. Judicial temperament is often hard to predict; but for what it's worth, I was struck in a wide-ranging conversation by Roberts's sense of humor, apparent modesty and above all his Jimmy Stewart—like reverence for the ideal of law shaped by reasoned argument rather than by ideology. "If I were inclined to do something that I would find politically satisfying and that I didn't feel I could adequately defend in an opinion," Roberts told me, "it would embarrass me to put that out in front of" the Clinton appointees on the court, whom he has known for years and respects.

After talking to Roberts and Snyder, in fact, I had the impression that they would agree in more cases than they disagreed, and that both had the sheer legal ability that sometimes distinguishes judges who care about working to identify the right answer from those who are driven by ideological agendas.

"John is one of the most brilliant minds in this or probably any other city, and he clearly meets anybody's tests for qualifications and legal background," Snyder says.

"I can't see much difference in terms of how Allen and I would approach cases," Roberts says. "He thinks there is an answer, and the harder you work, the more likely you are to get it, and to get it right. I think we share that." The Senate—and the nation—may never find that out.

Consider the source and the audience

- This article appeared in the *New York Times Magazine*. Although Rosen is the legal writer for the *New Republic*, a liberal opinion magazine, the *Times* serves a more general audience. How is this fact reflected in Rosen's tone and conclusions?

Lay out the argument, the values, and the assumptions

- What is Rosen's main goal here? What kind of tone would he like to see on courts such as the U.S. Court of Appeals for the D.C. Circuit?
- Why does he think that tone is in danger?
- How does he think it can be preserved?

Uncover the evidence

- What different kinds of evidence does Rosen assemble to make his case? Is it a persuasive combination? What if Snyder and Roberts were less likable guys and more ideologically extreme? Would that have damaged Rosen's argument?

Evaluate the conclusion

- Who does Rosen hold responsible for the way judicial confirmations do or do not proceed today? Is he right?

Sort out the political implications

- If the trend discussed by Rosen continues, what is it likely to mean for our court system? Does the fact that Roberts is now chief justice mean that the trend is over?
- Why do senators listen to interest groups anyway? Can that be changed? How?

● ●

10.2 No More Mr. Nice Guy
The Supreme Court's Stealth Hard-liner
Jeffrey Toobin, *New Yorker*

Why We Chose This Piece

In "No More Mr. Nice Guy," the New Yorker's Jeffrey Toobin asks the question: What is Chief Justice John Roberts's true ideological nature? The short answer is, Don't look for this man to move to the left anytime soon. But the longer answer is nuanced and complicated, as Toobin explores the kinds of conservative views Roberts holds. This article is long and complex because of the legal detail, but we like it because it provides a respectful view of the range of ideology on the Court, and even the shades of difference among those who ultimately vote the same way. Read it carefully and absorb the views of Chief Justice Roberts. Consider the decisions he has written or joined since this article was written: upholding the Affordable Care Act, striking down the Defense of Marriage Act, and striking down those that set the stage for the demise of affirmative action and the Voting Rights Act. Can you imagine a conversation between him and President Barack Obama on issues of race or executive power?

When John G. Roberts, Jr., emerges from behind the red curtains and takes his place in the middle of the Supreme Court bench, he usually wears a pair of reading glasses, which he peers over to see the lawyers arguing before him. It's an old-fashioned look for the Chief Justice of the United States, who is fifty-four, but, even with the glasses, there's no mistaking that Roberts is the youngest person on the Court. (John Paul Stevens, the senior Associate Justice, who sits to Roberts's right, is thirty-five years older.) Roberts's face is unlined, his shoulders are broad and athletic, and only a few wisps of gray hair mark him as changed in any way from the judge who charmed the Senate Judiciary Committee at his confirmation hearing, in 2005.

On April 29th, the last day of arguments for the Court's current term, the Justices heard *Northwest Austin Municipal Utility District No. 1 v. Holder*, a critical case about the future of the Voting Rights Act. Congress originally passed the law in 1965, and three years ago overwhelmingly passed its latest reauthorization, rejecting arguments that improvements in race relations had rendered the act unnecessary. Specifically, the bill, signed by President George W. Bush in 2006, kept in place Section 5 of the law, which says that certain jurisdictions, largely in the Old South, have to obtain the approval of the Justice Department before making any changes to their electoral rules, from the location of polling places to the boundaries of congressional districts. A small utility district in Texas challenged that part of the law, making the same argument that members of Congress had just discounted—that this process, known as preclearance, amounted to a form of discrimination against the citizens of the New South.

Selection published: May 25, 2009

Roberts said little to the lawyer for the plaintiff, but when Neal K. Katyal, the Deputy Solicitor General, took to the lectern to defend the Voting Rights Act, the Chief Justice pounced. "As I understand it, one-twentieth of one per cent of the submissions are not precleared," Roberts said. "That, to me, suggests that they are sweeping far more broadly than they need to to address the intentional discrimination under the Fifteenth Amendment"—which guarantees the right to vote regardless of race.

"I disagree with that, Mr. Chief Justice," Katyal said. "I think what it represents is that Section 5 is actually working very well—that it provides a deterrent." According to Katyal, the fact that the Justice Department cleared almost all electoral changes proved, in effect, that the South had been trained, if not totally reformed.

Roberts removed his glasses and stared down at Katyal. "That's like the old elephant whistle," he said. "You know, 'I have this whistle to keep away the elephants.' You know, well, that's silly. 'Well, there are no elephants, so it must work.'"

Roberts was relentless in challenging Katyal: "So your answer is that Congress can impose this disparate treatment forever because of the history in the South?"

"Absolutely not," Katyal said.

"When can they—when do they have to stop?"

"Congress here said that twenty-five years was the appropriate reauthorization period."

"Well, they said five years originally, and then another twenty years," Roberts said, referring to previous reauthorizations of the act. "I mean, at some point it begins to look like the idea is that this is going to go on forever."

And this, ultimately, was the source of Roberts's frustration—and not just in this case. In a series of decisions in the past four years, the Chief Justice has expressed the view that the time has now passed when the Court should allow systemic remedies for racial discrimination. The previous week, the Court heard a challenge by a group of white firefighters in New Haven who were denied promotions even though they had scored better than black applicants on a test. Roberts was, if anything, even more belligerent in questioning the lawyer defending the city. "Now, why is this not intentional discrimination?" he asked. "You are going to have to explain that to me again, because there are particular individuals here," he said. "And they say they didn't get their jobs because of intentional racial action by the city." He added, "You maybe don't care whether it's Jones or Smith who is not getting the promotion," he said. "All you care about is who is getting the promotion. All you care about is his race."

When Antonin Scalia joined the Court, in 1986, he brought a new gladiatorial spirit to oral arguments, and in subsequent years the Justices have often used their questions as much for campaign speeches as for requests for information. Roberts, though, has taken this practice to an extreme, and now, even more than the effervescent Scalia, it is the Chief Justice, with his slight Midwestern twang, who dominates the Court's public sessions.

Roberts's hard-edged performance at oral argument offers more than just a rhetorical contrast to the rendering of himself that he presented at his confirmation hearing. "Judges are like umpires," Roberts said at the time. "Umpires don't make the rules. They apply them. The role of an umpire and a judge is critical. They make sure everybody plays by the rules. But it is a limited role. Nobody ever went to a ballgame to see the umpire." His jurisprudence as Chief Justice, Roberts said, would be characterized by "modesty and humility." After four years on the Court, however, Roberts's record is not that of a humble moderate but, rather, that of a doctrinaire conservative. The kind of humility that Roberts favors reflects a view that the Court should almost always defer to the existing power relationships in society. In every major case since he became the nation's seventeenth Chief Justice, Roberts has sided with the prosecution over the defendant, the state over the condemned, the executive branch over the legislative, and the corporate defendant over the individual plaintiff. Even more than Scalia, who has embodied judicial conservatism during a generation of service on the Supreme Court, Roberts has served the interests, and reflected the values, of the contemporary Republican Party.

Two days after the argument in the Voting Rights Act case, David H. Souter announced his resignation, giving President Barack Obama his first chance to nominate a Justice to the Court. The first Democratic nominee to the Court in fifteen years will confront what is now, increasingly, John Roberts's Court. Along with Scalia, Clarence Thomas, Samuel A. Alito, Jr., and (usually) Anthony Kennedy, the majority of the Court is moving right as the rest of the country—or, at least, the rest of the federal government—is moving left. At this low moment in the historical reputation of George W. Bush, his nominee for Chief Justice stands in signal contrast to what appears today to be a failed and fading tenure as President. Roberts's service on the Court, which is, of course, likely to continue for decades, offers an enduring and faithful reflection of the Bush Presidency.

The Justices of the Supreme Court, as a rule, spare themselves unnecessary tedium. Their public hearings are lean and to the point; they hear lawyers' arguments and, later, announce their decisions. Still, one relic of more leisurely times remains. Several times a month, before the start of the day's oral arguments, the Justices allow attorneys to be sworn in as members of the Supreme Court bar in person, a process that can take fifteen minutes. (Most lawyers now conduct the swearing-in process by mail.) Rehnquist barely tolerated the practice, rushing through it and mumbling the names, and several colleagues (notably Souter) display an ostentatious boredom that verges on rudeness.

John Roberts, in contrast, welcomes each new lawyer with a smile, and when fathers or mothers put forth their lawyer children for admission—a tradition of sorts at the Court—the Chief makes sure to acknowledge "your son" and "your daughter" on the record. Everyone beams. It's a small thing, of course, but just one example of Roberts's appealing behavior in public, much as the nation viewed it during his testimony before the Judiciary Committee. At the time, Senator Dick Durbin, an Illinois Democrat who voted against Roberts's confirmation, nonetheless observed that he was so ingratiating that he had "retired the trophy" for performance by a judicial nominee. When, early in his tenure, a light bulb exploded in the courtroom in the middle of a hearing, Roberts quipped, "It's a trick they play on new Chief Justices all the time." Laughter broke the tension.

Roberts was born in Buffalo on January 27, 1955, and raised in northern Indiana, where his father was an executive with a steel company and his mother a homemaker. (He has three sisters.) Jackie, as he was known, was educated at Catholic schools, and graduated from La Lumiere, at the time an all-boys parochial boarding school in LaPorte. He was the classic well-rounded star student—valedictorian and captain of the football team. He went on to Harvard, majored in history, and graduated in three years, summa cum laude.

At Harvard Law School, Roberts continued to excel, in an even more competitive atmosphere. "He was extremely smart," said Laurence Tribe, the liberal scholar who taught Roberts constitutional law and grew to know him through his work on the *Law Review*. "He was really very good at being thoughtful and careful and not particularly conspicuous. He was very lawyerly, even as a law student." In the mid-seventies, the atmosphere at Harvard still reflected the tumult of the sixties. Roberts stood out as a conservative, though not a notably intense one. "On the *Law Review*, John was the managing editor, so that meant he gave us our work assignments every day," Elizabeth Geise, who was a year behind Roberts in law school, said. "He was very honest, straightforward, lot of integrity, fair. He was conservative, and we all knew that. That was unusual in those days. You couldn't think of a guy who was a straighter arrow." After graduating magna cum laude, in 1979, Roberts first clerked for Henry J. Friendly, of the federal appeals court in New York, who was legendary for his scholarship and erudition, but was not known as an especially partisan figure.

From New York, Roberts moved to the Supreme Court, where he became a clerk for Associate Justice William H. Rehnquist, and it was in Washington that his political education began. Rehnquist, appointed by Richard Nixon in 1972, was, in his first decade as a Justice, almost a fringe right-wing figure on the Court, which was then dominated by William J. Brennan, Jr. But Ronald Reagan's election to the Presidency, which took place just a few months into Roberts's clerkship, lifted Rehnquist to power and, more broadly, gave flight to the conservative legal movement.

At that early stage of the Reagan era, conservatives had a problem, because there were no institutions where like-minded lawyers could be nurtured; the Federalist Society, the conservative legal group, was not founded until 1982. "Roberts got a lot of attention because he clerked for Rehnquist," said Steven Teles, a professor of political science at Johns Hopkins and the author of "The Rise of the Conservative Legal Movement." "Without the Federalist Society, there were not a lot of other ways for the Administration to make sure that they were getting true conservatives. The Rehnquist clerkship marked Roberts as someone who could be trusted."

As a former law clerk to Rehnquist, not to mention his immediate successor as Chief Justice, Roberts was an obvious choice to deliver the annual lecture named for Rehnquist at the University of Arizona law school in February. Roberts is a gifted public speaker—relaxed, often funny, sometimes self-deprecating—and he began his speech with a warm remembrance of his mentor. Like Barack Obama, Roberts can make reading from a prepared text look almost spontaneous. "I first met William Rehnquist more than twenty-eight years ago," he told the audience in Tucson. "The initial meeting left a strong impression on me. Justice Rehnquist was friendly and unpretentious. He wore scuffed Hush Puppy shoes. That was my first lesson. Clothes do not make the man. The Justice sported long sideburns and Buddy Holly glasses long after they were fashionable. And he wore loud ties that I am confident were never fashionable."

Before long, though, Roberts steered away from nostalgic reverie and into constitutional controversy. He maintained his relaxed and conversational cadence, but his words reflected a sharply partisan world view. "When Justice Rehnquist came onto the

Court, I think it's fair to say that the practice of constitutional law—how constitutional law was made—was more fluid and wide-ranging than it is today, more in the realm of political science," Roberts said. "Now, over Justice Rehnquist's time on the Court, the method of analysis and argument shifted to the more solid grounds of legal arguments—what are the texts of the statutes involved, what precedents control. Rehnquist, a student both of political science and the law, was significantly responsible for that seismic shift." Rehnquist joined the Court toward the end of its liberal heyday—the era when the Justices expanded civil-rights protections for minorities, established new barriers between church and state, and, most famously, recognized a constitutional right to abortion for women. This period, in Roberts's telling, was the bad old days.

These sentiments reflect a common view for conservatives like Roberts. "There really was a sense at the time among the lawyers in his Administration that Reagan had a mandate for comprehensive change in the nature of government," Teles said. "They thought a lot of what the liberals had done in creating, say, affirmative action was simply interest-group politics and not really 'law' at all, and it was their job to restore professionalism to the legal profession in government."

"I heard about John, and I immediately tried to hire him," Charles Fried, the Harvard law professor who was Reagan's second Solicitor General, said. Kenneth Starr, who was chief of staff to William French Smith, Reagan's Attorney General, had hired Roberts as a special assistant to Smith. Roberts then went to work at the White House, as an associate counsel.

All the lawyers who worked for Reagan were, in some general sense, conservative, but there is a difference between those, like Roberts, who came of age during Reagan's first term in office and those who prospered in his second. "The Department of Justice in the first term was full of serious, principled people," Teles said. "They didn't see themselves as part of the Christian right, or even necessarily part of a larger political movement, but they did think of themselves as real lawyers who were reacting to what they thought of as the excesses of liberalism." They believed, Teles said, "in what they called judicial restraint and strict constructionism. Roberts comes out of this world." Liberal critics, in turn, regard this view as unduly deferential to the status quo and thus a kind of abdication of the judicial role.

The legal philosophy of Edwin Meese III, which promoted an "originalist" view of the Constitution, dominated Reagan's second term. Originalists, whose ranks now include Scalia and Thomas, believe that the Constitution should be interpreted in line with the intentions and beliefs of its framers. "John was not part of the Meese crowd," one lawyer who worked with Roberts in the Reagan years said. "They cared more about a strict separation of powers, and even some limitations on executive and government power."

Originalists and judicial-restraint conservatives generally reach similar conclusions on legal issues, but their reasoning differs. Both, for example, believe that the Constitution does not protect a woman's right to abortion. "An originalist on abortion would say that at the time of the Constitution, or of the adoption of the Fourteenth Amendment, abortion was prohibited, and that's it," Akhil Reed Amar, a professor at Yale Law School, said. "A conservative like Roberts, on the other hand, wouldn't look immediately at the question of whether all abortions should be outlawed, but examine the specific restriction on abortion rights at issue in the case and probably uphold it. He'd avoid the culture-war rhetoric and gradually begin cutting back on abortion rights without making lots of noise about getting rid of it altogether." In 2007, Roberts joined Kennedy's opinion that followed this approach in upholding a federal anti-abortion law. The Court's two originalists, Scalia and Thomas, wrote a separate concurring opinion in that case, urging, as they had before, that Roe v. Wade be overturned once and for all.

In documents from the Reagan era that were made public during Roberts's confirmation hearing, the young lawyer emerges as a loyal (and low-level) foot soldier in the Reagan revolution. On issues where there was disagreement within the Administration, Roberts's memos generally show him supporting the more conservative position, especially on matters of race and civil rights. Roberts said that affirmative action required the "recruiting of inadequately prepared candidates," and sought a narrow scope for Title IX, the law that mandates equal rights for men and women in educational settings. In 1981, Roberts wrote that a revision of the Voting Rights Act would "establish essentially a quota system for electoral politics by creating a right to proportional racial representation." (Reagan signed the revision anyway.)

Roberts's reputation soared in his White House years. "He was already on that superstar trajectory," said Henny Wright, a lawyer, now living in Dallas, who became friends with Roberts in Washington at the time. "He was pretty much like he is today, except without the bald spot. Extremely attractive, in every sense of the word. He's smart, he's funny, he's gregarious, he's good-looking. In those days, he was never too busy to play a round of golf. He's not a very good golfer, but, unlike a lot of golfers, he doesn't let that ruin his day or your day." Roberts's wit even came through in the usually stultifying format of the interoffice memo. In 1983, Fred Fielding, the White House counsel, asked Roberts to evaluate a proposal then in circulation to create a kind of super appeals court to assist the Supreme Court with its ostensibly pressing workload. In response, Roberts noted, "While some of the tales of woe emanating from the court are enough to bring tears to the eyes, it is true that only Supreme Court justices and schoolchildren are expected to and do take the entire summer off."

With the completion of oral arguments in the Voting Rights Act case, the Court has now entered the most contentious weeks of its year. The Justices almost always save their most controversial cases for the end of the term, and this year tensions may run higher than usual. For starters, the Supreme Court Building is now in the sixth year of a renovation—the first since it was dedicated, in 1935—that has forced each of the Justices to move to temporary chambers. The Justices do not take kindly to such disruptions, especially because they are now, by historical standards, a very old Court. John Paul Stevens just turned eighty-nine, and four Justices (Ruth Bader Ginsburg, Scalia, Kennedy, and Stephen Breyer) are in their seventies. The renovation project will also involve closing the entrance to the Court at the top of its iconic front steps—a change that is said to be a security measure but that several Justices regard as a distressing symbol. Souter's impending departure, and unknown replacement, is another source of anxiety.

The substance of the Court's work, of course, contributes most to the strains among the Justices. The Chief Justice has not yet embraced one particular judicial principle as his special interest—in the way that Rehnquist chose federalism and states' rights—but Roberts is clearly moved by the subject of race, as illustrated by his combative performance during the Texas and New Haven arguments. His concerns reflect the views that prevailed at the Reagan White House: that the government should ignore historical or even continuing inequities and never recognize or reward individuals on the basis of race. In a recent case, a majority of the Justices applied a provision of the Voting Rights Act to reject part of a Texas redistricting plan that was found to hurt Hispanic voters. Roberts dissented from that decision, writing, in an unusually direct expression of disgust, "It is a sordid business, this divvying us up by race."

Race was also at the center of the most important opinion so far in his career as Chief Justice—a case that also displayed his pugnacious style in oral argument. *Parents Involved in Community Schools v. Seattle School District No. 1* concerned a challenge to the city's racial-integration plan. The Seattle plan assigned students to schools based on a variety of factors, including how close the student lived to the school and whether siblings already attended, but the goal of maintaining racial diversity was considered as well. At the oral argument, on December 4, 2006, the Chief Justice tore into Michael F. Madden, the lawyer for the Seattle school district.

"You don't defend the choice policy on the basis that the schools offer education to everyone of the same quality, do you?" he asked, and Madden said that he did defend it on those grounds.

"How is that different from the 'separate but equal' argument?" Roberts went on. "In other words, it doesn't matter that they're being assigned on the basis of their race because they're getting the same type of education."

"Well, because the schools are not racially separate," the lawyer said. "The goal is to maintain the diversity that existed within a broad range in order to try to obtain the benefits that the educational research shows flow from an integrated education."

Roberts wouldn't let the issue go. "Well, you're saying every—I mean, everyone got a seat in *Brown* as well; but, because they were assigned to those seats on the basis of race, it violated equal protection. How is your argument that there's no problem here because everybody gets a seat distinguishable?"

"Because segregation is harmful," Madden said. "Integration, as this Court has recognized . . . has benefits."

In the *Seattle* case, the Court ruled by a five-to-four vote that the integration plan did indeed violate the equal-protection clause of the Constitution, and Roberts assigned himself the opinion. The Chief Justice said that the result in the *Seattle* case was compelled by perhaps the best-known decision in the Court's history, *Brown v. Board of Education*. In that ruling, in 1954, the Court held that school segregation was unconstitutional and rejected the claim that segregated schools were "separate but equal." In Roberts's view, there was no legal difference between the intentionally segregated public schools of Topeka, Kansas, at issue in *Brown*, and the integration plan in *Seattle*, five decades later. In the most famous passage so far of his tenure as Chief Justice, Roberts wrote, "The way to stop discrimination on the basis of race is to stop discriminating on the basis of race."

Roberts's opinion drew an incredulous dissent from Stevens, who said that the Chief Justice's words reminded him of "Anatole France's observation" that the "majestic equality" of the law forbade "rich and poor alike to sleep under bridges, to beg in the streets, and to steal their bread." For dozens of years, the Court had drawn a clear distinction between laws that kept black students out of white schools (which were forbidden) and laws that directed black and white students to study together (which were allowed); Roberts's decision sought to eliminate that distinction and, more generally, called into question whether any race-conscious actions by government were still constitutional. "It is my firm conviction that no Member of the Court that I joined in 1975 would have agreed with today's decision," Stevens concluded.

In Roberts's first term, when Alito also joined the Court, there were fewer controversial cases than usual, as well as an apparent effort by the Justices to reach more unanimous decisions. But the *Seattle* case came down on June 28, 2007, which was the last day of Roberts's second full term as Chief Justice and a year of routs for liberals on the Court. That same day, the Justices overturned a ninety-six-year-old precedent in antitrust law and thus made it harder to prove collusion by corporations. Also that year they upheld the federal Partial Birth Abortion Ban Act, in Kennedy's opinion, even though the Court had rejected a nearly identical law just seven years earlier. The case of *Ledbetter v. Goodyear*, brought by a sympathetic grandmother who had been paid far less than men doing the same work at the tire company, became a political flashpoint because the conservative majority, in an opinion by Alito, imposed seemingly insurmountable new burdens on plaintiffs in employment-discrimination lawsuits. (Ginsburg, in an unusual move, read her dissent from the bench.) In all these cases, Roberts and Alito joined with Scalia, Clarence Thomas, and Kennedy to make the majority. On this final day, Breyer offered an unusually public rebuke to his new colleagues. "It is not often in the law that so few have so quickly changed so much," Breyer said.

Roberts's sure-handed sense of public relations has deserted him only once during his tenure so far. The Chief Justice, as the leader of the federal judiciary, is obligated to prepare an annual report, which historically has been a fairly anodyne document—a set of modest requests to Congress, like faster confirmation of judges or new construction funds for courthouses. In 2006, however, Roberts devoted his entire report to arguing for raises for federal judges, and he even went so far as to call the status quo on salaries a "constitutional crisis." Most federal judges are paid a hundred and sixty-nine thousand dollars, and at that point they had not had a real raise in fifteen years. This request to Congress was universally popular among Roberts's colleagues, who were long used to watching their law clerks exceed their own salaries in their first year of private practice.

Congress, however, snubbed the Chief Justice. Six-figure salaries, lifetime tenure, and the opportunity to retire at full pay did not look inadequate to the elected officials, who make the same amount as judges and must face ordinary voters. Roberts's blindness on the issue may owe something to his having inhabited a rarefied corner of Washington for the past three decades.

In 1986, after his service in the Reagan White House, Roberts went to the Washington law firm of Hogan & Hartson, where he developed a successful practice as an appellate advocate. "John's a very, very conservative fellow, and I'm the opposite, but that was never a problem for us," E. Barrett Prettyman, Jr., a longtime partner at the firm and a co-counsel with Roberts on dozens of cases, said. "Our work was mostly corporate, some criminal, a few individuals as clients. The key to his success was that he was very clear, very articulate, and never confusing."

When George H. W. Bush won the Presidency, in 1988, his new Solicitor General, Kenneth Starr, hired Roberts again, this time as his principal deputy. Near the end of the first Bush's term, Roberts was nominated to the United States Court of Appeals for the D.C. Circuit, but Democrats in the Senate, sensing a victory in the approaching 1992 election, refused to let him come up for a vote. So, for Bill Clinton's eight years in office, Roberts went back to Hogan & Hartson, where, according to his financial-disclosure forms, he made more than a million dollars a year. In 1996, Roberts, then forty-one, married Jane Sullivan, a fellow-lawyer, also in her forties, who now works as a legal recruiter. In 2000, they adopted two children, who are both now eight years old.

While at Hogan, Roberts became a lunchtime regular at the table of J. William Fulbright, the former Arkansas senator, in the firm's cafeteria. Fulbright was affiliated with Hogan from the time of his departure from office, in 1974, until his death, in 1995, and he presided over a salon of sorts for partners with an interest in politics. "It was a politically diverse group, and they'd just get together and talk about the issues of the day," David Leitch, who was also a partner at Hogan, said. "John is interested in political issues, he is interested in the process of politics. He used to like to handicap elections." Roberts took a direct role in the contested 2000 election, travelling to Tallahassee to assist George W. Bush's legal team in the recount litigation. He was rewarded for his efforts the following year, when Bush, like his father before him, nominated Roberts to the D.C. Circuit. He was confirmed two years later, and he served there until Bush chose him for the Supreme Court.

In one respect, Roberts's series of prestigious jobs all amounted to doing the same thing for more than twenty years—reading and writing appellate briefs and, later, appellate decisions. During the heart of his career, Roberts's circle of professional peers consisted entirely of other wealthy and accomplished lawyers. In this world, a hundred and sixty-nine thousand dollars a year might well look like an unconscionably low wage. "Some judges have actually left the bench because they could make more money in private practice, and some Justices have complained privately about how it's almost impossible to educate your family on that kind of money," Prettyman said. "You don't want an unhappy court, judges who are worried about their salaries. John saw that."

Roberts's career as a lawyer marked him in other ways as well. In private practice and in the first Bush Administration, a substantial portion of his work consisted of representing the interests of corporate defendants who were sued by individuals. For example, shortly before Roberts became a judge, he successfully argued in the Supreme Court that a woman who suffered from carpal-tunnel syndrome could not win a recovery from her employer, Toyota, under the Americans with Disabilities Act. Likewise, Roberts won a Supreme Court ruling that the family of a woman who died in a fire could not use the federal wrongful-death statute to sue the city of Tarrant, Alabama. In a rare loss in his thirty-nine arguments before the Court, Roberts failed to persuade the Justices to uphold a sixty-four-million-dollar fine against the United Mine Workers, which was imposed by a Virginia court after a strike.

One case that Roberts argued during his tenure in the Solicitor General's office in George H. W. Bush's Administration, *Lujan v. National Wildlife Federation*, seems to have had special resonance for him. The issue involved the legal doctrine known as "standing"—one of many subjects before the Supreme Court that appear to be just procedural in nature but are in fact freighted with political significance. "One of the distinctive things about American courts is that we have all these gatekeeper provisions that keep courts from getting involved in every single dispute," Samuel Issacharoff, a professor at New York University School of Law, says. "The doctrine of standing says that you only want lawsuits to proceed if the plaintiffs are arguing about a real injury done to them, not simply that they want to be heard on a public-policy question." Liberals and conservatives have been fighting over standing for decades. "Standing is a technical legal doctrine, but it is shorthand for whether courts have a role in policing the conduct of government," Issacharoff says. "Typically, the public-interest advocates, usually on the liberal side of the spectrum, favor very loose standing doctrines, and people who want to protect government from scrutiny, who tend to be on the conservative side, want to require more and more specific standing requirements."

Lujan v. National Wildlife Federation was one of the Rehnquist Court's most important standing cases. The environmental group had challenged the Reagan Administration's effort to make as much as a hundred and eighty million acres of federal land available for mining. In an argument before the Court on April 16, 1990, Roberts said that the mere allegation that a member of the National Wildlife Federation used land "in the vicinity" of the affected acres did not entitle the group to standing to bring the case. "That sort of interest was insufficient to confer standing, because it was in no way distinct from the interest any citizen could claim, coming in the courthouse and saying, 'I'm interested in this subject,'" Roberts told the Justices. By a vote of five to four, the Justices agreed with Roberts and threw out the case. According to Issacharoff, "*Lujan* was the first big case that said, Just because you are really devoted to a cause like the environment, that doesn't mean we are going to let you into the courthouse."

As a lawyer and now as Chief Justice, Roberts has always supported legal doctrines that serve a gatekeeping function. In *DaimlerChrysler v. Cuno*, a group of taxpayers in Toledo, Ohio, went to court to challenge local tax breaks that were given to the carmaker to expand its operations in the city; the Supreme Court held that the plaintiffs lacked standing. In a broadly worded opinion that relied in part on the *Lujan* case, Roberts suggested that most state and local activities were off limits to challenge from taxpayers. "Affording state taxpayers standing to press such challenges simply because their tax burden gives them an interest in the state treasury," Roberts wrote, "would interpose the federal courts as virtually continuing monitors of the wisdom and soundness of state fiscal administration, contrary to the more modest role Article III envisions for federal courts." As usual with Roberts's jurisprudence, the citizen plaintiffs were out of luck.

In the past four years, Roberts and Scalia, while voting together most of the time, have had a dialogue of sorts about how best to address the Court's liberal precedents. For example, Roberts wrote a narrow opinion in 2007 holding that the McCain-Feingold campaign-finance law did not apply to certain political advertisements in Wisconsin. Scalia agreed with Roberts's conclusion in the case, but he said that the Chief Justice should have gone farther and declared the whole law unconstitutional, on free-speech grounds. Scalia insisted that Roberts was just being coy, that his opinion had in fact overruled an earlier ruling that upheld the campaign-finance law, but that he wouldn't come out and say it. "This faux judicial restraint is judicial obfuscation," Scalia wrote.

In a case about the free-speech rights of students, Roberts wrote the opinion approving the suspension of a high-school student in Alaska for holding a sign that said "BONG HiTS 4 JESUS" on a street off school grounds. The Chief Justice said the school had the right to "restrict student speech at a school event, when that speech is reasonably viewed as promoting illegal drug use." Thomas, characteristically, wrote a concurring opinion urging the Court to go farther and hold that students have no First Amendment rights at all. But the larger point remained that Roberts, Scalia, and Thomas voted together in that case, as they do virtually all the time. "These kinds of distinctions among the conservatives are just angels-on-the-head-of-a-pin stuff," says Theodore B. Olson, the former Solicitor General, who remains a frequent advocate before the Court. "Roberts is just what he said he would be in his hearing—a judge who believes in humility and judicial restraint." Like the other conservatives, for instance, Roberts has been a consistent supporter of death sentences, and he wrote the Court's opinion holding that lethal injection does not amount to the sort of cruel and unusual punishment prohibited by the Eighth Amendment. Many liberals, too, feel that Roberts is far more similar to his conservative colleagues than he appeared to be at the time of his confirmation hearing. According to Harvard's Laurence Tribe, "The Chief Justice talks the talk of moderation while walking the walk of extreme conservatism."

On issues of Presidential power, Roberts has been to Scalia's right—a position that's in keeping with his roots in the Reagan Administration. "John was shaped by working at the White House, where you develop a mind-set of defending Presidential power," the lawyer who worked with Roberts in the Reagan years said. Just a few days before Bush appointed Roberts to the Supreme Court, in 2005, Roberts joined an opinion on the D.C. Circuit in *Hamdan v. Rumsfeld* that upheld the Bush Administration's position on the treatment of detainees at Guantánamo Bay. (With Roberts recused from the case, the Supreme Court overruled that decision in 2006, by a five-to-three vote, with Kennedy joining the liberals.) Scalia has occasionally shown a libertarian streak, but Roberts, true to his White House past, has consistently voted to uphold the prerogatives of the executive, especially the military, against the other branches. Last year, Roberts dissented from Kennedy's opinion for a five-to-four Court in *Boumediene v. Bush*, which held that the Military Commissions Act of 2006 violated the rights of Guantánamo detainees. Roberts saw the case as mostly a contest between the executive branch and the rest of the federal government. "Today the Court strikes down as inadequate the most generous set of procedural protections ever afforded aliens detained by this country as enemy combatants," Roberts wrote in his dissent. "One cannot help but think . . . that this decision is not really about the detainees at all, but about control of federal policy regarding enemy combatants."

Roberts's solicitude for the President and the military extends to lower-profile cases as well. In *Winter v. National Resources Defense Council*, the question was whether the Navy had to comply with a federal environmental law protecting dolphins and other wildlife while conducting submarine exercises off California. Roberts said no. "We do not discount the importance of plaintiffs' ecological, scientific, and recreational interests in marine mammals," the Chief Justice wrote. "Those interests, however, are plainly outweighed by the Navy's need to conduct realistic training exercises to ensure that it is able to neutralize the threat posed by enemy submarines." Though Roberts was writing for only a five-to-four majority, he added, "Where the public interest lies does not strike us as a close question."

On the morning of January 20th, the Supreme Court held a small reception for the Justices and their guests before they all headed across First Street to the Capitol for the Inauguration of Barack Obama. Friends present say that Roberts was nervous that morning. He was used to appearing before crowds, of course, but this was the first time that he would be performing the most public of the Chief Justice's duties—administering the Presidential oath of office—and the audience, in person and by broadcast, would be in the many millions. In keeping with his perfectionist nature, Roberts had rehearsed the oath ceremony and had long since committed the words to memory.

Through intermediaries, Roberts and Obama had agreed how to divide the thirty-five-word oath for the swearing in. Obama was first supposed to repeat the clause "I, Barack Hussein Obama, do solemnly swear." But, when Obama heard Roberts begin to speak, he interrupted Roberts before he said "do solemnly swear." This apparently flustered the Chief Justice, who then made a mistake in the next line, inserting the word "faithfully" out of order. Obama smiled, apparently recognizing the error, then tried to follow along. Roberts then garbled another word in the next passage, before correctly reciting, "preserve, protect, and defend the Constitution of the United States."

At the lunch in the Capitol that followed, the two men apologized to each other, but Roberts insisted that he was the one at fault. For the day, Roberts lost some of his customary equanimity as he brooded about making such a public mistake. (He went to the White House the next day, and the oath was repeated, correctly, to forestall any challenges to its legality.) Since then, Roberts has put the embarrassment behind him and even made it the subject of a little humor at his own expense. On January 26th, he presided over the installation of the new leader of the Smithsonian Institution. "Those of you who have read it will see from the program that the Smithsonian some time ago adopted the passing of a key in lieu of the administration of an oath," Roberts said. "I don't know who was responsible for that decision. But I like him."

Still, the flubbed oath will always link Roberts and Obama, whose lives reflect considerable similarities as well as major differences. They belong to roughly the same generation—Roberts is six years older—and received similar educations. Roberts and Obama graduated from Harvard Law School in 1979 and 1991, respectively—Obama had taken time off to work as a community organizer in Chicago—and both served on the *Law Review*. (Obama was president, the top position; Roberts, in his capacity as managing editor, was just below that.) They share an even-tempered disposition, obvious but unshowy intelligence, and fierce ambition leavened by considerable charm.

But the distinctions between these two men are just as apparent. Obama is the first President in history to have voted against the confirmation of the Chief Justice who later administered his oath of office. In his Senate speech on that vote, Obama praised Roberts's intellect and integrity and said that he would trust his judgment in about ninety-five per cent of the cases before the Supreme Court. "In those five per cent of hard cases, the constitutional text will not be directly on point. The language of the statute will not be perfectly clear. Legal process alone will not lead you to a rule of decision," Obama said. "In those circumstances, your decisions about whether affirmative action is an appropriate response to the history of discrimination in this country or whether a general right of privacy encompasses a more specific right of women to control their reproductive decisions . . . the critical ingredient is supplied by what is in the judge's heart." Obama did not trust Roberts's heart. "It is my personal estimation that he has far more often used his formidable skills on behalf of the strong in opposition to the weak," the Senator said. The first bill that Obama signed as President was known as the Lilly Ledbetter Fair Pay Act; it specifically overturned the interpretation of employment law that Roberts had endorsed in the 2007 case.

In a way, Obama offers a mirror image of the view of the Supreme Court that Roberts presented in his tribute to Rehnquist in Tucson. To Obama, what Roberts called the "solid grounds of legal arguments" was only the beginning of constitutional interpretation, not the end. In his statement announcing Souter's resignation, on May 1st, the President defined the qualities he was looking for in a Justice in a very different way from Roberts's description of Rehnquist. "I will seek someone who understands that justice isn't about some abstract legal theory or footnote in a casebook. It is also about how our laws affect the daily realities of people's lives—whether they can make a living and care for their families; whether they feel safe in their homes and welcome in their own nation," Obama said. "I view that quality of empathy, of understanding and identifying with people's hopes and struggles, as an essential ingredient for arriving at just decisions and outcomes."

The differences between Roberts and Obama include such issues as abortion and affirmative action, but they extend beyond such familiar legal battlegrounds to what Roberts called, in his Tucson speech, "the nature of the Court itself." "When Justice Rehnquist went on the Court, a minority of the Justices had been former federal judges," Roberts observed. "Today, for the first time in its history, every member of the Court was a federal court-of-appeals judge before joining the Court—a more legal perspective, and less of a policy perspective."

Obama does not regard the all-former-judge makeup of the Supreme Court as an unalloyed virtue. "The obvious sources of candidates have been people already on the bench and people who are distinguished academic legal scholars and teachers," Gregory Craig, the White House counsel, told me in February. "But he's also looking for lawyers who have been public defenders or prosecutors, or representing points of view with respect to immigration or the Innocence Project. He doesn't think you have to be a member of the circuit courts of appeals to be on the Supreme Court." Obama has spoken fondly of Earl Warren, the fourteenth Chief Justice, who came to the Court from the governorship of California.

When Vice-President Biden publicly mocked Roberts about his gaffe at a ceremony shortly after the Inauguration, Obama shot him a scathing look of rebuke. (Biden later called Roberts to apologize.) Still, there is no disputing that the President and the Chief Justice are adversaries in a contest for control of the Court, and that both men come to that battle well armed. Obama has at most one more chance to take the oath of office, and Roberts will probably have a half-dozen more opportunities to get it right. But each time Roberts walks down the steps of the Capitol to administer the oath, he may well be surrounded—and eventually outvoted—by Supreme Court colleagues appointed by Barack Obama.

Consider the source and the audience

- Toobin is writing for the *New Yorker* audience—a sophisticated, educated, and most likely liberal group of readers. Toobin himself seems to be more liberal than not. Does that mean that his analysis of Roberts's views is suspect? Would a conservative writer present Roberts's views differently?
- Toobin is himself a graduate of Harvard Law, where he was a member of its *Law Review*. Does the fact that he has a legal background and can rely on his readers to be well-educated mean that you approach the article differently than you might a similar piece in a more mass-oriented magazine like *Time* or *Newsweek*?

Lay out the argument, the values, and the assumptions

- What views does Toobin attribute to Roberts, and why does he think they aren't consistent with "Mr. Nice Guy?" What does that tell you about Toobin's own views?
- What is the difference between Roberts's brand of conservatism and that of Justices Scalia and Thomas? Does Toobin think it makes much practical difference on the Court?
- Toobin says President Obama's Court might be the mirror image of Roberts's. How so?

Uncover the evidence

- Toobin relies partly for his claims on the opinions of observers of Chief Justice Roberts, but his primary source is Roberts's own words, whether in speeches, in legal opinions, or in oral arguments before the Court. Is that persuasive to you? What evidence might be more persuasive?

Evaluate the conclusion

- Toobin's argument is complex, but his conclusions might be summarized as a caution to readers not to be fooled by Roberts's smiling face, partly because Toobin seems to agree with Obama's view that Roberts is more likely to side with the strong rather than the weak, or as Toobin says, he defers to existing power relationships in society. Is that conclusion borne out by Justice Roberts's legal opinions and arguments?
- If you could ask Roberts, do you think he would disagree with Toobin's conclusions?

Sort out the political implications

- Toobin imagines a Court led by Roberts but peopled in part by Obama's appointees. Obama's first appointee was Sonia Sotomayor. How do you think her behavior on the Court will compare to Roberts's?
- Toobin also implies that Roberts presented himself one way during his Senate confirmation hearings but behaves in a slightly different way on the Court. Did Roberts misrepresent himself, or was he merely cagey? Can the Senate find out with accuracy what is in the mind of presidential nominees?

10.3 Supreme Court Weighs Cases Redefining Legal Equality

Adam Liptak, *New York Times*

Why We Chose This Piece

Adam Liptak wrote this piece in the New York Times *just days before the Supreme Court handed down major decisions on marriage equality, affirmative action, and voting rights. Even though there was much good analysis written after the fact, this article stands out for its clear analysis of the equality issues involved. In a nutshell, there are two American visions of equality—one that focuses more on equal treatment, the other on equal results—and they are at odds with each other. As Liptak points out, and as the Court's decisions bear out, a majority of justices on the Court tend to endorse the former view, which entails rejecting the latter. Why would this lead to judgments that seem inconsistent?*

Within days, the Supreme Court is expected to issue a series of decisions that could transform three fundamental social institutions: marriage, education and voting.

The extraordinary run of blockbuster rulings due in the space of a single week will also reshape the meaning of legal equality and help define for decades to come one of the Constitution's grandest commands: "the equal protection of the laws."

If those words require only equal treatment from the government, the rulings are likely to be a mixed bag that will delight and disappoint liberals and conservatives in equal measure. Under that approach, same-sex couples who want to marry would be better off at the end of the term, while blacks and Hispanics could find it harder to get into college and to vote.

But a tension runs through the cases, one based on different conceptions of equality. Some justices are committed to formal equality. Others say the Constitution requires a more dynamic kind of equality, one that takes account of the weight of history and of modern disparities.

The four major cases yet to be decided concern same-sex marriage, affirmative action in higher education and the fate of the Voting Rights Act of 1965, which places special burdens on states with a history of racial discrimination.

Formal equality would require that gay couples be treated just like straight couples when it comes to marriage, white students just like black students when it comes to admissions decisions and Southern states just like Northern ones when it comes to federal oversight of voting. The effect would be to help gay couples, and hurt blacks and Latinos.

But such rulings—"liberal" when it comes to gay rights, "conservative" when it comes to race—are hard to reconcile with the historical meaning of the 14th

---

Selection published: June 22, 2013

Amendment's equal protection clause, adopted in the wake of the Civil War and meant to protect the newly freed black slaves. It would be odd, said David A. Strauss, a law professor at the University of Chicago, for that amendment to help gays but not blacks.

"What's weird about it would be the retreat on race, which is the paradigm example of what the 14th Amendment is meant to deal with," he said, "coupled with fairly aggressive action on sexual orientation."

But actual as opposed to formal racial equality has fallen out of favor in some circles, Professor Strauss said. "One thing that seems to be going on with these historically excluded groups," he said, "is that they come to be thought of as just another interest group. Blacks seem to have crossed that line."

Justice Antonin Scalia appeared to express that view during the argument in February in the voting rights case, *Shelby County v. Holder*, No. 12-96. "Whenever a society adopts racial entitlements," he said, "it is very difficult to get out of them through the normal political processes."

Gay men and lesbians have yet to achieve formal legal equality. They are not protected against job discrimination in much of the nation, may not marry their same-sex partners in most of it and do not have their marriages recognized by the federal government in any of it. The fact that they are asking for equal treatment may help their cause in the cases challenging the federal Defense of Marriage Act, or DOMA, which for purposes of federal benefits defines marriage as the union of a man and a woman, and Proposition 8, the California voter initiative that banned same-sex marriage there.

But Chief Justice John G. Roberts Jr. suggested in March that ordinary politics would sort things out. "As far as I can tell," he told a lawyer challenging the federal marriage law in *United States v. Windsor*, No. 12-307, "political figures are falling over themselves to endorse your side of the case."

In the three months since that argument, three more states have adopted same-sex marriage, raising the total to 12, along with the District of Columbia.

Kenji Yoshino, a law professor at New York University, said the two different conceptions of equal protection are animated by different concerns. One is skeptical of government classifications based on race and similar characteristics, whatever their goals. The other tries to make sure that historically disfavored groups are not subordinated.

"Under Jim Crow," Professor Yoshino said, "both horses ran in the same direction." Southern states enacted laws that drew formal distinctions, and those distinctions oppressed blacks.

"These days," Professor Yoshino said, "the two horses are running in opposite directions."

Consider the case of Abigail Fisher, a white woman who was denied admission to the University of Texas. She says the university, an arm of the state government, should not classify people on the basis of race because that violates a colorblind conception of the Constitution's equal protection clause.

Defenders of the university's affirmative action program say the purpose of the classification must figure in the equal protection analysis. "What we're really trying to do is try to make sure there aren't castes in our society, and we will try to lift up castes," Professor Yoshino said.

A formal conception of equality helps Ms. Fisher in her case, *Fisher v. University of Texas*, No. 11-345. A dynamic one helps the university.

Whichever side loses a major Supreme Court case is likely to say the decision was an example of judicial activism. That term can be an empty insult, but political scientists try to give it meaning. They say a court is activist when it strikes down a law as unconstitutional. There is a chance the court will be activist in that sense twice this week.

It may strike down central provisions of the federal marriage law and of the Voting Rights Act. Should that happen, said Pamela Harris, an adviser to the Supreme Court Institute at Georgetown's law school, "the left will be saying out of one side of its mouth, 'How dare you strike down the considered judgment of Congress in the Voting Rights Act?' " In the same breath, she said, liberals will add, "But great job on DOMA."

There is another possibility: one or more of the cases could fizzle, said Walter E. Dellinger, who served as acting solicitor general in the Clinton administration and filed an influential brief in the Proposition 8 case, *Hollingsworth v. Perry*, No. 12-144. It argued that the failure of officials in California to appeal the judgment against them deprived the Supreme Court of jurisdiction to decide the case, and it was discussed at the argument in March.

Mr. Dellinger said all four remaining blockbuster cases suffer from plausible procedural flaws that could lead to their dismissal. "I've never heard of this before," he said of such an end-of-term possibility.

An effort to harmonize all of the court's big decisions may in the end prove impossible. "It's hard to imagine somebody happy with everything they do, except Justice Kennedy," Professor Strauss said, referring to the member of the court at its ideological center, Justice Anthony M. Kennedy.

That may be just as well for the court's reputation. In giving something to liberals and something to conservatives, as it often does, Professor Strauss said, "the court has avoided putting itself in a position where either side wants to declare war on them."

Consider the source and the audience

- Liptak is writing this article in the widely read *New York Times* before the Court handed down its controversial decisions. What is his purpose?

Lay out the argument, the values, and the assumptions

- The article argues that the Court has taken two fundamentally different approaches to understanding equality. What are they?
- How do those two values of equality relate to each other? Can they coexist?
- Why do some people endorse the more substantive view that equality needs to make up for past injustice? Why might others be more inclined to the more procedural equal treatment view?

Uncover the evidence

- The thrust of Liptak's argument is in laying out two views of equality and looking at how the Court might rule with respect to them. He cites previous cases and legal experts. Is there any other kind of evidence that would help you understand his argument?

Evaluate the conclusion

- In the final event, we know that Liptak's conclusions were pretty much right. When the Court handed down its rulings, it gave warning to advocates of affirmative action that the policy was on thin ice; it struck down part of the Voting Rights Act that required some states to get new voting laws cleared by the Department of Justice; it struck down the Defense of Marriage Act; and it punted on the California proposition banning gay marriage, sending it back to the lower court that struck it down. Which of these are applications of procedural equality, and which are applications of equality of result?

Sort out the political significance

- Liptak argues that whether the Court goes with the procedural view or the substantive view, both liberals and conservatives will be simultaneously pleased and unhappy with some of the decisions. He suggests that there is no way to make everyone happy. Is he correct?

10.4 The Cost of Compromise

Linda Greenhouse, *New York Times*

Why We Chose This Piece

When the Supreme Court handed down the rulings we discuss in the previous reading, Court-watchers were interested to see that Justice Ruth Bader Ginsberg, unlike some of her younger liberal colleagues, not only dissented from the majority opinion putting affirmative action on notice, but read her dissent from the bench. In this New York Times blog post, veteran Court reporter Linda Greenhouse takes a few minutes to speculate on why that is so, and comes to some interesting conclusions about the value of compromise on the Court, and the power of a dissenting voice.

Selection published: July 10, 2013

In his 2011 memoir, "Five Chiefs," the retired Supreme Court Justice John Paul Stevens offered a mildly eyebrow-raising reflection on *Brown v. Board of Education*. The landmark school desegregation decision is celebrated not only for its outcome but also for the unanimity that Chief Justice Earl Warren extracted from his wary colleagues. But the price of unanimity may have been too high, Justice Stevens suggested. He observed that the court's compromise order to desegregate "with all deliberate speed," rather than immediately, turned into a recipe for hardly any speed at all.

The court's "belated and somewhat tentative command," Justice Stevens wrote with reference to the similarly unanimous follow-up opinion known as Brown II, "may have done more to encourage resistance to the clear message contained in Earl Warren's original opinion than would have a dissenting opinion joined by only one or two justices."

Justice Stevens knows a thing or two about dissenting opinions, having written more during his 34-year Supreme Court career than any justice in history: 720 of them. (The distant runner-up is Justice William O. Douglas, with 486.) A persuasive dissent can do the court a favor, Justice Stevens wrote in his memoir: "Responses by the majority may not only clarify and strengthen the court's reasoning, but also demonstrate to the public that the dissenter's views were carefully considered before they were rejected."

I've been thinking about Justice Stevens's views on dissent ever since reading Justice Ruth Bader Ginsburg's solitary opinion two weeks ago dissenting from the court's affirmative-action ruling, *Fisher v. University of Texas*. The vote was 7 to 1, with Justice Elena Kagan recused. Justice Anthony M. Kennedy's majority opinion either did (as most people seem to think) or didn't (as I believe) raise the constitutional bar for universities seeking to justify taking race into account in their admission policies. The long-awaited decision (more than eight months from argument to opinion) had been widely and reasonably expected to begin the process of dismantling affirmative action in university admissions. The fact that it didn't do so, or at most did so only marginally, was obviously the product of a compromise, and has to be counted as a rare liberal victory against the court's conservative tide.

Justices Stephen G. Breyer and Sonia Sotomayor, members of the court's embattled liberal bloc, signed it without comment. Why did Justice Ginsburg, who is also one of the liberals, choose otherwise? And why, in her pithy four-page opinion, did she feel moved to call out her colleagues—not quite in so many words, of course, but unmistakably—as hypocrites?

The question the court chose to address in the *Fisher* case was how convincingly a university must prove that it considered and reasonably rejected all possible "race-neutral alternatives" before turning to the overt use of race in admitting a diverse student body. Justice Kennedy's 13-page opinion, so analytically barren that it would merit description on Wikipedia as a "stub," assumed without much discussion that Texas' "top ten-percent" law, under which the students in the top 10 percent of every graduating high school class in the state are guaranteed admission to the flagship Austin campus, meets the test of racial neutrality. The issue was whether Texas was constitutionally justified in going outside the bounds of the 10-percent plan to include racial and ethnic background, among other criteria, in selecting about 20 percent of the class. The 10-percent plan, in other words, was assumed by the majority to be the race-neutral baseline.

But of course, as Justice Ginsburg pointed out, that plan achieves diversity only because so many of the state's high schools are effectively segregated by race or ethnicity. She noted that the Legislature enacted the plan into law in 1997 "with racially segregated neighborhoods and schools front and center stage" in legislators' minds. "It is race consciousness, not blindness to race, that drives such plans," Justice Ginsburg said, adding that "only an ostrich" could think otherwise. Her point wasn't to disapprove the use of race. Quite the opposite: "I have several times explained why government actors, including state universities, need not be blind to the lingering effects of an overtly discriminatory past." (That the University of Texas has such a past is indisputable; it was a 1950 Supreme Court decision ordering the university to integrate its law school, in a case argued by Thurgood Marshall, that helped set the justices on the road to *Brown* four years later.

Rather, Justice Ginsburg argued in her dissenting opinion, candor was to be preferred to obfuscation, and a court that reflexively denounces race-consciousness ought to acknowledge the race-consciousness of the very approach it holds up as an acceptable alternative.

After the decision was issued on June 24, there was lively discussion in court-watching circles about why Justice Ginsburg, who highlighted her position by taking the unusual step of reading her dissent from the bench, had gone this route. Given that her dissent contained many references to her own earlier opinions, one prominent theory was that Justice Ginsburg, at 80 the oldest member of the court, was in the process of nailing down her equal-protection legacy in the event that she is no longer on the court by the time the next chapter in the affirmative-action saga plays out. Since I believe that Justice Ginsburg is very much anchored in the here and now, I had my doubts about that explanation.

And then, the very next day, came the court's 5-to-4 decision in the voting rights case, *Shelby County v. Holder.* There, it seemed to me, was the answer to the puzzle.

In his majority opinion in *Shelby County,* Chief Justice John G. Roberts Jr. relied heavily on his opinion in a predecessor case four years ago that expressed strong constitutional doubts about the Voting Rights Act but stopped just short of pulling the trigger. The vote in that 2009 case, *Northwest Austin Municipal Utility District No. 1 v. Holder,* was 8 to 1. The lone dissenter was Justice Clarence Thomas, who wanted the court to declare unconstitutional the preclearance provision of the law's Section 5 and who made clear his scorn for the contortions the majority went through to sidestep what appeared to be the logical conclusion of its analysis.

The court's liberal bloc at the time—Justices Stevens, Ginsburg, Breyer, and David H. Souter—said nothing. They thus signed on to the chief justice's critique of Section 5—his now famous claim that "things have changed in the South," as well as his assertion that the Voting Rights Act's past accomplishment was not by itself "adequate justification to retain the preclearance requirements." By their signatures, the liberal justices even subscribed to the argument that "a departure from the fundamental principle of equal sovereignty requires a showing that a statute's disparate geographic coverage is sufficiently related to the problem that it targets."

"Fundamental principle of equal sovereignty"? This became a central element of the chief justice's majority opinion last month, the constitutional basis for his critique of requiring some states but not others to obtain the federal government's approval before making changes in voting procedures. In her dissenting opinion, perhaps the most powerful of her career, Justice Ginsburg shredded the assertion that any such "fundamental principle" could apply to this case. Quoting the court's foundational precedent in the voting rights area, *South Carolina v. Katzenbach* from 1966, she noted that the equal-sovereignty principle "applies only to the terms upon which states are admitted to the union, and not to the remedies for local evils which have subsequently appeared."

In his majority opinion, Chief Justice Roberts, understandably enough, reminded the dissenters of what they (two of them at the time, anyway) had seemingly agreed to just four years ago. "Eight members of the court subscribed to these views," he noted pointedly after summarizing the *Northwest Austin* decision. "The dissent analyzes the question presented as if our decision in *Northwest Austin* never happened," he wrote, adding: "For example, the dissent refuses to consider the principle of equal sovereignty, despite *Northwest Austin*'s emphasis on its significance." In one long paragraph, he offered more examples as well.

Why did the liberal justices sign on to the *Northwest Austin* opinion in 2009? Clearly, it was the price of the compromise to buy the Voting Rights Act a little more time. They must have expected—or desperately hoped—that Congress would take the hint and update the formula that determines which states and localities are covered by the Section 5 preclearance requirement. A near-unanimous opinion, they may have thought, would make a Congressional response more likely; that the court was speaking with close to one voice seemingly put the issue beyond partisanship. Only in hindsight is it clear that this expectation was doomed by Congressional dysfunction, leaving the liberal justices on a limb they had knowingly, if reluctantly, climbed.

Was the price of compromise too high back in 2009? In retrospect, the answer is yes. The liberal justices' acquiescence to near-unanimity placed a fig leaf on a truly radical project to curb the civil-rights enforcement authority that the framers of the 14th and 15th amendments explicitly gave to Congress. It's admittedly a long shot even in hindsight, but a powerful dissent four years ago might have been the clarion call that just might have shaken Congress out of its torpor and persuaded it to immunize the Voting Rights Act from the charge that the application of Section 5 was, in the chief justice's words, "based on decades-old data and eradicated practices."

Which brings us back to the *Fisher* case and Justice Ginsburg's solitary dissent. True, Justice Kennedy's 7-to-1 majority opinion changed little and again bought a little time, but affirmative action is, more visibly than ever, on life support. The Texas case proved a poor vehicle for making much headway on the conservatives' project, but there are other cases in the pipeline, with one from Michigan already on the docket for argument when the new term begins. As Justice Harry A. Blackmun once wrote in a different context, "a chill wind blows."

"Fool me once, shame on you," the old saying goes. "Fool me twice, shame on me." No one ever fooled Ruth Bader Ginsburg twice.

Consider the source and the audience

- Linda Greenhouse wrote this article as a blog post on the *New York Times* website. How can a blog post be different from an article appearing in the paper? How might it free its author to write for a more specialized audience? Would Greenhouse have couched this argument in more general terms if it were appearing in the paper?

Lay out the argument, the values, and the assumptions

- Greenhouse's argument is pretty sophisticated. Why does she feel that Justice Ginsburg got burned by her previous efforts at compromise in the voting rights case? What legal strategy does Greenhouse think Chief Justice Roberts was following? Why does she think it caused Ginsburg to dissent in the affirmative action case?
- When is compromise not the positive thing that most of us were taught to do to get along in a complex world?

Uncover the evidence

- What kind of evidence would you like to see to support Greenhouse's idea that Ginsburg dissented because she feared that, if she compromised, her vote would later be used to support a conclusion with which she disagreed?

Evaluate the conclusion

- Greenhouse thinks that Ginsburg feels that her good faith effort at compromise came back to haunt her in the voting rights case. Do you think that is why she dissented in the affirmative action case?

Sort out the political significance

- If you take the lessons from all the articles that mention Chief Justice Roberts in this chapter, what kind of decisions do you expect him to be making in the next ten or twenty years?

10.5 *Federalist* No. 78

Alexander Hamilton, *The Federalist Papers*

Why We Chose This Piece

Thus far we have read a number of articles that deal with the increasing power and political nature of the courts. Yet, as we noted in the introduction to this chapter, Hamilton claimed that the judiciary would be the least dangerous branch of government because it was the least powerful. Have things changed, or could we have anticipated the power of today's courts from Hamilton's own arguments?

This essay is fascinating, but it needs careful reading—several subarguments require some unraveling before we can be clear about Hamilton's thesis. The basic task he undertakes here is to justify why judges in federal courts should be appointed to hold their offices on good behavior—essentially that they be appointed for life unless they do something really wrong. (The conditions for impeaching a judge are the same as for impeaching a president—the commitment of high crimes and misdemeanors.) Hamilton first declares that the judiciary is the least powerful branch of the federal government, seeming to suggest that giving lifetime appointments to an institution that is not very powerful is not all that threatening in the first place. Then he embarks on a far more controversial argument. Federal judges require lifetime tenure to keep them politically independent from the other two branches not because they are not powerful but because they are the only ones who hold in their hands the power to determine if the laws of Congress violate the will of the people as expressed in the Constitution. Does Hamilton's famous justification of judicial review, a power that does not appear in the Constitution itself, contradict any aspect of what he said about the judiciary's being the weakest branch of government?

To the People of the State of New York: WE PROCEED now to an examination of the judiciary department of the proposed government. In unfolding the defects of the existing Confederation, the utility and necessity of a federal judicature have been clearly pointed out. It is the less necessary to recapitulate the considerations there urged, as the propriety of the institution in the abstract is not disputed; the only questions which have been raised being relative to the manner of constituting it, and to its extent. To these points, therefore, our observations shall be confined.

The manner of constituting it seems to embrace these several objects: Ist. The mode of appointing the judges. 2d. The tenure by which they are to hold their places. 3d. The partition of the judiciary authority between different courts, and their relations to each other.

First. As to the mode of appointing the judges; this is the same with that of appointing the officers of the Union in general, and has been so fully discussed in the two last numbers, that nothing can be said here which would not be useless repetition.

Selection published: May 28, 1788

Second. As to the tenure by which the judges are to hold their places; this chiefly concerns their duration in office; the provisions for their support; the precautions for their responsibility.

According to the plan of the convention, all judges who may be appointed by the United States are to hold their offices DURING GOOD BEHAVIOR; which is conformable to the most approved of the State constitutions and among the rest, to that of this State. Its propriety having been drawn into question by the adversaries of that plan, is no light symptom of the rage for objection, which disorders their imaginations and judgments. The standard of good behavior for the continuance in office of the judicial magistracy, is certainly one of the most valuable of the modern improvements in the practice of government. In a monarchy it is an excellent barrier to the despotism of the prince; in a republic it is a no less excellent barrier to the encroachments and oppressions of the representative body. And it is the best expedient which can be devised in any government, to secure a steady, upright, and impartial administration of the laws.

Whoever attentively considers the different departments of power must perceive, that, in a government in which they are separated from each other, the judiciary, from the nature of its functions, will always be the least dangerous to the political rights of the Constitution; because it will be least in a capacity to annoy or injure them. The Executive not only dispenses the honors, but holds the sword of the community. The legislature not only commands the purse, but prescribes the rules by which the duties and rights of every citizen are to be regulated. The judiciary, on the contrary, has no influence over either the sword or the purse; no direction either of the strength or of the wealth of the society; and can take no active resolution whatever. It may truly be said to have neither FORCE nor WILL, but merely judgment; and must ultimately depend upon the aid of the executive arm even for the efficacy of its judgments.

This simple view of the matter suggests several important consequences. It proves incontestably, that the judiciary is beyond comparison the weakest of the three departments of power;[1] that it can never attack with success either of the other two; and that all possible care is requisite to enable it to defend itself against their attacks. It equally proves, that though individual oppression may now and then proceed from the courts of justice, the general liberty of the people can never be endangered from that quarter; I mean so long as the judiciary remains truly distinct from both the legislature and the Executive. For I agree, that "there is no liberty, if the power of judging be not separated from the legislative and executive powers."[2] And it proves, in the last place, that as liberty can have nothing to fear from the judiciary alone, but would have every thing to fear from its union with either of the other departments; that as all the effects of such a union must ensue from a dependence of the former on the latter, notwithstanding a nominal and apparent separation; that as, from the natural feebleness of the judiciary, it is in continual jeopardy of being overpowered, awed, or influenced by its coordinate branches; and that as nothing can contribute so much to its firmness and independence as permanency in office, this quality may therefore be justly regarded as an indispensable ingredient in its constitution, and, in a great measure, as the citadel of the public justice and the public security.

The complete independence of the courts of justice is peculiarly essential in a limited Constitution. By a limited Constitution, I understand one which contains certain specified exceptions to the legislative authority; such, for instance, as that it shall pass no bills of attainder, no ex-post-facto laws, and the like. Limitations of this kind can be preserved in practice no other way than through the medium of courts of justice, whose duty it must be to declare all acts contrary to the manifest tenor of the Constitution void. Without this, all the reservations of particular rights or privileges would amount to nothing.

Some perplexity respecting the rights of the courts to pronounce legislative acts void, because contrary to the Constitution, has arisen from an imagination that the doctrine would imply a superiority of the judiciary to the legislative power. It is urged that the authority which can declare the acts of another void, must necessarily be superior to the one whose acts may be declared void. As this doctrine is of great importance in all the American constitutions, a brief discussion of the ground on which it rests cannot be unacceptable.

There is no position which depends on clearer principles, than that every act of a delegated authority, contrary to the tenor of the commission under which it is exercised, is void. No legislative act, therefore, contrary to the Constitution, can be valid. To deny this, would be to affirm, that the deputy is greater than his principal; that the servant is above his master; that the representatives of the people are superior to the people themselves; that men acting by virtue of powers, may do not only what their powers do not authorize, but what they forbid.

If it be said that the legislative body are themselves the constitutional judges of their own powers, and that the construction they put upon them is conclusive upon the other departments, it may be answered, that this cannot be the natural presumption, where it is not to be collected from any particular provisions in the Constitution. It is not otherwise to be supposed, that the Constitution could intend to enable the representatives of the people to substitute their WILL to that of their constituents. It is far more rational to suppose, that the courts were designed to be an intermediate body between the people and the legislature, in order, among other things, to keep the latter within the limits assigned to their authority. The interpretation of the laws is the proper and peculiar province of the courts. A constitution is, in fact, and must be regarded by the judges, as a fundamental law. It therefore belongs to them to ascertain its meaning, as well as the meaning of any particular act proceeding from the legislative body. If there should happen to be an irreconcilable variance between the two, that which has the superior obligation and validity ought, of course, to be preferred; or, in other words, the Constitution ought to be preferred to the statute, the intention of the people to the intention of their agents.

Nor does this conclusion by any means suppose a superiority of the judicial to the legislative power. It only supposes that the power of the people is superior to both; and that where the will of the legislature, declared in its statutes, stands in opposition to that of the people, declared in the Constitution, the judges ought to be governed by the latter rather than the former. They ought to regulate their decisions by the fundamental laws, rather than by those which are not fundamental.

This exercise of judicial discretion, in determining between two contradictory laws, is exemplified in a familiar instance. It not uncommonly happens, that there are two statutes existing at one time, clashing in whole or in part with each other, and neither of them containing any repealing clause or expression. In such a case, it is the province of the courts to liquidate and fix their meaning and operation. So far as they can, by any fair construction, be reconciled to each other, reason and law conspire to dictate that this should be done; where this is impracticable, it becomes a matter of necessity to give effect to one, in exclusion of the other. The rule which has obtained in the courts for determining their relative validity is, that the last in order of time shall be preferred to the first. But this is a mere rule of construction, not derived from any positive law, but from the nature and reason of the thing. It is a rule not enjoined upon the courts by legislative provision, but adopted by themselves, as consonant to truth and propriety, for the direction of their conduct as interpreters of the law. They thought it reasonable, that between the interfering acts of an EQUAL authority, that which was the last indication of its will should have the preference.

But in regard to the interfering acts of a superior and subordinate authority, of an original and derivative power, the nature and reason of the thing indicate the converse of that rule as proper to be followed. They teach us that the prior act of a superior ought to be preferred to the subsequent act of an inferior and subordinate authority; and that accordingly, whenever a particular statute contravenes the Constitution, it will be the duty of the judicial tribunals to adhere to the latter and disregard the former.

It can be of no weight to say that the courts, on the pretense of a repugnancy, may substitute their own pleasure to the constitutional intentions of the legislature. This might as well happen in the case of two contradictory statutes; or it might as well happen in every adjudication upon any single statute. The courts must declare the sense of the law; and if they should be disposed to exercise WILL instead of JUDGMENT, the consequence would equally be the substitution of their pleasure to that of the legislative body. The observation, if it prove any thing, would prove that there ought to be no judges distinct from that body.

If, then, the courts of justice are to be considered as the bulwarks of a limited Constitution against legislative encroachments, this consideration will afford a strong argument for the permanent tenure of judicial offices, since nothing will contribute so much as this to that independent spirit in the judges which must be essential to the faithful performance of so arduous a duty.

This independence of the judges is equally requisite to guard the Constitution and the rights of individuals from the effects of those ill humors, which the arts of designing men, or the influence of particular conjunctures, sometimes disseminate among the people themselves, and which, though they speedily give place to better information, and more deliberate reflection, have a tendency, in the meantime, to occasion dangerous innovations in the government, and serious oppressions of the minor party in the community. Though I trust the friends of the proposed Constitution will never concur with its enemies,[3] in questioning that fundamental principle of republican government, which admits the right of the people to alter or abolish the established Constitution, whenever they find it inconsistent with their happiness, yet it is not to be inferred from this principle, that the representatives of the people, whenever a momentary inclination happens to lay hold of a majority of their constituents, incompatible with the provisions in the existing Constitution, would, on that account, be justifiable in a violation of those provisions; or that the courts would be under a greater obligation to connive at infractions in this shape, than when they had proceeded wholly from the cabals of the representative body. Until the people have, by some solemn and authoritative act, annulled or changed the established form, it is binding upon themselves collectively, as well as individually; and no presumption, or even knowledge, of their sentiments, can warrant their representatives in a departure from it, prior to such an act. But it is easy to see, that it would require an uncommon portion of fortitude in the judges to do their duty as faithful guardians of the Constitution, where legislative invasions of it had been instigated by the major voice of the community.

But it is not with a view to infractions of the Constitution only, that the independence of the judges may be an essential safeguard against the effects of occasional ill humors in the society. These sometimes extend no farther than to the injury of the private rights of particular classes of citizens, by unjust and partial laws. Here also the firmness of the judicial magistracy is of vast importance in mitigating the severity and confining the operation of such laws. It not only serves to moderate the immediate mischiefs of those which may have been passed, but it operates as a check upon the legislative body in passing them; who, perceiving that obstacles to the success of iniquitous intention are to be expected from the scruples of the courts, are in a manner compelled, by the very motives of the injustice they meditate, to qualify their attempts. This is a circumstance calculated to have more influence upon the character of our governments, than but few may be aware of. The benefits of the integrity and moderation of the judiciary have already been felt in more States than one; and though they may have displeased those whose sinister expectations they may have disappointed, they must have commanded the esteem and applause of all the virtuous and disinterested. Considerate men, of every description, ought to prize whatever will tend to beget or fortify that temper in the courts: as no man can be sure that he may not be to-morrow the victim of a spirit of injustice, by which he may be a gainer to-day. And every man must now feel, that the inevitable tendency of such a spirit is to sap the foundations of public and private confidence, and to introduce in its stead universal distrust and distress.

That inflexible and uniform adherence to the rights of the Constitution, and of individuals, which we perceive to be indispensable in the courts of justice, can certainly not be expected from judges who hold their offices by a temporary commission. Periodical appointments, however regulated, or by whomsoever made, would, in some way or other, be fatal to their necessary independence. If the power of making them was committed either to the Executive or legislature, there would be danger of an improper complaisance to the branch which possessed it; if to both, there would be an unwillingness to hazard the displeasure of either; if to the people, or to persons chosen by them for the special purpose, there would be too great a disposition to consult popularity, to justify a reliance that nothing would be consulted but the Constitution and the laws.

There is yet a further and a weightier reason for the permanency of the judicial offices, which is deducible from the nature of the qualifications they require. It has been frequently remarked, with great propriety, that a voluminous code of laws is one of the inconveniences necessarily connected with the advantages of a free government. To avoid an arbitrary discretion in the courts, it is indispensable that they should be bound down by strict rules and precedents, which serve to define and point out their duty in every particular case that comes before them; and it will readily be conceived from the variety of controversies which grow out of the folly and wickedness of mankind, that the records of those precedents must unavoidably swell to a very considerable bulk, and must demand long and laborious study to acquire a competent knowledge of them. Hence it is, that there can be but few men in the society who will have sufficient skill in the laws to qualify them for the stations of judges. And making the proper deductions for the ordinary depravity of human nature, the number must be still smaller of those who unite the requisite integrity with the requisite knowledge. These considerations apprise us, that the government can have no great option between fit character; and that a temporary duration in office, which would naturally discourage such characters from quitting a lucrative line of practice to accept a seat on the bench, would have a tendency to throw the administration of justice into hands less able, and less well qualified, to conduct it with utility and dignity. In the present circumstances of this country, and in those in which it is likely to be for a long time to come, the disadvantages on this score would be greater than they may at first sight appear; but it must be confessed, that they are far inferior to those which present themselves under the other aspects of the subject.

Upon the whole, there can be no room to doubt that the convention acted wisely in copying from the models of those constitutions which have established GOOD BEHAVIOR as the tenure of their judicial offices, in point of duration; and that so far from being blamable on this account, their plan would have been inexcusably defective, if it had wanted this important feature of good government. The experience of Great Britain affords an illustrious comment on the excellence of the institution.

Notes

1. The celebrated Montesquieu, speaking of them, says: "Of the three powers above mentioned, the judiciary is next to nothing." *Spirit of Laws*, vol. I., page 186.
2. Idem, page 181.
3. Vide "Protest of the Minority of the Convention of Pennsylvania," Martin's Speech, etc.

Consider the source and the audience

- Hamilton is writing to audiences who are skeptical of the power in the new Constitution he wants them to ratify. Article III of the Constitution, setting out the judiciary, is among the briefest and least specific of the constitutional provisions precisely because so many people objected to a strong and powerful federal court system. How is this factor likely to shape the arguments he makes here?

Lay out the argument, the values, and the assumptions

- We know from a variety of sources that Hamilton was an advocate of a strong federal government. In this essay, how does he balance his own preferences with the necessity to persuade people who fear a strong government?

- What are Hamilton's major arguments for lifetime tenure of federal judges?
- Why does he think that judicial review does not unduly elevate the Court over the legislature?
- How does he think judges can be kept from exercising their will rather than their judgment?

Uncover the evidence

- Does Hamilton provide any evidence to support his arguments? What are the advantages and limitations of relying on logic and rhetoric to support one's arguments?

Evaluate the conclusion

- Hamilton believes that there "can be no room to doubt" that federal judges should be appointed for life, and he incidentally believes that it is okay to give them the power to strike down the laws passed by Congress if they do not, in their judgment, conform to the Constitution. Has he made his case?
- Is his argument consistent with his initial contention that the courts will constitute the least dangerous and weakest branch of government?

Sort out the political implications

- In what ways does judicial politics today depart from Hamilton's plan? Is the judiciary truly independent of the other two branches? Does politics intrude, despite Hamilton's precaution of providing lifetime tenure?
- What would Hamilton think about the Supreme Court's ruling in *Bush v. Gore?*

Public Opinion

How much should public opinion count in a democracy? Do we want our representatives to be slaves to what we say we want? Do we think they should ignore us and steer their own course? When Bill Clinton was running for president, he was nicknamed "Slick Willie" for his practice of changing his issue stances according to the polls. Eight years later, George W. Bush promised that his administration would not be run by pollsters because, he said, true leaders make up their own minds and are not swayed by public opinion. The difference in these two leadership styles boils down to a difference over a fundamental question of democracy: Should what citizens think matter to their representatives, or should those representatives follow their own judgment and consciences?

People who support Bush's view on this issue claim that citizens are too ignorant, busy, or irrational to have opinions of the quality that we want represented in government, and that our representatives are better qualified to know what we want. Opponents of that view claim that no one is better qualified than the American public to decide what Americans want, and that the essence of democracy is responsiveness to public opinion. Many social scientists claim that even though people are busy and do not focus on politics on a daily basis, they still gather enough information to make informed choices about the things that affect their interests.

Regardless of whether they think public opinion ought to matter, most politicians act as if it does matter. Elected officials, after all, have to contend with what the public thinks during elections, even if they disregard polls at other times. And, as it turns out, few politicians disregard polls altogether. Indeed, nationwide, pollsters have gotten into the habit of asking Americans what they think about a variety of issues, and they have scientifically honed the instruments with which they measure opinions. They do this for lots of reasons: Marketers want to find out what consumers want to buy, politicians want to know what voters want them to do, and everyday Americans want to know what their neighbors and colleagues are up to. There is no denying that, in American politics today, polling is big business.

The articles in this chapter illustrate the debates surrounding the role of public opinion polls in democratic governance. An article from the *American Spectator*, a conservative opinion journal, laments the ignorance of the American public on a host of issues and is pessimistic about its effect on public policy. The second article, from the *Chronicle of Higher Education*, discusses the use of "Big Data" to forecast presidential elections and the controversy surrounding it. In the third piece, Mark Mellman, a Democratic pollster, questions the interpretation of a poll on Americans' views on abortion. In the fourth piece, from the *Washington Monthly*, an investigative, anti-establishment journal, Joshua Green compares the polling efforts of Presidents Bill Clinton and George W. Bush. Finally, we turn to George Gallup, the father of opinion polling in America, for the classic defense of public opinion's role in democratic government.

● ●

11.1 Party On, Dudes!
Ignorance Is the Curse of the Information Age
Matthew Robinson, *American Spectator*

Why We Chose This Piece

One of the great debates among scholars of public opinion is whether the American public is informed regarding politics and policy. If not, then public opinion polls may measure nothing but a bunch of noise. The author of this article is clear where he stands in the debate. Matthew Robinson bemoans the ignorance of the American public and its general unfitness for the task of self-governance. In a way, he is writing about all of us. As you read the article, poll yourself. Do you think the Constitution guarantees you a job? Do you know who Alexander Hamilton is? Can you identify the chief justice of the U.S. Supreme Court? Do you know what DNA is? Do you know who won the battle of Yorktown? Can you correctly estimate the proportion of the U.S. population that is homeless or the number of abortions performed every year?

Also, ask yourself whether these kinds of questions matter. If you don't know who won the battle of Yorktown, does that mean you don't have a well-thought-out position on abortion? If you have forgotten who exactly Alexander Hamilton was, does that mean that you can't cast an informed vote in a presidential election? In other words, how important is this kind of knowledge to our ability to formulate opinions on public matters and to understand our own political interests? If we do not match the democratic ideal of interested and informed citizens, should our opinions count?

Selection published: March/April 2002

Almost any look at what the average citizen knows about politics is bound to be discouraging. Political scientists are nearly unanimous on the subject of voter ignorance. The average American citizen not only lacks basic knowledge but also holds beliefs that are contradictory and inconsistent. Here is a small sample of what Americans "know":

Nearly one-third of Americans (29 percent) think the Constitution guarantees a job. Forty-two percent think it guarantees health care. And 75 percent think it guarantees a high school education.

Forty-five percent think the communist tenet "from each according to his abilities, to each according to his needs" is part of the U.S. Constitution.

More Americans recognize the Nike advertising slogan "Just Do It" than know where the right to "life, liberty, and the pursuit of happiness" is set forth (79 percent versus 47 percent). 90 percent know that Bill Gates is the founder of the company that created the Windows operating system. Just over half (53 percent) correctly identified Alexander Hamilton as a Founding Father.

Fewer than half of adults (47 percent) can name their own Representative in Congress. Fewer than half of voters could identify whether their congressman voted for the use of force in the Persian Gulf War.

Just 30 percent of adults could name Newt Gingrich as the congressman who led Republican congressional candidates in signing the Contract with America. Six months after the GOP took Congress, 64 percent admitted they did not know.

A 1998 poll by the Pew Research Center for the People and the Press showed that 56 percent of Americans could not name a single Democratic candidate for president; 63 percent knew the name "Bush," but it wasn't clear that voters connected the name to George W. Bush.

According to a January 2000 Gallup poll, 66 percent of Americans could correctly name Regis Philbin when asked who hosts *Who Wants to Be a Millionaire*, but only 6 percent could correctly name Dennis Hastert when asked to name the Speaker of the House of Representatives in Washington.

Political scientists Michael X. Delli Carpini and Scott Keeter studied 3,700 questions surveying the public's political knowledge from the 1930's to the present. They discovered that people tend to remember or identify trivial details about political leaders, focusing on personalities or simply latching onto the policies that the press plays up. For example, the most commonly known fact about George Bush while he was president was that he hated broccoli, and during the 1992 presidential campaign, although 89 percent of the public knew that Vice President Quayle was feuding with the television character Murphy Brown, only 19 percent could characterize Bill Clinton's record on the environment.

Their findings demonstrate the full absurdity of public knowledge: More people could identify Judge Wapner (the longtime host of the television series *The People's Court*) than could identify Chief Justices Warren Burger or William Rehnquist. More people had heard of John Lennon than of Karl Marx. More Americans could identify comedian-actor Bill Cosby than could name either of their U.S. senators. More people knew who said, "What's up, Doc," "Hi ho, Silver," or "Come up and see me sometime" than "Give me liberty or give me death," "The only thing we have to fear is fear itself," or "Speak softly and carry a big stick." More people knew that Pete Rose was accused of gambling than could name any of the five U.S. senators accused in the late 1980s of unethical conduct in the savings and loan scandal.

In 1986, the National Election Survey found that almost 24 percent of the general public did not know who George Bush was or that he was in his second term as vice president of the United States. "People at this level of inattentiveness can have only the haziest idea of the policy alternatives about which pollsters regularly ask, and such ideas as they do have must often be relatively innocent of the effects of exposure to elite discourse," writes UCLA political science professor John R. Zaller.

All of this would appear to be part of a broader trend of public ignorance that extends far beyond politics. Lack of knowledge on simple matters can reach staggering levels. In a 1996 study by the National Science Foundation, fewer than half of American adults polled (47 percent) knew that the earth takes one year to orbit the sun. Only about 9 percent could describe in their own words what a molecule is, and only 21 percent knew what DNA is.

Esoteric information? That's hard to say. One simple science-related question that has grown to have major political importance is whether police ought to genetically tag convicted criminals in the hopes of linking them to unsolved crimes. In other words, should police track the DNA of a convicted burglar to see if he is guilty of other crimes? Obviously issues of privacy and government power are relevant here. Yet how can a poll about this issue make sense if the citizenry doesn't understand the scientific terms of debate? Asking an evaluative question seems pointless.

The next generation of voters—those who will undoubtedly be asked to answer even tougher questions about politics and science—are hardly doing any better on the basics. A 2000 study by the American Council of Trustees and Alumni found that 81 percent of seniors at the nation's fifty-five top colleges scored a D or F on high school-level history exams. It turns out that most college seniors—including those from such elite universities as Harvard, Stanford, and the University of California—do not know the men or ideas that have shaped American freedom. Here are just a few examples from Losing America's Memory: Historical Illiteracy in the 21st Century, focusing on people's lack of knowledge about our First Citizen—the man whose respect for the laws of the infant republic set the standard for virtue and restraint in office.

Barely one in three students knew that George Washington was the American general at the battle of Yorktown—the battle that won the war for independence.

Only 42 percent could identify Washington with the line "First in war, first in peace, first in the hearts of his countrymen."

Only a little more than half knew that Washington's farewell address warned against permanent alliances with foreign governments.

And when it comes to actually explaining the ideas that preserve freedom and restrain government, the college seniors performed just as miserably.

More than one in three were clueless about the division of power set forth in the U.S. Constitution.

Only 22 percent of these seniors could identify the source of the phrase "government of the people, by the people, and for the people" (from Lincoln's Gettysburg Address).

Yet 99 percent of college seniors knew the crude cartoon characters Beavis and Butthead, and 98 percent could identify gangsta rapper Snoop Doggy Dogg.

Apparent ignorance of basic civics can be especially dangerous. Americans often "project" power onto institutions with little understanding of the Constitution or the law. Almost six of ten Americans (59 percent) think the president, not Congress, has the power to declare war. Thirty-five percent of Americans believe the president has the power to adjourn Congress at his will. Almost half (49 percent) think he has the power to suspend the Constitution (49 percent). And six in ten think the chief executive appoints judges to the federal courts without the approval of the Senate.

Some political scientists charge that American ignorance tends to help institutions and parties in power. That is hardly the active vigilance by the citizenry that the founders advocated. Political scientists continue to debate the role of ignorance and the future of democracy when voters are so woefully ignorant. As journalist Christopher Shea writes, "Clearly, voter ignorance poses problems for democratic theory: Politicians, the representatives of the people, are being elected by people who do not know their names or their platforms. Elites are committing the nation to major treaties and sweeping policies that most voters don't even know exist."

Professors Delli Carpini and Keeter discovered, for example, that most Americans make fundamental errors on some of the most contested and heavily covered political questions. "Americans grossly overestimate the average profit made by American corporations, the percentage of the U.S. population that is poor or homeless, and the percentage of the world population that is malnourished," they write. "And, despite twelve years of antiabortion administrations, Americans substantially underestimate the number of abortions performed every year."

With most voters unable to even name their congressperson or senators during an election year, the clear winner is the establishment candidate. Studies by Larry Bartels at Princeton University show that mere name recognition is enough to give incumbents a 5-percentage-point advantage over challengers: Most voters in the election booth can't identify a single position of the incumbent, but if they've seen the candidate's name before, that can be enough to secure their vote. (In many cases, voters can't even recognize the names of incumbents.)

Media polls are typically searching in vain for hard-nosed public opinion that simply isn't there. Polls force people to say they are leaning toward a particular candidate, but when voters are asked the more open-ended question "Whom do you favor for the presidency?" the number of undecided voters rises. The mere practice, in polling, of naming the candidates yields results that convey a false sense of what voters know. When Harvard's "Vanishing Voter Project" asked voters their presidential preferences without giving the names of candidates, they routinely found that the number of undecided voters was much higher than in media polls. Just three weeks before the 2000 election, 14 percent of voters still hadn't made up their minds.

Even when polling covers subjects on which a person should have direct knowledge, it can yield misleading results because of basic ignorance. The non-partisan Center for Studying Health System Change (HSC) found that how people rate their health care is attributable to the type of plan they *think* they are in more than their actual health insurance. The center asked twenty thousand privately insured people what they thought of their coverage, their doctor, and their treatment. But instead of just taking their opinions and impressions, the center also looked at what coverage each respondent actually had.

Nearly a quarter of Americans misidentified the coverage they had. Eleven percent didn't know they were in an HMO, and another 13 percent thought they were in an HMO but were *not*. Yet when people believed they were in a much-maligned HMO (even when they actually had another kind of insurance), their perceived satisfaction with their health care was lower than that of people who believed they had non-HMO coverage (even when they were in an HMO). Similarly, on nearly all ten measures studied by the center, those HMO enrollees who thought they had a different kind of insurance gave satisfaction ratings similar to those who actually had those other kinds of insurance.

Once center researchers adjusted for incorrect self-identification, the differences between HMO and non-HMO enrollees nearly vanished. Even on something as personal as health care, citizens display a striking and debilitating ignorance that quietly undermines many polling results.

After looking at the carnage of polls that test voter knowledge rather than impressions, James L. Payne concluded in his 1991 book *The Culture of Spending*:

> Surveys have repeatedly found that voters are remarkably ignorant about even simple, dramatic features of the political landscape. The vast majority of voters cannot recall the names of congressional candidates in the most recent election; they cannot use the labels "liberal" and "conservative" meaningfully; they do not know which party controls Congress; they are wildly wrong about elementary facts about the federal budget; and they do not know how their congressmen vote on even quite salient policy questions. In other words, they are generally incapable of rewarding or punishing their congressman for his action on spending bills.

Ignorance of basic facts such as a candidate's name or position isn't the only reason to question the efficacy of polling in such a dispiriting universe. Because polls have become "players in the political process," their influence is felt in the policy realm, undercutting efforts to educate because they assume respondents' knowledge and focus on the horse race. Is it correct to say that Americans oppose or support various policies when they don't even have a grasp of basic facts relating to those policies? For instance, in 1995, GrassRoots Research found that 83 percent of those polled underestimated the average family's tax burden. Taxes for a four-person family earning $35,000 are 54 percent higher than most people think. Naturally when practical-minded Americans look at political issues, their perceptions of reality influence which solutions they find acceptable. If they perceive that there are fewer abortions or lower taxes than there really are, these misperceptions may affect the kinds of policy prescriptions they endorse. They might change their views if introduced to the facts. In this sense, the unreflective reporting on public opinion about these policy issues is deceptive.

The Wall Street Journal editorial page provides another example of how ignorance affects public debate. Media reports during the 1995 struggle between the Republicans in Congress and the Clinton White House continually asserted that the public strongly opposed the GOP's efforts to slow the growth of Medicare spending. A poll by Public Opinion Strategies asked one thousand Americans not what they felt but what they actually *knew* about the GOP plan. Twenty-seven percent said they thought the GOP would cut Medicare spending by $4,000 per recipient. Almost one in four (24 percent) said it would keep spending the same. Another 25 percent didn't know. Only 22 percent knew the correct answer: The plan would increase spending to $6,700 per recipient.

Public Opinion's pollsters then told respondents that true result of the GOP plan and explained: "[U]nder the plan that recently passed by Congress, spending on Medicare will increase 45 percent over the next seven years, which is twice the projected rate of inflation." How did such hard facts change public opinion about Medicare solutions? Six of ten Americans said that the GOP's proposed Medicare spending was too *high*. Another 29 percent said it was about right. Only 2 percent said it was too *low*.

Indeed polling and the media may gain their ability to influence results from voter ignorance. When a polling question introduces new facts (or any facts at all), voters are presented with a reframed political issue and thus may have a new opinion. Voters are continually asked about higher spending, new programs, and the best way to solve social ills with government spending. But how does the knowledge base (or lack of knowledge) affect the results of a polling question? That is simply unknown. When asked in a June 2000 *Washington Post* poll how much money the federal government gives to the nation's public schools, only 31 percent chose the correct answer. Although only 10 percent admitted to not knowing the correct answer, fully 60 percent of registered voters claimed they knew but were wrong. Is there any doubt that voters' knowledge, or lack thereof, affects the debate about whether to raise school spending to ever higher levels?

Reporters often claim that the public supports various policies, and they use such sentiment as an indicator of the electoral prospects of favored candidates. But this, too, can be misleading. Take, for instance, the results of a survey taken by The Polling Company for the Center for Security Policy about the Strategic Defense Initiative. Some 54 percent of respondents thought that the U.S. military had the capability to destroy a ballistic missile before it could hit an American city and do damage. Another 20 percent didn't know or refused to answer. Only 27 percent correctly said that the U.S. military could not destroy a missile.

What's interesting is that although 70 percent of those polled said they were concerned about the possibility of ballistic missile attack, the actual level of ignorance was very high. The Polling Company went on to tell those polled that "government documents indicate that the U.S. military cannot destroy even a single incoming missile." The responses were interesting. Nearly one in five said they were "shocked and angry" by the revelation. Another 28 percent said they were "very surprised," and 17 percent were "somewhat surprised." Only 22 percent said they were "not surprised at all." Finally 14 percent were "skeptical because [they] believe that the documents are inaccurate."

Beyond simply skewing poll results, ignorance is actually amplified by polling. Perhaps the most amazing example of the extent of ignorance can be found in Larry Sabato's 1981 book *The Rise of Political Consultants*. Citizens were asked: "Some people say the 1975 Public Affairs Act should be repealed. Do you agree or disagree that it should be repealed?" Nearly one in four (24 percent) said they wanted it repealed. Another 19 percent wanted it to remain in effect. Fifty-seven percent didn't know what should be done. What's interesting is that there was no such thing as the 1975 Public Affairs Act. But for 43 percent of those polled, simply asking that question was enough to create public opinion.

Ignorance can threaten even the most democratic institutions and safeguards. In September 1997, the Center for Media and Public Affairs conducted one of the largest surveys ever on American views of the Fourth Estate. Fully 84 percent of Americans are willing to "turn to the government to require that the news media give equal coverage to all sides of controversial issues." Seven in ten back court-imposed fines for inaccurate or biased reporting. And just over half (53 percent) think that journalists should be licensed. Based on sheer numbers—in the absence of the rule of law and dedication to the Bill of Rights—there is enough support to put curbs on the free speech that most journalists (rightly) consider one of the most important bulwarks of liberty.

In an era when Americans have neither the time nor the interest to track politics closely, the power of the pollster to shape public opinion is almost unparalleled when united with the media agenda.

For elected leaders, voter ignorance is something they have to confront when they attempt to make a case for new policies or reforms. But for the media, ignorance isn't an obstacle. It's an opportunity for those asking the questions—whether pollster or media polling director—to drive debate. As more time is devoted to media pundits, journalists, and pollsters, and less to candidates and leaders, the effect is a negative one: Public opinion becomes more important as arbiter for the chattering classes. But in a knowledge vacuum, public opinion also becomes more plastic and more subject to manipulation, however well intentioned.

Pollsters often try to bridge the gap in public knowledge by providing basic definitions of terms as part of their questions. But this presents a new problem: By writing the questions, pollsters are put in a position of power, particularly when those questions will be used in a media story. The story—if the poll is the story—is limited by the questions asked, the definitions supplied, and the answers that respondents are given to choose from.

The elevation of opinion without context or reference to knowledge exacerbates a problem of modern democracies. Self-expression may work in NEA-funded art, but it robs the political process of the communication and discussion that marries compromise with principle. Clearly "opinion" isn't the appropriate word for the melange of impressions and sentiment that are presented as the public's beliefs in countless newspaper and television stories. If poll respondents lack a solid grasp of the facts, surveys give us little more than narcissistic opinion.

As intelligent and precise thinking declines, all that remains is a chaos of ideologies in which the lowest human appetites rule. In her essay "Truth and Politics," historian Hannah Arendt writes: "Facts inform opinions, and opinions, inspired by different interests and passions, can differ widely and still be legitimate as long as they respect factual truth. Freedom of opinion is a farce unless factual information is guaranteed and facts themselves are not in dispute."

If ignorance is rife in a republic, what do polls and the constant media attention to them do to deliberative democracy? As Hamilton put it, American government is based on "reflection and choice." Modern-day radical egalitarians—journalists and pollsters who believe that polls are the definitive voice of the people—may applaud the ability of the most uninformed citizen to be heard, but few if any of these champions of polling ever write about or discuss the implications of ignorance to a representative democracy. This is the dirtiest secret of polling.

Absent from most polling stories is the honest disclosure that American ignorance is driving public affairs. Basic ignorance of civic questions gives us reason to doubt the veracity of most polls. Were Americans armed with strongly held opinions and well-grounded knowledge of civic matters, they would not be open to manipulation by the wording of polls. This is one of the strongest reasons to question the effect of polls on representative government.

Pollsters assume and often control the presentation of the relevant facts. As a blunt instrument, the pollster's questions fail to explore what the contrary data may be. This is one reason that public opinion can differ so widely from one poll to another. When the citizens of a republic lack basic knowledge of political facts and cannot process ideas critically, uninformed opinion becomes even more potent in driving people. Worse, when the media fail to think critically about the lines of dispute on political questions, polls that are supposed to explore opinion will simplify and even mislead political leaders as well as the electorate.

When the media drive opinion by constant polling, the assumption of an educated public undermines the process of public deliberation that actually educates voters. Ideas are no longer honed, language isn't refined, and debate is truncated. The common ground needed for compromise and peaceful action is eroded because the discussion about facts and the parameters of the question are lost. In the frenzy to judge who wins and who loses, the media erode what it is to be a democracy. Moments of change become opportunities for spin, not for new, bold responses to the exigencies of history.

Not only are polls influenced, shaped, and even dominated by voter ignorance, but so is political debate. The evidence shows that ignorance is being projected into public debate because of the pervasiveness of polls. Polls are leading to the democratization of ignorance in the public square by ratifying ill-formed opinions, with the march of the mob instigated by an impatient and unreflective media. Polls—especially in an age marked by their proliferation—are serving as broadcasting towers of ignorance.

Political science professor Rogan Kersh notes, "Public ignorance and apathy toward most policy matters have been constant (or have grown worse) for over three decades. Yet the same period has seen increasing reliance on finely tuned instruments for measuring popular opinion, and more vigorous applications of the results in policy making." And here is the paradox in the Age of Polls: Pollsters and political scientists are still unclear about the full consequences of running a republic on the basis of opinion polls. The cost of voter ignorance is high, especially in a nation with a vast and sprawling government that, even for the most plugged-in elites, is too complicated to understand. Media polling that does not properly inform viewers and readers of its limitations serves only to give the facade of a healthy democracy, while consultants, wordsmiths, and polling units gently massage questions, set the news agenda, and then selectively report results. It is like the marionette player who claims (however invisible the strings) that the puppet moves on his own.

Consider the source and the audience

- Robinson is an editor at the *American Spectator*, a conservative opinion journal. How might the conservative nature of the journal affect the evaluation of public opinion presented here?

Lay out the argument, the values, and the assumptions

- What is Robinson's view of how democracy should work? Is there a place for public opinion polls in his view? For voting? What views should be represented?
- Robinson believes that American public discourse is in trouble because of unscrupulous pollsters, shoddy journalism, and ignorant voters. Are polls influenced by voter ignorance, or is voter ignorance a product of manipulative polls?
- Does Robinson show a link between voter ignorance and bad public policy? Do voters need the information he believes they don't have in order to make sound political decisions?

Uncover the evidence

- Robinson's chief concern is voter ignorance, and he cites a lot of poll evidence and scholarly opinion to illustrate it. Do we need to know anything more about the polling evidence he cites in order to evaluate it?
- Does Robinson provide evidence that voter ignorance and irresponsible polling actually drive public affairs?

Evaluate the conclusion

- Robinson makes a number of observations about the American voter. Are the conclusions he draws from them clear? Do they necessarily follow from his assumptions and evidence?

Sort out the political implications

- If Robinson were writing the rules, what role would the American public play in U.S. government? What role would the media play?

11.2 The Rise of the Poll Quants (or, Why Sam Wang Might Eat a Bug)

Tom Bartlett, *Chronicle of Higher Education*

Why We Chose This Piece

Many students may be familiar with the book (or, more likely, the movie) Moneyball, *in which the general manager of the Oakland A's uses a player's previous performance to predict his future success (or failure). Sabermetrics—the analysis of baseball through objective evidence—has become all the rage. Baseball is known for*

Selection published: November 5, 2012

having statistics on almost everything imaginable, so there are plenty of data to analyze. But it is not just baseball that is flooded with data. The public is inundated with data in today's presidential elections as well. The question is: What to do with all of that data? Some people—such as the subjects of this article—believe that, as with baseball, the data can be used to more accurately predict future outcomes (in this case, the winner of the election). Others, generally pundits whose job is to talk about elections, are skeptical. Like the scouts in Moneyball *who complained that relying totally on statistics takes out the human element in evaluation, some pundits question the predictive power of the data. We chose this article because it does a nice job of discussing this debate, and it presents the "science" aspect of political science. As the article makes clear, this debate is far from settled. Pay attention in 2014. You will likely hear many of the same arguments made when predicting who will win various gubernatorial seats or which party will control Congress.*

If you watched *Meet the Press* this past weekend, you learned that the presidential election was "statistically tied" and could be a "photo finish." The Associated Press predicted a "nail biter." *The Philadelphia Inquirer* threw up its hands, saying the vote was just "too close to call."

Sam Wang begs to differ. By day, Wang is a neuroscientist at Princeton University, where his lab uses lasers to monitor the chemical signals of cells in the cerebellum. He co-wrote a recent paper that found that mathematics and science majors are more likely than humanities students to have a sibling on the autism spectrum.

But in the evenings, after his wife and 5-year-old daughter are in bed, the 45-year-old turns his attention to polls. Since 2004, Wang has used his considerable data-crunching chops to forecast elections, publishing his results on Princeton Election Consortium, a very popular blog with an extremely dull name. He expects to log around one million hits on Election Day alone.

His posts are engaging and often droll, but it's the numbers that are the real draw. Wang, as I write this, believes that President Obama has a 99.8-percent chance of winning the election. No need for nail biting.

Actually, 99.8 percent is his Bayesian prediction, which refers to the branch of logic that uses statistics to determine probabilities. In another model, which assumes that opinions could fluctuate in either direction—what he calls random drift—Obama has a 98.2-percent chance of winning. The upshot: According to Wang, it is "highly implausible" that Mitt Romney will add the White House to his list of homes.

In 2008, Nate Silver made forecasting elections nerd-cool. Silver was already known as a baseball statistician when he turned his mathematical talents to national politics. As he writes in his new book *The Signal and the Noise: Why So Many Predictions Fail—but Some Don't*, he figured that someone "could look like a genius simply by doing some fairly basic research into what really has predictive power in a political campaign."

He became that someone, starting a blog he titled FiveThirtyEight, after the total number of Electoral College votes, which has since been snatched up by *The New York Times*. His posts attract hundreds of comments, and he has more than 300,000 followers on Twitter.

Wang doesn't have nearly as large an audience, but it's been growing. He got into the game for pretty much the same reasons as Silver: He thought he could bring some statistical rigor to a discourse dominated by talking heads nattering on about the number of yard signs in a random neighborhood or the volume of cheering at a swing-state rally. "I'm use[d] to solving the problem of taking a data set and extracting something when there's a lot of noise," Wang says. "That's something I do every day in my work. The presidential race was something that was crying out for that."

He learned from Silver's quick success that audiences wanted more than statistical breakdowns. They wanted explanation, banter, personality. His posts are still driven by numbers, but you also get a dose of Wang's sense of humor, like the way he has relentlessly mocked the notion of Romney's momentum ("Ro-mentum!") in recent weeks. He slapped John Dickerson, who writes about politics for *Slate*, for arguing that Romney was "peaking at just the right moment." Wrote Wang: "Ah, yes. The Great Election of October 13, 2012. I remember it well."

Like Silver, his posts attract hundreds of comments, but he moderates them to keep the discussion on track. Wang is not interested in fostering the kind of low-brow, partisan blather that's the hallmark of sites like *The Huffington Post* and *The Daily Caller*. He favors quantitative comments, mixed with the occasional crack about the possibility that Wolf Blitzer is an android.

The newest kid on the forecasting block is Drew Linzer, an assistant professor of political science at Emory University, who started a site called Votamatic this past summer. He designed it as a companion to his published research and as a way of informing an audience slightly broader than the people who thumb through political-science journals in their spare time. He's succeeded: Votamatic gets tens of thousands of hits a day.

So what exactly do these guys do? Basically, they take polls, aggregate the results, and make predictions. They each do it somewhat differently. Silver factors in state polls and national polls, along with other indicators, like monthly job numbers. Wang focuses on state polls exclusively. Linzer's model looks at historical factors several months before the election but, as voting draws nearer, weights polls more heavily.

At the heart of all their models, though, are the state polls. That makes sense because, thanks to the Electoral College system, it's the state outcomes that matter. It's possible to win the national vote and still end up as the head of a cable-television channel rather than the leader of the free world. But also, as Wang explains, it's easier for pollsters to find representative samples in a particular state. Figuring out which way Arizona or even Florida might go isn't as tough as sizing up a country as big and diverse as the United States. "The race is so close that, at a national level, it's easy to make a small error and be a little off," Wang says. "So it's easier to call states. They give us a sharper, more accurate picture."

But the forecasters don't just look at one state poll. While most news organizations trot out the latest, freshest poll and discuss it in isolation, these guys plug it into their models. One poll might be an outlier; a whole bunch of polls are likely to get closer to the truth. Or so the idea goes. Wang uses all the state polls, but gives more weight to those that survey likely voters, as opposed to those who are just registered to vote. Silver has his own special sauce that he doesn't entirely divulge.

Both Wang and Linzer find it annoying that individual polls are hyped to make it seem as if the race is closer than it is, or to create the illusion that Romney and Obama are trading the lead from day to day. They're not. According to the state polls, when taken together, the race has been fairly stable for weeks, and Obama has remained well ahead and, going into Election Day, is a strong favorite. "The best information comes from combining all the polls together," says Linzer, who projects that Obama will get 326 electoral votes, well over the 270 required to win. "I want to give readers the right information, even if it's more boring."

While it may not seem likely, poll aggregation is a threat to the supremacy of the punditocracy. In the past week, you could sense that some high-profile media types were being made slightly uncomfortable by the bespectacled quants, with their confusing mathematical models and zippy computer programs. The *New York Times* columnist David Brooks said pollsters who offered projections were citizens of "sillyland."

Maybe, but the recent track record in sillyland is awfully solid. In the 2008 presidential election, Silver correctly predicted 49 of 50 states. Wang was off by only one electoral vote. Meanwhile, as Silver writes in his book, numerous pundits confidently predicted a John McCain victory based on little more than intestinal twinges.

Simon Jackman thinks we're in the midst of a shift in the world of political predictions. His poll-averaging model, Pollster, which is published by *The Huffington Post*, is forecasting a narrow Obama win (277 electoral votes). Jackman, who is a professor of political science at Stanford University and author of *Bayesian Analysis for the Social Sciences*, thinks that models like his and the others present "a real challenge to the conventional great oracle pundit." Most journalists are ill equipped to interpret data, he says (and few journalists would disagree), so they view statistics with skepticism and occasionally, in the case of Brooks, disdain. "The data-driven people are going to win in the long run," Jackman says.

He sees it as part of the rise of what's being called Big Data—that is, using actual information to make decisions. As Jackman points out, Big Data is already changing sports and business, and it may be that pundits are the equivalents of the baseball scouts in Michael Lewis's book *Moneyball*, caring more about the gracefulness of a batter's swing than whether he gets on base. "Why," Jackman wonders, "should political commentary be exempt from this movement?"

That's John Sides's point, too. Sides, an associate professor of political science at George Washington University who blogs for The Monkey Cage and has written for FiveThirtyEight, is exasperated by articles that speculate on momentum and refer vaguely to polls. "Some polls say? Which polls say?," Sides exclaims. "It's not that all of politics can be explained by science. It's just that, for God's sake, we can bring a little bit of science into our analysis of politics."

Last week the professional pundit and MSNBC host Joe Scarborough ranted that people like Silver, Wang, Linzer, and Jackman—who think the presidential race is "anything but a tossup"—should be kept away from their computers "because they're jokes." Silver responded by challenging Scarborough to bet $1,000 on Romney (in the form of a donation to the American Red Cross) if he was so sure. This led to hand-wringing about whether it was appropriate for someone affiliated with *The New York Times* to make crass public wagers.

But the bet seemed like an important symbolic moment. The poll aggregators have skin in the game. They've made statistical forecasts and published them, not just gut-feeling guesses on Sunday-morning talk shows. And, in Silver's case, as a former professional poker player, he is willing to back it up with something tangible. Alex Tabarrok, an economist and blogger for Marginal Revolution, applauded, calling such bets a "tax on bullshit."

Wang is willing to put it on the line as well, albeit in a more gustatory manner. If Romney wins Pennsylvania, a state many pundits have called a tossup, he wrote on his blog that he will "eat a bug." If Romney wins Ohio, he will eat "a really big bug."

He promised to post the photos, too.

What will the poll quants be doing on election night? Linzer says he will be "watching TV with my laptop and ignoring my friends." Wang doesn't really enjoy election night because the information dribbles in, and nothing is entirely clear until the next morning. It's frustrating for a numbers guy. If he had the willpower, he says, he would avoid the spectacle and go to bed early. Instead, he will probably do what he did in 2008. "I was with a bunch of people who were Obama supporters. They were very pleased about Obama being ahead on election night, and I was concerned that early Virginia returns didn't match my projections," he says. "That tells you something about how quasi-autistic we are over here."

Consider the source and the audience

- The *Chronicle of Higher Education* is read primarily by academics and college and university administrators. Why would they be interested in an article on polling?

Lay out the argument, the values, and the assumptions

- Why are the statisticians and the pundits at odds?
- Why do people like Wang and Silver believe their methods are better than those used by political pundits? What problems do the pundits have with the statisticians' methods?
- Why did the statisticians believe that the race was not very close even though national polling indicated that it was?

Uncover the evidence

- Wang and the other statisticians rely on polls to make their predictions. Do we need to know more about their methods? How do their methods differ? Why might that matter?
- What kinds of evidence do pundits often use?

Evaluate the conclusion

- The argument made in this article is easy to evaluate. Were the statisticians correct in their predictions? Why might pundits still not be convinced of the accuracy of the predictions?
- Simon Jackman states that "the data-driven people are going to win in the long run." Why does he feel this way? Do you agree?

Sort out the political implications

- Why might it be problematic if election forecasts are inaccurate, or does it matter?
- Do election forecasts serve an important purpose, or do they simply have entertainment value for the public? How might campaigns view them differently than the public does?

11.3 Pro-Life and Pro-Choice

Mark Mellman, TheHill.com

Why We Chose This Piece

It seems like hundreds of polls are released every day that tell people how Americans feel about numerous issues. Interpreting those poll results can be hard work. It is easy simply to accept the results of the polls at face value, but sometimes you need to dig a little deeper to understand what—if anything—the poll results actually mean.

Here, Mark Mellman, a Democratic pollster, questions the interpretation of a Gallup poll probing Americans' opinions on abortion. We chose this piece because, unlike Matthew Robinson, the author of the first selection in this chapter, Mellman wants you to be critical of polls, not skeptical of them. He is, after all, a pollster, and he believes that when polls are implemented correctly, they can provide valuable information. Also, the focus of the article is abortion, a highly salient, emotionally charged issue. Yet even on an issue such as abortion, results may differ based on how the question is asked.

Finally, Mellman's critique is interesting because Gallup isn't some ragtag polling operation. It is considered by many to be the granddaddy of polling organizations. Indeed, the namesake of the organization, and also the author of the last piece in this chapter, is thought of as the father of opinion polling in America. Gallup is an organization that has credibility; as a result, people may be willing to accept its poll results as fact, something that Mellman clearly believes is problematic.

Selection published: May 19, 2009

Obtaining meaningful poll results requires asking meaningful questions. It seems obvious, but too often this basic rule is observed in the breech.

Typically, after some useless result escapes into the ether, reporters and interest groups proceed to spin some new theory of public opinion based on faulty analysis of a meaningless question.

Last week's Gallup poll on abortion followed this oft-repeated pattern. Gallup confined itself to reporting the accurate, if misleading, result—"51 percent of Americans call[ing] themselves 'pro-life' on the issue of abortion and 42 percent 'pro-choice.' This is the first time a majority of U.S. adults have identified themselves as pro-life since Gallup began asking this question in 1995."

A *Wall Street Journal* blog twisted the result to suggest a substantive interpretation not in evidence—"A majority of Americans now say they oppose abortion rights, according to a Gallup poll released today." Leave it to those who want to make all abortions illegal to move way beyond the facts, citing the poll results as proof the anti-abortion cause "is a vibrant, growing, youthful movement."

What did these Gallup results actually reveal about American public opinion? Damn little.

First, as Professor Charles Franklin points out, the sample for this particular Gallup poll was much more Republican than most others Gallup has done, leading more respondents to identify themselves as "pro-life."

More problematic is the language itself. While the political class readily identifies with words like "pro-choice" and "pro-life," many voters do not. In a large national survey we conducted, fewer than half of respondents defined the term "pro-choice" in a way even remotely connected to the abortion debate. Only 28 percent made explicit reference to abortion in their response. Another 20 percent offered a vague definition, usually about trusting women.

Half, however, were not even close. "Having the choice to change your mind if you want to—about anything." "The choice to live, the choice to die." "Choosing your religion for me." Thus, questions asking voters to embrace one of these labels are not necessarily even tapping into the abortion debate, because so few know what the terms mean.

In addition, accepting one of those labels does not necessarily relate to real public policy choices in any meaningful way. For instance, in our survey, nearly a third of those who called themselves "pro-life" reject the view that "the government should pass more laws restricting the availability of abortions," saying instead "the government should not interfere with a woman's access to abortion." Would anti-choice leaders hold up as one of their own a politician who opposed laws restricting abortion?

That is exactly where the American people are—by 62 percent to 27, voters oppose additional legal restrictions on the availability of abortion.

Roe v. Wade is at the heart of the public policy debate. A week after Gallup's poll, CNN and Opinion Research Corp. defined the decision this way: "The 1973 *Roe v. Wade* decision established a woman's constitutional right to an abortion at least in the first three months of pregnancy." Sixty-eight percent wanted to keep *Roe* in place—hardly the position of those celebrating Gallup's result. Just 30 percent supported overturning *Roe*.

In short, the data tell us Americans oppose government restrictions on abortion and want to keep *Roe* in place, while identifying themselves as pro-life—a term many do not understand.

Useful poll questions on public policy meet at least two key criteria. They use words and concepts respondents understand and they employ categories that reflect the real terms of the debate. Asking people whether they are "pro-choice" or "pro-life" meets neither of those criteria and therefore does more to obscure the debate than to illuminate it.

Consider the source and the audience

- Does the fact that Mellman is a Democratic pollster matter? How might his background affect his argument?

Lay out the argument, the values, and the assumptions

- Why does Mellman believe the result of the Gallup poll is "misleading"? What problems does Mellman have with the question Gallup asked?
- Is it just the Gallup organization that he is critical of, or someone or something else?

Uncover the evidence

- How does Mellman demonstrate that the results are misleading?

Evaluate the conclusion

- What does Mellman ultimately conclude regarding where Americans stand on the issue of abortion? How does he know this?

Sort out the political implications

- Poll results are often reported in the media with little context or information regarding how the poll was conducted. Why might this be problematic?
- Is it important in a democracy that the public have confidence in poll results?

11.4 The Other War Room
Joshua Green, *Washington Monthly*

Why We Chose This Piece

At first glance, it might appear odd to be reading an article about how pollsters were used by two former presidents, one of whom was president before many of you were in elementary school. However, we include this article because it provides not only

Selection published: April 2002

clear insight into two very different presidential approaches to polling the public, but also two different views of presidential leadership. The article remains as relevant today as it was at the time it was written, early in George W. Bush's first term.

Bill Clinton was famous for his polling activities, and his opponents often accused him of being too "poll driven"—that is, willing to change his policies according to what his pollsters told him the American people wanted to hear. George W. Bush ran for president, in part, on his independence from polls in formulating policy stances. This article doesn't dispute that fact, but it argues that Bush used polls, too—just in a different way.

During President Barack Obama's first term, we know that he polled slightly more than Bush and slightly less than Clinton. His pollsters tend to remain out of the public eye, and his political advisers, not Obama himself, appear to digest the poll results. As you read the article, ask yourself whether Obama's use of polling and leadership style are more in line with Clinton's or Bush's. Or do they fall somewhere in between?

On a Friday afternoon late last year, press secretaries from every recent administration gathered in the Ward Room of the White House at the invitation of Ari Fleischer, press secretary to President Bush. There was no agenda. It was just one of those unexpectedly nice things that seemed to transpire during the brief period after September 11 when people thought of themselves as Americans first and Democrats and Republicans second. Over a lunch of crab cakes and steak, Republicans such as Fleischer and Marlin Fitzwater traded war stories with Joe Lockhart, Mike McCurry, and assorted other Democrats. Halfway through lunch, President Bush dropped by unexpectedly and launched into an impromptu briefing of his own, ticking off the items on his agenda until he arrived at the question of whether it was preferable to issue vague warnings of possible terrorist threats or to stay quietly vigilant so as not to alarm people. At this point, former Clinton press secretary Dee Dee Myers piped up, "What do the poll numbers say?" All eyes turned to Bush. Without missing a beat, the famous Bush smirk crossed the president's face and he replied, "In this White House, Dee Dee, we don't poll on something as important as national security."

This wasn't a stray comment, but a glimpse of a larger strategy that has served Bush extremely well since he first launched his campaign for president—the myth that his administration doesn't use polling. As Bush endlessly insisted on the campaign trail, he governs "based upon principle and not polls and focus groups."

It's not hard to understand the appeal of this tactic. Ever since the Clinton administration's well-noted excesses—calling on pollsters to help determine vacation spots and family pets—polling has become a kind of shorthand for everything people dislike about Washington politics. "Pollsters have developed a reputation as Machiavellian plotters whose job it is to think up ways to exploit the public," says Andrew Kohut, director of the Pew Research Center for the People and the Press. Announcing that one ignores polls, then, is an easy way of conveying an impression of leadership, judgment, and substance. No one has recognized and used this to such calculated effect as Bush.

When he announced he would "bring a new tone to Washington," he just as easily could have said he'd banish pollsters from the White House without any loss of effect. One of the most dependable poll results is that people don't like polling.

But in fact, the Bush administration is a frequent consumer of polls, though it takes extraordinary measures to appear that it isn't. This administration, unlike Clinton's, rarely uses poll results to ply reporters or congressional leaders for support. "It's rare to even hear talk of it unless you give a Bush guy a couple of drinks," says one White House reporter. But Republican National Committee filings show that Bush actually uses polls much more than he lets on, in ways both similar and dissimilar to Clinton. Like Clinton, Bush is most inclined to use polls when he's struggling. It's no coincidence that the administration did its heaviest polling last summer, after the poorly received rollout of its energy plan, and amid much talk of the "smallness" of the presidency. A *Washington Monthly* analysis of Republican National Committee disbursement filings revealed that Bush's principal pollsters received $346,000 in direct payments in 2001. Add to that the multiple boutique polling firms the administration regularly employs for specialized and targeted polls and the figure is closer to $1 million. That's about half the amount Clinton spent during his first year; but while Clinton used polling to craft popular policies, Bush uses polling to spin unpopular ones—arguably a much more cynical undertaking.

Bush's principal pollster, Jan van Lohuizen, and his focus-group guru, Fred Steeper, are the best-kept secrets in Washington. Both are respected but low-key, proficient but tight-lipped, and, unlike such larger-than-life Clinton pollsters as Dick Morris and Mark Penn, happy to remain anonymous. They toil in the background, poll-testing the words and phrases the president uses to sell his policies to an often-skeptical public; they're the Bush administration's Cinderella. "In terms of the modern presidency" says Ron Faucheux, editor of *Campaigns & Elections*, "van Lohuizen is the lowest-profile pollster we've ever had." But as Bush shifts his focus back toward a domestic agenda, he'll be relying on his pollsters more than ever.

Bush's Brain

On the last day of February, the Bush administration kicked off its renewed initiative to privatize Social Security in a speech before the National Summit on Retirement Savings in Washington, D.C. Rather than address "Social Security," Bush opted to speak about "retirement security." And during the brief speech he repeated the words "choice" (three times), "compound interest" (four times), "opportunity" (nine times) and "savings" (18 times). These words were not chosen lightly. The repetition was prompted by polls and focus groups. During the campaign, Steeper honed and refined Bush's message on Social Security (with key words such as "choice," "control," and "higher returns"), measuring it against Al Gore's attack through polls and focus groups ("Wall Street roulette," "bankruptcy" and "break the contract"). Steeper discovered that respondents preferred Bush's position by 50 percent to 38 percent, despite the conventional wisdom that tampering with Social Security is political suicide. He learned, as he explained to an academic conference last February, that "there's a great deal of cynicism about the federal government being able to do anything right, which translated to the federal government not having the ability to properly invest people's Social Security dollars." By couching Bush's rhetoric in poll-tested phrases that reinforced this notion, and adding others that stress the benefits of privatization, he was able to capitalize on what most observers had considered to be a significant political disadvantage. (Independent polls generally find that when fully apprised of Bush's plan, including the risks, most voters don't support it.)

This is typical of how the Bush administration uses polls: Policies are chosen beforehand, polls used to spin them. Because many of Bush's policies aren't necessarily popular with a majority of voters, Steeper and van Lohuizen's job essentially consists of finding words to sell them to the public. Take, for instance, the Bush energy plan. When administration officials unveiled it last May, they repeatedly described it as "balanced" and "comprehensive," and stressed Bush's "leadership" and use of "modern" methods to prevent environmental damage. As *Time* magazine's Jay Carney and John Dickerson revealed, van Lohuizen had poll-tested pitch phrases for weeks before arriving at these as the most likely to conciliate a skeptical public. (Again, independent polls showed weak voter support for the Bush plan.) And the "education recession" Bush trumpeted throughout the campaign? Another triumph of opinion research. Same with "school choice," the "death tax," and the "wealth-generating private accounts" you'll soon hear more about when the Social Security debate heats up. Even the much-lauded national service initiative Bush proposed in his State of the Union address was the product of focus grouping. Though publicly Bush prides himself on never looking in the mirror (that's "leadership"), privately, he's not quite so secure. His pollsters have even conducted favorability ratings on Ari Fleischer and Karen Hughes.

Bush's public opinion operation is split between Washington, D.C., where van Lohuizen's firm, Voter/Consumer Research, orchestrates the primary polling, and Southfield, Mich., where Steeper's firm, Market Strategies, runs focus groups. What the two have in common is Karl Rove. Like many in the administration, Steeper was a veteran of the first Bush presidency, and had worked with Rove on campaigns in Illinois and Missouri. Van Lohuizen has been part of the Bush team since 1991, when Rove hired him to work on a campaign to raise the local sales tax in Arlington, Texas, in order to finance a new baseball stadium for Bush's Texas Rangers.

Like previous presidential pollsters, van Lohuizen also serves corporate clients, including Wal-Mart, Qwest, Anheuser-Busch, and Microsoft. And like his predecessors, this presents potential conflicts of interest. For example, van Lohuizen polls for Americans for Technology Leadership, a Microsoft-backed advocacy group that commissioned a van Lohuizen poll last July purporting to show strong public support for ending the government's suit against the company. At the time, Bush's Justice Department was deciding to do just that. Clinton pollster Mark Penn also did work for Microsoft and Clinton took heat for it. Bush has avoided criticism because few people realize he even *has* a pollster.

The nerve center of the Bush polling operation is a 185-station phone bank in Houston through which van Lohuizen conducts short national polls to track Bush's "attributes," and longer polls on specific topics about once a month. These are complemented by Steeper's focus groups.

One real difference between Bush and Clinton is that, while Clinton was the first to read any poll, Bush maintains several degrees of separation from his pollsters. Both report to Matthew Dowd, the administration's chief of polling, stationed at the RNC, who then reports to Rove. "Rove is a voracious consumer of polls," says a Republican pollster. "He gets it, sifts through it, analyzes it, and gives the president the bottom line." In other words, when it comes to polling, Rove serves as Bush's brain.

Poll Vault

The practice of presidents poll-testing their message dates back to John F. Kennedy, who wished to pursue a civil rights agenda but knew that he would have to articulate it in words that the American public in the 1960s would accept. Alarm about being known to use polls is just as old. Kennedy was so afraid of being discovered that he kept the polling data locked in a safe in the office of his brother, the attorney general. Lyndon Johnson polled more heavily than Kennedy did and learned, through polling, that allowing Vietnam to become an issue in 1964 could cost him re-election. Richard Nixon brought polling—and paranoia over polling—to a new level, believing that his appeal to voters was his reputation as a skilled policymaker, and that if people discovered the extent to which he was polling, they would view him as "slick" and desert him. So he kept his poll data in a safe in his home. But though presidents considered it shameful, polling became an important tool for governing well. Nixon was smart enough to make good use of his polls, once opting to ban oil drilling off the California coast after polling revealed it to be highly unpopular with voters. Jimmy Carter's pollster, Pat Caddell, was the first rock-star pollster, partying with celebrities and cultivating a high-profile image as the president's Svengali (an image considerably tarnished when Caddell's polling for another client, Coca-Cola, became the rationale for the disastrous "New Coke" campaign in the 1980s).

Ronald Reagan polled obsessively throughout his presidency. His pollster, Richard Wirthlin, went so far as to conduct them "before Reagan was inaugurated, while he was being inaugurated, and the day after he was inaugurated," says an administration veteran. He was the first to use polls to sell a right-wing agenda to the country, but he knew enough to retreat when polls indicated that he couldn't win a fight. (Wirthlin's polls convinced Reagan not to cut Social Security, as he'd planned.) By contrast, his successor, George H. W. Bush, practically eschewed polls altogether. "There was a reaction against using polls because they reacted against everything Reagan," says Ron Hinckley, a Bush pollster. "They wanted to put their own name on everything. But their efforts to not be like Reagan took them into a framework of dealing with things that ultimately proved fatal." Indeed, in his first two years in office, Bush is said to have conducted just two polls. Even at Bush's highest point—after the Gulf War, when his approval rating stood at 88 percent—Hinckley says that his economic numbers were in the 40s. "We were in a hell of a lot of trouble," he says, "and nobody wanted to listen."

Bill Clinton, of course, polled like no other president. In addition to polling more often and in greater detail than his predecessors, he put unprecedented faith in his pollsters, elevating them to the status of senior advisers. His tendency to obsess over polls disconcerted even those closest to him, and his over-reliance on polls led to some devastating errors, such as following a Morris poll showing that voters wouldn't accept a candid acknowledgment of his relationship with Monica Lewinsky. But the truth about Clinton's use of polls is more nuanced than is generally understood.

Early in his administration, Clinton drifted away from the centrist agenda he campaigned on and staked out policy positions that appealed to his base. Like Reagan, he polled on how best to sell them to the American people. Healthcare reform is the most instructive example. Describing Clinton's handling of healthcare reform in their book *Politicians Don't Pander: Political Manipulation and the Loss of Democratic Responsiveness*, political scientists Lawrence R. Jacobs and Robert Y. Shapiro conclude: "The fundamental political mistake committed by Bill Clinton and his aides was in grossly overestimating the capacity of a president to 'win' public opinion and to use public support as leverage to overcome known political obstacles—from an ideologically divided Congress to hostile interest groups." The authors call this kind of poll-tested message "crafted talk." Clinton learned its shortcomings firsthand and modified his subsequent use of polls. He fired his pollster, Stanley Greenberg, in favor of centrist pollsters such as Dick Morris and Mark Penn. Though widely ridiculed for it in the press, after the disastrous midterm elections in 1994, Clinton began responding to voters' wishes, moving toward the political center.

Oftentimes these were largely symbolic nuggets like supporting school uniforms or choosing Christopher Reeve to speak at the 1996 Democratic National Convention (Reeve outpolled Walter Cronkite and John F. Kennedy, Jr.). But they also included important policies such as reforming welfare, balancing the budget, and putting 100,000 new police officers on the streets. Many of these centrist policies initially met strong resistance from congressional Democrats, the agencies, and interest groups, as well as liberals within the White House. But the fact that the policies polled well became a powerful tool of persuasion for Clinton and his centrist aides to use. Nor was Clinton afraid to act in spite of the polls, which he did on Bosnia, Haiti, the Mexican bailout, and affirmative action. Indeed, according to senior aides, it was forbidden to discuss foreign policy in the weekly polling meeting Clinton held in the White House residence. (Although, in a priceless irony, Clinton was sufficiently worried about appearing to be poll-driven that Morris drafted a list for him of the "unpopular actions you have taken despite polls.")

"The Circle Is Tight"

When George W. Bush launched his campaign for president, he did so with two prevailing thoughts in mind: to avoid his father's mistakes and to distinguish himself from Bill Clinton. To satisfy the first, Bush needed a tax cut to rival the one being offered by Steve Forbes, at the time considered Bush's most formidable rival for the GOP nomination. But to satisfy the second, Bush needed to engage in some tricky maneuvering. A van Lohuizen poll conducted in late 1998 showed tax cuts to be "the least popular choice" on his agenda among swing voters. So Bush faced a dilemma: He had to sell Americans a tax cut most didn't want, using a poll-crafted sales pitch he didn't want them to know about. In speeches, Bush started listing the tax cut after more popular items like saving Social Security and education. In March 2001, with support still flagging, he began pitching "tax cuts and debt relief" rather than just tax cuts—his polling showed that the public was much more interested in the latter. After plenty of creative math and more poll-tested phrases, Bush's tax cut finally won passage (a larger one, in fact, than he'd been offering in '98).

In a way, Bush's approach to polling is the opposite of Clinton's. He uses polls but conceals that fact, and, instead of polling to ensure that new policies have broad public support, takes policies favored by his conservative base and polls on how to make them seem palatable to mainstream voters. This pattern extends to the entire administration. Whereas Clinton's polling data were regularly circulated among the staff, Bush limits his to the handful of senior advisers who attend Rove's "strategy meetings." According to White House aides, the subject is rarely broached with the president or at other senior staff meetings. "The circle is tight," Matthew Dowd, Bush's chief of polling, testifies. "Very tight." As with Kennedy and Nixon, the Bush administration keeps its polling data under lock and key. Reagan circulated favorable polling data widely among congressional Republicans in an effort to build support. Clinton did likewise and extended this tactic to the media, using polls as political currency to persuade reporters that he was on the right side of an issue. "You don't see it like you did in the Dick Wirthlin days," says a top Republican congressman. "The White House pollster won't meet with the caucus to go through poll data. It just doesn't happen." Says a White House reporter, "The Clinton folks couldn't wait to call you up and share polling data, and Democratic pollsters who worked for the White House were always calling you to talk about it. But there's a general dictate under Bush that they don't use polls to tell them what to think." This policy extends to the president's pollsters, who are discouraged from identifying themselves as such. The strategy seems to be working. A brief, unscientific survey of White House reporters revealed that most couldn't name van Lohuizen as the Bush's primary pollster (most guessed Dowd, who doesn't actually poll). For his part, van Lohuizen sounded genuinely alarmed when I contacted him.

Crafted Talk

It's no mystery why the Bush administration keeps its polling operation in a secure, undisclosed location. Survey after survey shows that voters don't want a president slavishly following polls—they want "leadership" (another word that crops up in Bush's speeches with suspicious frequency). So it's with undisguised relish that Dowd tells me, "It was true during the campaign, it's true now. We don't poll policy positions. Ever."

But voters don't like a president to ignore their desires either. One of the abiding tensions in any democracy is between the need for leaders to respond to public opinion but also to be willing to act in ways that run counter to it. Good presidents strike the right balance. And polls, rightly used, help them do it.

But used the wrong way, polls become a way to cheat the system and evade this tension altogether. As Jacobs and Shapiro explain in *Politicians Don't Pander*, with the exception of the latter Clinton years, presidents since 1980 have increasingly used polls to come up with the "crafted talk" that makes their partisan, interest-group-driven policies seem more mainstream than they really are. Consider the Republican stimulus plan unveiled last winter: So heavily did it tilt toward corporate interests that focus group participants refused to believe that it was real—yet Bush pitched it for months as a "jobs" package.

Presidents, of course, must occasionally break with public opinion. But there's a thin line between being principled and being elitist. For many years, Democrats hurt themselves and the country by presuming they knew better than voters when it came to things like welfare, crime, and tax increases. Clinton used polling to help Democrats break this habit. Bush is more intent on using it to facilitate the GOP's own peculiar political elitism—the conviction that coddling corporations and cutting taxes for the rich will help the country, regardless of the fact that a majority of voters disagree.

Bush's attempt to slip a conservative agenda past a moderate public could come back to hurt him, especially now that his high approval ratings might tempt him to overreach. Recent history shows that poll-tested messages are often easy to parry. During the debate over Clinton's healthcare plan, for instance, Republican opponents launched their own poll-tested counterattack, the famous "Harry and Louise" ads, which were broadcast mainly on airport cable networks such as "CNN Airport" where well-traveled congressmen would be sure to spot them and assume they were ubiquitous. Because lawmakers and voters never fully bought Clinton's policy, it couldn't withstand the carefully tested GOP rebuttal.

A similar fate befell the GOP when it took over Congress in 1995, after campaigning on a list of promises dubbed the "Contract With America." As several pollsters and political scientists have since pointed out, the Contract's policies were heavily geared toward the party's conservative base but didn't register with voters—things like corporate tax cuts and limiting the right to sue. The GOP's strategy was to win over the press and the public with poll-tested "power phrases." Education vouchers, for instance, were promoted as a way of "strengthening rights of parents in their children's education," and Republicans were instructed by RNC chairman Haley Barbour to repeat such phrases "until you vomit." But when it came to proposals such as cutting Medicare, Republicans discovered that their confidence in being able to move public opinion—"preserving" and "protecting" Medicare—was misplaced. Clinton successfully branded them as "extremists," and this proposal, along with many of the Contract's provisions, never made it beyond the House.

Like so many other Republican ideas, Barbour's has been reborn under Bush. "What's happened over time is that there's a lot more polling on spin," says Jacobs. "That's exactly where Bush is right now. He's not polling to find out issues that the public supports so that he can respond to their substantive interests. He's polling on presentation. To those of us who study it, most of his major policy statements come off as completely poll concocted." Should this continue, the administration that condemns polling so righteously may not like what the polls wind up saying.

Consider the source and the audience
- The *Washington Monthly* is an independent investigative political journal that prides itself on its ability to take on both liberals and conservatives, and whose mission statement makes clear its goal of influencing Washington insiders. How does this article fit that profile?

Lay out the argument, the values, and the assumptions
- What does Green believe the role of public opinion ought to be in a democracy? How does he differ here from Matthew Robinson (the author of the first article in this chapter)?

- When should a president listen to public opinion, and when should he not? What role can polls play here?
- Is there a legitimate way for politicians to use public opinion and an illegitimate one?

Uncover the evidence

- Where does Green go to investigate public opinion—gathering in the Bush administration? Given how "tight the circle is," how can he know what he claims to know?
- Whether or not Bush uses polls is a matter for factual investigation. What kind of evidence does Green rely on to support his claim that Bush uses polls to "spin" policy stances he has already taken and make them palatable to the public?

Evaluate the conclusion

- What are the differences between Green's and Robinson's conclusions? What role does each think public opinion plays in policymaking, and whom does each hold responsible for the manipulation of public opinion?
- Is Green right in saying that those who manipulate public opinion to advance a more extreme ideological agenda will be vulnerable to attack from moderate opponents more in tune with the public?

Sort out the political implications

- What does it mean for the future of democracy if more polls are being done to "spin" policy than to create and direct it?

11.5 Will the Polls Destroy Representative Democracy?

George Horace Gallup and Saul Forbes Rae, "The Pulse of Democracy"

Why We Chose This Piece

This selection is a concluding chapter of a book that polling pioneer George Horace Gallup coauthored about the role of polls in democracy. We include it because, counter to some of the articles we have read in this chapter, this is a classic statement of confidence in the American people particularly, and in the central role of public opinion in a democracy generally. Gallup's book was written in 1940. Are his arguments still relevant today?

Selection published: 1940

Another accusation leveled at the modern polls is based on the assumption that they intensify the "band-wagon" instinct in legislators and undermine the American system of representative government. "Ours is a representative democracy," a newspaper editorial suggested soon after the polls had become prominent in 1936, "in which it is properly assumed that those who are chosen to be representatives will think for themselves, use their best judgment individually, and take the unpopular side of an argument whenever they are sincerely convinced that the unpopular side is in the long run in the best interests of the country."

The point has been made more recently by a student of public opinion. "If our representatives were told," it has been written, "that 62% of the people favored payment of the soldier's bonus or 65% favored killing the World Court Treaty, the desire of many of them to be re-elected would lead them to respond to such statistics by voting for or against a measure not because they considered it wise or stupid but because they wanted to be in accord with what was pictured to them as the will of the electorate."[1]

Beyond such criticisms, and at the root of many objections to the polls of public opinion, lies a fundamental conflict between two opposed views of the democratic process and what it means. This conflict is not new—it is older than American political theory itself. It concerns the relationship between representative government and direct democracy, between the judgments of small exclusive groups and the opinions of the great mass of the people. Many theorists who criticize the polls do so because they fear that giving too much power to the people will reduce the representative to the role of rubber stamp. A modern restatement of this attitude may be found in an article written by Colonel O. R. Maguire in the November, 1939, issue of the *United States Law Review*.[2]

Colonel Maguire quotes James Madison: "... pure democracies ... have ever been spectacles of turbulence and contention; have ever been found incompatible with personal security or the rights of property; and have in general been as short in their lives as they have been violent in their deaths."

To support these statements made by an eighteenth-century conservative who feared the dangers of "too much democracy," Maguire insists that the ordinary man is incapable of being a responsible citizen, and leans heavily on the antidemocratic psychological generalizations of Ross, Tarde, and Le Bon. He follows James Madison and the English Conservative, Edmund Burke, in upholding the conception of representative government under which a body of carefully chosen, disinterested public representatives "whose wisdom may best discern the true interest of their country, and whose patriotism and love of justice will be least likely to sacrifice it to temporary or partial considerations," interpret the real will of the people. Under such conditions, it is argued, "it may well happen that the public voice, pronounced by the representatives of the people, will be more consonant to the public good than if pronounced by the people themselves, convened for that purpose." The polls are condemned because, in his view, they invite judgments on which the people are ignorant and ill-informed, on which discussion must be left to representatives and specialists. Finally, a grim picture is drawn of the excesses that will follow the growth of "direct democracy": "... the straw ballot will undermine and discourage the influence of able and conscientious public men and elevate to power the demagogue who will go to the greatest extremes in taking from those who have and giving to those who have not, until there has been realized the prophecy of Thomas Babington Macaulay that America will be as fearfully plundered from within by her own people in the twentieth century as Rome was plundered from without by the Gauls and Vandals."

This case against government by public opinion reveals suspicion not only of the public-opinion surveys, but also of the mass of the people. By and large, the thesis that the people are unfit to rule, and that they must be led by their natural superiors—the legislators and the experts—differs only in degree, and not in essence, from the view urged by Mussolini and Hitler that the people are mere "ballot cattle," whose votes are useful not because they represent a valuable guide to policy, but merely because they provide "proof" of the mass support on which the superior regime is based. It must not be forgotten that the dictators, too, urge that the common people, because of their numbers, their lack of training, their stupidity and gullibility, must be kept as far away as possible from the elite whose task it is to formulate laws for the mass blindly to obey.

Many previous statements and charges of just this kind can be found throughout history. Every despot has claimed that the people were incapable of ruling themselves, and by implication decided that only certain privileged leaders were fit for the legislative task. They have argued that "the best" should rule—but at different times and in different places the judgments as to who constituted "the best" have been completely contradictory. In Burke's England or Madison's America, it was the peerage or the stable wealthier classes—"the good, the wise, and the rich." In Soviet Russia, the representatives of the proletariat constitute "the best."

But the history of autocracy has paid eloquent testimony to the truth of Lord Acton's conclusion that "Power corrupts—absolute power corrupts absolutely." The possible danger of what has been called "the never-ending audacity of elected persons" emphasizes the need for modifying executive power by the contribution of the needs and aspirations of the common people. This is the essence of the democratic conception: political societies are most secure when deeply rooted in the political activity and interest of the mass of the people and least secure when social judgment is the prerogative of the chosen few.

The American tradition of political thought has tried to reconcile these two points of view. Since the beginning of the country's history, political theorists have disagreed on the extent to which the people and their opinions could play a part in the political decision.

"Men by their constitutions," wrote Jefferson, "are naturally divided into two parties: 1.—Those who fear and distrust the people and wish to draw all powers from them into the hands of the higher classes; 2.—Those who identify themselves with the people, have confidence in them, cherish and consider them as the most wise depository of the public interests."[3] Jefferson himself believed that the people were less likely to misgovern themselves than any small exclusive group, and for this reason urged that public opinion should be the decisive and ultimate force in American politics.

His opponents have followed Alexander Hamilton, whose antidemocratic ideas provide an armory for present-day conservatives. "All communities divide themselves into the few and the many," Hamilton declared. "The first are the rich and well-born, the others are the mass of the people. The voice of the people has been said to be the Voice of God; and however generally this maxim has been quoted and believed, it is not true in fact. The people seldom judge or determine right." Those who have followed the Federalist philosophy have largely been concerned with the liberties and property of the minority and have continually urged the necessity of building checks against the people's power.

Those who favor rule of "the best," through the gifted representative, and those who desire to give the common people more power are frequently at loggerheads because their arguments do not meet each other. The need exists to find the right balance between the kind of mass judgments and comments obtained by the public-opinion polls and the opinions of legislators. Both extreme views contain a kernel of truth. No one would deny that we need the best and the wisest in the key positions of our political life. But the democrat is right in demanding that these leaders be subject to check by the opinions of the mass of the people. He is right in refusing to let these persons rule irresponsibly. For in its most extreme form, the criticism that opposes any effort, like the modern polls, to make the people more articulate, that inveighs against the perils of a "direct democracy," leads directly to antidemocratic government. If it is argued that legislators understand better than the people what the people want, it is but a short step to give legislators the power to decree what the people *ought* to want. Few tendencies could be more dangerous. When a special group is entrusted with the task of determining the values for a whole community, we have gone a long way from democracy, representative or any other kind.

The debate hinges to some extent on which particular theory of the representatives' role is accepted. There is the view which the English Conservative, Edmund Burke, advanced in the eighteenth century to the electors of Bristol: "His unbiased opinion, his mature judgment, his enlightened conscience, he ought not to sacrifice to you; to any man, or to any set of men living. These he does not derive from your pleasure. They are a trust from Providence, for the abuse of which he is deeply answerable. Your representative owes you, not his industry only, but his judgment; and he betrays instead of serving you, if he sacrifices it to your opinion." This view has been restated more sharply in the words of the Southern Senator who is reported to have told a state delegation: "Not for hell and a brown mule will I bind myself to your wishes." But, on the other hand, it must be remembered that the electors of Bristol rejected Burke after his address, and that there are many in our own day who take the view that one of the legislator's chief tasks in a democracy must be to "represent."

Unless he is to be the easy prey of special interests and antisocial pressure, he must have access to the expression of a truly "public" opinion, containing the views of all the groups in our complex society. For free expression of public opinion is not merely a right which the masses are fortunate to possess—it is as vital for the leaders as for the people. In no other way can the legislators know what the people they represent want, what kinds of legislation are possible, what the people think about existing laws, or how serious the opposition may be to a particular political proposal. A rigid dictatorship, or any organization of political society which forbids the people to express their own attitudes, is dangerous not only to the people, but also to the leaders themselves, since they never know whether they are sitting in an easy chair or on top of a volcano. *People who live differently think differently*. In order that their experience be incorporated into political rules under which they are to live, their thinking must be included in the main body of ideas involved in the process of final decisions. That is why the surveys take care to include those on relief as well as those who draw their income from investments, young as well as old, men and women of all sorts from every section of the country, in the sample public.

Another form which the case against the people takes is the argument that we are living today in a society so complex and so technical that its problems cannot be trusted to the people or their representatives, but must be turned over to experts. It has been urged that only those who know *how* to legislate should have the power of decreeing what type of legislation *ought* to exist. The Technocracy movement put this view squarely before the American public. If it is true, it means that the kind of mass value judgments secured by the polls and surveys is quite useless in political life. It means that the people and their representatives must abdicate before the trained economist, the social worker, the expert in public finance, in tariffs, in rural problems, in foreign affairs. These learned persons, the argument runs, are the only ones who know and understand the facts, therefore, they alone are competent to decide on matters of policy.

There is something tempting about the view that the people should be led by an aristocracy of specialists. But Americans have learned something from the experience of the past decade. They have learned, in the first place, that experts do not always agree about the solutions for the ills of our times. "Ask six economists their opinion on unemployment," an English wag has suggested, "and you will get seven different answers—two from Mr. John Maynard Keynes."

The point is obviously exaggerated. Certainly today a vast body of useful, applicable knowledge has been built up by economists and other specialists—knowledge which is sorely needed to remedy the ills of our time. But all that experts can do, even assuming we can get them to agree about what need be done, is to tell *how* we can act.

The objectives, the ends, the basic values of policy must still be decided. The economist can suggest what action is to be taken if a certain goal is to be reached. He, speaking purely as an economist, cannot say what final goal *should* be reached. The lawyer can administer and interpret the country's laws. He cannot say what those laws should be. The social worker can suggest ways of aiding the aged. He cannot say that aiding aged persons is desirable. The expert's function is invaluable, but its value lies in judging the means—not the ends—of public policy.

Thus the expert and his techniques are sorely needed. Perhaps Great Britain has gone even further than the United States in relating expert opinion to democratic government. The technique of the Royal Commission, and the other methods of organizing special knowledge, are extremely valuable ways of focusing the attention of the general public on specific evils and on solutions of them. In these Commissions, expert opinion is brought to bear, and opportunities for collective deliberation are created for those with special knowledge of political and economic questions. But even these Royal Commissions must remain ineffective until the general public has passed judgment on whether or not their recommendations should be implemented into legislation.

As a corollary of this view that expert opinion can bear only on specific questions of means, on the technical methods by which solutions are to be achieved, we must agree that most people do not and, in the nature of things, cannot have the necessary knowledge to judge the intimate details of policy. Repeated testing by means of the poll technique reveals that they cannot be expected to have opinions or intelligent judgments about details of monetary policy, of treaty making, or on other questions involving highly specialized knowledge. There are things which cannot be done by public opinion, just as there are things which can only be done by public opinion. "The people who are the power [sic] entitled to say what they want," Bryce wrote, "are less qualified to say how, and in what form, they are to obtain it; or in other words, public opinion can determine ends, but is less fit to examine and select means to those ends."[4]

All this may be granted to the critics. But having urged the need for representatives and experts, we still need to keep these legislators and experts in touch with the public and its opinions. We still have need of declarations of attitudes from those who live under the laws and regulations administered by the experts. For only the man on relief can tell the administrator how it feels to be on relief. Only the small businessman can express his attitude on the economic questions which complicate his existence. Only women voters can explain their views on marriage and divorce. Only all these groups, taken together, can formulate the general objectives and tendencies which their experience makes them feel would be best for the common welfare. For the ultimate values of politics and economics, the judgments on which public policy is based, do not come from special knowledge or from intelligence alone. *They are compounded from the day-to-day experience of the men and women who together make up the society we live in.*

That is why public-opinion polls are important today. Instead of being attempts to sabotage representative government, kidnap the members of Congress, and substitute the taxi driver for the expert in politics, as some critics insist, public-opinion research is a necessary and valuable aid to truly representative government. The continuous studies of public opinion will merely *supplement*, not destroy, the work of representatives. What is evident here is that representatives will be better able to represent if they have an accurate measure of the wishes, aspirations, and needs of different groups within the general public, rather than the kind of distorted picture sent them by telegram enthusiasts and overzealous pressure groups who claim to speak for all the people, but actually speak only for themselves. Public-opinion surveys will provide legislators with a new instrument for estimating trends of opinion, and minimize the chances of their being fooled by clamoring minorities. For the alternative to these surveys, it must be remembered, is not a perfect and still silence in which the Ideal Legislator and the Perfect Expert can commune on desirable policies. It is the real world of competing pressures, vociferous demonstrations, and the stale cries of party politics.

Does this mean that constant soundings of public opinion will inevitably substitute demagoguery for statesmanship? The contrary is more likely. The demagogue is no unfamiliar object. He was not created by the modern opinion surveys. He thrives, not when the people have power, facts, information, but when the people are insecure, gullible, see and hear only one side of the case. The demagogue, like any propagandist of untruths, finds his natural habitat where there is no method of checking on the truth or falsity of his case. To distinguish demagogues from democratic leaders, the people must know the facts, and must act upon them.

Is this element secured by having no measurement of public opinion, or by having frequent, accurate measurement? When local Caesars rise to claim a large popular support for their plans and schemes, is it not better to be able to refer to some more tangible index of their true status than their own claims and speeches? The poll measurements have, more than once, served in the past to expose the claims of false prophets.

As the polls develop in accuracy, and as their returns become more widely accepted, public officials and the people themselves will probably become more critical in distinguishing between the currents of opinion which command the genuine support of a large section of the public and the spurious claims of the pressure groups. The new methods of estimating public opinion are not revolutionary—they merely supplement the various intuitive and haphazard indices available to the legislator with a direct, systematic description of public opinion. Politicians who introduced the technique of political canvassing and door-to-door surveys on the eve of elections, to discover the voting intentions and opinions of the public in their own districts, can hardly fail to acknowledge the value of canvassing the people to hear their opinions, not only on candidates, but on issues as well. It is simply a question of substituting more precise methods for methods based on impressions. Certainly people knew it was cold long before the invention of the thermometer, but the thermometer has helped them to know exactly how cold it is, and how the temperature varies at different points of time. In the same way, politicians and legislators employed methods for measuring the attitudes of the public in the past, but the introduction of the sampling referendum allows their estimates to be made against the background of tested knowledge.

Will the polls of the future become so accurate that legislators will automatically follow their dictates? If this happened would it mean rule by a kind of "mobocracy"? To the first point, it may be suggested that although great accuracy can be achieved through careful polling, no poll can be completely accurate in every single instance over a long period of time. In every sampling result there is a small margin of error which must never be overlooked in interpreting the results. The answer to the second question depends essentially on the nature of the judgments which people make, and on the competence of the majority to act as a directive force in politics.

There has always been a fear of the majority at the back of the minds of many intelligent critics of the polls. Ever since the time of Alexis de Tocqueville, the phrase, "tyranny of the majority," has been used widely by critics of democratic procedure, fearful lest the sheer weight of numbers should crush intelligent minorities and suppress the criticism that comes from small associations which refuse to conform to the majority view. It has been asserted that the same tendencies to a wanton use of power which exist in a despotism may also exist in a society where the will of the majority is the supreme sovereign power.

What protection exists against this abuse of power by a majority scornful of its weaker critics and intolerant of dissenting opinions? The sages of 1787 were fully aware of the danger, and accordingly created in the Bill of Rights provisions whereby specific guarantees—free speech, free association, and open debate—were laid down to ensure the protection of the rights of dissident minorities.

Obviously, such legal provisions cannot guarantee that a self-governing community will never make mistakes, or that the majority will always urge right policies. No democratic state can ever be *certain* of these things. Our own history provides abundant evidence pointing to the conclusion that the majority can commit blunders, and can become intolerant of intelligent minority points of view. But popular government has never rested on the belief that such things *cannot* happen. On the contrary, it rests on the sure knowledge that they *can* and *do* happen, and further, that they can and do happen in autocracies—with infinitely more disastrous consequences. The democratic idea implies awareness that the people *can* be wrong—but it attempts to build conditions within which error may be discovered and through which truth may become more widely available. It recognizes that people can make crucial mistakes when they do not have access to the facts, when the facts to which they have access are so distorted through the spread of propaganda and half-truths as to be useless, or when their lives are so insecure as to provide a breeding ground for violence and extremes.

It is important to remember that while the seismograph does not create earthquakes, this instrument may one day help to alleviate such catastrophes by charting the place of their occurrence, their strength, and so enabling those interested in controlling the effects of such disasters to obtain more knowledge of their causes. Similarly, the polls do not create the sources of irrationalism and potential chaos in our society. What they can do is to give the people and the legislators a picture of existing tendencies, knowledge of which may save democracy from rushing over the edge of the precipice.

The antidote for "mobocracy" is not the suppression of public opinion, but the maintenance of a free tribunal of public opinion to which rival protagonists can make their appeals. Only in this atmosphere of give-and-take of rival points of view can democratic methods produce intelligent results. "The clash and conflict of argument bring out the strength and weakness of every case," it has been truly said, "and that which is sound tends to prevail. Let the cynic say what he will. Man is not an irrational animal. Truth usually wins in the long run, though the obsessions of self-interest or prejudice or ignorance may long delay its victory."

There is a powerful incentive to expose the forces which prevent the victory of truth, for there is real value in the social judgments that are reached through widespread discussion and debate. Although democratic solutions may not be the "ideally best," yet they have the fundamental merit of being solutions which the people and their representatives have worked out in co-operation. There is value in the method of trial and error, for the only way people will ever learn to govern themselves is by governing themselves.

Thus the faith to which the democrat holds is not found so much in the inherent wisdom of majorities as in the value of rule by the majority principle. The democrat need not depend upon a mystic "general will" continually operating to direct society toward the "good life." He merely has to agree that the best way of settling conflicts in political life is by some settled rule of action, and that, empirically, this lies in the majority principle. For when the majority is finally convinced, the laws are immeasurably more stable than they would be were they carried out in flagrant opposition to its wishes. In the long run, only laws which are backed by public opinion can command obedience.

"The risk of the majority principle," it has been said "is the least dangerous, and the stakes the highest, of all forms of political organization. It is the risk least separable from the process of government itself. When you have made the commonwealth reasonably safe against raids by oligarchies or depredations by individual megalomaniacs; when you have provided the best mechanisms you can contrive for the succession to power, and have hedged both majorities and minorities about with constitutional safeguards of their own devising, then you have done all that the art of politics can ever do.

For the rest, insurance against majority tyranny will depend on the health of your economic institutions, the wisdom of your educational process, the whole ethos and vitality of your culture."[5] In short, the democrat does not have to believe that man is infinitely perfectible, or that he is infinitely a fool. He merely has to realize that under some conditions men judge wisely and act decently, while under other conditions they act blindly and cruelly. His job is to see that the second set of conditions never develops, and to maximize the conditions which enable men to govern themselves peacefully and wisely.

The "tyranny of the majority" has never been America's biggest problem. It is as great a danger to contemplate the "tyranny of the minority," who operate under cover of the Bill of Rights to secure ends in the interests of a small group. The real tyranny in America will not come from a better knowledge of how majorities feel about the questions of the day which press for solution. Tyranny comes from ignorance of the power and wants of the opposition. Tyranny arises when the media of information are closed, not when they are open for all to use.

The best guarantee for the maintenance of a vigorous democratic life lies not in concealing what people think, but in trying to find out what their ultimate purposes are, and in seeking to incorporate these purposes in legislation. It demands exposing the weakness of democracy as well as its values. Above all, it is posited on the belief that political institutions are not perfect, that they must be modified to meet changing conditions, and that a new age demands new political techniques.

Notes

1. C. W. Smith, *Public Opinion in a Democracy*, New York, 1939, p. 411.
2. O. R. Maguire, "The Republican Form of Government and the Straw Poll—an Examination," *U.S. Law Review*, November, 1939.
3. Herbert Agar, *Pursuit of Happiness*, p. 42.
4. James Bryce, *The American Commonwealth*, p. 347.
5. Max Lerner, *It Is Later Than You Think*, 1938, p. 111.

Consider the source and the audience

- Gallup was writing a book to showcase his science of polling and its possibilities. Would that fact affect his message?

Lay out the argument, the values, and the assumptions

- Gallup and Rae discuss two views of the democratic process. To which of these views do they adhere?
- What is public opinion capable of doing, and what are its limitations?
- What is the worst form of government that Gallup and Rae can imagine? How do they think the monitoring of public opinion can help avert that form of government?

Uncover the evidence

- From what sources do Gallup and Rae draw the evidence for their argument? Are historical example and philosophical principle sufficient to make their case? Could they offer any kind of empirical evidence?

Evaluate the conclusion

- Is democracy doomed if it is not based on the public's own determination of what it wants?
- Can public opinion be an effective check on the dangers inherent in democracy?

Sort out the political implications

- How much democracy would Gallup and Rae favor? What role do they see for polls? What would they think of the uses to which polling is put today?

12

Political Parties

The U.S. Constitution is silent on the subject of political parties, but our founders were not. James Madison warned against the dangers of factional divisions among the population in *The Federalist Papers* (see Reading 13.4), and George Washington echoed that warning when he left office after serving two terms as the first president of the new nation (see Reading 12.5). And yet, parties were present in the early days of the republic, and they are present today.

Defined as groups that unite under a common label to control government and to promote their ideas and policies, parties have become an integral part of the American political system. Two parties in particular, the Democrats and the Republicans, have dominated the political scene for approximately 150 years.

Defenders of parties say that they strengthen American democracy—serving to recruit candidates, to define their policy agendas, and to run their campaigns, as well as providing a link between voters and the people they elect, greater political accountability, and continuity and stability in government. Some people go so far as to say that it is political parties that make democracy possible.[1]

Critics, however, say that parties are captives of special interests, that their divisive partisanship turns off voters, that they narrow voters' political choices, that they provide a haven for corruption, and that they are driven by an untouchable elite. Some critics want to do away with parties altogether; others want to change the rules to empower more parties; still others want to reduce the power of all parties.

The selections in this chapter look at some recent debates about the role of political parties. We begin with an article on the difficulties the Republican Party has had winning the votes of racial and ethnic minorities. The author of the second article, conservative David Frum, believes that concern about the viability of the Republican Party in the future is exaggerated. In the third selection, former Republican representative Steve LaTourette claims that Republicans cannot be successful if they continue to nominate candidates who are more ideologically extreme than the general election electorate. Fourth, Kurt Andersen argues in *New York* magazine that neither major party is acceptable and instead pushes for the creation of a third party. Finally, we look at a classic, George Washington's farewell address, in which he celebrates American government but points out the pitfalls he sees before it, chief of which is the danger of partisan division.

Note

1. E. E. Schattschneider, *Party Government* (New York: Farrar and Rinehart, Inc., 1942).

• •

12.1 GOP v. Voting Rights Act
William Yeomans, Reuters

Why We Chose This Piece

After Barack Obama's victory in 2012, conversation among pundits and politicos centered around what was wrong with the Republican Party and how it would brand itself going forward. At the center of this debate were arguments about the party's inability to win the votes of racial and ethnic minorities. With Latinos in particular likely to comprise a greater percentage of the electorate in the future, Republican electoral success may hinge on the GOP's willingness to reach out to these voters. We chose this blog entry because the author highlights this very issue, but from a slightly different perspective. He argues that it is not so much what Republican candidates are doing on the campaign trail that threatens the party's relationship with racial and ethnic minorities, but instead what they are doing in the courts. How might the Republican Party make inroads with racial and ethnic minorities?

The Republican Party is in danger of reaping what it has sown.

Much has been written about the GOP's problem with minority voters. Quite simply, the party has managed to alienate every nonwhite constituency in the nation.

This is not an accidental or sudden phenomenon. Ever since Republicans chose almost 50 years ago to pursue a Southern strategy, to embrace and promote white voters' opposition to civil rights, the party has been on a path toward self-segregation.

Successive Republican administrations have pursued agendas that included retreating on civil rights enforcement and opposing government programs that increase minority opportunity. That steady progression culminated in Mitt Romney's disastrous showing among African-American, Latino and Asian voters.

Now, even as Republican leaders are openly lamenting that the party is doomed unless it can reverse its downward spiral with minority voters, the Supreme Court has announced that it would hear *Shelby County v. Holder* next month—the latest challenge to the constitutionality of section 5 of the Voting Rights Act.

Selection published: January 10, 2013

252

Clear-eyed GOP strategists must have cringed with recognition that the five Republican-appointed Supreme Court justices are threatening to put the final nail in the party's coffin.

Put bluntly, if the court's Republican majority strikes down this recently reauthorized, core provision of the Voting Rights Act—the most effective and revered of all civil rights statutes—the backlash will likely ensure that Republican presidential candidates will struggle for a generation to win more than a handful of minority votes. The specter of justices appointed by the Republican Party joining in the effort to suppress minority votes will likely ignite a new movement among minorities and their allies to protect the franchise against GOP attack.

Section 5 of the Voting Rights Act requires that jurisdictions with a record of voting transgressions subjected the law must obtain pre-clearance for any change in election rules from either the Justice Department or a three-judge court in Washington, D.C. This requirement grew out of the inability of litigation to address many jurisdictions' determined efforts to prevent African-Americans from voting. The Justice Department's best attempts in suing to enforce the 15th Amendment, which prohibits denial of the vote based on race, proved inadequate.

Because of local jurisdictions' lack of cooperation and, in some instances, the recalcitrance of racist judges, individual cases proved time-consuming and expensive to pursue. Frustratingly, even when plaintiffs won an order blocking one tactic for disenfranchisement, a jurisdiction could just adopt a new method—requiring a fresh round of litigation.

Only after years of litigation had produced unsatisfactory results and the heroic efforts of civil rights activists and ordinary citizens had exposed massive injustice did Congress finally step forward. Pushed by President Lyndon B. Johnson, Congress passed the Voting Rights Act in 1965.

Section 5 has proven so successful, its opponents now argue, that its own achievements should kill it. They contend that conditions in the jurisdictions subject to the law have changed—in part because of the act's accomplishments—making the federal oversight imposed by Section 5 no longer warranted. Congress, however, made extensive findings to the contrary in 2006 and reauthorized Section 5 for 25 years by unanimous vote in the Senate and an overwhelming majority in the House of Representatives.

Indeed, as Judge David S. Tatel's opinion for the D.C. Circuit Court in *Shelby County* amply demonstrates, Congress acted well within its power in reauthorizing Section 5. The ruling noted that Congress, examining the record only since 1982, acted on the basis of 626 attorney general objections blocking discriminatory changes; more than 800 proposed voting changes that were withdrawn or modified after the Justice Department requested more information before it would approve them; 653 successful cases under Section 2 of the act, which allows lawsuits to redress discrimination; tens of thousands of election observers being sent to covered jurisdictions; 105 successful Section 5 enforcement actions; 25 unsuccessful suits seeking approval of voting changes; and the invisible deterrent effect, which can restrain jurisdictions that know their election practices must survive Section 5 review.

Faced with this overwhelming evidence that Section 5 is still justified in the jurisdictions still subject to it, opponents are making a second argument. Some jurisdictions, they point out, that are not covered by Section 5 behave just as badly—revealing the imprecision of the section's coverage formula. The formula captures jurisdictions that administered a discriminatory device (such as a literacy test) and where registration or turnout in the presidential elections of 1964, 1968, or 1972 fell below 50 percent. There was never any magic to the formula, which was reverse-engineered to capture the worst offenders.

The formula was always under-inclusive. It fails, for example, to include such states as Arkansas, Tennessee and Oklahoma, where racial discrimination was no stranger. It was also over-inclusive, capturing jurisdictions where voting discrimination was not as severe. That is why Congress built into the act a bailout provision, which allows jurisdictions that have maintained clean records for 10 years to go to court to end federal oversight. Dozens of jurisdictions have done just that.

It is true that several states not covered by Section 5 have been hotbeds of voting law controversy in recent cycles—notably Ohio, Pennsylvania and Florida (only five counties are covered). The correct response to this misbehavior, however, is not to release the covered jurisdictions. It is to ensure adequate legal remedies against abuses in these others as well.

Despite Congress's recent reauthorization of Section 5, unanimous recognition of its success, and a voluminous record compiled by Congress in support of its continued necessity, the Republican appointees to the court appear eager to throw it out. In 2009, these justices put it in their sights—by accepting the case *NAMUDNO v. Holder*—but then failed to pull the trigger. They instead decided the matter through creative statutory interpretation. Chief Justice John Roberts' opinion, however, gratuitously expressed serious concern about Section 5's constitutionality and made it clear that the court would not likely hold its fire a second time.

Shelby County presents that second time.

The Republican Party planted the seeds of this judicial disaster decades ago. Building on the resentment of white Southerners toward *Brown v. Board of Education* and the demise of Jim Crow, Richard M. Nixon implemented his Southern strategy to appeal to angry white voters. He then fed this beast by appointing conservative judges who would reverse civil rights progress.

President Ronald Reagan identified conservative ideologues for the bench who could be counted on to reject effective civil rights enforcement. He elevated Associate Justice William Rehnquist to chief justice and then tried to push through confirmation of the ultra-conservative Robert Bork, who had opposed the Civil Rights Act of 1964. This proved too much for the Senate.

Reagan also appointed Justices Antonin Scalia and Anthony Kennedy. Both have voted consistently against minority civil rights plaintiffs, while showing enthusiastic support for whites challenging civil rights remedies. President George H. W. Bush continued this pattern when he appointed Clarence Thomas, age 41, to the court. Thomas was not chosen on the basis of his experience or distinction as a legal thinker, but because of his race and conservative ideology—which featured strong opposition to civil rights remedies.

President George W. Bush's appointments of Roberts and Samuel Alito, who cut their teeth as attorneys in Reagan's Justice Department, completed this decades-long Republican effort to create a solid right-wing majority on the Supreme Court that would consistently oppose minorities' civil rights claims.

With that project now complete, the Republican appointees are poised to take on the Voting Rights Act.

While forces hostile to the act spent the years since the 2006 reauthorization trying to convince the public that Section 5 is no longer necessary, the two years leading to the 2012 election undermined their work. Following strong GOP gains in the 2010 election, Republican-led statehouses across the nation launched efforts to suppress minority voting by restricting early voting, blocking voting on Sunday, imposing draconian registration requirements, purging voting lists and passing photo ID requirements.

Early post-election accounts suggest that these noxious tactics backfired and actually increased minority enthusiasm and turnout in the affected jurisdictions.

These suppression efforts should make it far harder for opponents of Section 5 to argue that it is no longer necessary. Fortunately, Section 5 blocked photo identification laws enacted by South Carolina and Texas and limited the restrictions on early voting adopted by Florida. A three-judge court relied on Section 5 to block Texas' most recent redistricting plans for its congressional, senate and state house seats—finding that the legislature acted with the intent to discriminate on the basis of race. Section 5 should also prevent Alabama and Mississippi from implementing recently authorized photo identification laws.

The two years since the 2010 midterm election present overwhelming evidence that covered jurisdictions are not yet ready to conduct elections without federal supervision.

Days after Romney was humbled by a historic lack of minority support, the Republican-appointed Supreme Court justices plunged ahead—agreeing to review Section 5 and threatening to make it significantly more difficult for the Republican Party to improve its standing with minority voters.

Just as Romney's defeat reflected decades of Republican policy hostile to the interests of minorities, the court's recent decision to hear *Shelby County* reflects decades of effort to pack the court with right-wing ideologues who will oppose minority interests.

The Republicans' best hope to avoid further alienating minority voters lies in Kennedy, the Republican-appointed justice most likely to break with his conservative colleagues. All eyes will be on him as he decides whether his legacy will include being the justice whose vote brought down America's most effective civil rights law.

His vote may well determine the prospects of the Republican Party for years to come—and the health of our democracy.

Consider the source and the audience

- The author is a law professor who spent close to thirty years at the Department of Justice, where he litigated civil rights cases in the federal courts involving voting rights. What kind of perspective does that give him on this issue?
- He also served as Sen. Ted Kennedy's chief counsel on the Judiciary Committee. One might presume that this makes him a Democrat. How does this make you view the persuasiveness of his argument? Would the argument be any different if it were written by a Republican?

Lay out the argument, the values, and the assumptions

- How has Section 5 of the Voting Rights Act affected the ability of racial and ethnic minorities to vote? Why does the author believe that the Court's decision on the constitutionality of it could threaten the GOP's ability to win the voters of racial and ethnic minorities in the future?
- What are the constitutional arguments in favor of Section 5? Against it?
- According to the author, what led to the disconnect between the GOP and racial and ethnic minorities?

Uncover the evidence

- The author provides several examples of actions taken by the GOP that he believes have hurt the Republican Party with racial and ethnic minority voters. Does he provide any empirical evidence that this is indeed the case?
- Does the author show evidence that racial and ethnic minorities would blame the GOP if Section 5 is overturned? Can he?

Evaluate the conclusion

- Yeomans believes the challenge to Section 5 is based on race. What might be an alternative view regarding why conservatives question its constitutionality?
- Since Yeoman's blog post was published, the Supreme Court issued a ruling that, for all intents and purposes, eliminated Section 5. Does the Court's ruling really matter to Yeomans's argument? In other words, has damage already been done by the fact that the constitutionality of Section 5 has been called into question by conservatives?

Sort out the political implications

- If Republicans continue to alienate racial and ethnic minorities, as Yeomans has suggested, what might that mean for the future of the Republican Party? Does the Democratic Party face some of the same concerns?

12.2 Conservatives, Don't Despair
David Frum, CNN

Why We Chose This Piece

After Barack Obama's reelection in 2012, many commentators questioned the Republican Party's ability to be competitive in national elections (see Reading 12.1 for one such example). Here, David Frum says "not so fast." In fact, he explicitly

Selection published: November 13, 2012

challenges those, including conservatives, who question whether Republican candidates can be successful because of the increasing electoral influence of racial and ethnic voters. Can Frum's argument be reconciled with Yeomans's claims in the previous reading?

The mood among American conservatives is now one of apocalyptic despair.

Having convinced themselves that this election arrayed freedom against tyranny, they now must wonder: Did their country just democratically vote in favor of tyranny?

On Fox News election night, Bill O'Reilly explained the meaning of the election: The "white establishment" was now outnumbered by minorities. "The demographics are changing. It's not a traditional America anymore." And these untraditional Americans "want stuff. They want things. And who is going to give them things? President Obama. He knows it, and he ran on it."

O'Reilly's analysis is echoed across the conservative blogosphere. The (non-white) takers now outnumber the (white) makers. They will use their majority to pillage the makers and redistribute to the takers. In the process, they will destroy the sources of the country's wealth and end the American experiment forever.

You'll hear O'Reilly's view echoed wherever conservatives express themselves.

Happily, the view is wrong, and in every respect.

America is not a society divided between "makers" and "takers." Instead, almost all of us proceed through a life cycle where we sometimes make and sometimes take as we pass from schooling to employment to retirement.

The line between "making" and "taking" is not a racial line. The biggest government program we have, Medicare, benefits a population that is 85% white.

President Barack Obama was not re-elected by people who want to "take." The president was re-elected by people who want to work—and who were convinced, rightly or wrongly, that the president's policies were more likely to create work than were the policies advocated by my party.

The United States did not vote for socialism. It could not do so, because neither party offers socialism. Both parties champion a free enterprise economy cushioned by a certain amount of social insurance. The Democrats (mostly) want more social insurance; the Republicans want less. National politics is a contest to move the line of scrimmage, in a game where there's no such thing as a forward pass, only a straight charge ahead at the defensive line. To gain three yards is a big play.

Whatever you think of the Obama record, it's worth keeping in mind that by any measure, free enterprise has been winning the game for a long, long time to this point.

Compare the United States of 2012 with the United States of 1962. Leave aside the obvious points about segregation and discrimination, and look only at the economy.

In 1962, the government regulated the price and route of every airplane, every freight train, every truck and every merchant ship in the United States. The government regulated the price of natural gas. It regulated the interest on every checking account and the commission on every purchase or sale of stock. Owning a gold bar was a serious crime that could be prosecuted under the Trading with the Enemy Act. The top rate of income tax was 91%.

It was illegal to own a telephone. Phones had to be rented from the giant government-regulated monopoly that controlled all telecommunications in the United States. All young men were subject to the military draft and could escape only if they entered a government-approved graduate course of study. The great concern of students of American society—of liberals such as David Riesman, of conservatives such as Russell Kirk and of radicals such as Dwight Macdonald—was the country's stultifying, crushing conformity.

Even if you look only at the experiences of white heterosexual men, the United States of 2012 is a freer country in almost every way than the United States of 1962.

Obama has changes in mind that conservatives and Republicans will oppose. He will want to raise taxes; he will want to sustain social spending at a permanently higher level; he has in mind new regulations over health care, energy production and banking. He'll win some; he'll lose some. To the extent that his wins prove injurious, future Republican Congresses and administrations will struggle to undo them. That's politics: a contest that never ends and in which the only certainty is the certainty of constant change.

The Republican challenge next is to reassemble a new coalition for limited government and private enterprise. That coalition must include Americans of all ethnicities. To assume from the start that only certain ethnicities will contribute, and that others aspire only to grab, is not only ugly prejudice; it is also self-destructive delusion.

People of all backgrounds want to create, save and contribute to society. A party of the center-right should make them all feel at home, regardless of how they pronounce their last name, the complexion of their skin or the way in which they express love and build family.

The Roman Catholic Church deems despair a mortal sin. To abandon hope is to reject the reality of goodness and to forswear future action. The United States is a great and good country, and it remains great and good even when we do not get all our own way politically. The United States is a tolerant and free country, which means that there are no "tipping points" beyond which it becomes impossible to correct mistakes.

Fifty years ago, Marxism was still a live intellectual force in British universities. Marxists taught that human society must inevitably evolve into a socialist dictatorship of the proletariat. The great British conservative historian Hugh Trevor-Roper scoffed at this arrogance. He said, "When radicals scream that victory is indubitably theirs, sensible conservatives knock them on the nose. It is only very feeble conservatives who take such words as true and run round crying for the last sacraments."

We need more sensible conservatives. As for the feeble conservatives, they should take a couple of aspirin and then stay quietly indoors until the temper has subsided and they are ready to say and do something useful again.

Consider the source and the audience

- The author is a conservative commentator who worked as a special assistant to George W. Bush. How might the fact that Frum is conservative influence his argument? How might it affect his credibility?

Lay out the argument, the values, and the assumptions

- Frum distinguishes between "makers" and "takers." What does he mean by this distinction?
- According to Frum, why was Barack Obama reelected? What must Republicans do to win presidential elections in the future? Why does he believe that the future could be bright for the Republican Party?

Uncover the evidence

- What kinds of evidence does Frum include to support his claim that Republicans need not despair? Is this enough? If not, what other kinds of evidence might have made his argument more persuasive?

Evaluate the conclusion

- Has Frum convinced you that the Republican Party is not out of sync with Americans?

Sort out the political implications

- If Frum is correct, what can we expect national elections to look like in the future? What if he is wrong?

• •

12.3 The Senate's "Manchurian Candidates"
Steve LaTourette, Politico

Why We Chose This Piece

William Yeomans, the author of Reading 12.1, believes that the Republican Party's lack of success is due to its alienation of racial and ethnic minority voters. Former Republican representative Steve LaTourette agrees with Yeomans that Republicans have had difficulty winning elections, although in this case he is referring to recent Senate elections. Yet LaTourette blames the lack of electoral success on something quite different: In LaTourette's view, the GOP has nominated candidates that are unelectable.

Selection published: November 11, 2012

This article is interesting for a few reasons. First, it dovetails nicely with the first two readings in this chapter. Students are able to compare multiple arguments explaining a single topic (the inability of Republicans to win in several recent elections). Second, it introduces students to issues regarding representation as a result of an increasingly polarized Congress. And finally, the fact that it is written by a former member of Congress who is a member of the party he is criticizing adds an intriguing component.

In the 1962 film "The Manchurian Candidate," Staff Sergeant Raymond Shaw is brainwashed into becoming an unwitting accomplice for an international communist conspiracy. Shaw, a good man and a patriot, is conditioned into taking actions that advance a cause that he does not support.

Over the past two election cycles, Republican primary voters in several states have been subject to the Manchurian Candidate treatment—helping to hand at least five U.S. Senate seats, and control of the Senate, to the Democratic Party.

In Nevada in 2010, Senate Majority Leader Harry Reid retained his seat, despite abysmal approval ratings, because Nevada Republican primary voters had chosen possibly the one person in the entire state who couldn't defeat Harry Reid—Sharron Angle.

That same year, Delaware Republican primary voters defeated Rep. Mike Castle—the one Republican who could win statewide in the deep blue state. Instead, choosing to go with Christine O'Donnell, a candidate whose first general election ad famously declared, "I am not a witch."

Republicans left a third seat on the table in the 2010 midterms, when Colorado Republican primary voters chose right-wing firebrand Ken Buck over former Colorado Lt. Gov. Jane Norton. Despite a historic Republican wave, Democrat Michael Bennet was able to prevail over Buck in the general election.

In 2012, this disastrous trend continued. In Missouri, Republican primary voters chose Rep. Todd Akin. Akin's primary campaign received a big assist from Democratic incumbent Claire McCaskill, who spent money in the GOP primary painting Akin as the most conservative of her challengers. McCaskill's money was well spent and she got her wish. Akin won the primary and within weeks of winning became a national albatross for Republicans after comments about "forcible rape." McCaskill, who was one of the highest priority targets for the National Republican Senatorial Committee, cruised to reelection.

The Missouri Senate seat wasn't the only unforced error by Republicans in 2012. In Indiana, Republican primary voters ousted longtime Sen. Dick Lugar and instead chose tea party favorite Richard Mourdock. The once safe Indiana Senate seat suddenly was lost to the GOP after Mourdock made comments about rapes that resulted in pregnancies were "God's will."

That is five Senate seats in two cycles essentially given away. Five seats that Republicans could have and should have won, which were lost because Republican primary voters chose candidates that could not win in a general election.

I do not believe that Republican primary voters in any of these five states intended to elect a Democrat in November by selecting a candidate that could not win. I do not believe that any of these Republican primary voters intended to hand Harry Reid and the Democrats control of the Senate. That is, in fact, however, what they actually did.

What could possibly explain this behavior then? How could good and loyal Republican primary voters be convinced to take actions that actually aided Reid and his liberal Democratic majority in the Senate? In short, because Republican primary voters were convinced by a handful of special interest groups that the problem was Republicans and that the answer to what ailed our party was a circular firing squad.

Over the past decade or so, the dysfunction in Washington has rightfully frustrated voters of all ideological stripes. Washington is broken and few serious people in either party will argue that point. Ultra-conservative special interests took that justified anger and frustration with the dysfunction in Washington and funneled it—not against Democrats—but instead against candidates they deemed not to be "pure" ideologically.

Republican primary voters were conditioned by these ultra conservative special interest groups into believing the way that we could change a Washington crippled by partisanship was by nominating even more bitterly partisan candidates.

The results for Republicans—and for the nation—of this process have been nothing short of devastating. We have a paralyzing gridlock in Washington, even as we stare into the jaws of incredibly serious challenges as a nation.

It is time for Republican soul-searching. It is time for grass-roots Republicans all across the country to recognize that they have been manipulated by the special interests.

If Republicans are going to build the coalitions necessary to win all across this country, if we are to restore the American people's faith in our party and in our ability to govern, then it is time we start nominating serious people. It is time our party stops nominating Manchurian candidates, and start nominating people who are committed to coming to Washington to make this city work for the people of this country.

More than 23 million Americans are looking for work, real wages have declined, and we face a debt crisis that could shake the very foundations of this country. These challenges will not be solved by one party. They will require two parties willing to work together to find common-sense solutions. It is time Republicans do our part to make sure that our party is one-half of that equation.

Consider the source and the audience

- Steve LaTourette is a former Republican representative from Ohio (and a current member of Congress at the time he wrote this op-ed piece). How might this fact make him view the problems facing the Republican Party differently from, say, a pundit or an academic?

Lay out the argument, the values, and the assumptions

- Why does LaTourette title this article "The Senate's 'Manchurian Candidates'"?
- According to LaTourette, why has the Republican Party lost Senate seats that it had no business losing? Who is responsible for those losses?

Uncover the evidence

- LaTourette claims that Republicans nominated candidates who were too conservative to win. Does he provide evidence for this claim? How can he be sure that a more moderate Republican candidate could have won?

Evaluate the conclusion

- LaTourette was generally thought of as a moderate representative. How might a more conservative member of Congress respond to him?
- How might LaTourette's conclusion mesh with those of the previous two readings? How might it be different?

Sort out the political implications

- What do the examples that LaTourette provides mean for representation? What might they mean for the Republican Party going forward?

12.4 Introducing the Purple Party
Kurt Andersen, *New York* magazine

Why We Chose This Piece

One of the topics that regularly drive discussions of political parties in the United States is whether voters need more options. Since the Civil War, the Democratic and Republican Parties have dominated American politics. While third-party movements have emerged over the course of that time, they have rarely been successful. Many Americans, including Kurt Andersen, the author of this article, believe that the two-party system does not give Americans sufficient choice. In this New York *magazine piece, Andersen "creates" his own party—one that he believes represents the views of more Americans than either of the two major parties. Is it possible for two parties to represent all voters? What might be the benefits of such a system?*

Before I was old enough to vote, I worked as a volunteer for George McGovern's presidential primary campaign, then voted for him in the November election, then for Carter (twice), then Mondale, Dukakis, Clinton (twice), Gore, and Kerry. I'm nine for nine; I've never voted for a Republican for president, like most people I know—and, I expect, like most New Yorkers.

However, except for McGovern (I was 18; the Vietnam War was on; his opponent was Richard Nixon), I cast none of those votes very enthusiastically. In the last four mayoral

---

Selection published: April 24, 2006

elections, I've voted for the Republican three times—Giuliani in 1993 and 1997, and Bloomberg last fall. Each of those Republican votes felt a little less transgressive and weird.

I don't consider myself a true Democrat. Yet my mayoral votes notwithstanding, I am not now nor have I ever been a Republican, and could never be unless the Lincoln Chafee–Olympia Snowe–John McCain wing of the party were to take decisive control, or hell freezes over. For me, what has happened politically in New York City stays in New York City.

But the thing is, in my political ambivalence I'm not such a freak these days. Fully a third of New Yorkers who voted in the last two elections behaved as I did, voting for Kerry and Bloomberg. Nationally, more and more Americans are clearly disaffected with both big parties. In 2005, for the first time since 1997, the percentages of people telling pollsters they feel generically "very positive" toward the Democrats or Republicans fell to single digits. And antipathy is running at historical highs as well—40 percent negatives for both parties, give or take a few points—which suggests that a huge number of nominal Democrats are voting more against the Bushes and Cheneys (and Santorums and Brownbacks) than they are for the Kerrys and Gores.

Less than a third of the electorate are happy to call themselves Republicans, and only a bit more say they're Democrats—but between 33 and 39 percent now consider themselves neither Democrat nor Republican. In other words, there are more of us than there are of either of them.

What's changed hardly at all over the past 30 years, however, is people's sense of where, in rough terms, they stand ideologically. Almost half of Americans consistently call themselves moderates.

We are people without a party. We open-minded, openhearted moderates are alienated from the two big parties because backward-looking ideologues and p.c. hypocrites are effectively in charge of both. Both are under the sway of old-school clods who consistently default to government intrusion where it doesn't belong—who want to demonize video-game makers and criminalize abortion and hate speech and flag-burning, who are committed to maintaining the status quos of the public schools and health-care system, and who decline to make the hard choices necessary (such as enacting a high gasoline tax or encouraging nuclear energy) to move the country onto a sustainable energy track. Both line up to reject sensible, carefully negotiated international treaties when there's too much sacrifice involved and their special-interest sugar daddies object—the Kyoto Protocol for the Republicans, the Central American Free Trade Agreement for the Democrats.

Some lifelong Republicans (such as my mother) abandoned ship in the nineties when the Evangelicals and right-to-lifers finally loomed too large in her party and Gingrich and company tried to defund public broadcasting and the national cultural endowments. As for us lifelong non-Republicans, we don't want taxes to be any higher than necessary, but the tax-cutting monomania of the GOP these days is grotesque selfishness masquerading as principle—and truly irresponsible, given the free-spending, deficit-ballooning policies it's also pursuing. We are appalled by the half-cynical, half-medieval mistrust and denial of science—the crippling of stem-cell research, the refusal to believe in man-made climate change. And Republicans' ongoing willingness to go racist for political purposes (as Bush's supporters did during the 2000 primaries) is disgusting. Demagoguery is endemic to both parties, but when it comes to exploiting fundamentally irrelevant issues (such as the medical condition of Terri Schiavo), the GOP takes the cake.

Republicans used to brag that theirs was the party of fresh thinking, but who's braindead now? All the big new ideas they have trotted out lately—privatizing Social Security, occupying a big country with only 160,000 troops, Middle Eastern democracy as a force-fed contagion—have given a bad name to new paradigms.

As for the Democrats, the Republicans still have a point: Where are the brave, fresh, clear approaches passionately and convincingly laid out? When it comes to reforming entitlements, the Democrats have absolutely refused to step up. Because the teachers unions and their 4 million members are the most important organized faction of its political base, the party is wired to oppose any meaningful experimentation with charter schools or other new modes. Similarly, after beginning to embrace the inevitability of economic globalization in the nineties, and devising ways to minimize our local American pain, the Democrats' scaredy-cat protectionist instincts seem to be returning with a vengeance. On so many issues, the ostensibly "progressive" party's habits of mind seem anything but.

However, what makes so much of the great middle of the electorate most uncomfortable about signing on with the Democratic Party is the same thing that has made them uncomfortable since McGovern—the sense that the anti-military instincts of the left half of the party, no matter how sincere and well meaning, render prospective Democratic presidents untrustworthy as guardians of national security. It's no accident that Bill Clinton was elected and reelected (and Al Gore won his popular majority) during the decade when peace reigned supreme, after the Cold War and before 9/11.

The Bush administration's colossal mismanagement of the occupation of Iraq is not about to make lots of Americans discover their inner pacifist, either. Rather, they will simply crave someone who is sensible, thoughtful, and competent as well as "tough" in his geopolitical m.o. If Iraq is souring most Americans on the Republican brand of dreamy, wishful, recklessly sketchy foreign policy, the result will not and should not be a pendulum swing to its dreamy, wishful, recklessly sketchy left-wing Democratic counterpart.

Wait, wait, the vestigial Democrat in me pleads, Hillary Clinton and Joe Biden are certainly not peace-at-any-price appeasers, and, Howard Dean aside, most of the party bigwigs have strenuously, carefully avoided endorsing a cut-and-run approach in Iraq.

The problem is "strenuously" and "carefully": People know tactical dissembling when they see it, whether it's liberal Democrats hiding their true feelings about military force or Republican Supreme Court nominees hiding their true feelings about abortion law. And Democrats who are sincerely tough-minded on national security are out of sync not only with much of their base but also with one of the party's core brand attributes. The Democrats remain the antiwar party, notwithstanding the post-9/11 growth of the liberal-hawk caucus—just as the Republicans are still the white party, notwithstanding George Bush's manifest friendliness to individual people of color.

So the simple question is this: Why can't we have a serious, innovative, truth-telling, pragmatic party without any of the baggage of the Democrats and Republicans? A real and enduring party built around a coherent set of ideas and sensibility—neither a shell created for a single charismatic candidate like George Wallace or Ross Perot, nor a protest party like the Greens or Libertarians, with no hope of ever getting more than a few million votes in a presidential election. A party that plausibly aspires to be not a third party but the third party—to winning, and governing.

Let the present, long-running duopoly of the Republicans and Democrats end. Let the invigorating and truly democratic partisan flux of the American republic's first century return. Let there be a more or less pacifist, anti-business, protectionist Democratic Party on the left, and an anti-science, Christianist, unapologetically greedy Republican Party on the right—and a robust new independent party of passionately practical progressives in the middle.

It's certainly time. As no less a wise man than Alan Greenspan said last month, the "ideological divide" separating conservative Republicans and liberal Democrats leaves "a vast untended center from which a well-financed independent presidential candidate is likely to emerge in 2008 or, if not then, in 2012."

And it's possible—indeed, for a variety of reasons, more so than it's been in our lifetimes. In 1992, a megalomaniacal kook with no political experience, running in a system stacked powerfully against third parties, won 19 percent of the presidential vote against a moderate Democrat and moderate Republican—and in two states, Perot actually beat one of the major-party candidates. In 1912, former president Teddy Roosevelt, running as a third-party progressive, got more votes than Taft, the Republican nominee. The Republicans, remember, began as a dicey new party until their second nominee, Lincoln, managed to get elected president.

It wouldn't be easy or cheap to create this party. It would doubtless require a rich visionary or two—a Bloomberg, a Steve Jobs, a Paul Tudor Jones—to finance it in the beginning. And since a new party hasn't won the presidency in a century and a half, it would have to struggle for credibility, to convince a critical mass of voters that a vote for its candidates would be, in the near term, an investment in a far better political future and not simply a wasted ballot.

Is this a quixotic, wishful conceit of a few disgruntled gadflies? Sure. This is only a magazine; we're only writers. But the beautiful, radical idea behind democracy was government by amateurs. As the historian Daniel J. Boorstin wrote, "An enamored amateur need not be a genius to stay out of the ruts he has never been trained in." We have a vision if not a true platform, sketches for a party if not quite a set of blueprints. Every new reality must start with a set of predispositions, a scribbled first draft, an earnest dream of the just possibly possible. In our amateur parlor-game fashion we are very serious about trying to get the conversation started, and moving in the right direction.

And New York, as it happens, is the ideal place to give birth to such a movement. This city's spirit—clear-sighted, tough-minded, cosmopolitan, hardworking, good-humored, financially acute, tolerant, romantic—should infuse the party. Despite our lefty reputation, for a generation now this city's governance has tended to be strikingly moderate, highly flexible rather than ideological or doctrinaire. While we have a consistent and overwhelming preference for Democratic presidential candidates, for 24 of the past 28 years the mayors we have elected—Koch, Giuliani, Bloomberg—have been emphatically independent-minded moderates whose official party labels have been flags of convenience. (And before them, there was John Lindsay—elected as a Republican and reelected as an independent before becoming an official Democrat in order to run for president.) Moreover, New York's stealth-independent-party regime has worked: bankruptcy avoided, the subways air-conditioned and graffiti-free, crime miraculously down, the schools reorganized and beginning to improve.

We're certainly not part of red-state America, but when push comes to shove we are really not blue in the D.C.–Cambridge–Berkeley–Santa Monica sense. We are, instead, like so much of the country, vividly purple. And so—for now—we'll call our hypothetical new entity the Purple Party.

"Centrist" is a bit of a misnomer for the paradigm we envision, since that suggests an uninspired, uninspiring, have-it-both-ways, always-split-the-difference approach born entirely of political calculation. And that's because one of the core values will be honesty. Not a preachy, goody-goody, I'll-never-lie-to-you honesty of the Jimmy Carter type, but a worldly, full-throated and bracing candor. The moderation will often be immoderate in style and substance, rather than tediously middle-of-the-road. Pragmatism will be an animating party value—even when the most pragmatic approach to a given problem is radical.

Take health care. The U.S. system requires a complete overhaul, so that every American is covered, from birth to death, whether he is employed or self-employed or unemployed. What?!? Socialized medicine? Whatever. Half of our medical costs are already paid by government, and the per capita U.S. expenditure ($6,280 per year) is nearly twice what the Canadians and Europeans and Japanese pay—suggesting that we could afford to buy our way out of the customer-service problems that afflict other national health systems. Beyond the reformist virtues of justice and sanity, our party would make the true opportunity-society argument for government-guaranteed universal health coverage: Devoted as the Purple Party is to labor flexibility and entrepreneurialism, we want to make it as easy as possible for people to change jobs or quit to start their own businesses, and to do that we must break the weirdly neo-feudal, only-in-America link between one's job and one's medical care.

But the Purple Party wouldn't use its populist, progressive positions on domestic issues like health to avoid talking about military policy, the way Democrats tend to do. We would declare straight out that, alas, the fight against Islamic jihadism must be a top-priority, long-term, and ruthless military, diplomatic, and cultural struggle.

We would be unapologetic in our support of a well-funded military and (depoliticized) intelligence apparatus, and the credible threat of force as a foreign policy tool. We would seldom accuse Democrats of being dupes and wimps or Republicans of being fearmongers and warmongers—but we would have the guts and the standing to do both.

And as we defend our country and civilization against apocalyptic religious fanatics for whom politics and religious belief are one and who consider America irredeemably heathen, we will be especially keen about adhering to the Founders' (and, for that matter, Christ's) ideal concerning the separation of religion and politics—to render to government the things that are its and to God the things that are his. Our party will enthusiastically embrace people of all religious beliefs, but we will never claim special divine virtue for our policies—we'll leave that to the Pat Robertsons and Osama bin Ladens. Where to draw the line is mostly a matter of common sense. Public reminders to honor one's parents and love one's neighbor, and not to lie, steal, or commit adultery or murder? Fine. Genesis taught as science in public schools, and government cosmologists forced by their PR handlers to give a shout-out to creationism? No way. Kids who want to wear crucifixes or yarmulkes or head scarves to those same schools? Sure, why not? And so on.

Our new party will be highly moral (but never moralistic) as well as laissez-faire. In other words, the Purple Party will be both liberal and American in the old-fashioned senses.

So: Are you in?

Consider the source and the audience

- Andersen is writing for *New York* magazine, which is intended primarily for New Yorkers. He often writes as though he is speaking directly to New Yorkers. Does his argument seem to be one that would resonate only with New Yorkers, or does it have a broader appeal?

Lay out the argument, the values, and the assumptions

- What does Andersen see as being wrong with the two major parties?
- In Andersen's eyes, what would a centrist party stand for?

Uncover the evidence

- Much of Andersen's argument is about his personal experience with the parties. What evidence does he provide that others might agree with him?

Evaluate the conclusion

- Does Andersen successfully make the case for a third party? Would his specific party have broad appeal?
- How would members of the Democratic and Republican Parties respond to Andersen's criticisms of them?
- Would Steve LaTourette, the author of Reading 12.3, likely agree with Anderson? Or does LaTourette see a place for moderates in one of the two major parties?

Sort out the political implications

- How would American politics change if a viable third party like the one Andersen proposes existed?
- What challenges would such a party face?

• •

12.5 Farewell Address
George Washington

Why We Chose This Piece

On the brink of leaving office, President George Washington prepared this address to the nation he had led since its birth. Eager to retire (this address was originally intended to mark his departure four years earlier, but he was persuaded to stay on), he was also anxious to point out to the young nation where danger might lie in its future. Chief among his concerns were political parties, fiscal responsibility, and foreign policy.

Here we excerpt Washington's remarks with respect to parties since, contrary to many modern observers, he saw party as an evil influence on politics and government. Like his colleague James Madison, who with Alexander Hamilton helped prepare earlier drafts of this address, he feared factional forces that would divide the nation against itself. The founders had tried to keep parties out of their new Constitution, and Washington was concerned that geographical and ideological divisions were admitting them through the back door. They had the potential, he believed, to spell doom for the fledgling republic. That the republic still stands is not to say that his argument has no merit, for many of his concerns find an echo in present-day politics.

Friends and Citizens:

The period for a new election of a citizen to administer the executive government of the United States being not far distant, and the time actually arrived when your thoughts must be employed in designating the person who is to be clothed with that important trust, it appears to me proper, especially as it may conduce to a more distinct expression of the public voice, that I should now apprise you of the resolution I have formed, to decline being considered among the number of those out of whom a choice is to be made. . . .

The impressions with which I first undertook the arduous trust were explained on the proper occasion. In the discharge of this trust, I will only say that I have, with good intentions, contributed towards the organization and administration of the government the best exertions of which a very fallible judgment was capable. Not unconscious in the outset of the inferiority of my qualifications, experience in my own eyes, perhaps still more in the eyes of others, has strengthened the motives to diffidence of myself; and every day the increasing weight of years admonishes me more and more that the shade of retirement is as necessary to me as it will be welcome. Satisfied that if any

Selection delivered: September 17, 1796

circumstances have given peculiar value to my services, they were temporary, I have the consolation to believe that, while choice and prudence invite me to quit the political scene, patriotism does not forbid it. . . .

Here, perhaps, I ought to stop. But a solicitude for your welfare, which cannot end but with my life, and the apprehension of danger, natural to that solicitude, urge me, on an occasion like the present, to offer to your solemn contemplation, and to recommend to your frequent review, some sentiments which are the result of much reflection, of no inconsiderable observation, and which appear to me all-important to the permanency of your felicity as a people. These will be offered to you with the more freedom, as you can only see in them the disinterested warnings of a parting friend, who can possibly have no personal motive to bias his counsel. Nor can I forget, as an encouragement to it, your indulgent reception of my sentiments on a former and not dissimilar occasion.

Interwoven as is the love of liberty with every ligament of your hearts, no recommendation of mine is necessary to fortify or confirm the attachment.

The unity of government which constitutes you one people is also now dear to you. It is justly so, for it is a main pillar in the edifice of your real independence, the support of your tranquility at home, your peace abroad; of your safety; of your prosperity; of that very liberty which you so highly prize. But as it is easy to foresee that, from different causes and from different quarters, much pains will be taken, many artifices employed to weaken in your minds the conviction of this truth; as this is the point in your political fortress against which the batteries of internal and external enemies will be most constantly and actively (though often covertly and insidiously) directed, it is of infinite moment that you should properly estimate the immense value of your national union to your collective and individual happiness; that you should cherish a cordial, habitual, and immovable attachment to it; accustoming yourselves to think and speak of it as of the palladium of your political safety and prosperity; watching for its preservation with jealous anxiety; discountenancing whatever may suggest even a suspicion that it can in any event be abandoned; and indignantly frowning upon the first dawning of every attempt to alienate any portion of our country from the rest, or to enfeeble the sacred ties which now link together the various parts.

For this you have every inducement of sympathy and interest. Citizens, by birth or choice, of a common country, that country has a right to concentrate your affections. The name of American, which belongs to you in your national capacity, must always exalt the just pride of patriotism more than any appellation derived from local discriminations. With slight shades of difference, you have the same religion, manners, habits, and political principles. You have in a common cause fought and triumphed together; the independence and liberty you possess are the work of joint counsels, and joint efforts of common dangers, sufferings, and successes.

But these considerations, however powerfully they address themselves to your sensibility, are greatly outweighed by those which apply more immediately to your interest. Here every portion of our country finds the most commanding motives for carefully guarding and preserving the union of the whole.

The North, in an unrestrained intercourse with the South, protected by the equal laws of a common government, finds in the productions of the latter great additional resources of maritime and commercial enterprise and precious materials of manufacturing industry. The South, in the same intercourse, benefiting by the agency of the North, sees its agriculture grow and its commerce expand. Turning partly into its own channels the seamen of the North, it finds its particular navigation invigorated; and, while it contributes, in different ways, to nourish and increase the general mass of the national navigation, it looks forward to the protection of a maritime strength, to which itself is unequally adapted. The East, in a like intercourse with the West, already finds, and in the progressive improvement of interior communications by land and water, will more and more find a valuable vent for the commodities which it brings from abroad, or manufactures at home. The West derives from the East supplies requisite to its growth and comfort, and, what is perhaps of still greater consequence, it must of necessity owe the secure enjoyment of indispensable outlets for its own productions to the weight, influence, and the future maritime strength of the Atlantic side of the Union, directed by an indissoluble community of interest as one nation. Any other tenure by which the West can hold this essential advantage, whether derived from its own separate strength, or from an apostate and unnatural connection with any foreign power, must be intrinsically precarious.

While, then, every part of our country thus feels an immediate and particular interest in union, all the parts combined cannot fail to find in the united mass of means and efforts greater strength, greater resource, proportionably greater security from external danger, a less frequent interruption of their peace by foreign nations; and, what is of inestimable value, they must derive from union an exemption from those broils and wars between themselves, which so frequently afflict neighboring countries not tied together by the same governments, which their own rival ships alone would be sufficient to produce, but which opposite foreign alliances, attachments, and intrigues would stimulate and embitter. Hence, likewise, they will avoid the necessity of those overgrown military establishments which, under any form of government, are inauspicious to liberty, and which are to be regarded as particularly hostile to republican liberty. In this sense it is that your union ought to be considered as a main prop of your liberty, and that the love of the one ought to endear to you the preservation of the other.

These considerations speak a persuasive language to every reflecting and virtuous mind, and exhibit the continuance of the Union as a primary object of patriotic desire. Is there a doubt whether a common government can embrace so large a sphere? Let experience solve it. To listen to mere speculation in such a case were criminal. We are authorized to hope that a proper organization of the whole with the auxiliary agency of governments for the respective subdivisions, will afford a happy issue to the experiment. It is well worth a fair and full experiment. With such powerful and obvious motives to union, affecting all parts of our country, while experience shall not have demonstrated its impracticability, there will always be reason to distrust the patriotism of those who in any quarter may endeavor to weaken its bands.

In contemplating the causes which may disturb our Union, it occurs as matter of serious concern that any ground should have been furnished for characterizing parties by geographical discriminations, Northern and Southern, Atlantic and Western; whence designing men may endeavor to excite a belief that there is a real difference of local interests and views. One of the expedients of party to acquire influence within particular districts is to misrepresent the opinions and aims of other districts. You cannot shield yourselves too much against the jealousies and heartburnings which spring from these misrepresentations; they tend to render alien to each other those who ought to be bound together by fraternal affection. The inhabitants of our Western country have lately had a useful lesson on this head; they have seen, in the negotiation by the Executive, and in the unanimous ratification by the Senate, of the treaty with Spain, and in the universal satisfaction at that event, throughout the United States, a decisive proof how unfounded were the suspicions propagated among them of a policy in the General Government and in the Atlantic States unfriendly to their interests in regard to the Mississippi; they have been witnesses to the formation of two treaties, that with Great Britain, and that with Spain, which secure to them everything they could desire, in respect to our foreign relations, towards confirming their prosperity. Will it not be their wisdom to rely for the preservation of these advantages on the Union by which they were procured? Will they not henceforth be deaf to those advisers, if such there are, who would sever them from their brethren and connect them with aliens?

To the efficacy and permanency of your Union, a government for the whole is indispensable. No alliance, however strict, between the parts can be an adequate substitute; they must inevitably experience the infractions and interruptions which all alliances in all times have experienced. Sensible of this momentous truth, you have improved upon your first essay, by the adoption of a constitution of government better calculated than your former for an intimate union, and for the efficacious management of your common concerns. This government, the offspring of our own choice, uninfluenced and unawed, adopted upon full investigation and mature deliberation, completely free in its principles, in the distribution of its powers, uniting security with energy, and containing within itself a provision for its own amendment, has a just claim to your confidence and your support. Respect for its authority, compliance with its laws, acquiescence in its measures, are duties enjoined by the fundamental maxims of true liberty. The basis of our political systems is the right of the people to make and to alter their constitutions of government. But the Constitution which at any time exists, till changed by an explicit and authentic act of the whole people, is sacredly obligatory upon all. The very idea of the power and the right of the people to establish government presupposes the duty of every individual to obey the established government.

All obstructions to the execution of the laws, all combinations and associations, under whatever plausible character, with the real design to direct, control, counteract, or awe the regular deliberation and action of the constituted authorities, are destructive of this fundamental principle, and of fatal tendency. They serve to organize faction, to give it an artificial and extraordinary force; to put, in the place of the delegated will of the nation the will of a party, often a small but artful and enterprising minority of the community; and, according to the alternate triumphs of different parties, to make the public administration the mirror of the ill-concerted and incongruous projects of faction, rather than the organ of consistent and wholesome plans digested by common counsels and modified by mutual interests.

However combinations or associations of the above description may now and then answer popular ends, they are likely, in the course of time and things, to become potent engines, by which cunning, ambitious, and unprincipled men will be enabled to subvert the power of the people and to usurp for themselves the reins of government, destroying afterwards the very engines which have lifted them to unjust dominion.

Towards the preservation of your government, and the permanency of your present happy state, it is requisite, not only that you steadily discountenance irregular oppositions to its acknowledged authority, but also that you resist with care the spirit of innovation upon its principles, however specious the pretexts. One method of assault may be to effect, in the forms of the Constitution, alterations which will impair the energy of the system, and thus to undermine what cannot be directly overthrown. In all the changes to which you may be invited, remember that time and habit are at least as necessary to fix the true character of governments as of other human institutions; that experience is the surest standard by which to test the real tendency of the existing constitution of a country; that facility in changes, upon the credit of mere hypothesis and opinion, exposes to perpetual change, from the endless variety of hypothesis and opinion; and remember, especially, that for the efficient management of your common interests, in a country so extensive as ours, a government of as much vigor as is consistent with the perfect security of liberty is indispensable. Liberty itself will find in such a government, with powers properly distributed and adjusted, its surest guardian. It is, indeed, little else than a name, where the government is too feeble to withstand the enterprises of faction, to confine each member of the society within the limits prescribed by the laws, and to maintain all in the secure and tranquil enjoyment of the rights of person and property.

I have already intimated to you the danger of parties in the State, with particular reference to the founding of them on geographical discriminations. Let me now take a more comprehensive view, and warn you in the most solemn manner against the baneful effects of the spirit of party generally.

This spirit, unfortunately, is inseparable from our nature, having its root in the strongest passions of the human mind. It exists under different shapes in all governments, more or less stifled, controlled, or repressed; but, in those of the popular form, it is seen in its greatest rankness, and is truly their worst enemy.

The alternate domination of one faction over another, sharpened by the spirit of revenge, natural to party dissension, which in different ages and countries has perpetrated the most horrid enormities, is itself a frightful despotism. But this leads at length to a more formal and permanent despotism. The disorders and miseries which result gradually incline the minds of men to seek security and repose in the absolute power of an individual; and sooner or later the chief of some prevailing faction, more able or more fortunate than his competitors, turns this disposition to the purposes of his own elevation, on the ruins of public liberty.

Without looking forward to an extremity of this kind (which nevertheless ought not to be entirely out of sight), the common and continual mischiefs of the spirit of party are sufficient to make it the interest and duty of a wise people to discourage and restrain it.

It serves always to distract the public councils and enfeeble the public administration. It agitates the community with ill-founded jealousies and false alarms, kindles the animosity of one part against another, foments occasionally riot and insurrection. It opens the door to foreign influence and corruption, which finds a facilitated access to the government itself through the channels of party passions. Thus the policy and the will of one country are subjected to the policy and will of another.

There is an opinion that parties in free countries are useful checks upon the administration of the government and serve to keep alive the spirit of liberty. This within certain limits is probably true; and in governments of a monarchical cast, patriotism may look with indulgence, if not with favor, upon the spirit of party. But in those of the popular character, in governments purely elective, it is a spirit not to be encouraged. From their natural tendency, it is certain there will always be enough of that spirit for every salutary purpose. And there being constant danger of excess, the effort ought to be by force of public opinion, to mitigate and assuage it. A fire not to be quenched, it demands a uniform vigilance to prevent its bursting into a flame, lest, instead of warming, it should consume.

Consider the source and the audience

- Although this address was never given by Washington in person, it was clearly intended to be. To whom is Washington addressing his words primarily? The American public? Fellow politicians? Political adversaries?

Lay out the argument, the values, and the assumptions

- What are Washington's basic assumptions about human nature? What is the link between human nature and parties?
- What values does Washington believe government should protect above all else?
- In what ways does Washington think parties threaten those values?

Uncover the evidence

- What evidence does Washington provide to support his contention that a unified country is a good thing?
- Is that evidence sufficient to convince people that parties are consequently bad, or should he have provided something more?

Evaluate the conclusion

- Washington makes a powerful logical and rhetorical case. Are passion, logic, and eloquence enough to convince you?
- What does Washington want Americans to do about the dangers of parties?

Sort out the political implications

- In what ways do modern-day politics support or weaken Washington's contention? Would he think that his fears had been realized, or that they were unnecessary?

13

Interest Groups

French philosopher Alexis de Tocqueville, writing about American culture and government during his trip to the United States in the early 1830s, noted that "Americans of all ages, all conditions, and all dispositions, constantly form associations. They not only have commercial and manufacturing companies, in which all take part, but associations of a thousand other kinds—religious, moral, serious, futile, general, or restricted, enormous or diminutive."[1] Tocqueville's observation more than 180 years ago still applies today. In fact, while we often criticize Americans for their lack of political engagement, more than 80 percent of us belong to at least one interest group.[2] An interest group is simply an organization of individuals who share a common political goal and unite for the purpose of influencing government decisions.

Indeed, one theory of representative democracy notes the incredible importance of interest groups in our society. Believers in pluralist democracy argue that while individually we may not have much power to influence government, our voices are magnified through our membership in interest groups. Representatives may discount our single vote, or ignore our single letter, but they are likely to listen to the Sierra Club, the National Rifle Association (NRA), or AARP (formerly the American Association of Retired Persons) when their professional representatives, known as lobbyists, come to call.

We may be, as Tocqueville wrote, a country of "joiners," but that doesn't necessarily mean we hold interest groups in the highest regard. The founders were quite wary of factions (their term for interest groups) because they feared it would then be easy for a majority to suppress the minority. James Madison made this argument persuasively in *Federalist* No. 10, included in this chapter. Today, when there are more interest groups than at any other time in our history, citizens often view interest groups as defenders of "special interests"—interests that, as far as Madison was concerned, do not represent the general public good. Interest groups such as the NRA and the Association of Trial Lawyers of America seem to have immense influence with elected officials, but their views are not necessarily consistent with the majority of the public. We also are skeptical of the role of interest groups in elections, and we fear that interest group money buys or unduly influences elected officials' votes. While political scientists haven't conclusively demonstrated this to be true, they have found evidence that money buys access, which could indirectly influence votes.

The articles in this chapter examine several aspects of interest groups. The first analyzes the leadership style of the executive vice president and CEO of one of the most prominent—and controversial—interest groups in American politics. The next article, from the *Huffington Post*, examines the role of interest groups that lobby the government on behalf of for-profit educational institutions. Third, Dave Levinthal, in a piece in *Politico*, looks at how interest groups are finding a new use for super PACs, the organizations that played such a significant role in the 2012 elections. Finally, we close with Madison's famous *Federalist* No. 10, in which he warns against the negative effects of factions.

Notes

1. Alexis de Tocqueville, *Democracy in America*, Richard D. Heffner, ed. (New York: New American Library, 1956), 198.
2. *The Public Perspective*, April/May 1995.

• •

13.1 Shy No More, N.R.A.'s Top Gun Sticks to Cause

Sheryl Gay Stolberg and Jodi Kantor, *New York Times*

Why We Chose This Piece

Perhaps no interest group has received more discussion from the media in the last few years than the National Rifle Association (NRA). It seems hard to find someone who doesn't have a strong opinion—positively or negatively—on the NRA. Moreover, few interest groups have the kind of influence over elected officials that the NRA enjoys. There have been many examples of politicians who have voted for the NRA's position on a gun-related issue for fear of being targeted by the organization in the next election.

With alarm over several high-profile incidents where innocent people have lost their lives to a gunman—Sandy Hook Elementary School the most recent—and President Barack Obama's call for stricter gun control legislation, the NRA once again is front and center in the public's eye.

We chose to include this piece for two reasons. First, it gives you a close look at the NRA and its controversial leader, Wayne LaPierre. Second, it is different from many

---

Selection published: April 13, 2013

of the selections in this reader because it focuses more on a person, as opposed to an issue. How might the personality of the leader of an interest group determine how successful a group is? What other factors might determine an interest group's success?

Victims of the massacre in Newtown, Conn., had just been laid to rest when Wayne LaPierre, the chief executive of the National Rifle Association, met with his board of directors in early January. A national tide of grief had prompted new attacks on his group and a White House push for more gun control measures, while Mr. LaPierre—who had called for armed guards in every school—was pilloried as a "gun nut" on the cover of *The New York Post*.

"They call us crazy, but no one—no other organization in the world—has spent more millions over more decades to keep Americans safe," said Mr. LaPierre, shown in January at a Senate hearing on gun violence.

"I don't know why the N.R.A. or the Second Amendment and lawful gun owners have to somehow end up in a story every time some crazy person goes off and kills children," he complained to Cleta Mitchell, a board member, who says Mr. LaPierre was "horrified" by the deaths and "insanely angry" that he and the N.R.A. were being blamed.

"These people are out to get us and the Second Amendment," she recalls him telling the board, "and we're not going to let them."

Now, as the Senate takes up gun control measures, the no-compromise strategy Mr. LaPierre has honed over his 35 years with the association is facing its most difficult test in decades. Lawmakers may defy Mr. LaPierre by extending background checks on some gun purchases, which the N.R.A. opposes. But since that grim January planning meeting, Mr. LaPierre has prevented what he and his group feared most: bans on assault weapons and high-capacity magazines.

Though Mr. LaPierre has long been on the public stage, today he provokes perhaps more debate than ever about who exactly he is. Supporters see him as a steadfast Second Amendment purist; critics cast him as a paranoid figure who believes, as he said last year, in "a massive Obama conspiracy" to seize the nation's firearms or as a cynical mouthpiece who is paid nearly $1 million a year to warn of crackdowns and crises he knows will never come.

"Wayne reminds me of the clowns at the circus," one of his most vocal detractors, Gov. Dannel P. Malloy of Connecticut, said after his state passed new gun control laws this month. "They get the most attention. That's what he's paid to do."

Once so bookish that he was known for his copious note-taking and so clumsy with a gun that colleagues laughed at his shooting, Mr. LaPierre, 64, helped invent the modern N.R.A. and transformed himself along with it into a right-wing folk hero and a reliable source of polarizing statements.

Liberals search for explanations as to how a man who is no one's idea of a highly polished spokesman can be so effective, and they accuse Mr. LaPierre of buying influence with campaign cash and intimidating lawmakers by "scoring," or issuing public report cards, on how they vote. But what his critics often overlook is the iron relationship Mr. LaPierre has forged with many N.R.A. members.

Week after week, year after year, he is on the road, traveling to gun shows and hotel ball-room fund-raisers, where he dispenses affirmation and absolution, telling firearms enthusi-asts that their N.R.A. ties have nothing to do with violence and everything to do with freedom.

The attendees form a ready-made base that Mr. LaPierre can draw on whenever he sees a threat to gun rights, and after spending much of his career building the member-ship—now nearly five million, the group says—he knows it well.

"We've got one guy on our committee, he's 72 years old, he's got a two-foot-long gray ponytail, and twice Wayne has picked him out at the national convention to give him a hug, to say, 'You're my trouper,'" said Gary Kamp, a judge in Cape Girardeau, Mo., who helped host a recent "Friends of the N.R.A." dinner there for educational and training charities.

N.R.A. members admire Mr. LaPierre, who declined to be interviewed for this article, as "a guy who will never fold," said Grover Norquist, the antitax crusader who is anoth-er board member.

"We are so used to electing politicians who go to Washington, D.C., and trim their sails and trade favors and do things they say they would never do," Mr. Norquist said. "If you are going to ask people to write $25 checks, you have to signal to people, 'I'm not folding; don't you think about folding.' And him not folding reminds everybody that we haven't given up."

"Have they lost their minds?"

Three months and a day after the Newtown massacre, Mr. LaPierre, dressed in his trade-mark business suit and starched white shirt, arrived with a security detail at a conven-tion hall overlooking the Potomac for the annual Conservative Political Action Conference, a gathering of thousands of activists sponsored, in part, by the N.R.A.

From the earliest days after the shooting, Mr. LaPierre had been working to counter any legislative impact: sowing concerns about background checks, which in the late 1990s he supported; introducing his "National School Shield" plan to arm teachers, administrators and other school personnel; and making sure his base felt protected as the national trauma sank in.

But on stage that day, Mr. LaPierre kept going back to himself. He was introduced by a slick video montage produced by his organization of television commentary that made him out to be a member of the lunatic fringe, with pundits proclaiming him "whacked" and "the lobbyist for mass murderers," which he used as the starting point for a 30-minute speech about how his opponents are really the irrational ones.

"They call us crazy, but no one—no other organization in the world—has spent more millions over more decades to keep Americans safe," Mr. LaPierre said, referring to the association's gun safety efforts.

He lashed out at "Janet Napolitano's Department of Homeland Security" by playing a self-defense video from the agency advising office workers to use "whatever means are available" to overpower a shooter, while showing images of a hand pulling scissors from a drawer. "To protect our children in school, we recommend a trained professional with a gun," Mr. LaPierre thundered. "They recommend scissors, and they say we're crazy?"

And he had nothing but ridicule for Vice President Joseph R. Biden Jr., who had recent-ly advised women to go outside and fire "two blasts" from a shotgun into the air if they heard an intruder.

"Honestly," Mr. LaPierre asked, "have they lost their minds over at the White House?"

It was a typically combative speech, and like many of Mr. LaPierre's other recent public performances, it was mystifying to some who knew him as a young man.

As a teenager growing up in Roanoke, Va., Mr. LaPierre had no apparent interest in hunting or guns, but a deep interest in politics, recalled Tom Lisk, a childhood neighbor who later worked for the rifle association.

He volunteered for the 1972 presidential campaign of George McGovern, a Democrat (back then Democrats were the dominant party in Virginia); earned a master's degree in government and politics from Boston College; and then worked for a Virginia state delegate and gun rights advocate, Vic Thomas. Mr. LaPierre essentially fell into his job at the N.R.A. through Mr. Thomas, and he began working as a state lobbyist covering New York and New England.

He earned a reputation as being more shy and studious than ideological, accumulating stacks of yellow legal pads filled with detailed notes. Later, he recruited Mr. Lisk by telling him that the rifle association was "a great place to learn politics, learn about lobbying." Being passionate about firearms was not a job requirement, Mr. Lisk said; he remembers Mr. LaPierre as more of a hockey fan.

John Aquilino, a former N.R.A. director of public education, said, "Wayne is not a gunny, he's not ex-military, he's not a hunter, he's not a trapper." What interested the young lobbyist was strategy.

He was deliberate and courteous, even to opponents, once surprising Naomi Paiss, a gun control advocate about to debate him on television, by warmly congratulating her on her approaching wedding. His fantasy, he told Mr. Aquilino, was to retire from the N.R.A. and open an ice cream shop in Maine. Instead he spent decades expanding the organization—founded in 1871 by Civil War commanders dismayed by their troops' poor marksmanship—into a universe of its own.

The association's skilled lobbying arm, the direct-mail hailstorms that help influence elections, the women's council, the television network, the sports stars and celebrities (including the rock musician Ted Nugent and the actor Tom Selleck) who sit on its board are all, to some degree, the handiwork of Mr. LaPierre. Outreach to minorities has also been a LaPierre priority, said Roy Innis, the national chairman of the Congress of Racial Equality, who serves on the N.R.A. board.

On Mr. LaPierre's watch, gun rights have expanded across the country; 41 states now issue permits to carry concealed weapons "in large part because of Wayne's leadership," the association's Web site boasts.

"He has built a membership and advocacy organization that is the model for other nonprofit organizations, liberal and conservative alike," said Anthony D. Romero, the executive director of the American Civil Liberties Union, an occasional ally of the N.R.A.

Devoted to the cause

And as Mr. LaPierre took over the association, it also took him over. Since becoming its executive vice president and chief executive in 1991, he has devoted himself to the organization, serving as spokesman but also top administrator. He spends his weekends traveling to N.R.A. gatherings across the country, sometimes making multiple stops in a single weekend.

His wife, Susan, helps raise money for the association and is a co-chairwoman of its women's leadership forum, which sponsors an annual luncheon that last year featured two prominent political spouses, Callista Gingrich and Ann Romney.

Years ago, Mr. LaPierre hoped to strike out as a consultant, Mr. Lisk said, an idea he abandoned when he realized how completely he had become identified with the gun issue.

Along the way Mr. LaPierre's language has steadily grown more operatic, filled with warnings about government agents who were "jackbooted thugs" (1995), "an Islamic ex-con with two aliases and no job" (2002) and a "U.N.-declared official day of hate" (2011).

"After Hurricane Sandy, we saw the hellish world that the gun prohibitionists see as their utopia," he wrote in February, conjuring images far worse than reality. "Looters ran wild in south Brooklyn. There was no food, water or electricity."

Former colleagues say he speaks that way because that is what his job demands; Mr. LaPierre learned early on the dangers of appearing to back down. After his "jackbooted thugs" remark, he apologized, only to face his members' ire, according to Richard Feldman, a former lobbyist for the association who now runs a rival gun rights group.

In small settings, people who know him say, he is mild-mannered and thoughtful.

"You ask if he is the same in private as he is in public—not at all," said Ms. Mitchell, the board member, who is also a lawyer and a Fox News commentator. "In real life, he's one of the shyest, kindest, most unassuming, total lack of ego, nonconfrontational— he hates confrontation—individuals I have ever met."

Gun control advocates say the gap between the public and private leader is dictated by simple demographic reality. Because gun ownership has been declining for decades, "the N.R.A. knows it has to motivate a shrinking base," said Josh Sugarmann, the executive director of the Violence Policy Center. "They have to reach out to the fringes."

The more besieged N.R.A. members feel, the more committed they are, with regular jumps in membership after mass shootings, as was the case after Newtown.

"Illegitimi non carborundum," Mr. LaPierre sometimes tells associates. It is a mock-Latin phrase for "Don't let the bastards wear you down."

Changed circumstances

With the Senate scheduled to begin voting on gun control measures this week, the question in Washington is not only which restrictions will pass. It is also whether Mr. LaPierre, having done more to expand gun rights than perhaps any other official in N.R.A. history, can keep winning now that the Newtown massacre has changed the national debate.

Already, two N.R.A. allies—Senators Patrick J. Toomey, Republican of Pennsylvania, and Joe Manchin III, Democrat of West Virginia—have broken with Mr. LaPierre to sponsor legislation extending background checks, which a bipartisan group of senators has embraced.

"The N.R.A. didn't lose many fights in the old days, and they don't lose many fights now," said Charlie Cook, the editor of the nonpartisan Cook Political Report. "But circumstances have changed."

Mr. LaPierre is being uncomfortably squeezed: from the right by organizations like Gun Owners of America, whose members regard themselves as even more ardent defenders of the Second Amendment, and from the left by new opponents like Gabrielle Giffords, the former congresswoman, shooting victim and Glock owner, who says her goal is common-sense gun laws.

Gun control advocates are moving to cast Mr. LaPierre and his organization—which once used the slogan "I am the N.R.A." to show its reach across American society—as extreme and out of sync even with its own members. A *New York Times*/CBS News survey in January found that 68 percent of households with N.R.A. members support background checks on all potential gun buyers; some sales, including those at gun shows, are now exempt.

New York and several other states have significantly tightened gun laws since the Newtown shooting. And longtime N.R.A. activities like sponsoring Nascar races, including one this weekend at the Texas Motor Speedway in Fort Worth, are generating controversy. (A Nascar spokesman said the organization would review sponsorships, given "current circumstances.")

All of that raises a question about Mr. LaPierre's leadership.

"The question for the N.R.A. is whether eventually he appeals to only so narrow a segment of the population that he consigns himself to irrelevance," said Senator Richard Blumenthal, a Connecticut Democrat and gun control advocate. "And I believe he is fast approaching that point of almost making a caricature of himself."

Mr. LaPierre is fighting back. Last week, as the Senate voted to bring the Toomey-Manchin bill up for debate, the N.R.A. notified lawmakers that unless the measure was changed, it would take the highly unusual step of scoring a procedural vote, meaning that a lawmaker's N.R.A. rating could suffer just for agreeing to allow the Senate to vote. "It was a message," said Ms. Mitchell, the board member. "There are no free passes. We are keeping score."

Consider the source and the audience

- The authors of this article seem to be targeting a broad audience. Why would this article be of interest to a wide variety of readers of the *New York Times*?
- The focus of this piece, Wayne LaPierre, declined to be interviewed for this article. How might that affect the depiction of how he is portrayed? Does the fact that he refused to be interviewed make the depiction less credible? Why might he not have wanted to be interviewed?

Lay out the argument, the values, and the assumptions

- According to the article, what is LaPierre's leadership style? How has his style changed?
- Why do some people—even detractors—think his style is effective? What are some criticisms of his style?

Uncover the evidence

- The authors of this article rely heavily on interviews with others. Whom did they interview? What credibility do those interviewed have to discuss LaPierre's leadership style and actions as the president of the NRA? Are there voices missing from the article from whom you would want to hear?

Evaluate the conclusion

- The authors of the article do not make normative claims about the success of LaPierre's leadership style. Instead, they let others make the arguments for them. Who is more persuasive? Does LaPierre's leadership style seem effective, or might it create problems for the NRA? How might your answer to this question be influenced by your own views on gun control?

Sort out the political implications

- Is it problematic in a representative democracy that groups representing some interests may be more powerful and influential than groups representing other interests? Is it inevitable?

13.2 For-Profit Colleges Mount Unprecedented Battle for Influence in Washington

Chris Kirkham, *Huffington Post*

Why We Chose This Piece

When you think about interest groups lobbying government—in other words, attempting to persuade policymakers to support their positions—organizations like the NRA (the subject of Reading 13.1), AARP, or the American Civil Liberties Union likely come to mind. Yet there are literally thousands of interests that must be protected, many by organizations not nearly as visible as some of the groups mentioned previously but quite powerful nonetheless. One such group that has become more influential in recent years is the for-profit college lobby, the focus of this reading.

We chose this article because the issues it discusses deal with higher education and therefore should be quite relevant to most of you. Additionally, while many of you are probably familiar with for-profit universities, you are likely less aware that there is a major power struggle at stake between for-profit and not-for-profit colleges and universities that plays out in Washington. The outcome of this battle will likely have a substantial effect on the future of higher education.

The morning after an 11th-hour deal to avert a government shutdown earlier this month, as many in Washington were still catching up on lost sleep, a group representing the for-profit college industry raced to send an online plea marked "urgent."
After a lobbying and campaign finance blitz totaling millions of dollars over the past year, the industry appeared to be on the verge of getting a special provision in the budget bill that would block increased government oversight of their schools. The matter was still not decided, they insisted.

Selection published: June 25, 2011

"We need you to make calls this weekend!" urged the letter from the group to its more than 1,600 member colleges. "Members and staff are meeting over the weekend to finalize the details of the [bill]. We encourage you TODAY and throughout this weekend to contact the offices of your Congressman/Senators urging them to support inclusion of the . . . amendment in the final package."

The email communique was a last-ditch bid to protect the massive federal subsidies that have fueled the spectacular growth of what is now a multibillion-dollar, publicly traded industry in higher education. With student loan defaults growing alongside profits at many of the largest companies, the government is seeking more accountability for colleges that promise training for careers, but leave students with unsustainable debts.

As the stakes for this fast-growing industry rise, so have the dollars spent on an expansive lobbying campaign to ensure the government money keeps flowing.

Some of the largest publicly traded college corporations receive nearly 90 percent of their revenues from federal student aid programs. While government money fuels increased enrollments and record profits, the industry has poured increasing amounts of those proceeds into an unprecedented effort to preempt the rules through greater influence in Washington.

In other words, an industry that derives a vast majority of its revenue from federal funding is actively using that money to fight government efforts for accountability.

The last-minute scramble earlier this month was only the latest chapter in the industry's yearlong battle against increased federal oversight of their schools.

Overall, the industry spent more than $8.1 million on lobbying in 2010, up from $3.3 million in 2009, according to a *Huffington Post* analysis of lobbying data compiled by the Center for Responsive Politics.

Figure 13.2.1   Lobbying Expenditures by For-Profit Colleges

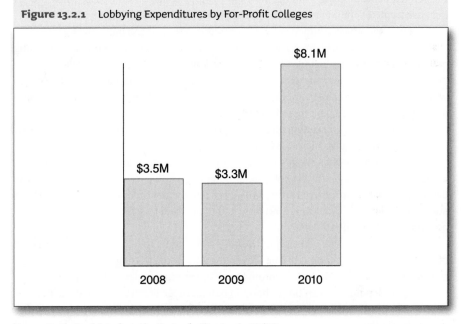

Source: Analysis of data from the Center for Responsive Politics.

In addition, campaign spending from the industry's political action committees and executives increased to more than $2 million from $1.1 million between the 2008 and 2010 election cycles, according to a *Huffington Post* analysis of campaign finance records from the Sunlight Foundation's website, TransparencyData. The industry's political action committees and executives spent nearly twice as much on Democrats as on Republicans.

Industry representatives say the uptick in spending for a business that derives most of its money from the government is not at all unusual in Washington.

"It's not unique in any sense," said Harris Miller, the president and chief executive of the Association of Private Sector Colleges and Universities, "any more than it is for traditional higher education lobbying to get earmarks for their schools, or Boeing or defense contractors using their money to promote an agenda, which is to win a contract of the U.S. government."

For-profit college companies and trade associations have hired a dream team of Washington insiders to lobby on their behalf, however, bringing on 14 former members of Congress, including former Democratic House Leader Dick Gephardt. Some of the most powerful lobby shops in Washington have been employed in the fight: Tony Podesta and the Podesta Group; former Clinton special counsel Lanny J. Davis; numerous former staffers from the Department of Education and the education oversight committees on Capitol Hill.

Until scrutiny of the schools intensified last year, when the Obama administration announced plans for new accountability rules, many of the colleges' parent companies were known on Wall Street for their exemplary profit margins.

The stakes for industry executives and shareholders have been huge. Andrew Clark, the chief executive at Bridgepoint Education Inc., which owns two online colleges, brought home more than $20 million in compensation last year. Corinthian Colleges Inc., which owns a string of more than 100 campuses across the nation, saw profits increase from $4.5 million in 1999 to more than $146 million in 2010.

Revenues for publicly traded college corporations topped $20 billion last year.

The industry has not been shy about funneling its money into marketing. Ubiquitous advertisements for the colleges fill subway cars in major cities and are plastered on billboards along highways across the country. *Advertising Age* listed The Apollo Group, which owns the University of Phoenix, as one of the top 100 spenders on U.S. advertising in 2009: The company spent in excess of $377 million, more than Apple Inc.

But the outcomes for students at such schools have prompted deep concerns about the federal government's increased investments.

Students at for-profit colleges default on federal loans at double the rate of their counterparts at nonprofit schools, according to recently released data from the Department of Education. And although only 10 percent of students nationwide attend such institutions, they account for nearly half of all student loan defaults, leaving the government to pick up the tab.

On average, the tuition at many of the largest for-profit colleges is nearly twice that of in-state tuition at four-year public universities and more than five times the average tuition at community colleges, according to a Senate report released last year.

Critics have pointed to an unfair bargain behind those statistics: Students and taxpayers take on all the risk while the schools reap all the rewards, in the form of profits from federal money.

"Going to college should not be like going to a casino, where the odds are stacked against you and the house always wins," Sen. Tom Harkin (D-Iowa), a vocal critic of for-profit colleges, said at a Senate hearing last fall.

For their part, for-profit colleges argue that they provide educational opportunities for many Americans who would otherwise have no such options, and that additional regulation could deny such students advancement.

"It does literally threaten the existence of hundreds if not thousands of programs, and threaten the ability of hundreds of thousands of students to continue to get an education," said Miller, of the Association of Private Sector Colleges and Universities.

Advertisements in Washington newspapers and on websites across the country have broadcast the same message: The Department of Education is trying to prevent students from going to college, especially low-income students who have struggled in other educational fields.

Education advocacy groups, meanwhile, argue the for-profit college rhetoric skill-fully twists reality.

"They've mastered the art of marketing," said Jose Cruz, vice president for Higher Education Policy at the Education Trust, a student advocacy organization. "In an attempt to protect the most important revenue source, which are the federal subsidies, they have launched this campaign to appeal to Americans' belief in choice and opportunity, particularly for those who have been traditionally underserved."

As the industry pours more money into lobbying, marketing and campaign finance, both Republicans and Democrats in Congress have shown their support.

Figure 13.2.2   Campaign Contributions in 2010

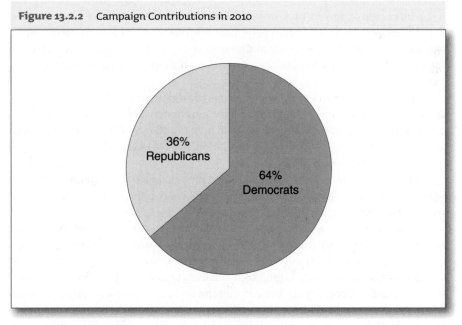

Source: *Huffington Post* analysis of data from the Sunlight Foundation.

Figure 13.2.3 Top Individual Recipients of Campaign Funding (over $30K)

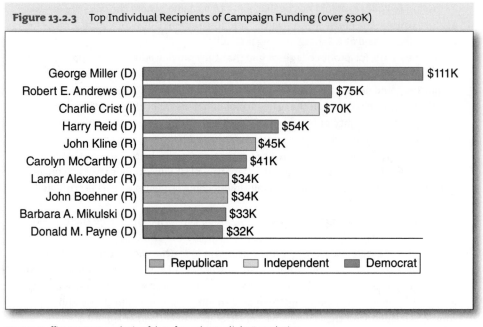

Source: *Huffington Post* analysis of data from the Sunlight Foundation.

Its increased clout was on display during a House vote in February, when more than 50 House Democrats, including House Minority Leader Nancy Pelosi (D-Calif.) and incoming Democratic National Committee chairwoman Debbie Wasserman Schultz (D-Fla.), joined Republicans in voting to block new regulations on the industry.

And during this month's budget fight, a bipartisan group of House members pushed to prohibit the Department of Education from moving forward with such regulations later this year. The Senate eventually stripped from the budget bill the rider that would have exempted for-profits from further regulation, but the industry has vowed to continue seeking such an exemption.

Many of the lawmakers who voted in support of the exemption in February, and who signed on to a letter urging its inclusion in the budget earlier this month, were the most well-compensated by the for-profit college industry.

"These burdensome and unnecessary regulations unfairly single out the private sector of postsecondary education and will negatively affect the landscape of our nation's higher education system," read a letter from six Democratic and six Republican House members urging that the budget compromise include a provision to block additional regulations. Five of the signatories were among the top 10 recipients of campaign cash from the industry, receiving more than $20,000 apiece in the last election cycle.

Figure 13.2.4   Top Organizations Receiving Campaign Funding

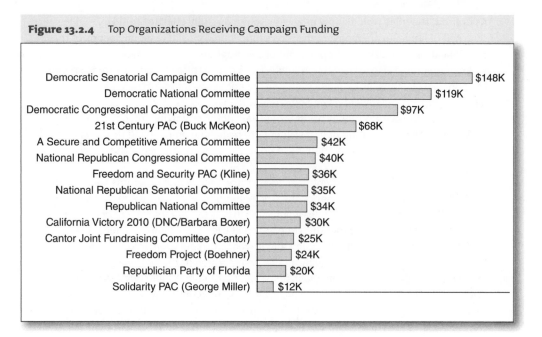

Democratic Senatorial Campaign Committee — $148K
Democratic National Committee — $119K
Democratic Congressional Campaign Committee — $97K
21st Century PAC (Buck McKeon) — $68K
A Secure and Competitive America Committee — $42K
National Republican Congressional Committee — $40K
Freedom and Security PAC (Kline) — $36K
National Republican Senatorial Committee — $35K
Republican National Committee — $34K
California Victory 2010 (DNC/Barbara Boxer) — $30K
Cantor Joint Fundraising Committee (Cantor) — $25K
Freedom Project (Boehner) — $24K
Republican Party of Florida — $20K
Solidarity PAC (George Miller) — $12K

Source: Huffington Post analysis of data from the Sunlight Foundation.

An Existential Threat

The rules at issue, developed by the Department of Education, are known as "gainful employment" regulations. It's an effort to measure the quality of for-profit college and nonprofit vocational college programs by analyzing student outcomes in the workplace, gauging whether the schools set students up for careers that will allow them to pay off debts.

Rules requiring that vocational colleges prepare students for "gainful employment in a recognized occupation" have been on the books since the 1970s, adopted following a series of problems with unscrupulous, fly-by-night trade schools that didn't provide the training they promised. This marks the first time the Department of Education has ever sought to officially define those rules written into the law by Congress.

For-profit colleges say that would pose an existential threat to the industry.

The Department of Education, on the other hand, has said the regulations are designed as both a consumer protection measure for students and a student aid accountability test for the federal government. A final version is expected within months.

The rules have been in the works since 2009, and were first drafted and presented to the public by the Department last summer. According to the draft version, the Department of Education would track students after leaving college and evaluate them using two criteria: whether they are paying down the principal on their student loans and whether graduates have attained an income that allows them to manage debts.

Programs at certain for-profit colleges and other vocational college programs that do not meet targets for student loan repayment or debt levels would be restricted from receiving federal student aid or forced to disclose debt levels to prospective students.

As drafted, the rules would allow programs to remain fully eligible for aid even if less than half of students are repaying the interest on loans, plus at least one penny of the principal after graduating or dropping out of the program.

Programs could also remain fully eligible if less than a third of students are repaying the principal on loans, as long as graduates are not spending more than 20 percent of discretionary income toward paying off student loans.

Student advocacy groups say the standards are not overly stringent, since each scenario would allow more than half of students to be behind on repaying the balance of their loans. The industry says there have not been enough studies of the effects the rules would have on the industry.

The rules would not punish entire schools; rather, individual programs that fail to meet the standards could face sanctions. The regulation would not go into effect until the 2012–'13 school year and the rules would punish only the worst 5 percent of offenders during the first year, giving programs time to adjust their curriculum or reduce costs.

"There hasn't been much discussion about what the regulation actually would do," said David Hawkins, director of public policy and research at the National Association for College Admission Counseling, whose member colleges include mostly nonprofits. "Instead there has been this hyperbolic, grand debate about limiting student choice. Really what the debate is about is the federal government drawing a line, beyond which they will be prepared to say, 'I'm sorry, we cannot fund this program anymore.'"

The Department of Education estimates the rules would completely restrict federal aid to about 5 percent of for-profit college programs, and that 55 percent of such schools would have to warn students about average debt levels.

Industry estimates, of course, are much higher. A study financed by the Association of Private Sector Colleges and Universities estimated that 33 percent of students at such schools would be affected.

Rep. Robert Andrews (D-N.J.), an opponent of the regulations who is also one of the top campaign recipients from the industry, said he disagrees with the government's focus on measuring debts compared to earnings. Instead, he said gainful employment should be measured by job placement that increases a graduate's income.

"I think the question is how we do this, not if we do it," Andrews said. "If they don't place enough students up to a fair standard, kick them out of the program. Whether they're owned by a for-profit, nonprofit or public institution."

Davis, the Democratic lobbyist and former special counsel to Bill Clinton, questioned why the regulations should not be applied to all sectors of higher education.

"If we're looking at the problem of excessive student debt, it is a problem and there needs to be a national solution," Davis said. "I, as a liberal Democrat, would say the national solution isn't cracking down on poor people who default."

Revolving Door Culture

Many critics of the for-profit sector who have long argued for more oversight say the rules proposed by the Obama administration are simply a reaction to a loose regulatory approach practiced during the administration of George W. Bush.

During those years, the corporations and their regulators developed a distinct revolving-door culture, where administration and congressional officials shifted from policy work for the government to advocacy work for the industry.

Both Bush Education Secretaries, Rod Paige and Margaret Spellings, have worked in connection with for-profit college corporations since leaving their posts. And for the majority of the Bush years, the assistant secretary overseeing higher education in Washington was Sally Stroup, a former lobbyist for the University of Phoenix, the largest of the for-profit college corporations. After leaving the administration in 2006, she became a top aide for the House Education and Labor Committee, now known as Education and Workforce.

That same year, current House Speaker John Boehner (R-Ohio), then the chairman of the lower chamber's education committee, helped to successfully pass legislation that lifted restrictions on federal student aid flowing to online college programs.

The provision nixed a previous rule that required schools to have at least half of students attending ground campus classes in order to be eligible for federal student aid. The old rule's elimination allowed for unprecedented growth at primarily online, for-profit schools.

Defining The Message

The final gainful employment rules were supposed to be released last fall, but the Department of Education delayed publishing them after receiving more than 90,000 comments from the public—the most ever received on any regulation in the Department's history. Many of the comments came from identical email form letters set up by colleges and trade associations for employees and students to send out—the byproduct of an extensive online marketing campaign.

Some of the form letters sent in as comments were not even filled out. One filed by Alyssa Hoskins of Edinburgh, Ind., read, "I am a career college student at [INSTITUTION] studying [PROGRAM]. [INSTITUTION] is providing me with the education and training necessary to obtain the job I've always wanted as a [CAREER]."

One anonymous comment from an employee at Herzing University included an email from the university president, Renee Herzing, stating that, "If you have not already you need to make a comment/letter through this web site. . . . E-mail me to confirm that you entered a comment—we (are) counting our total comments."

The lobbying efforts directed at members of Congress in recent months have been similarly strategic. During a "Hill Day" organized by the Association of Private Sector Colleges and Universities last month, the trade group handed out a series of tip sheets for students talking to the media, which were first obtained by CampusProgress, an advocacy group affiliated with the Center for American Progress.

Most of the instructions dealt with potential questions about student loan debt or recruiting tactics.

"Should a reporter ask if or how much debt you incurred at a career institution, you can firmly but politely reply: 'I made an adult decision to invest in my education, and I am confident in my ability to meet my financial responsibilities,'" one bullet point read. "Should the reporter continue to push on the debt point, you can politely but firmly reply: 'I have answered that question, and am happy to talk more about how my degree/diploma/certificate has enhanced my career prospects.'"

The Association of Private Sector Colleges and Universities has represented the industry for decades. But last year, two of the larger publicly traded education companies, Education Management Corp. and ITT Educational Services Inc., joined other colleges to form a separate lobbying organization called the Coalition for Educational Success.

They brought on Davis, a former legal counsel to Bill Clinton, to lobby on their behalf last fall—a time when scrutiny of the sector was reaching an all-time high.

The Department of Education had announced new rules, Sen. Tom Harkin (D-Iowa) had begun a series of hearings probing abuses in the industry, and the Government Accountability Office had released scathing findings from an undercover investigation of recruiting tactics at 15 for-profit schools.

The coalition and other corporations have brought on a wide array of lobbying expertise over the past year, employing many with deep connections to the committees and constituencies who could control the debate.

Figure 13.2.5 2010 Lobbying Spent by Individual Companies

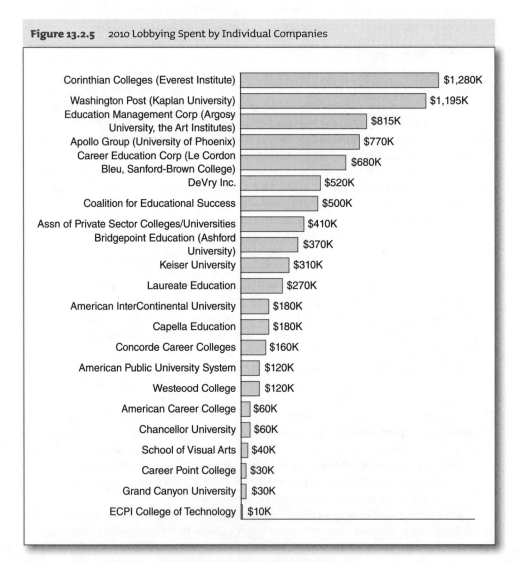

Source: Analysis of data from the Center for Responsive Politics.

Other major Democratic lobbying powers hired on for the fight include the Podesta Group, hired by Career Education Corp. and APSCU; and Steve Elmendorf, a major organizer for John Kerry's 2004 presidential campaign, who was hired by the Washington Post Co.'s Kaplan Inc.

College corporations have also focused on outreach to minority lawmakers and interest groups, fueling the debate about access to education for disadvantaged groups.

One of the lobbyists hired from the Podesta Group is Paul Braithwaite, a former executive director of the Congressional Black Caucus, whose members have been split on the question of the gainful employment regulations. Former Maryland Congressman Albert Wynn Jr., a longtime member of the CBC, was hired by Bridgepoint Education Inc. of San Diego.

Other lobbyists had backgrounds with the National Association of Latino Elected Officials, on education committees in both the House and Senate, and as staffers with the Department of Education.

Corinthian Colleges Inc. brought on Gephardt, the former Democratic House leader for 14 years, and a number of his former staff members.

Aside from Davis, none of the lobbyists or firms mentioned in this article returned phone calls and emails seeking comment; but trade groups for the industry have defended the increased advocacy, arguing they are no different from other industries seeking to be part of the debate.

"I wouldn't say that it's unusual for companies that feel regulation is going to either put them out of business, or drastically change their business, to advocate for their point of view," said Penny Lee, the managing director of the coalition.

Davis, who was lobbying for the Coalition for Educational Success until last week, said the outreach to Democrats has been a way to shift debate on the issue away from a traditional anti-government, pro-business perspective.

"I had an argument to make that was not a conservative, anti-regulation argument, and that was unusual," Davis said. "I think they reached out to other liberal and Democratic lobbyists for exactly the same reason. It's the 'man bites dog' point of view, because I'm criticizing my own fellow Democrats in the administration."

Growing Reach

The for-profit college industry's influence has been noticeable during public hearings in Washington.

At a hearing last September focusing on recruitment practices at for-profit colleges, Sen. John McCain (R-Ariz.) read aloud an op-ed letter written by Davis and published by *The Huffington Post* and other publications. The letter criticized Democratic support for the gainful employment rules.

"We've done a battle on many occasions," McCain said, but later pointed out that, "I find myself in complete agreement with Lanny Davis."

He then walked out of the hearing in protest, without noting the fact that Davis was being paid more than $40,000 to lobby on behalf of a number of schools.

Sen. Al Franken (D-Minn.) noted that fact later in the hearing.

"Lanny Davis is being paid by the industry to make these arguments that we get regurgitated here," Franken said. "I would appreciate it if the other members would stay, instead of making a comment, quoting a paid lobbyist—with great umbrage—and then leaving."

For-profit education companies gave more than $18,000 to McCain in the last election cycle, making him one of the top recipients in the Senate.

McCain and other Republicans on the Senate Health, Education, Labor and Pensions Committee wrote a letter to committee chairman Harkin last week, asking him to reconsider holding a scheduled May hearing on for-profit colleges.

"Should you decide to decline this request, we will not participate in the next hearing on for-profit institutions," the letter stated, calling the previous hearings "disorganized and prejudicial."

The letter was released the same day the budget amendment was finalized, without the rider that would prevent regulations. Most of the Republicans who signed the letter have either not attended previous Senate hearings on for-profit colleges or have walked out in protest.

That letter and others sent by Republicans and Democrats fighting against regulations over the past few months have also focused on two lines of attack pushed by industry lobbyists: one against the Department of Education, and another against the Government Accountability Office.

Rather than focusing on the substance of the rules at issue, the industry has instead tended to assert that it is under attack by the federal government.

The coalition in particular has been vocal in criticizing the GAO, Congress' independent investigative arm, over corrections made to an undercover investigation of for-profit college recruiting last year. The group has sued the GAO and publicly attacked the agency. Members of Congress have followed suit, calling into question the report's findings.

The GAO has stuck by its conclusions in the report, which was updated to include tweaks to language and more elaborate descriptions after GAO lawyers reviewed undercover footage. Lobbyists for the industry say the changes should invalidate the entire report.

The video evidence shown, however, is compelling: Recruiters encouraged investigators posing as prospective students to falsify federal financial aid documents and refused to provide details about tuition costs until they had signed paperwork to enroll in classes.

"I don't recall any kind of frontal assault the way they have mounted this one against the GAO," said Barmak Nassirian, associate executive director of the American Association of Collegiate Registrars & Admissions Officers, which mostly represents nonprofit colleges. "We saw with our own eyes how they were lying to and defrauding students."

The coalition has also sought to discredit the Department of Education by accusing department officials of conspiring to develop the regulations with Wall Street short sellers—investors who profit when stocks tumble. The theory is based on four meetings that Department of Education officials had with short sellers who had done analysis on publicly traded for-profit schools, and a number of mostly one-way emails from four hedge fund managers to officials in the department.

Representatives of for-profit colleges, who are also invested in how stocks fare on the market, have met privately and publicly with top-level Department of Education officials and the Office of Management and Budget on nearly 50 occasions over the past year, according to public schedules posted by the department.

Critics Get Cash

Some of the most vocal regulatory critics in Congress have also been the most well-compensated by the industry.

Rep. John Kline (R-Minn.), who chairs the House Education and the Workforce Committee, received more than $40,000 in campaign contributions during the last election cycle. His political action committee, the Freedom & Security PAC, received an additional $35,000.

Kline was instrumental in introducing the legislation in the House that aimed to block the gainful employment rules, and led the effort earlier this month to have the prohibition included in the budget bill.

Rep. Howard "Buck" McKeon (R-Calif.), another longtime member of the education committee, received more than $20,000 from the industry in his personal campaign and more than $65,000 to his political action committee, the 21st Century PAC.

While McKeon was serving on the committee during the Bush administration, he owned stock in one company, Corinthian Colleges Inc., at the time the restrictions on online programs were being lifted.

Staffers for McKeon and Kline did not respond to requests seeking comment.

Democrats who have opposed regulations on for-profit colleges have also been rewarded with contributions. Reps. Andrews and Carolyn McCarthy (D-N.Y.), who signed onto the letter pushing for the budget bill rider, are among the top five recipients of campaign cash: Andrews received more than $70,000, and McCarthy more than $41,000, during the last election cycle.

Andrews said he has been involved with the industry for a long time and believes that career programs can offer many benefits for students.

"I do what I do based upon what I think is right," he said. "I'm interested in the outcome for the student and the taxpayer, not on the outcome for the school. But I also disagree with people who say that by definition for-profit education is bad. I think bad education is bad, and I think we ought to come up with a measure to figure that out."

One notable exception is Rep. George Miller (D-Calif.), the former chairman of the education committee until this year, who took in more than $105,000 from the industry—the most of any single candidate in Congress.

His son also works for a lobbying firm in California that lobbies for Education Management Corp., the second-largest publicly traded college corporation.

But Miller has supported the Department of Education's proposed regulations, and has been critical of attempts to delay or water them down.

A spokeswoman for Miller said the contributions are "completely separate" from any policy work. "The fact is that Rep. Miller has a long and successful track record of holding for-profit schools accountable and reforming this industry," said the spokeswoman, Melissa Salmanowitz.

Other top recipients of campaign money who have not supported the industry include Senate Majority Leader Harry Reid (D-Nev.), who took in more than $50,000; and Iowa Democrat Harkin, who received about $13,000 but has held a series of highly critical hearings probing the industry.

Looking at the February House vote, however, Democrats who supported the amendment to block regulations received on average nearly twice as much in political donations as Democrats who opposed the regulations.

Harris Miller, the president of the trade group representing for-profit colleges (who is not related to George Miller), downplayed the importance that political contributions play in changing policy, pointing to the donations to many who have actively opposed the industry.

"I know some people like to think there's this simplistic correlation between writing a check and getting a vote," he said. "I wish it were that easy."

Consider the source and the audience

- Chris Kirkham is a business reporter. Why would the for-profit university lobby be of interest to him?

Lay out the argument, the values, and the assumptions

- Why are for-profit universities spending so much money on lobbying? What is at stake? How has the group become so powerful?
- Why are for-profit universities and government entities such as the Department of Education and the Government Accountability Office at odds?
- Does Kirkham seem to come down on one side or the other in the debate?

Uncover the evidence

- What evidence do for-profit universities and their opponents provide to support their positions? Empirical data? Logic? Or is this really more of a normative debate over the role of government and its regulatory powers?

Evaluate the conclusion

- Is this disagreement a battle over money or something else?
- Are you convinced that the for-profit universities play an important role in higher education?

Sort out the political implications

- How might a congressperson's vote on these issues affect his or her standing in the home district?

● ●

13.3 Super PACs Get New Use—as Lobbying Arms on Hill

Dave Levinthal, *Politico*

Why We Chose This Piece

A super PAC is an organization that is registered with the Federal Election Commission that pledges to donate no money to candidates, but can air ads explicitly urging for their election or defeat. They often, although certainly not always, are associated with specific interest groups. Donations to super PACs are unlimited and can come from anyone, so they are quite controversial.

Super PACs were created as a result of two recent Supreme Court rulings. They played a significant role in the 2012 election, spending more than $567 million on behalf of or in opposition to candidates and political parties.[1] However, according to this article published in Politico, interest groups are also using super PACs for a different purpose. We chose this article because it focuses on lobbying—a central concept to understanding interest groups— but not in the traditional way that is normally discussed in most American Government textbooks. Moreover, super PACs are likely to continue to be a significant part of the political landscape for the foreseeable future, and it is important that students understand what they are and what they do.

There's a second act for super PACs.

From autism research to dentists, a growing number of issue-based organizations are preparing to use these powerful political committees not for their prescribed purpose—advocating for the election or defeat of candidates—but as de facto lobbying arms on Capitol Hill.

The advantage?

Super PACs may raise and spend as much money as they please, including from corporations, unions and individuals, to broadcast whatever they want about politicians within the context of their particular special interest. Traditional issue ads, in contrast, don't allow for full-throated attacks or endorsements, and the nonprofit groups that often sponsor them can't by law have a primary purpose in engaging in politics like super PACs can.

So for some issue interest groups, super PACs are a potentially major complement to—if not upgrade over—traditional, Capitol Hill lobbying in their ability to bring heat on lawmakers and twist their arms toward their agendas.

Selection published: September 25, 2012

"If you're a lobbyist, you're talking with a legislator and mention you're forming a super PAC, their ears are really going to perk up just because you said the words 'super PAC,'" said Shana Glickfield, a partner at public affairs firm Beekeeper Group. "It's such a big, scary thing—and can give you an extra edge of influence."

That's precisely why Craig Snyder, a former lobbyist for Autism Speaks and a chief of staff to former Sen. Arlen Specter, is now president of the new Autism Super PAC.

The super PAC—which is not affiliated with other autism education organizations— plans to produce an advertising campaign aimed at convincing both President Barack Obama and Republican Mitt Romney to endorse its agenda, which includes demands to double federal autism research dollars by 2017 and create an autism research office within the National Institutes of Health. Formed last month, the group has already bankrolled pricey political polling indicating Americans are overwhelmingly supportive of increased federal autism funding.

If the candidates ignore the super PAC, Snyder said he's prepared to launch a yet-to-be-produced advertising barrage against either candidate, regardless of who ultimately wins the White House. These ads, he said, would be "hard-hitting" in tone and tenor.

"There will be political consequences for ignoring our community and this issue," Snyder said.

"As a super PAC, you can speak to power with so much more clarity—both the money in and message out are more open than they'd be otherwise," he added. "Whatever you think of the *Citizens United* decision and super PACs, if these are going to be the rules, why not use them for causes you feel are important?"

The National Association of Realtors—among the first issue-based organizations to form a super PAC—has augmented its already sizable lobbying firepower with its own super PAC that's rewarded like-minded lawmakers with hundreds of thousands of dollars in advertising air cover.

Through July, the National Association of Realtors Congressional Fund super PAC boasted spending nearly $826,000 to boost various pro-development lawmakers such as Reps. Gary Miller (R-Calif.) and Gary Peters (D-Mich.) and congressional candidate Marc Veasey (D-Texas). And it still reported having $1 million in the bank.

A Realtor super PAC ad lauding Rep. Fred Upton (R-Mich.), for example, repeatedly praised the House Energy and Commerce Committee chairman for his development-friendly legislation and stances, such as fighting for tax deductions on second homes. A pro-Peters ad says the congressman "fights every day for safe and affordable home financing for all responsible borrowers." Both overtly call for the lawmakers' reelection.

"The super PAC—it's a complement to our other outreach and it's another form of lobbying, in a sense," said Scott Reiter, the association's political director who also runs the super PAC.

"You'll definitely see more and more mainstream groups looking at super PACs," he added.

Officials from special interest groups such as Gun Owners of America and the Drug Policy Alliance have yet to form super PACs, but they confirm they would consider doing do.

The American Dental Association and the Cooperative of American Physicians are among established issue-focused organizations that have already formed super PACs.

The ADA's super PAC has spent at least $323,000 in radio ads, direct mail and polling to support Reps. Paul Gosar (R-Ariz.) and Mike Simpson (R-Idaho) as well as Republican House candidates Scott Keadle of North Carolina and Fred Costello of Florida—all dentists by trade. About half of this super PAC's money comes in the form of contributions from Citibank, according to federal disclosure reports.

Of course, forming a super PAC isn't without political risk.

Siding too much with one political party could make it difficult to do business in Washington and risk losing bipartisan credibility.

And campaign finance reformers have vilified super PACs as a primary symptom of a political finance regime run amok, where big money raised from corporate sources and wealthy individuals unduly games the system.

But a 2011 federal court decision and subsequent Federal Election Commission ruling is making issue-focused super PACs even easier to create. The hybrid PAC is a single political committee that may operate as a traditional PAC and a super PAC at the same time, so long as the money for each are kept in separate accounts.

It's particularly attractive since many special interest groups already have a traditional PAC. These existing PACs need only send a letter to the FEC to announce they're going hybrid. At least 45 hybrid PACs have materialized, federal records show.

They include special interests ranging from the Fraternity and Sorority Political Action Committee and PURO PAC, which advocates for the cigar industry, to the Harbor Trucking Association Federal Political Action Committee and Gay and Lesbian Victory Fund Federal PAC.

Big-ticket congressional issues coming up after Nov. 7, including the budget deficit, tax reform and sequestration, almost invite super PAC activity, said James Bonham, chairman of Manatt, Phelps & Phillips' federal government affairs and public policy practice.

For super PACs sporting big financial reserves after Election Day, "it's going to be pretty hard to keep that cash sitting in an account—if it's there, it'll be spent, even if it's not on an election."

Note

1.   *Wall Street Journal*, http://projects.wsj.com/super-pacs/.

Consider the source and the audience

- *Politico* is a publication that is read by many D.C. political insiders. Why would this article interest them? Would it likely appear in a more broadly read publication?

Lay out the argument, the values, and the assumptions

- Why are interest groups turning to super PACs to lobby members of Congress? How is this lobbying different from the more traditional lobbying in which interest groups normally engage?
- What risks might come with forming a super PAC?

Uncover the evidence

- Is there any evidence that the use of super PACs is influencing members of Congress? How would we know?

Evaluate the conclusion

- Does the author take a clear position one way or the other on whether this new use of super PACs is a positive thing? Based on what you've read here, is it? How come?

Sort out the political implications

- What might be some consequences of the movement toward super PACs being used as lobbying tools?
- Super PACs are viewed negatively by many, including campaign finance reform advocates. Why do you think this is the case? Are there any positive aspects of super PACs? What might they be?

• •

13.4 *Federalist* No. 10

James Madison, *The Federalist Papers*

Why We Chose This Piece

Of all the Federalist Papers, *perhaps none has received as much scrutiny and discussion as Madison's Federalist No. 10. One simply cannot be a student of interest groups without understanding Madison's argument in this essay. Whereas supporters of pluralist democracy—a theory of representative democracy that holds that citizen membership in groups is the key to political power—argue that interest groups are an essential component of a republic, Madison claims that the formation of interest groups—or factions, as he calls them—can potentially threaten the very health of a society. In Federalist No. 10, Madison argues that the proposed new republic offers the perfect opportunity to control "the violence of faction" while, at the same time, not limiting individual freedoms. How does Madison's view of factions in 1787 compare with our view of interest groups today?*

To the People of the State of New York:

Among the numerous advantages promised by a well constructed Union, none deserves to be more accurately developed than its tendency to break and control the

_____

Selection published: November 23, 1787

violence of faction. The friend of popular governments never finds himself so much alarmed for their character and fate, as when he contemplates their propensity to this dangerous vice. He will not fail, therefore, to set a due value on any plan which, without violating the principles to which he is attached, provides a proper cure for it. The instability, injustice, and confusion introduced into the public councils, have, in truth, been the mortal diseases under which popular governments have everywhere perished; as they continue to be the favorite and fruitful topics from which the adversaries to liberty derive their most specious declamations. The valuable improvements made by the American constitutions on the popular models, both ancient and modern, cannot certainly be too much admired; but it would be an unwarrantable partiality, to contend that they have as effectually obviated the danger on this side, as was wished and expected. Complaints are everywhere heard from our most considerate and virtuous citizens, equally the friends of public and private faith, and of public and personal liberty, that our governments are too unstable, that the public good is disregarded in the conflicts of rival parties, and that measures are too often decided, not according to the rules of justice and the rights of the minor party, but by the superior force of an interested and overbearing majority. However anxiously we may wish that these complaints had no foundation, the evidence, of known facts will not permit us to deny that they are in some degree true. It will be found, indeed, on a candid review of our situation, that some of the distresses under which we labor have been erroneously charged on the operation of our governments; but it will be found, at the same time, that other causes will not alone account for many of our heaviest misfortunes; and, particularly, for that prevailing and increasing distrust of public engagements, and alarm for private rights, which are echoed from one end of the continent to the other. These must be chiefly, if not wholly, effects of the unsteadiness and injustice with which a factious spirit has tainted our public administrations.

By a faction, I understand a number of citizens, whether amounting to a majority or a minority of the whole, who are united and actuated by some common impulse of passion, or of interest, adversed to the rights of other citizens, or to the permanent and aggregate interests of the community.

There are two methods of curing the mischiefs of faction: the one, by removing its causes; the other, by controlling its effects.

There are again two methods of removing the causes of faction: the one, by destroying the liberty which is essential to its existence; the other, by giving to every citizen the same opinions, the same passions, and the same interests.

It could never be more truly said than of the first remedy, that it was worse than the disease. Liberty is to faction what air is to fire, an aliment without which it instantly expires. But it could not be less folly to abolish liberty, which is essential to political life, because it nourishes faction, than it would be to wish the annihilation of air, which is essential to animal life, because it imparts to fire its destructive agency.

The second expedient is as impracticable as the first would be unwise. As long as the reason of man continues fallible, and he is at liberty to exercise it, different opinions will be formed. As long as the connection subsists between his reason and his self-love, his opinions and his passions will have a reciprocal influence on each other; and the former will be objects to which the latter will attach themselves. The diversity in the faculties of men, from which the rights of property originate, is not less an insuperable obstacle to a uniformity of interests. The protection of these faculties is the first object of government. From the protection of different and unequal faculties of acquiring property, the possession of different degrees and kinds of property immediately results; and from the influence of these on the sentiments and views of the respective proprietors, ensues a division of the society into different interests and parties.

The latent causes of faction are thus sown in the nature of man; and we see them everywhere brought into different degrees of activity, according to the different circumstances of civil society. A zeal for different opinions concerning religion, concerning government, and many other points, as well of speculation as of practice; an attachment to different leaders ambitiously contending for preeminence and power; or to persons of other descriptions whose fortunes have been interesting to the human passions, have, in turn, divided mankind into parties, inflamed them with mutual animosity, and rendered them much more disposed to vex and oppress each other than to co-operate for their common good. So strong is this propensity of mankind to fall into mutual animosities, that where no substantial occasion presents itself, the most frivolous and fanciful distinctions have been sufficient to kindle their unfriendly passions and excite their most violent conflicts. But the most common and durable source of factions has been the various and unequal distribution of property. Those who hold and those who are without property have ever formed distinct interests in society. Those who are creditors, and those who are debtors, fall under a like discrimination. A landed interest, a manufacturing interest, a mercantile interest, a moneyed interest, with many lesser interests, grow up of necessity in civilized nations, and divide them into different classes, actuated by different sentiments and views. The regulation of these various and interfering interests forms the principal task of modern legislation, and involves the spirit of party and faction in the necessary and ordinary operations of the government.

No man is allowed to be a judge in his own cause, because his interest would certainly bias his judgment, and, not improbably, corrupt his integrity. With equal, nay with greater reason, a body of men are unfit to be both judges and parties at the same time; yet what are many of the most important acts of legislation, but so many judicial determinations, not indeed concerning the rights of single persons, but concerning the rights of large bodies of citizens? And what are the different classes of legislators but advocates and parties to the causes which they determine? Is a law proposed concerning private debts? It is a question to which the creditors are parties on one side and the debtors on the other. Justice ought to hold the balance between them. Yet the parties are, and must be, themselves the judges; and the most numerous party or, in other words, the most powerful faction must be expected to prevail. Shall domestic manufactures be encouraged, and in what degree, by restrictions on foreign manufactures? are questions which would be differently decided by the landed and the manufacturing classes, and probably by neither with a sole regard to justice and the public good. The apportionment of taxes on the various descriptions of property is an act which seems to require the most exact impartiality; yet there is, perhaps, no legislative act in which greater opportunity and temptation are given to a predominant party to trample on the rules of justice. Every shilling with which they overburden the inferior number, is a shilling saved to their own pockets.

It is in vain to say that enlightened statesmen will be able to adjust these clashing interests, and render them all subservient to the public good. Enlightened statesmen will not always be at the helm. Nor, in many cases, can such an adjustment be made at all without taking into view indirect and remote considerations, which will rarely prevail over the immediate interest which one party may find in disregarding the rights of another or the good of the whole.

The inference to which we are brought is, that the CAUSES of faction cannot be removed, and that relief is only to be sought in the means of controlling its EFFECTS.

If a faction consists of less than a majority, relief is supplied by the republican principle, which enables the majority to defeat its sinister views by regular vote. It may clog the administration, it may convulse the society; but it will be unable to execute and mask its violence under the forms of the Constitution. When a majority is included in a faction, the form of popular government, on the other hand, enables it to sacrifice to its ruling passion or interest both the public good and the rights of other citizens. To secure the public good and private rights against the danger of such a faction, and at the same time to preserve the spirit and the form of popular government, is then the great object to which our inquiries are directed. Let me add that it is the great desideratum by which this form of government can be rescued from the opprobrium under which it has so long labored, and be recommended to the esteem and adoption of mankind.

By what means is this object attainable? Evidently by one of two only. Either the existence of the same passion or interest in a majority at the same time must be prevented, or the majority, having such coexistent passion or interest, must be rendered, by their number and local situation, unable to concert and carry into effect schemes of oppression. If the impulse and the opportunity be suffered to coincide, we well know that neither moral nor religious motives can be relied on as an adequate control. They are not found to be such on the injustice and violence of individuals, and lose their efficacy in proportion to the number combined together, that is, in proportion as their efficacy becomes needful.

From this view of the subject it may be concluded that a pure democracy, by which I mean a society consisting of a small number of citizens, who assemble and administer the government in person, can admit of no cure for the mischiefs of faction. A common passion or interest will, in almost every case, be felt by a majority of the whole; a communication and concert result from the form of government itself; and there is nothing to check the inducements to sacrifice the weaker party or an obnoxious individual. Hence it is that such democracies have ever been spectacles of turbulence and contention; have ever been found incompatible with personal security or the rights of property; and have in general been as short in their lives as they have been violent in their deaths. Theoretic politicians, who have patronized this species of government, have erroneously supposed that by reducing mankind to a perfect equality in their political rights, they would, at the same time, be perfectly equalized and assimilated in their possessions, their opinions, and their passions.

A republic, by which I mean a government in which the scheme of representation takes place, opens a different prospect, and promises the cure for which we are seeking. Let us examine the points in which it varies from pure democracy, and we shall comprehend both the nature of the cure and the efficacy which it must derive from the Union.

The two great points of difference between a democracy and a republic are: first, the delegation of the government, in the latter, to a small number of citizens elected by the rest; secondly, the greater number of citizens, and greater sphere of country, over which the latter may be extended.

The effect of the first difference is, on the one hand, to refine and enlarge the public views, by passing them through the medium of a chosen body of citizens, whose wisdom may best discern the true interest of their country, and whose patriotism and love of justice will be least likely to sacrifice it to temporary or partial considerations. Under such a regulation, it may well happen that the public voice, pronounced by the representatives of the people, will be more consonant to the public good than if pronounced by the people themselves, convened for the purpose. On the other hand, the effect may be inverted. Men of factious tempers, of local prejudices, or of sinister designs, may, by intrigue, by corruption, or by other means, first obtain the suffrages, and then betray the interests, of the people. The question resulting is, whether small or extensive republics are more favorable to the election of proper guardians of the public weal; and it is clearly decided in favor of the latter by two obvious considerations:

In the first place, it is to be remarked that, however small the republic may be, the representatives must be raised to a certain number, in order to guard against the cabals of a few; and that, however large it may be, they must be limited to a certain number, in order to guard against the confusion of a multitude. Hence, the number of representatives in the two cases not being in proportion to that of the two constituents, and being proportionally greater in the small republic, it follows that, if the proportion of fit characters be not less in the large than in the small republic, the former will present a greater option, and consequently a greater probability of a fit choice.

In the next place, as each representative will be chosen by a greater number of citizens in the large than in the small republic, it will be more difficult for unworthy candidates to practice with success the vicious arts by which elections are too often carried; and the suffrages of the people being more free, will be more likely to centre in men who possess the most attractive merit and the most diffusive and established characters.

It must be confessed that in this, as in most other cases, there is a mean, on both sides of which inconveniences will be found to lie. By enlarging too much the number of electors, you render the representatives too little acquainted with all their local circumstances and lesser interests; as by reducing it too much, you render him unduly attached to these, and too little fit to comprehend and pursue great and national objects. The federal Constitution forms a happy combination in this respect; the great and aggregate interests being referred to the national, the local and particular to the State legislatures.

The other point of difference is, the greater number of citizens and extent of territory which may be brought within the compass of republican than of democratic government; and it is this circumstance principally which renders factious combinations less to be dreaded in the former than in the latter. The smaller the society, the fewer probably will be the distinct parties and interests composing it; the fewer the distinct parties and interests, the more frequently will a majority be found of the same party; and the smaller the number of individuals composing a majority, and the smaller the compass within which they are placed, the more easily will they concert and execute their plans of oppression. Extend the sphere, and you take in a greater variety of parties and interests; you make it less probable that a majority of the whole will have a common motive to invade the rights of other citizens; or if such a common motive exists, it will be more difficult for all who feel it to discover their own strength, and to act in unison with each other. Besides other impediments, it may be remarked that, where there is a consciousness of unjust or dishonorable purposes, communication is always checked by distrust in proportion to the number whose concurrence is necessary.

Hence, it clearly appears, that the same advantage which a republic has over a democracy, in controlling the effects of faction, is enjoyed by a large over a small republic,—is enjoyed by the Union over the States composing it. Does the advantage consist in the substitution of representatives whose enlightened views and virtuous sentiments render them superior to local prejudices and schemes of injustice? It will not be denied that the representation of the Union will be most likely to possess these requisite endowments. Does it consist in the greater security afforded by a greater variety of parties, against the event of any one party being able to outnumber and oppress the rest? In an equal degree does the increased variety of parties comprised within the Union, increase this security? Does it, in fine, consist in the greater obstacles opposed to the concert and accomplishment of the secret wishes of an unjust and interested majority? Here, again, the extent of the Union gives it the most palpable advantage.

The influence of factious leaders may kindle a flame within their particular States, but will be unable to spread a general conflagration through the other States. A religious sect may degenerate into a political faction in a part of the Confederacy; but the variety of sects dispersed over the entire face of it must secure the national councils against any danger from that source. A rage for paper money, for an abolition of debts, for an equal division of property, or for any other improper or wicked project, will be less apt to pervade the whole body of the Union than a particular member of it; in the same proportion as such a malady is more likely to taint a particular county or district, than an entire State.

In the extent and proper structure of the Union, therefore, we behold a republican remedy for the diseases most incident to republican government. And according to the degree of pleasure and pride we feel in being republicans, ought to be our zeal in cherishing the spirit and supporting the character of Federalists.

PUBLIUS.

Consider the source and the audience

- *Federalist* No. 10 was an editorial, written anonymously under the name "Publius," in an effort to get the citizens of New York to sign on to the Constitution. *Federalist* No. 10 was especially aimed at people who feared the possibilities for corruption in a large country. How does that fact affect how Madison couches his arguments about factions?

Lay out the argument, the values, and the assumptions

- What does Madison believe are the root causes of factions?
- Why does he think factions are problematic?
- Does he want to control the causes of factions or the effects of them—and why? What's the difference? Why does he think the root causes of factions cannot be controlled, but the effects of factions can?
- How, in Madison's view, will the new republic contain the dangers of factions? What is the key role that its size will play?

Uncover the evidence

- Does Madison provide any evidence to support his arguments, or are they all theory driven? Is there any type of evidence he could have added to make his argument more persuasive?

Evaluate the conclusion

- Hindsight is 20/20. Historical works allow us to go back and ask, "Was the author right?" Was he? Has the Constitution limited the power of factions?
- Even if Madison was right—specifically, in saying that the Constitution would control the effects of factions—was his premise correct? Are factions bad? What good, if any, can come from them?

Sort out the political implications

- Conditions have changed since Madison's day. With phones, e-mails, and fax machines, we can now get in touch with someone on the other side of the country in seconds. The landmass of the United States is significantly larger than it was when Madison was writing; yet, in a sense, the country is much smaller today. Does the shrinking of America negate the force of Madison's argument about the containment of the ill effects of factions?
- What would Madison say if he could come back today? Would he think his expectations in *Federalist* No. 10 had been borne out? Would he be pleased or displeased? Why?

14

Voting and Elections

Elections are at the very heart of a representative democracy, based on the principle that the public interest is best served by many individuals each choosing those leaders they feel will make decisions in their particular interests. Politics is about power, after all. It's about winners and losers, and nowhere is this more evident than in elections in the United States. Parties, interest groups, individuals, and candidates throw hundreds of millions of dollars into campaigns for one reason: so that their team (or at least their candidate) will win and their interests will be served.

Because winning is what really counts in electoral politics, campaigns have become more expensive, more negative, and more long-lived. Political consulting has become a lucrative business. Today's candidates have not only policy advisers but also campaign strategists, pollsters, opposition researchers, and speechwriters all working to put, and keep, them in office.

Even with the rise of candidate-centered elections, we still measure who wins and who loses based on how well the two major parties do. The importance of winning means that parties must have a strategy. The party needs a message. It must make clear what it stands for and what it will do if it wins. The party that has the more effective, persuasive message typically will set the agenda for the next few years.

All campaign strategy is created with voters in mind. Who votes? Who doesn't? How will the candidate do among women voters? African Americans? The poor? The educated? The first major theory of voting developed in the 1940s argued that campaigns don't matter because we simply vote with the groups with which we identify. If we are wealthy, we vote Republican. If we come from a blue-collar family, we vote Democratic. If we are Protestant, we vote Republican. If we are Jewish, we vote Democratic. Although more recently many political scientists have criticized this theory of voting, campaigns still devise their strategies as if it were valid. During the next election, pay attention. You will surely hear pundits make such comments as "Candidate X must win at least 60 percent of the white vote to be successful" or "Candidate Y is really struggling with women. If he can't improve women's perceptions of him, he will lose." Candidates keep altering their strategies to make themselves more appealing to certain groups that are essential for them to win. They can't rest on their laurels; they must continually try to expand that winning electoral coalition.

Obviously, campaign strategy depends on who the voters are. But just as important may be who the voters aren't, and unfortunately most of us aren't voters. The United States prides itself on being the model democracy, the one that others should look to as an example. But in this model democracy, only about half of all eligible voters will cast their ballots in a presidential election. This percentage is even worse when we look at midterm elections, where voter turnout hovers around 35 percent, or primaries and caucuses, where turnout is even lower. In 1996, 915 people came to Wyoming's Republican caucus meeting! And in contrast to the Olympic medal count, in which the United States prides itself on finishing toward the top, few people seem to care that we consistently rank near the very bottom of the list regarding voter turnout in industrialized countries.

In this chapter we look at some recent controversies and debates that have surrounded elections in the United States. First, Sasha Issenberg presents the reason why he believes that Barack Obama won the 2012 presidential election. Next, we examine an editorial, by Michael Waldman, that encourages Congress to support a bill that he thinks will update an antiquated voter registration system. The third article, written by John Wonderlich for the *Huffington Post*, argues that Obama has been hypocritical regarding his actions as they relate to money and transparency in politics. We conclude with the concession speech by one of the most famous electoral losers of the past decade and a half—former vice president Al Gore, who shows how elections promote stability when all agree on the rules of the game, even when they dislike the outcome.

• •

14.1 A Vast Left-Wing Competency

How Democrats Became the Party of Effective Campaigning—and Why the GOP Isn't Catching up Anytime Soon
Sasha Issenberg, *Slate*

Why We Chose This Piece

Heading into the 2012 presidential election, Barack Obama's reelection was far from certain. Although the unemployment rate was declining, it remained above 8 percent for most of the race and never dropped below 7.8 percent, a rate that is still considered to be high. When survey respondents were asked whether the county was headed in the right direction or on the wrong track, majorities consistently gave the

---

Selection published: November 7, 2012

negative response. Moreover, President Obama's approval rating rarely was above 50 percent, and respondents consistently said they disapproved of his handling of the economy. Yet on Election Day Obama was reelected by a fairly healthy margin. The question that scholars must ask, then, is why? How could an incumbent president whose numbers were not very positive win with relative ease? The author of this piece, journalist and author Sasha Issenberg, has a theory and presents it here. We chose this piece for two reasons. First, it provides one possible explanation for the result of the 2012 presidential election. Second, that explanation focuses more on the candidate's campaign than on the candidate's characteristics. Some political scientists argue that campaigns don't matter; Issenberg clearly disagrees.

A polarizing incumbent wins a closely fought but decisive re-election despite mixed public opinion about his first term. His lead was steady and consistent throughout, and he was boosted on Election Day by strong turnout from core constituencies despite suggestions that his supporters could suffer from weakened enthusiasm the second time. The storyline was clear: The president won in large part because of superior tactics and improved technique.

In 2004, the incumbent who won that tactical victory was George W. Bush, and as Democrats learned more about his campaign's successful application of first-generation "microtargeting" procedures, they began to see their opponent's powers as more mundane than mystical. Five weeks after Bush's re-election, *Washington Post* columnist E. J. Dionne diagnosed the Democrats as suffering from "Rove Envy" and described the longing the party had "for the strategic clarity and organizational acumen" Republicans showed in campaigns. Indeed Bush's win had ratified what both sides recognized as a long-standing culture gap between the parties. Republicans were the party that was competent about politics, bringing the discipline of the corporate suite to the campaign war room. Democrats, who had resigned themselves to the reality of the Will Rogers quip about not being "an organized political party," committed themselves to building a new infrastructure for innovation and collaboration among separate interest groups and rival consultants.

Tuesday night's results testify to many dramatic changes, particularly demographic and ideological ones, that mark life in Obama's America. But within the practice of politics, no shift seems more dramatic than the role reversal between the two parties on campaigning competence. Today, there is only one direction in which envy can and should be directed: Democrats have proved themselves better—more disciplined, rigorous, serious, and forward-looking—at nearly every aspect of the project of winning elections.

After losing even more dramatically in 2008, Republicans acknowledged that Obama's campaign was tactically superior and technically more advanced than John McCain's, and the party's operatives leafed through David Plouffe's memoir, *The Audacity to Win*, for clues on what the Democrats did right. (Spoiler alert: The book revealed almost nothing about the mechanics of an Obama campaign.) But that curiosity never translated into serious self-examination.

The Republican political class could look at so much else working in Obama's favor—that candidate's unique appeal, a broad distaste for Bush, voter anxieties about economic crisis, strategic inconsistencies in McCain's approach—that few undertook the same self-examination that the electioneering left did in the wake of 2004. But in 2012, a seemingly vulnerable incumbent president's solid victory will be attributed to tactics, and the other side will surely hustle to catch up. But the innovation terrain in politics has changed over the last eight years, and it will be a lot harder for Republicans to return to parity with their opponents.

"It is a rude awakening," says Blaise Hazelwood, who served as political director of the Republican National Committee during Bush's re-election and worked this year as part of Mitt Romney's targeting team. "There was a false sense of security, a sense that we figured out how to do this microtargeting—we'd figured it out how do to it pretty well—and now there are other things for the party to focus on."

It is no coincidence that in both 2004 and 2012 the engines of radical innovation were the campaigns of incumbent presidents. We tend to underappreciate how radically different a presidential re-election is from any other enterprise in American political life. It is the rare chance for candidates to disrupt the cycle of short-term, election-year priorities and invest in their own research agendas instead of being forced to follow a consultant-driven marketplace.

For Bush, this proved a unique opportunity to synthesize information from consumer-data warehouses with voter registration records and apply some of the same statistical modeling techniques that companies used to segment customers so that they could market to them individually. In Obama's case, the continuity provided by a re-election campaign encouraged a far broader set of research priorities, perhaps most important the adoption of randomized-control experiments, used in the social sciences to address elusive questions about voter behavior.

Following their 2004 loss, Democrats found it relatively easy to catch up with Republicans in the analysis of individual consumer data for voter targeting. By 2006, Democrats were at least at parity when it came to statistical modeling techniques, and they were exploring ways to integrate them with other modes of political data analysis. Already the public-opinion firms of the left saw themselves as research hubs in a way that their peers on the right didn't, a disparity that stretched back a generation. When polling emerged in the early 1980s as a new (and lucrative) specialty within the consulting world, the people who flowed into it on the Republican side tended to be party operatives; former political and field directors who had been consumers of polls quickly realized that it was a better business to be *producers* of them.

Those who went into the polling business on the left were political consultants, too, but many of them also possessed serious scholarly credentials and had derailed promising academic careers to go into politics. Now that generation—Stan Greenberg, Celinda Lake, Mark Mellman, Diane Feldman, among others—preside over firms that see themselves not only as vendors of a stable set of campaign services but patrons of methodological innovation. When microtargeting tools made it possible to analyze the electorate as a collection of individuals rather than merely demographic and geographic subgroups, many of the most established Democratic pollsters in Washington invested in developing expertise in this new approach. Their Republican rivals, by contrast, tended to see the new tools as a threat to their business model.

Concern that the technical supremacy of Rove and his crew would ensure the Democrats' future as a minority party drove consultants who usually competed with one another to collaborate on previously unimaginable research projects. Major donors like George Soros decided not to focus their funding on campaigns to win single elections, as they had in the hopes of beating Bush in 2004, but instead to seed institutions committed to learning how to run better campaigns. Liberals, generally in awe of the success that Republicans had during the 1980s and 1990s in building a think-tank and media infrastructure to disseminate conservative ideas, responded by building a vast left-wing campaign research culture through groups like the Analyst Institute (devoted to scientific experimentation), Catalist (a common voter-data resource), and the New Organizing Institute (improved field tactics).

With an eager pool of academic collaborators in political science, behavioral psychology, and economics linking up with curious political operatives and hacks, the left has birthed an unexpected subculture. It now contains a full-fledged electioneering intelligentsia, focused on integrating large-scale survey research with randomized experimental methods to isolate particular populations that can be moved by political contact.

"There is not much of a commitment to that type of research on the right," says Daron Shaw, a University of Texas at Austin political scientist who worked on both of George W. Bush's presidential campaigns. "There is no real understanding of the experimental stuff."

If Republicans brought consumer data into politics during Bush's re-election, Democrats are mastering the techniques that give campaigns the ability to understand what actually moves voters. As a result, Democrats are beginning to engage a wider set of questions about what exactly a campaign is capable of accomplishing in an election year: not just how to modify nonvoters' behavior to get them to the polls, but what exactly can change someone's mind outside of the artificial confines of a focus group.

"The asset that Karl Rove and his team built during the Bush era, with consumer data—that was good and valuable, but it's static data," says Cyrus Krohn, a former Republican National Committee e-campaign director and founder of the political-tech startup Crowdverb. "The Democrats have figured out how to harness dynamic data on top of static data."

For Republicans concerned about their prospects as a party able to run successful campaigns in the 21st century, the heartening news should be that this election ended in much the same way that 2004 did. The heartbreak of losing a race many thought was winnable should drive a sclerotic political class to sacrifice their short-term professional priorities for the sake of innovation—and the closeness of the outcome should lead them to invest in methods that help them around the margins in the future. But the gap between the sides may be too large for mere enthusiasm to close it anytime soon.

Consider the source and the audience

- Sasha Issenberg is author of *The Victory Lab: The Secret Science of Winning Campaigns*. How might his perspective as a journalist who studies campaigns be different from those who run them?

Lay out the argument, the values, and the assumptions

- Why does Issenberg believe that Barack Obama was reelected in 2012?
- What had changed between 2004 and 2012?

Uncover the evidence

- Issenberg provides no empirical data to support his argument. Can he make an argument such as this without providing statistics directly related to tactics and technique? What kinds of statistics might he have supplied?

Evaluate the conclusion

- While it is true that public opinion was divided on Obama and he would face a tough reelection, how do we know that Obama won because of tactics and technique? What other explanations might exist? What data would you need to test those propositions?

Sort out the political implications

- If Issenberg is correct, what might be the implications for the future of the Democratic and Republican Parties? How might this affect the 2016 presidential election?

14.2 On Voting, Listen to John Lewis
Michael Waldman, Reuters

Why We Chose This Piece

In any democracy, citizens should be concerned both that all eligible voters have equal access to the voting booth and that no one besides those eligible voters can gain access to the polls. However, not everyone is convinced that American elections meet those criteria. In this article, the author, Michael Waldman, argues that our system of voting is antiquated and, as a result, can make it difficult for some people to participate and in other cases actually prevents people from voting. Waldman supports a bill that is being pushed by civil rights activist John Lewis that he believes will fix this problem.

We chose this piece because it highlights one of the many concerns over the U.S. electoral system as it relates to voting. Why would something that might make it easier to vote be so controversial?

President Barack Obama emphasized the need to modernize the U.S. election system in his Inaugural Address. One bill to do just that is set to be introduced Wednesday by the civil rights hero Representative John Lewis (D-Ga.)—who knows a thing or two about how to expand democracy.

Selection published: January 23, 2013

Under his reform plan, states would have to take responsibility to make sure that every eligible voter is on the rolls. How? By taking existing computerized voter rolls, and expanding them with names voluntarily collected when citizens deal with government—including the Department of Motor Vehicles for drivers' licenses, the Social Security Administration or other agencies. Any voter could opt in with the click of a mouse.

The proposed bill would bring our antiquated system into the 21st century. The "Voter Empowerment Act," introduced by Lewis with Rep. Steny Hoyer (D-Md.) and Senator Kirsten Gillibrand (D-N.Y.), could transform the way we choose our leaders.

This proposed plan meets the concerns of left and right. It offers a chance for an armistice in the endless trench warfare over voting. Instead of joylessly repeating the same fights over "voter fraud" and potential suppression, here is a reform that helps solve both problems at once.

It would be fairly easy. Voters could correct their record at the polling place on Election Day. Best of all, when voters move, their registration moves with them. No longer would citizens lose eligibility when they change addresses, as happens so often now in our highly mobile society.

Such a reform could add up to 50 million citizens to the rolls, permanently. It would cost less than the current system—because computers are cheaper than piles of paper. It would also curb the potential for fraud and error on voter rolls.

This would mark a true paradigm shift in the way we register voters. After all, Lewis accomplished a similar feat almost 50 years ago.

Lewis led the voting rights march in Selma, Alabama, on March 7, 1965. When the young minister reached the Edmund Pettus Bridge that day, police clubs and dogs assailed the protesters before a national television audience. Lewis was badly beaten and ended up in the hospital. But his physical courage and moral tenacity helped spur passage of the landmark, and still vital, Voting Rights Act of 1965.

Last year, Lewis, as a senior member of Congress, powerfully decried the varied efforts to limit voting, such as harsh ID requirements passed in some states. Courts blocked or postponed almost all these laws. Lewis' answer to these actions goes far beyond simply avoiding new restrictive measures, or seeking partisan advantage.

For it was again clear on Election Day that even at its best, America's voting system is a mess. Polling places veered toward chaos. Thousands waited in long, frustrating lines. In Palm Beach County, Florida, for example, some citizens stood for seven hours waiting to vote, partly because the state legislature had slashed early voting hours. The *Orlando Sentinel* reported that in central Florida alone, some 49,000 voters were deterred by endless queues. Many voters gave up.

Long lines were only the most visible problem, however. In Ohio, hundreds of thousands were forced to cast "provisional ballots" that were never counted. Had the presidential race been close and come down to the Buckeye State, as many predicted, we might still be waiting to know who won. One Obama campaign counsel told me plans were afoot to provide lawyers for individual voters—meaning each ballot would be litigated to the hilt.

The biggest problems stem from our outdated voter registration system. Rife with error, it relies on a blizzard of paper records. The rolls nationwide contained millions of dead people, according to a report last year from the Pew Center on the States, and countless duplicates and errors. If you have ever tried to get your name removed from a voter roll when you move to a new town, you know how hard it can be.

This idea has been supported by Republicans as well as Democrats. Jon Hunstman, the GOP presidential candidate, for example, backed a version when he was governor of Utah. Trevor Potter, a former Republican Federal Election Commission chairman, supports it. Bob Bauer, the Obama campaign's chief lawyer, has long championed the approach.

In recent years, 25 states have implemented some of this bill's provisions, with little partisan fuss. In 2012, hundreds of thousands of voters nationwide were added to the rolls through data transfers from computerized lists. (The Brennan Center, which I lead, first developed the proposal several years ago.)

Could this measure garner bipartisan support in bitterly divided Washington, D.C.? That is less clear.

Already, the Heritage Foundation is preparing to do battle. It convened four conservative secretaries of state for a meeting Thursday to attack the case for modernization. Voting rights advocates are readying a response.

More ominously, conservative columnist George F. Will recently fired a harsh shot. He warned that the Obama administration and Attorney General Eric Holder want to federalize elections as a first step toward forcing every American to vote. That's absurd. We can have universal voter registration while still leaving the choice to exercise that right to individuals.

Will concedes that as many as 60 million eligible citizens are not registered but insists they are merely displaying their satisfaction with the status quo. No doubt some nonvoters are blissed out by our current politics. But it is more likely that many more are frustrated by an inept system. In 2008, according to a comprehensive analysis by California Institute of Technology and Massachusetts Institute of Technology professors, at least 2 million people tried to vote but could not because of voter registration problems.

Other steps could help ease Election Day problems. National standards should ensure adequate opportunities to vote early everywhere in the country. We need to do more to invest in technology and to train poll workers, who are often earnest volunteers ill-equipped to handle the crush of voters. The federal Election Assistance Commission, now moribund, should be revived to help states.

Nevada's Democratic secretary of state, Ross Miller, has another approach, suggesting that driver's license photos be included in polling place signature books. If voters don't have an ID, a photo could be snapped that would serve as their ID going forward. The plan's success would clearly depend on the details. Done right, it could help point to an end to the divisive voter ID battles of recent years.

All these moves could be vital. But none more so that making sure that all citizens are registered long before Election Day. In 1965, Lewis paid with his blood for the right for every American to vote. Today, digital technology offers a new chance to march forward from Selma.

Consider the source and the audience

- John Lewis is not the author of this article, but the focus of it. The author mentions Lewis's fight to expand voting rights in the sixties. Are the issues being raised here the same as those during the sixties? How might they be different? Does the fact that Lewis is one of the sponsors of the bill give it more credibility?
- Michael Waldman is the author of the article. He is president of the Brennan Center for Justice at New York University School of Law. Among other things, the Brennan Center advocates for voter reform. What aspects of Waldman's affiliation with the Brennan Center make his position more credible? Is there anything about his affiliation that might make his argument less credible?

Lay out the argument, the values, and the assumptions

- What is John Lewis's solution to modernizing the U.S. electoral system?
- Why does Lewis believe this will improve the system?

Uncover the evidence

- Does the author provide any evidence that the proposed bill will do what it is intended to do?

Evaluate the conclusion

- Waldman argues that the proposed bill meets the concerns of both the left and the right. Why does he believe that? Do you agree?
- He also notes that the bill has bipartisan support. Why, then, do you think it has been so difficult to get it passed?
- What potential negative consequences might come from passing the bill?

Sort out the political implications

- If the bill is passed, how might that affect the results of future elections? Will turnout likely increase? If so, among whom?
- What nonpartisan reforms, if any, could safeguard the electoral process without advantaging or disadvantaging any particular group?

● ●

14.3 Obama Versus Campaign Finance Laws
John Wonderlich, *Huffington Post*

Why We Chose This Piece

Few subjects generate more controversy than the role of money in politics. Some reformers believe that money buys election victories for candidates and influence for organizations such as business and labor. Others are not concerned about the amount of money in politics as long as donations and spending are transparent. And still others aren't supportive of transparency, believing that people should have the ability to donate money anonymously. The Supreme Court's ruling in Citizens United v. Federal Election Commission (2010) has raised the debate over money in politics to a fever pitch. In the Citizens United case, the Court ruled that corporations and unions could not be prohibited from using treasury funds to broadcast "electioneering communications." As a result of the ruling, many reformers were concerned that the floodgates were opened regarding the amount of money used in politics. One of those people who expressed strong opposition to the ruling was President Obama. Yet, in this piece published in the Huffington Post, *the author argues that Obama's actions have not lived up to his words.*

There's a certain conventional wisdom that President Obama wants stronger campaign finance laws, and to protect our democracy from the corrupting effects of money in politics.

It's a story that you should no longer believe.

The arc of the Obama presidency may be long, but so far, it has bent away from transparency for influence and campaign finance, and toward big funders.

There's the obvious examples, like promising (and failing) to put healthcare negotiations on C-SPAN, only to negotiate a secret agreement with a segment of the industry the reform effort sought to regulate.

But there's a longer pattern here too. Obama came to power as the outsider who would return merit to public policy, and raise up regular citizens' voices in the process, at the expense of the moneyed interests whose power had displaced regular people. (My career was kick-started, in part, by helping to inspire an amendment to a 2006 Senate bill sponsored by Obama and Salazar, an idea emerging from a series of blog posts on *Daily Kos*.)

Obama was the standard-bearer for post–*Citizens United* reform, sparring with Republican Senate opposition to ultimately fall a vote short of passing the DISCLOSE Act. 2010 was the high point for Obama's campaign finance rhetoric, where weekly speeches and Rose Garden addresses sought to affirm the dangers of dark money, and the need to understand whose money is buying Washington.

Selection published: February 15, 2013

How far we've come.

Since then, Obama embraced superPACs and C4, the vehicles of newly deregulated influence-buying, suggesting that they were a necessary evil, and suggesting that the only alternative would be unilateral disarmament. A reluctant participant in a rigged game. The rationale didn't ring true even then—the weak disclosure for these groups was justified by appeals to the same broken laws Obama spent 2010 railing against.

Then came the inauguration.

Obama reversed his policy of limiting donors for the inauguration celebration, and failed to post donation amounts online. (George W, Bush had amounts and ranges online for his inauguration donors.) He sold access to the inauguration, and to the presidency, to corporate donors, wheedling their way into the privileged positions that move their policy agendas forward. Obama did this *for a series of parties*, with no public interest justification whatsoever, and didn't disclose donor amounts. The transparency president couldn't publish donor amounts on the internet—of corporate donors. Private citizens can make hundreds of GIFs of a comical Rubio water swilling incident within three minutes, but the President of the United States can't post corporate donation amounts online.

Transparency president no more.

And now we've got the new c4. It's hard to understate how bad this new policy is for campaign finance. Today's *Los Angeles Times* (via Democracy 21) explains that Obama's new c4 has been set up to sell direct access to the president, for huge sums of cash, which will be disclosed online, quarterly, without specific dollar figures. The president who told us that secret money in politics undermines democracy has now created a huge funnel for donations, with accompanying disclosure that would have been considered cutting edge in 1992. Quarterly disclosure in ranges is the kind of disclosure you create when you don't want to be seen. This should be a policy innovation Obama is remembered for—a return to soft money and unlimited donations outside the confines of campaign finance law, with instant access to the White House for the most well-heeled donors, all, incredibly, in the name of empowering the grassroots. It's more egregious, direct, (and potentially corrupting) than the similar efforts of recent presidents who came before him, an evolutionary step forward for money in politics that is more legal, more normalized, and more powerful than it was before.

Maybe Obama has stopped talking about *Citizens United* because he's learned to use it to his advantage. Maybe his campaign finance rhetoric was fake all along, donning the visage of a reformer. It doesn't matter.

Obama is taking on money in politics by getting more money into his politics.

Obama has done valuable things for transparency. There are innovations that create value for everyone, and many good people in the White House have created valuable things that continue. But we should be clear about Obama's position on transparency when it comes to his political power.

It's time to stop worrying about how Obama can help fix campaign finance, and instead worry about how we fix what he's created.

Consider the source and the audience

- The author, John Wonderlich, is policy director for the Sunlight Foundation, an organization committed to the concept of open government. How is his background evident from his argument?
- To whom is Wonderlich addressing his argument? Is it Democrats? Republicans? Someone else?

Lay out the argument, the values, and the assumptions

- Wonderlich takes a clear position regarding the role of money in politics. What is it?
- Why does Wonderlich believe that Obama has changed his tune on campaign finance reform?

Uncover the evidence

- Wonderlich provides many examples of what he believes illustrate Obama's lack of commitment to campaign finance reform. Are they persuasive?

Evaluate the conclusion

- Has Wonderlich shown any negative consequences for Obama's actions?
- When evaluating an argument that is attacking the actions of a person, it is always a good idea to consider how the person who is the focus of the argument might respond. How do you think Obama might react to Wonderlich's criticisms?

Sort out the political implications

- Let's assume for a minute that Wonderlich is correct. What might that mean for the future of campaign finance reform?
- The amount of money in politics is usually thought of as having negative consequences on democracy. What positives might come from it?

● ●

14.4 Concession Speech
Al Gore

Why We Chose This Piece

Elections serve lots of purposes in democratic society: They give people a voice in their government, they lend legitimacy to leadership change, they offer an alternative to fighting in the streets when people disagree. Another function of elections is to provide political stability. The 2000 presidential election was unusual

---

Selection delivered: December 13, 2000

on several counts. A state's election results were contested, amid accusations of fraud and misleading ballot design; that state's supreme court was overruled by the U.S. Supreme Court in the matter of recounts; and the results of that contested state election gave an Electoral College victory to a candidate who had lost the popular vote. To top it off, the governor of the state in question was the brother of the candidate who was eventually declared the winner. In many societies, such a series of events could have led to rioting, violence, or revolution. But in the United States, where there is commitment to the Constitution and to the idea of procedural justice (that is, if the rules are fair, then the results will be fair), the outcome, though distressing to many, was accepted by most.

Among the disappointed was Vice President Al Gore, who believed that he would have won the election in Florida if all the votes had been counted, and who knew that he had won the popular vote in any case. The night of the election, he had called George W. Bush to concede, only to be told afterward that the networks had erred in projecting Bush the winner in Florida, and that this state was still in play. He called Bush back and retracted his concession. Over a month later, he finally phoned Bush again.

We chose to include this speech because it highlights how elections, even ones as odd as this one, serve to legitimate government when people agree on the rules. How did the country manage to go on after this event—as if nothing, really, had happened—with a majority of voters, including some of those who had voted for Gore, giving Bush high approval ratings as he came into office?

G ood evening.

Just moments ago, I spoke with George W. Bush and congratulated him on becoming the 43rd president of the United States, and I promised him that I wouldn't call him back this time.

I offered to meet with him as soon as possible so that we can start to heal the divisions of the campaign and the contest through which we just passed.

Almost a century and a half ago, Senator Stephen Douglas told Abraham Lincoln, who had just defeated him for the presidency, "Partisan feeling must yield to patriotism. I'm with you, Mr. President, and God bless you."

Well, in that same spirit, I say to President-elect Bush that what remains of partisan rancor must now be put aside, and may God bless his stewardship of this country.

Neither he nor I anticipated this long and difficult road. Certainly neither of us wanted it to happen. Yet it came, and now it has ended, resolved, as it must be resolved, through the honored institutions of our democracy.

Over the library of one of our great law schools is inscribed the motto, "Not under man but under God and law." That's the ruling principle of American freedom, the source of our democratic liberties. I've tried to make it my guide throughout this contest as it has guided America's deliberations of all the complex issues of the past five weeks.

Now the U.S. Supreme Court has spoken. Let there be no doubt, while I strongly disagree with the court's decision, I accept it. I accept the finality of this outcome which will be ratified next Monday in the Electoral College. And tonight, for the sake of our unity of the people and the strength of our democracy, I offer my concession.

I also accept my responsibility, which I will discharge unconditionally, to honor the new president elect and do everything possible to help him bring Americans together in fulfillment of the great vision that our Declaration of Independence defines and that our Constitution affirms and defends.

Let me say how grateful I am to all those who supported me and supported the cause for which we have fought. Tipper and I feel a deep gratitude to Joe and Hadassah Lieberman who brought passion and high purpose to our partnership and opened new doors, not just for our campaign but for our country.

This has been an extraordinary election. But in one of God's unforeseen paths, this belatedly broken impasse can point us all to a new common ground, for its very closeness can serve to remind us that we are one people with a shared history and a shared destiny.

Indeed, that history gives us many examples of contests as hotly debated, as fiercely fought, with their own challenges to the popular will.

Other disputes have dragged on for weeks before reaching resolution. And each time, both the victor and the vanquished have accepted the result peacefully and in the spirit of reconciliation.

So let it be with us.

I know that many of my supporters are disappointed.

I am too. But our disappointment must be overcome by our love of country.

And I say to our fellow members of the world community, let no one see this contest as a sign of American weakness. The strength of American democracy is shown most clearly through the difficulties it can overcome.

Some have expressed concern that the unusual nature of this election might hamper the next president in the conduct of his office. I do not believe it need be so.

President-elect Bush inherits a nation whose citizens will be ready to assist him in the conduct of his large responsibilities.

I personally will be at his disposal, and I call on all Americans—I particularly urge all who stood with us to unite behind our next president. This is America. Just as we fight hard when the stakes are high, we close ranks and come together when the contest is done.

And while there will be time enough to debate our continuing differences, now is the time to recognize that that which unites us is greater than that which divides us.

While we yet hold and do not yield our opposing beliefs, there is a higher duty than the one we owe to political party. This is America and we put country before party. We will stand together behind our new president.

As for what I'll do next, I don't know the answer to that one yet. Like many of you, I'm looking forward to spending the holidays with family and old friends. I know I'll spend time in Tennessee and mend some fences, literally and figuratively.

Some have asked whether I have any regrets and I do have one regret: that I didn't get the chance to stay and fight for the American people over the next four years, especially for those who need burdens lifted and barriers removed, especially for those who feel their voices have not been heard. I heard you and I will not forget.

I've seen America in this campaign and I like what I see. It's worth fighting for and that's a fight I'll never stop.

As for the battle that ends tonight, I do believe as my father once said, that no matter how hard the loss, defeat might serve as well as victory to shape the soul and let the glory out.

So for me this campaign ends as it began: with the love of Tipper and our family; with faith in God and in the country I have been so proud to serve, from Vietnam to the vice presidency; and with gratitude to our truly tireless campaign staff and volunteers, including all those who worked so hard in Florida for the last 36 days.

Now the political struggle is over and we turn again to the unending struggle for the common good of all Americans and for those multitudes around the world who look to us for leadership in the cause of freedom.

In the words of our great hymn, "America, America": "Let us crown thy good with brotherhood, from sea to shining sea."

And now, my friends, in a phrase I once addressed to others, it's time for me to go.

Thank you and good night, and God bless America.

Consider the source and the audience

- Gore is speaking to several audiences here. Who are they? Why does he address "our fellow members of the world community"?
- At the time, Gore was certainly considering a run for the presidency in the future. How might that have shaped his message?
- How could he have used this speech to rally supporters if he had wanted to?

Lay out the argument, the values, and the assumptions

- What personal values of Gore's become apparent in this speech? How do they affect his political views?
- What is Gore's view of the common good here? How does that differ from partisan advantage, and when should the former take precedence over the latter?
- When should a political outcome be accepted even when one doesn't like it? How do the "honored institutions of our democracy" help to resolve contests like this? In what context does Gore refer to the Supreme Court and the Electoral College?

Uncover the evidence

- What kinds of evidence does Gore use to support his argument that the result of the election process should be accepted even if one doesn't agree with it, and that George W. Bush is the legitimate president of the United States?

Evaluate the conclusion

- Did Gore's use of symbolism and references to history, law, and religion convince supporters to accept the election result?
- Did they convince the world that the United States was a stable and solid nation?
- Did they convince the nation to put the trauma of the partisan backbiting behind it and move on?

Sort out the political implications

- Many electoral reforms were debated following the election, but few were enacted. Who would have resisted reform, and why?

15

The Media

Of all the things that have changed in the United States since the country's founding, it is perhaps the media that have changed the most. When once we got our news, often months old, from weekly papers and in Sunday sermons, we now can access worldwide news in real time on devices we carry in our pockets. We have truly experienced a revolution in communication in the last one hundred years.

In a democratic society, access to accurate, timely news is essential so that we can make informed decisions at the voting booth but also so that we can keep tabs on what government does, and keep our representatives honest. Free speech and press freedom were some of the key values preserved by the framers, who knew that a stifled press could not work to protect any of our other liberties.

The threat to press freedom that the authors of the Constitution were concerned about was the government, and they had reason to worry. During colonial times, printers had to get government approval for the work they turned out. Even after independence, the newspaper business was often subsidized by politicians in exchange for favorable coverage. It was not until mass-circulation papers acquired some measure of financial independence that journalistic objectivity and detachment from political patronage became economically feasible and, in fact, commercially savvy. The effort to appeal to a broad audience was enhanced if a paper did not risk alienating part of that audience by taking up controversial political positions.

The objectivity spawned by mass-circulation news organizations is jealously guarded today by partisans on both sides of the ideological spectrum who eagerly scan the media's output for signs of liberal or conservative bias. We know that, on average, journalists tend to be slightly more liberal than the average American—media owners and editorial writers slightly more conservative (the conservatives at Fox News and the liberals at MSNBC notwithstanding, of course). But in any case, most Americans are amply armed to deflect any political bias that sneaks into the media because we bring our own ideological filters to the business of reading the paper and watching the news.

We are less primed to watch for the effects of other kinds of pressures on the media that may have a more serious influence on the news that we get. Today, the mainstream media (major city newspapers and the television networks) are part of corporate America, where the drive for profits helps define the news and how it is presented and packaged. In addition to the commercial pressures coming from the corporate owners, journalists have to contend with the efforts of politicians to control the way they are presented by the media. But today's mainstream media also find themselves challenged by a new threat to their existence.

As news-seekers increasingly go online to get their information, as bloggers and tweeters and others set themselves up as free disseminators of the news, and as traditional sources of the news fail to find ways to charge people for accessing their work, the media landscape is being transformed in ways we don't yet quite appreciate. All these forces can make the journalist's public job—to present accurate and timely news to citizens and to provide a check on government—increasingly difficult.

The articles in this chapter deal with some of the pressures journalists face today. The first piece, by an Internet writer, speculates on the future of newspapers. The second looks at the way political ideologues can construct their own reality when they can tailor their media messages the way they want. The third piece argues that the Republicans are doing just that right now, to their detriment. The fourth claims that the Obama administration is using unprecedented means to bypass the mainstream media and is thus escaping being held accountable for its actions. The fifth argues that the new media are making government better, not worse. Finally, we look backward in time to the arguments made by media giant William Randolph Hearst, about the evils of government-controlled newspapers.

• •

15.1 Newspapers and Thinking the Unthinkable

Clay Shirky, *www.shirky.com*

Why We Chose This Piece

One of the main reasons people worry about the shrinking audience of the mainstream media is that, until now, it has been the big papers and networks that have funded the investigation and reporting of the news (that is, journalism) through the advertising they sell. They maintain bureaus in faraway places around the world and find and disseminate information about those places, as well as about locales closer to home.

Selection published: March 13, 2009

It is ironic and fitting that this article about the "unthinkable" end of newspapers is written by an expert on the Internet and is published on the Internet, at www .shirky.com (the author's Web site.) Shirky looks at the various attempts newspapers have made to stave off the challenge of the Internet, and he argues that the one possibility they don't consider is the unthinkable one, that we are in the midst of a revolution that spells their demise. Is he right that it is time to start thinking about the unthinkable?

Back in 1993, the Knight-Ridder newspaper chain began investigating piracy of Dave Barry's popular column, which was published by the *Miami Herald* and syndicated widely. In the course of tracking down the sources of unlicensed distribution, they found many things, including the copying of his column to alt.fan. dave_barry on usenet; a 2000-person strong mailing list also reading pirated versions; and a teenager in the Midwest who was doing some of the copying himself, because he loved Barry's work so much he wanted everybody to be able to read it.

One of the people I was hanging around with online back then was Gordy Thompson, who managed internet services at the *New York Times*. I remember Thompson saying something to the effect of "When a 14 year old kid can blow up your business in his spare time, not because he hates you but because he loves you, then you got a problem." I think about that conversation a lot these days.

The problem newspapers face isn't that they didn't see the internet coming. They not only saw it miles off, they figured out early on that they needed a plan to deal with it, and during the early 90s they came up with not just one plan but several. One was to partner with companies like America Online, a fast-growing subscription service that was less chaotic than the open internet. Another plan was to educate the public about the behaviors required of them by copyright law. New payment models such as micropayments were proposed. Alternatively, they could pursue the profit margins enjoyed by radio and TV, if they became purely ad-supported. Still another plan was to convince tech firms to make their hardware and software less capable of sharing, or to partner with the businesses running data networks to achieve the same goal. Then there was the nuclear option: sue copyright infringers directly, making an example of them.

As these ideas were articulated, there was intense debate about the merits of various scenarios. Would DRM or walled gardens work better? Shouldn't we try a carrot-and-stick approach, with education *and* prosecution? And so on. In all this conversation, there was one scenario that was widely regarded as unthinkable, a scenario that didn't get much discussion in the nation's newsrooms, for the obvious reason.

The unthinkable scenario unfolded something like this: The ability to share content wouldn't shrink, it would grow. Walled gardens would prove unpopular. Digital advertising would reduce inefficiencies, and therefore profits. Dislike of micropayments would prevent widespread use. People would resist being educated to act against their own desires. Old habits of advertisers and readers would not transfer online. Even ferocious litigation would be inadequate to constrain massive, sustained law-breaking. (Prohibition redux.) Hardware and software vendors would not regard copyright holders as allies, nor would they regard customers as enemies. DRM's requirement that the attacker be allowed to decode the content would be an insuperable flaw. And, per Thompson, suing people who love something so much they want to share it would piss them off.

Revolutions create a curious inversion of perception. In ordinary times, people who do no more than describe the world around them are seen as pragmatists, while those who imagine fabulous alternative futures are viewed as radicals. The last couple of decades haven't been ordinary, however. Inside the papers, the pragmatists were the ones simply looking out the window and noticing that the real world was increasingly resembling the unthinkable scenario. These people were treated as if they were barking mad. Meanwhile the people spinning visions of popular walled gardens and enthusiastic micropayment adoption, visions unsupported by reality, were regarded not as charlatans but saviors.

When reality is labeled unthinkable, it creates a kind of sickness in an industry. Leadership becomes faith-based, while employees who have the temerity to suggest that what seems to be happening is in fact happening are herded into Innovation Departments, where they can be ignored *en masse*. This shunting aside of the realists in favor of the fabulists has different effects on different industries at different times. One of the effects on the newspapers is that many of their most passionate defenders are unable, even now, to plan for a world in which the industry they knew is visibly going away.

* * *

The curious thing about the various plans hatched in the '90s is that they were, at base, all the same plan: "Here's how we're going to preserve the old forms of organization in a world of cheap perfect copies!" The details differed, but the core assumption behind all imagined outcomes (save the unthinkable one) was that the organizational form of the newspaper, as a general-purpose vehicle for publishing a variety of news and opinion, was basically sound, and only needed a digital facelift. As a result, the conversation has degenerated into the enthusiastic grasping at straws, pursued by skeptical responses.

"The *Wall Street Journal* has a paywall, so we can too!" (Financial information is one of the few kinds of information whose recipients don't want to share.) "Micropayments work for iTunes, so they will work for us!" (Micropayments work only where the provider can avoid competitive business models.) "The *New York Times* should charge for content!" (They've tried, with QPass and later TimesSelect.) "*Cook's Illustrated* and *Consumer Reports* are doing fine on subscriptions!" (Those publications forgo ad revenues; users are paying not just for content but for unimpeachability.) "We'll form a cartel!" (. . . and hand a competitive advantage to every ad-supported media firm in the world.)

Round and round this goes, with the people committed to saving newspapers demanding to know "If the old model is broken, what will work in its place?" To which the answer is: Nothing. Nothing will work. There is no general model for newspapers to replace the one the internet just broke.

With the old economics destroyed, organizational forms perfected for industrial production have to be replaced with structures optimized for digital data. It makes increasingly less sense even to talk about a publishing industry, because the core problem publishing solves—the incredible difficulty, complexity, and expense of making something available to the public—has stopped being a problem.

* * *

Elizabeth Eisenstein's magisterial treatment of Gutenberg's invention, *The Printing Press as an Agent of Change*, opens with a recounting of her research into the early history of the printing press. She was able to find many descriptions of life in the early 1400s, the era before movable type. Literacy was limited, the Catholic Church was the pan-European political force, Mass was in Latin, and the average book was the Bible. She was also able to find endless descriptions of life in the late 1500s, after Gutenberg's invention had started to spread. Literacy was on the rise, as were books written in contemporary languages, Copernicus had published his epochal work on astronomy, and Martin Luther's use of the press to reform the Church was upending both religious and political stability.

What Eisenstein focused on, though, was how many historians ignored the transition from one era to the other. To describe the world before or after the spread of print was child's play; those dates were safely distanced from upheaval. But what was happening in 1500? The hard question Eisenstein's book asks is "How did we get from the world before the printing press to the world after it? What was the revolution *itself* like?"

Chaotic, as it turns out. The Bible was translated into local languages; was this an educational boon or the work of the devil? Erotic novels appeared, prompting the same set of questions. Copies of Aristotle and Galen circulated widely, but direct encounter with the relevant texts revealed that the two sources clashed, tarnishing faith in the Ancients. As novelty spread, old institutions seemed exhausted while new ones seemed untrustworthy; as a result, people almost literally didn't know what to think. If you can't trust Aristotle, who can you trust?

During the wrenching transition to print, experiments were only revealed in retrospect to be turning points. Aldus Manutius, the Venetian printer and publisher, invented the smaller *octavo* volume along with italic type. What seemed like a minor change—take a book and shrink it—was in retrospect a key innovation in the democratization of the printed word. As books became cheaper, more portable, and therefore more desirable, they expanded the market for all publishers, heightening the value of literacy still further.

That is what real revolutions are like. The old stuff gets broken faster than the new stuff is put in its place. The importance of any given experiment isn't apparent at the moment it appears; big changes stall, small changes spread. Even the revolutionaries can't predict what will happen. Agreements on all sides that core institutions must be protected are rendered meaningless by the very people doing the agreeing. (Luther and the Church both insisted, for years, that whatever else happened, no one was talking about a schism.) Ancient social bargains, once disrupted, can neither be mended nor quickly replaced, since any such bargain takes decades to solidify.

And so it is today. When someone demands to know how we are going to replace newspapers, they are really demanding to be told that we are not living through a

325

revolution. They are demanding to be told that old systems won't break before new systems are in place. They are demanding to be told that ancient social bargains aren't in peril, that core institutions will be spared, that new methods of spreading information will improve previous practice rather than upending it. They are demanding to be lied to.

There are fewer and fewer people who can convincingly tell such a lie.

* * *

If you want to know why newspapers are in such trouble, the most salient fact is this: Printing presses are terrifically expensive to set up and to run. This bit of economics, normal since Gutenberg, limits competition while creating positive returns to scale for the press owner, a happy pair of economic effects that feed on each other. In a notional town with two perfectly balanced newspapers, one paper would eventually generate some small advantage—a breaking story, a key interview—at which point both advertisers and readers would come to prefer it, however slightly. That paper would in turn find it easier to capture the next dollar of advertising, at lower expense, than the competition. This would increase its dominance, which would further deepen those preferences, repeat chorus. The end result is either geographic or demographic segmentation among papers, or one paper holding a monopoly on the local mainstream audience.

For a long time, longer than anyone in the newspaper business has been alive in fact, print journalism has been intertwined with these economics. The expense of printing created an environment where Wal-Mart was willing to subsidize the Baghdad bureau. This wasn't because of any deep link between advertising and reporting, nor was it about any real desire on the part of Wal-Mart to have their marketing budget go to international correspondents. It was just an accident. Advertisers had little choice other than to have their money used that way, since they didn't really have any other vehicle for display ads.

The old difficulties and costs of printing forced everyone doing it into a similar set of organizational models; it was this similarity that made us regard *Daily Racing Form* and *L'Osservatore Romano* as being in the same business. That the relationship between advertisers, publishers, and journalists has been ratified by a century of cultural practice doesn't make it any less accidental.

The competition-deflecting effects of printing cost got destroyed by the internet, where everyone pays for the infrastructure, and then everyone gets to use it. And when Wal-Mart, and the local Maytag dealer, and the law firm hiring a secretary, and that kid down the block selling his bike, were all able to use that infrastructure to get out of their old relationship with the publisher, they did. They'd never really signed up to fund the Baghdad bureau anyway.

* * *

Print media does much of society's heavy journalistic lifting, from flooding the zone—covering every angle of a huge story—to the daily grind of attending the

City Council meeting, just in case. This coverage creates benefits even for people who aren't newspaper readers, because the work of print journalists is used by everyone from politicians to district attorneys to talk radio hosts to bloggers. The newspaper people often note that newspapers benefit society as a whole. This is true, but irrelevant to the problem at hand; "You're gonna miss us when we're gone!" has never been much of a business model. So who covers all that news if some significant fraction of the currently employed newspaper people lose their jobs?

I don't know. Nobody knows. We're collectively living through 1500, when it's easier to see what's broken than what will replace it. The internet turns 40 this fall. Access by the general public is less than half that age. Web use, as a normal part of life for a majority of the developed world, is less than half *that* age. We just got here. Even the revolutionaries can't predict what will happen.

Imagine, in 1996, asking some net-savvy soul to expound on the potential of craigslist, then a year old and not yet incorporated. The answer you'd almost certainly have gotten would be extrapolation: "Mailing lists can be powerful tools," "Social effects are intertwining with digital networks," blah blah blah. What no one would have told you, could have told you, was what actually happened: craigslist became a critical piece of infrastructure. Not the idea of craigslist, or the business model, or even the software driving it. Craigslist itself spread to cover hundreds of cities and has become a part of public consciousness about what is now possible. Experiments are only revealed in retrospect to be turning points.

In craigslist's gradual shift from 'interesting if minor' to 'essential and transformative,' there is one possible answer to the question "If the old model is broken, what will work in its place?" The answer is: Nothing will work, but everything might. Now is the time for experiments, lots and lots of experiments, each of which will seem as minor at launch as craigslist did, as Wikipedia did, as *octavo* volumes did.

Journalism has always been subsidized. Sometimes it's been Wal-Mart and the kid with the bike. Sometimes it's been Richard Mellon Scaife. Increasingly, it's you and me, donating our time. The list of models that are obviously working today, like *Consumer Reports* and NPR, like ProPublica and WikiLeaks, can't be expanded to cover any general case, but then nothing is going to cover the general case.

Society doesn't need newspapers. What we need is journalism. For a century, the imperatives to strengthen journalism and to strengthen newspapers have been so tightly wound as to be indistinguishable. That's been a fine accident to have, but when that accident stops, as it is stopping before our eyes, we're going to need lots of other ways to strengthen journalism instead.

When we shift our attention from 'save newspapers' to 'save society,' the imperative changes from 'preserve the current institutions' to 'do whatever works.' And what works today isn't the same as what used to work.

We don't know who the Aldus Manutius of the current age is. It could be Craig Newmark, or Caterina Fake. It could be Martin Nisenholtz, or Emily Bell. It could be some 19 year old kid few of us have heard of, working on something we won't recognize as vital until a decade hence. Any experiment, though, designed to provide new models for journalism is going to be an improvement over hiding from the real, especially in a year when, for many papers, the unthinkable future is already in the past.

For the next few decades, journalism will be made up of overlapping special cases. Many of these models will rely on amateurs as researchers and writers. Many of these models will rely on sponsorship or grants or endowments instead of revenues. Many of these models will rely on excitable 14 year olds distributing the results. Many of these models will fail. No one experiment is going to replace what we are now losing with the demise of news on paper, but over time, the collection of new experiments that do work might give us the journalism we need.

Consider the source and the audience

- Shirky writes about the Internet for people who are interested in Internet issues. This article does not appear in a book or magazine; it is self-published on the Web, exactly the kind of threat to traditional methods of disseminating information that the mainstream media worry about. How can you learn more about who Shirky is and what he thinks?

Lay out the argument, the values, and the assumptions

- Shirky is clearly comfortable with the Internet and sees the plight of the mainstream media without the fear that those who strive to save them feel. What does he think is worth saving in the traditional channels through which we get the news?
- What is the value of the comparison Shirky makes to the revolution brought on by the invention of the printing press?

Uncover the evidence

- Shirky's argument here is based largely on his own insights about the modern media and on historical analogy. What evidence does he use? Could he bring in other evidence, or is this sufficient?

Evaluate the conclusion

- Shirky says it is not newspapers we need to worry about saving, but rather journalism. What does he mean by that?
- How does he think journalism can be saved?

Sort out the political implications

- What would a world without newspapers look like? How might it change the practice of American politics?
- What will happen if we are not able to find a way to save journalism?

15.2 The Unskewed Election

In 2012, Facts Matter Less Than Ever.
Blame the Media

Ben Smith and Ruby Cramer, *BuzzFeed*

Why We Chose This Piece

As cable TV stations proliferate and more and more of us get our news online in ways that are tailored to our own specific interests and values, the actual news we get is tailored for us as well. Liberals get their news from liberal sources; conservatives get theirs from conservative sources; and, as this article from the website BuzzFeed argues, we begin to live in two separate realities. We chose this article because it nails a phenomenon that will likely get worse as fewer and fewer of us read a common newspaper with a common understanding of what the facts are.

Barack Obama may win in November, or Mitt Romney may win, but the 2012 election already has given us its most important new word and iconic idea: Unskewing.

The proprietor of UnskewedPolls.com, a previously obscure Virginia blogger named Dean Chambers, didn't like the results of a set of polls showing Mitt Romney losing. So he rearranged their samples, and announced that Romney was winning, a result greeted warmly by conservatives from Rick Perry to Matt Drudge.

Chambers' instant popularity on the right marked a kind of death knell for the aphorism often attributed to the late Senator Daniel Patrick Moynihan: "Everyone is entitled to his own opinion, but not his own facts," a claim that has faced an unusual assault this election year. The 2012 presidential cycle began on a stage set by utterly irrational demands for a president's birth certificate and wide and heated Republican rejection of a health care principle that, Democrats never tire of pointing out, was at one point a Republican idea. It rolled on this week to wide Republican doubt about the validity of the previously uncontroversial Bureau of Labor Statistics unemployment numbers. It has seen a hallucinatory gap in partisan perceptions of the economy, as Democrats suddenly began rating it "excellent" and "good" as the presidential campaign heated up.

There is a vast and longstanding political science literature devoted to explaining the human propensity to fit opinion and even fact to partisan convenience—support for a war, for instance, tends to flip when a new party takes the White House—but many of the political scientists who study just this say they've never seen it the gap this wide.

"It's different today than the Whigs and the Tories fighting it out a couple hundred years ago—and it's even different from the 50s or 60s—because today we have a hyperpartisan media," said Paul Kellstedt, an associate professor of political science at Texas

Selection published: October 7, 2012

A&M University, who has argued that standard measures of economic confidence fail to take into account the partisan skew.

"When people watch only Fox News, or only MSNBC, their minds are thrown into this preferred-world state," he said. "The accuracy motive fades a bit."

"When we encounter information that is inconvenient or disagreeable, we find ways to explain it away. We can do that with statistics almost as well as we can with any other type of information," said John Sides, an associate professor of political science at George Washington University and co-founder of the blog *The Monkey Cage*. "Now we have partisan news and partisan leaders to do that work for you. If you don't want to believe that Romney is losing, you go to UnskewedPolls.com, and it will tell you that he's not. "

More of the 2012 cycle's descents into fantasyland—the unskewing of polls and BLS paranoia most obvious among them—have featured Republicans than Democrats, prompting some on the left to argue that American conservatives have a particular hostility to reality. And certainly, the conservative movement has long nourished more skepticism of the mainstream media and of some forms of government authority than has the left.

But there's probably a simpler explanation for at least some of this: Mitt Romney has spent most of the year losing, and so the Republicans are the ones feeling compelled to re-imagine the polls. That Democrats share, at least, the impulse became clear Wednesday night when a CNN snap poll showed Romney winning overwhelmingly. The liberal twittersphere erupted with skepticism over a sample that, an easy misread suggested, was tilted toward Southern Whites. The progressive news site TalkingPoints Memo shared, then retracted, those doubts; others, like the enduring liberal blog Hullaballoo, which declared the poll "malpractice," didn't correct, and the episode prompted a wave of glee among conservatives who had watched the previous round of unskewing with some embarrassment.

An array of authors have blamed the shifting media for this deepening divide. *Slate*'s Farhad Manjoo's 2008 book on the subject presented itself as a cheeky manual on the problem of "learning to live in a post-fact society."

"Increasingly our arguments aren't over what we *should* be doing . . . but instead over what is *happening*," he wrote. "We're now fighting over competing versions of reality."

(2008 also featured a countervailing trend: The poll analyst Nate Silver came to prominence in part by arguing that polling, read accurately, *could* be trusted.)

Manjoo pointed to the rise of tailored online media as a key cause of the deepening divide, something echoed by academic researchers.

"We have more media choices, whether it's cable television or the internet, so it's easier to get information that's consistent with your predisposition," Cornell's Peter Enns told *BuzzFeed*.

And as online media shifts, new and ideological sources of information are shifting with it. MoveOn co-founder Eli Pariser published a book about how Google and other platforms are subtly tailoring users' experience to tell them what they want to hear, creating a "filter bubble"—before creating *Upworthy*, a site that packages progressive content to make it spread on the social web, perhaps the most effective online tool for extending those bubbles into that booming online space. (Pariser argues that the content will persuade and mobilize people across partisan bubbles.)

One central consequence of the divided new political realities is that conversation has grown difficult, and politics harder to talk about.

"It's not that I disagree," Andrew Sullivan wrote recently. "I cannot even begin to see how a conversation can begin. We have different experiences of reality. But that's why, I think, this election is so fascinating. It will, by default, offer us a direct take on the majority's perception of reality."

This fall's arguments over basic facts have been the strangest and most interesting features of a generally dull political cycle, and the main consolation may be that if a poor grasp on facts is a growing and disturbing feature of American politics it is not entirely new. Senator Moynihan's famous quote itself, in fact, appears to have been misattributed to him.

But unskewing reality is now a booming industry. Chambers, the original unskewer, has since launched Unskewed Media and Unskewed Politics sites. The former site trumpets skepticism on the jobs numbers from the Bureau of Labor Statistics.

The latter site, meanwhile, links an article by Chambers that seeks to explain away the methodological complication that Romney is now gaining in the despised media polls.

"I blew the whistle the on the skewed pollsters, predicted they would clean up their act, and bingo, the pollsters are producing more accurate polls using less skewed samples," Chambers writes. "It's not coincidence."

Consider the source and the audience

- *BuzzFeed* is a website designed to capture and disseminate viral Web content. Despite much of *BuzzFeed*'s frothy content, Ben Smith, its editor, was once a political reporter for *Politico*, and Ruby Cramer is the daughter of Richard Ben Cramer, one of the great political writers of the modern era. They know their political stuff. How does that context shape your perception of what you have read?
- Given the nature of their website, how deep do you expect their analysis to go?

Lay out the argument, the values, and the assumptions

- The authors say that the modern media are responsible for the fact that there is no consensus on what reality is. How does that happen?
- What effect does a disputed reality have for our political discourse?
- Who are the worst offenders at creating their own reality?

Uncover the evidence

- As evidence of the dueling reality, the authors give multiple examples of people who, when they do not like what reality is telling them, create an alternative. Do those examples convince you?
- They also talk to political scientists for insight into what the warring sets of facts are all about. What do they add to your understanding?

• •

15.3 Tearing Down the Conservative Echo Chamber

Joe Scarborough, *Politico*

Why We Chose This Piece

Joe Scarborough is a conservative Republican, once a member of the House of Representatives from Florida and now the host of a talk show on MSNBC called Morning Joe. Despite the fact that MSNBC has a reputation as a liberal station, and the fact that Scarborough's cohost is Mika Brzezinski, a Democrat, Scarborough's conservative credentials are strong. Writing several months after the 2012 election, he picks up the theme of the last selection you read, but he is very frank about claiming that the construction of a false reality is not currently shared by both parties; while Democrats have suffered from it in the past, it is a Republican media problem right now.

A "Morning Joe" discussion from Tuesday is sure to set off extremists within the Republican Party who remain more interested in defending the GOP's losing ways than charting a new course to victory. After Chuck Todd concluded that Republicans are afraid to leave the safe confines of conservative media outlets, I explained that such a response was short-sighted. After all, it was the Conservative Entertainment Complex that led Republican thought leaders, grass-roots activists and even the presidential candidate himself into believing that a GOP victory was imminent

---

Selection published: February 19, 2013

on Election Day. The Romney team was so isolated deep inside this conservative media bubble that they continued to believe victory was theirs well into the evening.

That embarrassing political tale proved that conservatives had finally become what they had once mocked: an insular movement so lost in its own echo chamber that it rarely made contact with those who didn't share their world view. This is, of course, the same trap that liberals fell into in Manhattan newsrooms and on college campuses throughout the 1960s and 70s during the rise of Richard Nixon, Ronald Reagan and the Silent Majority. And yes, there was a silent majority that liberal newspapers and TV anchors were blind to for the better part of a generation.

Middle-class Californians were so set on edge by the Watts riots and Berkeley protests of 1965 that they elected an aging actor as California's governor in 1966. Reagan was dismissed as an extremist and a lightweight by the national media. In fact, he was considered to be such a marginal figure that his Democratic opponent, the legendary Pat Brown, aided Reagan's cause in the GOP primary so the popular governor could face off against this extremist dunce in the general election. But with Watts and Berkeley as the backdrop to a radically changing political landscape, the cloistered liberal elite awakened to find that it was Democrats who voters began to view as extreme and out of touch.

Two years later, the radicalism of Chicago helped elect Richard Nixon and set American liberalism back on its heels for a generation. But the liberal elites were the last to take notice, in part, because they controlled major news networks and dominated the newsrooms of the major dailies to such a degree that they could construct their own self-reinforcing echo chamber. Perhaps that explains how they could be blindsided yet again by Ronald Wilson Reagan, the amiable dunce who just so happened to start a political revolution that crushed a sitting Democratic president and wiped out most of the Senate's most liberal icons in his 1980 Republican landslide.

That liberal echo chamber remained a boon for Republicans through Reagan's historic 49-state win in 1984 and George H.W. Bush's landslide victory over Michael Dukakis four years later. Despite the left's control of *The New York Times*, *Washington Post*, CBS, ABC and NBC News, the GOP won five of six presidential races from the rise of Reagan in 1966 to the election of his vice president in 1988.

Despite this electoral dominance, conservatives remained shut out of Hollywood, academia and the news media. The rise of an alternative conservative media in the early 1990s was hailed by Republicans like myself as a needed check on the left-wing biases of American media. Rush Limbaugh went national in 1990 and immediately caused a sensation. He led conservative opposition to the Bush tax increases in 1991 and after Bush the Elder lost, Limbaugh played a big role in helping elect conservatives like myself in the off-year election of 1994.

Fox News exploded onto the scene two years later and was a game changer for conservatives who had long been forced to watch the evening news broadcasts of anchors who had never voted for a Republican presidential candidate in their lives. Matt Drudge brought this alternative conservative revolution to the Internet a few years later and constantly exposed liberal hypocrisy and double standards in newsrooms across America.

The conservative alternative media machine was now firmly in place and all things were right in the Republican world. Democrats then proceeded to win the popular vote in five of six presidential elections.

Why is Rush Limbaugh batting one for six in presidential races? Why is Fox News one for five? Perhaps it is because two decades later, what many of us once considered to be an important balance to left-wing media bias have become the only outlets conservative politicians and thought leaders consider legitimate. That has proven to be a terrible calculation.

This assumption has now become so widespread on the right that any news analysis or media poll that runs counter to Republican interests is dismissed by the right as biased and irrelevant. This mindset took firm hold in 2012 so that the echo chamber syndrome that once made fools of left [sic] has now come back to undermine the right. Not only does this approach distort political reality by only reinforcing pre-existing worldviews, it also stifles intellectual debate inside the party. This in turn creates the kind of stale political environment that has been criticized of late by conservative thought leaders like Bill Kristol, John Podhoretz and Pete Wehner. Mr. Wehner wrote a column today in "Commentary" calling for the "intellectual unfreezing" of the right.

Conservatives should celebrate the gains they have made in the media world over the past two decades. But their greatest challenge moving forward is to begin breaking down the walls they have built that keeps them locked inside a comfort zone that distorts political reality and cedes great advantages to Democratic candidates. What conservatives must do instead is dare to think different, apply eternal truths to current realities and then start spreading their gospel of conservatism to the swing voters who have rejected them in five of six presidential races.

Two decades of losing should be evidence enough that simply talking to ourselves is not a winning strategy if we ever want to run the country again.

Consider the source and the audience

- Scarborough is a guest columnist for *Politico*, a Washington insider newspaper and website you have seen before in these pages. To whom is Scarborough directing his argument?

Lay out the argument, the values, and the assumptions

- Scarborough is pretty brutal in laying out his concerns. How did the rise of a conservative media, which he viewed as a good thing, turn into something dangerous for Republicans?
- What does he mean by the words *echo chamber?* Why do people get caught up in them?
- What does he think is the impact of the echo chamber on conservative intellectual development?

Uncover the evidence

- What kinds of evidence does Scarborough offer to support his argument?
- How does he try to make it more palatable for conservatives? Does pointing out that the Democrats were once in the same boat take away some of the sting?

Evaluate the conclusion

- Scarborough argues that if conservatives don't break out of their echo chamber they are going to keep losing national elections. Do you think that is a correct analysis?

Sort out the political significance

- Although the Republicans have been having a tough time winning at the national level, most congressional districts are gerrymandered so that conservatives face no real threat from the left. Do those Republican representatives have any incentive to leave the echo chamber?

15.4 Obama, the Puppet Master

Jim VandeHei and Mike Allen, *Politico*

Why We Chose This Piece

It is the business of the media to criticize politicians for not giving them access, and it is the business of the politicians to try to do an end-run around the media. New technology gives politicians a whole new bag of tricks to speak to the American people without filtering their words through the White House press corps. As you can see in this article, the White House press corps is not taking it well. VandeHei and Allen are the ultimate Washington insider journalism duo. VandeHei is a cofounder of Politico, *and Allen is his chief political reporter. Are the mainstream media elite necessary for the survival of democracy, or can bloggers, reporters for alternative press, cable news anchors, and Twitter and Facebook do the job? What are the strengths and the weaknesses of these alternatives?*

President Barack Obama is a master at limiting, shaping and manipulating media coverage of himself and his White House.

Not for the reason that conservatives suspect: namely, that a liberal press willingly and eagerly allows itself to get manipulated. Instead, the mastery mostly flows from a White House that has taken old tricks for shaping coverage (staged leaks, friendly interviews) and put them on steroids using new ones (social media, content creation, precision targeting). And it's an equal opportunity strategy: Media across the ideological spectrum are left scrambling for access.

The results are transformational. With more technology, and fewer resources at many media companies, the balance of power between the White House and press has

---

Selection published: February 18, 2013

tipped unmistakably toward the government. This is an arguably dangerous development, and one that the Obama White House—fluent in digital media and no fan of the mainstream press—has exploited cleverly and ruthlessly. And future presidents from both parties will undoubtedly copy and expand on this approach.

"The balance of power used to be much more in favor of the mainstream press," said Mike McCurry, who was press secretary to President Bill Clinton during the Monica Lewinsky scandal. Nowadays, he said, "The White House gets away with stuff I would never have dreamed of doing. When I talk to White House reporters now, they say it's really tough to do business with people who don't see the need to be cooperative."

McCurry and his colleagues in the Clinton White House were hardly above putting their boss in front of gentle questions: Clinton and Vice President Al Gore often preferred the safety of "Larry King Live" to the rhetorical combat of the briefing room. But Obama and his aides have raised it to an art form: The president has shut down interviews with many of the White House reporters who know the most and ask the toughest questions. Instead, he spends way more time talking directly to voters via friendly shows and media personalities. Why bother with *The New York Times* beat reporter when Obama can go on "The View"?

At the same time, this White House has greatly curtailed impromptu moments where reporters can ask tough questions after a staged event—or snap a picture of the president that was not shot by government-paid photographers.

The frustrated Obama press corps neared rebellion this past holiday weekend when reporters and photographers were not even allowed onto the Floridian National GolfClub, where Obama was golfing. That breached the tradition of the pool "holding" in the clubhouse and often covering—and even questioning—the president on the first and last holes.

Obama boasted Thursday during a Google+ Hangout from the White House: "This is the most transparent administration in history." The people who cover him day to day see it very differently.

"The way the president's availability to the press has shrunk in the last two years is a disgrace," said ABC News White House reporter Ann Compton, who has covered every president back to Gerald R. Ford. "The president's day-to-day policy development—on immigration, on guns—is almost totally opaque to the reporters trying to do a responsible job of covering it. There are no readouts from big meetings he has with people from the outside, and many of them aren't even on his schedule. This is different from every president I covered. This White House goes to extreme lengths to keep the press away."

One authentically new technique pioneered by the Obama White House is extensive government creation of content (photos of the president, videos of White House officials, blog posts written by Obama aides), which can then be instantly released to the masses through social media. They often include footage unavailable to the press.

Brooks Kraft, a contributing photographer to *Time*, said White House officials "have a willing and able and hungry press that eats this stuff up, partly because the news organizations are cash-strapped."

"White House handout photos used to be reserved for historically important events—9/11, or deliberations about war," Kraft said. "This White House regularly releases [day-in-the-life] images of the president . . . a nice picture of the president looking pensive . . . from events that could have been covered by the press pool. But I don't blame the White House for doing it, because networks and newspapers use them. So the White House has built its own content distribution network."

When Obama nominated Elena Kagan for the Supreme Court, she gave one interview—to White House TV, produced by Obama aides.

"There's no question that technology has significantly altered the playing field of competitive journalism," said Josh Earnest, principal deputy White House press secretary—and the voice of "West Wing Week," produced by the administration.

"Our ongoing challenge is to engage media outlets with audiences large and small—occasionally harnessing technology to find new ways to do so."

By no means does Obama escape tough scrutiny or altogether avoid improvisational moments. And by no means is Obama unique in wanting to control his public image and message—every president pushes this to the outer limits. His 2012 opponent, Mitt Romney, was equally adept at substance-free encounters with reporters.

But something is different with this White House. Obama's aides are better at using technology and exploiting the president's "brand." They are more disciplined about cracking down on staff that leak, or reporters who write things they don't like. And they are obsessed with taking advantage of Twitter, Facebook, YouTube and every other social media forums, not just for campaigns, but governing.

"They use every technique anyone has ever thought of, and some no one ever had," New York Times White House reporter Peter Baker told us. "They can be very responsive and very helpful at pulling back the curtain at times while keeping you at bay at others. And they're not at all shy about making clear when they don't like your stories, which is quite often."

Conservatives assume a cozy relationship between this White House and the reporters who cover it. Wrong. Many reporters find Obama himself strangely fearful of talking with them and often aloof and cocky when he does. They find his staff needlessly stingy with information and thin-skinned about any tough coverage. He gets more-favorable-than-not coverage because many staffers are fearful of talking to reporters, even anonymously, and some reporters inevitably worry access or the chance of a presidential interview will decrease if they get in the face of this White House.

Obama himself sees little upside to wide-ranging interviews with the beat reporters for the big newspapers—hence, the stiffing of even The New York Times since 2010. The president's staff often finds Washington reporters whiny, needy and too enamored with trivial matters or their own self-importance.

So the White House has escalated the use of several media manipulation techniques:

- The super-safe, softball interview is an Obama specialty. The kid glove interview of Obama and outgoing Secretary of State Hillary Clinton by Steve Kroft of CBS's "60 Minutes" is simply the latest in a long line of these. Obama gives frequent interviews (an astonishing 674 in his first term, compared with 217 for President George W. Bush, according to statistics compiled by Martha Joynt Kumar, a political scientist at Towson University), but they are often with network anchors or local TV stations, and rarely with the reporters who cover the White House day to day.

"This administration loves to boast about how transparent they are, but they're transparent about things they want to be transparent about," said Mark Knoller, the veteran CBS News reporter. "He gives interviews not for our benefit, but to achieve his objective." Knoller last talked to Obama in 2010—and that was when Knoller was in then-press secretary Robert Gibbs's office, and the president walked in.

- There's the classic weekend document dump to avoid negative coverage. By our count, the White House has done this nearly two dozen times, and almost always to minimize attention to embarrassing or messy facts. "What you guys call a document dump, we call transparency," the White House's Earnest shot back. If that's the case, the White House was exceptionally transparent during the Solyndra controversy, releasing details three times on a Friday.
- There is the iron-fisted control of access to White House information and officials. Top officials recently discouraged Cabinet secretaries from talking about sequestration. And even top officials privately gripe about the muzzle put on them by the White House.
- They are also masters of scrutiny avoidance. The president has not granted an interview to print reporters at *The New York Times*, *The Washington Post*, *The Wall Street Journal*, POLITICO and others in years. These are the reporters who are often most likely to ask tough, unpredictable questions.

Kumar, who works out of the White House press room and tallies every question a journalist asks the president, has found that in his first term Obama held brief press availabilities after photos ops or announcements one-third as often as George W. Bush did in his first term—107 to Bush's 355.

- While White House officials deny it is intentional, this administration—like its predecessors—does some good old-fashioned bullying of reporters: making clear there will be no interviews, or even questions at press conferences, if aides are displeased with their coverage.

Still, the most unique twist by this White House has been the government's generating and distributing of content.

A number of these techniques were on vivid display two weekends ago, when the White House released a six-month-old photo of the president shooting skeet, buttressing his claim in a *New Republic* interview that he fires at clay pigeons "all the time" at Camp David.

Obama and his team, especially newly promoted senior adviser Dan Pfeiffer, often bemoan the media's endless chase of superficial and distracting storylines. So how did the president's inner circle handle the silly dust-up about whether the president really did shoot skeet?

Pfeiffer and White House press secretary Jay Carney tweeted a link to the photo, with Pfeiffer writing that it was "[f]or all the skeeters" (doubters, or "skeet birthers"). Longtime adviser David Plouffe then taunted critics on Twitter: "Attn skeet birthers. Make our day—let the photoshop conspiracies begin!" Plouffe soon followed up with: "Day made. The skeet birthers are out in full force in response to POTUS pic. Makes for most excellent, delusional reading."

The controversy started with an interview co-conducted by Chris Hughes, a former Obama supporter and now publisher of *The New Republic*. The government created the content (the photo), released it on its terms (Twitter) and then used Twitter again to stoke stories about conservatives who didn't believe Obama ever shot a gun in the first place.

"The people you need to participate in the process are not always the people hitting 'refresh' on news websites," said Jen Psaki, the Obama campaign's traveling press secretary, who last week was appointed the State Department spokeswoman. "The goal is not to satisfy the requester, but doing what is necessary to get into people's homes and communicate your agenda to the American people."

Consider the source and the audience

- VandeHei and Allen are mainstream media elite writing for other mainstream media elite. How is that affecting their message? How does their argument sound to readers who are not inside their particular media bubble?

Lay out the argument, the values, and the assumptions

- VandeHei and Allen say that Obama is unprecedented in his avoidance of the mainstream media who know the most and ask the toughest questions, and they decry the president's efforts to talk directly to Americans through various social media. Are the mainstream media really the toughest questioners? Why would VandeHei and Allen think so?
- Why do the authors object to the White House production of content in an era when most news outlets cannot afford to produce their own?
- What is their objection to social media?

Uncover the evidence

- Who are the authors' sources for their claim that the mainstream media are being mistreated by the White House? Are the opinions of members of the mainstream media the best evidence for their claim? Who else would you have liked to hear from?

Evaluate the conclusion

- The authors suggest that the Obama administration is worse than previous administrations in its creation of content and its avoidance of the media. Do they successfully make this case?
- If it is true that the Obama administration uses social media more than previous administrations, why might that be?

Sort out the political significance

- Given that communication technology is changing so dramatically, how can the profession of journalism evolve along with it so that politicians can take advantage of new ways to contact citizens and yet still be held accountable?

· ·

15.5 Five (Weird) Ways Government Is Experimenting with Social Media

Ryan Holmes, HootSuite

Why We Chose This Piece

There isn't really any doubt that the developments in communication technology and social media are revolutionizing the way we make, report, and receive news, but we aren't yet sure what role the new media will play in our political world. Do they strengthen democracy, or allow politicians to get away without being held accountable, as the previous selection suggested? It's primarily speculation right now, but the author of the following piece has more experience than do most people. Do the following examples serve to enhance our democratic life?

On April 20, 2007, a young U.S. senator named Barack Obama sent his first tweet. "Thinking we're only one signature away from ending the war in Iraq," the future president tweeted, a bit optimistically. Since then, governments across the world have jumped onto social media. These days, voters are as likely to see political ads in their Facebook feeds as on TV, and Twitter Q&As with elected officials have become as common as fireside chats.

But beyond the usual applications, governments are also experimenting with using social media in surprising, progressive, and sometimes just plain weird ways. I've seen it from the front lines working at a social media company that makes tools to connect governments and other organizations with millions of users. Specialized command centers can now monitor trends on Twitter and Facebook in minute detail, enabling officials to do everything from forecast voting patterns to anticipate disasters before they happen.

Here are 5 unusual and powerful ways governments are harnessing social media:

Picking up the trash: Anyone who's waited all day in line at the DMV knows that government agencies aren't always keen on customer service. But does it have to be that way? Take something as simple as weekly garbage collection. In the city of Vancouver, confusing schedules were leading to overflowing bins on streets and in homes. So the city turned to Twitter. It set up a website where residents could sign up to be tweeted the night before garbage and recycling collection. Specialized bulk tweeting and scheduling tools made it possible. Result: cleaner streets and sparkling customer service at a fraction of the cost of traditional phone centers or email.

Defusing riots: The 2012 London Olympic Games were largely free from disturbances and disorder. Could social media have played a part? Prior to the games,

---

Selection published: June 11, 2013

U.K. police set up a dedicated social media task force. Using social media management tools, they followed known rabble rousers on Twitter, setting up streams to monitor conversations about the games and planned protests. When push came to shove, authorities were able to dialogue with antagonists in real time and, in some cases, pinpoint the exact location of troublemakers using geolocation features. All of the information was open and publicly accessible: All it took was the right tools to tap into it.

Detecting earthquakes before they happen: When a 5.9-magnitude earthquake shook the Northeast in 2011, many New Yorkers learned about it on Twitter—seconds before the shaking actually started. Tweets from people at the epicenter near Washington, D.C., outpaced the quake itself, providing a unique early warning system. (Conventional alerts, by contrast, can take two to 20 minutes to be issued.) Seeking to take advantage of these crowdsourced warnings, the U.S. Geological Survey is hard at work on TED, short for Twitter Earthquake Dispatch. It uses specialized software to gather real-time messages from Twitter, applying place, time, and keyword filters to create real-time accounts of shaking.

Preparing for the zombie apocalypse: Taking a page from Orson Welles, the Centers for Disease Control recently terrified readers with a blog post titled Preparedness 101: Zombie Apocalypse. "[Where] do zombies come from, and why do they love eating brains so much?" the author asks, before listing ways to prepare for the inevitable. The post, which also explained how to get ready for real emergencies, attracted more than 1,200 comments, with a lively debate ensuing between readers on the finer points of zombie culture and emergency preparedness. While not a social network in the strict sense of the word, the CDC blog does illustrate how governments can use online channels to engage and educate. More recent posts have focused on what the popular board game Pandemic can teach us about how disease spreads.

Forecasting elections: During the 2012 U.S. presidential election, Twitter developed a brand new political analysis tool called the Twindex, which gauged online conversations and sentiment around Barack Obama and Mitt Romney. As election day approached—and most traditional polls had Romney pulling ahead—the Twindex showed Obama trending sharply upward in all 12 swing states. Now, it may have been pure coincidence that Obama went on to win. Or maybe not. It's hard to dispute that buzz in the Twittersphere is tied to real-world sentiment. As analysts get better at quantifying that buzz, social media may become a crystal ball of sorts for peering into election results. Many campaigns are already investing in social media command centers, specialized software and screens for tracking social mentions, and trends in detail.

With the right social media management tools, agencies and officials are turning the torrent of social posts into a catalyst for better government (or, at least, some pretty cool apps). Keep an eye on your newsfeeds: Big data plus better software means these initiatives could be coming soon to a social network near you.

Consider the source and the audience

- HootSuite is a social media management tool, and Ryan Holmes is its CEO. How might that give him an understanding of what social media can do compared with, say, VandeHei and Allen in the previous selection?
- Holmes's piece was posted on business2community.com, a website for small businesses and entrepreneurs. How will that audience receive his message?

Lay out the argument, the values, and the assumptions

- Holmes doesn't make an argument so much as a claim: Social media are changing our world, including our political world, in creative and enterprising ways. What is Holmes's attitude toward that change?
- Do the changes Holmes mentions bring government closer to people or move it further away? Is government more or less responsive to citizens when it uses social media?

Uncover the evidence

- Holmes uses what we call anecdotal evidence—no data or figures, but several examples. Do you think that evidence bolsters his case?

Evaluate the conclusion

- Holmes is optimistic that the flood of information, "big data," and social media channels are a "catalyst for better government." Do you think that is true?

Sort out the political significance

- When you compare Holmes' conclusions with the conclusions of VandeHei and Allen in the previous article, you have two very different takes on the mainstream media versus the new media. Which is more persuasive?

15.6 Mr. Hearst Answers High School Girl's Query

William Randolph Hearst, *San Francisco Examiner*

Why We Chose This Piece

In times of war and national insecurity there are many pressures on the media, both from within government and without, to control their coverage of national affairs. In the days immediately after the September 11 terrorist attacks, President Bush's press

---

Selection published: October 8, 1935

secretary told a questioner that people needed to be very careful about what they said. Although he later retracted the statement, he was clearly warning people to be cautious about their comments on the government's antiterror efforts. Journalists covering the war in Afghanistan said that there were tighter limits on the information available to them than in previous military actions they had covered. During wartime there are security concerns that obviously demand secrecy, but governments also have an incentive to use national security as an excuse to control the information and images that go out to the public. The Vietnam War is a lesson in what public opinion can do to a war effort of which people do not approve.

Media censorship is an issue that pertains not just to the war on terror, as demonstrated by this editorial letter by William Randolph Hearst, the great newspaper publisher and editor. Hearst was often blamed for contributing to the sensationalism of the news in the early decades of the twentieth century, but, in fact, that gossipy, exaggerated, human-interest form of journalism allowed newspapers to garner sufficiently large circulations that they could afford to free themselves from the government financial support (and control) they had required before the Civil War. In this letter, written in response to a high school girl's question, Hearst makes clear that he thinks the worst fate that can befall the news is to be government controlled. Are his arguments valid today?

There is no such thing and can be no such thing as government control of NEWSPAPERS.

There may be and there is government control of publications, including daily papers.

But daily papers cease to be NEWSPAPERS as soon as they come under governmental control.

Please observe Germany and Russia and Italy, and all the nations where governments control the daily press.

Papers in such countries print only what the Government wants them to print.

The Government suppresses anything which it does not want printed; and if the editor prints anything which the Government does not approve, he goes to jail and the paper is compelled to suspend publication.

Consequently the public never get the full facts about anything.

They never get the actual NEWS.

They always get just one side of every question,—and that is the government side.

When I was last in England, I met an old friend who was London correspondent for what had once been a great German newspaper. He said: "I have been relieved of my post and am going back to Germany."

"Good heavens," I said, "what have you done?"

"Oh," he said, "I have not done anything, but I cannot send any news from London. My editor says that he is not allowed to print any more news from or about England excepting what the German Government gives him to print.

"He cannot print the real news. He must print what the Government desires to have the people believe. Consequently he says he has no need for a news correspondent. The foreign office of the Government hands him his so-called foreign news."

Again, when I was in Germany, a paper was closed up and its editor deprived of the privilege of ever again editing a paper because he had printed in his paper some absolutely true account of occurrences that the Government did not want printed.

In Russia the same conditions prevail in more aggravated form, and more drastic degree. Editors who do not print what the Government wants or who print what the Government does not want are sent to Siberia or shot.

Under such circumstances, there cannot be any real news or any real newspapers.

Consequently the people never know the TRUTH.

In a despotism perhaps this does not matter much.

It would not do the people any good if they did know the truth. They could not do anything about it. The iron heel of a military dictator is on their necks.

But in a democracy the people MUST know the facts, and must know all sides of all questions.

Good government in a democracy depends upon the enlightenment of the electorate. They cannot vote right unless they are completely informed.

They must have the right to read not merely one newspaper but many newspapers, and get all the facts and shades of opinion.

Free speech and free publication are the cornerstones of democracy—the keystones of liberty.

The first step towards tyranny is the suppression of free speech, and the government control of the press.

When the Government controls the press the people no longer get true accounts of what their Government is doing; and the successive steps to tyranny come quickly and surely.

Therefore, those who advocate government control of the press advocate the downfall of democracy and the end of liberty.

Consider the source and the audience

- This letter appeared on the front page of Hearst's *San Francisco Examiner*. What does the front-page placement of a letter better suited for the editorial pages tell us about how Hearst regarded his message?

Lay out the argument, the values, and the assumptions

- What is the relationship between Hearst's key values of truth and democracy? Can we have one without the other?
- What does he see as the citizen's role in democratic government? What happens if citizens are unable to perform that role?
- Would Hearst think that it is ever allowable to have government control of the press? What would happen if we did?

Uncover the evidence

- Is Hearst's use of comparative examples persuasive? Is what happens in Germany or Russia relevant to what happens in the United States? Why or why not?

Evaluate the conclusion

- Hearst is uncompromising in his conclusions on this subject. Is he unnecessarily harsh, or is government censorship an all-or-nothing proposition? What would he think would happen once the door to government control was opened?

Sort out the political implications

- Is censorship permissible under any conditions? When? How do we avoid setting a precedent?

16

Domestic Policy

So far we have spent a good deal of time looking at governmental actors and processes—the *who* and the *how* of politics. In this chapter we turn our attention to the *what*. What does government do with all the personnel, resources, and rules at its disposal? What is at stake in the nitty-gritty political struggles we have examined in this book?

When all is said and done, what government does (or does not do) is called policy. What the U.S. government does here in the United States is domestic policy; what it does in other countries is foreign policy (the subject of Chapter 17). Domestic policies can concern anything government decides is its business—transportation, drugs, security, defense, welfare, education, economic regulation, or environmental protection. The list is endless.

Some of the biggest political battles in the United States involve decisions regarding what is government's business and, if something is an appropriate target for government action, which level of government should act. Historically, the U.S. federal government had only a limited policymaking role. The Great Depression of the 1930s changed that dramatically, however, as people demanded that government do something to regulate the ailing economy, get them back to work, and provide them with some security. President Franklin Roosevelt's New Deal offered a way out of many of the social ills that plagued the country after the Depression, and it ushered in a new era of American policymaking.

Since the New Deal, in general (though in politics there are always exceptions) Democrats have tended to approve a larger role for the federal government in solving social problems, and they have tended to hold an expansive idea of what a social problem is. They are often reluctant to leave problems in the hands of the states, fearing uneven or inadequate responses. Republicans, on the other hand, have generally believed that problems should be solved first at the individual level, and then at the state level, with federal action a last resort except for such policy areas as national defense and domestic security.

Members of the two parties also differ in their constituencies, so they are often at odds about whom they think government action should assist. To give just a few examples,

Democrats tend to respond to issues affecting workers, minorities, and the environment, while Republicans are more responsive to issues affecting business, religious conservatives, and the military. Another way to think about this is to consider three kinds of policies: distributive policies, those that benefit targeted portions of the population (homeowners, for instance, or students, or veterans) and are paid for by all taxpayers; redistributive policies, which shift resources from the wealthier part of the population to the less well off; and regulatory policies, which seek to restrict or change the actions of a business or an individual. While both parties frequently support distributive policies (though they do not always agree on the groups that should be assisted), Democrats tend to favor redistributive polices, which Republicans are more likely to oppose. Democrats also favor regulation of business, whereas Republicans are more likely to favor regulation of personal and religious life.

Policymaking is tricky for lawmakers. Not only do they have to agree on the problem to be solved and on how to solve it, but also they need to monitor the policy once it is made to see if the solution works and to be sure that it does not cause new, unexpected problems. All kinds of political actors are joined in the enterprise of policymaking—members of Congress, but also the president, the bureaucracy, the courts, and groups of interested citizens along with their professional organizations and lobbyists. Policymaking is the main job of American government, and all the available political resources come to be involved in it.

The selections in this chapter look at a variety of different policies. The first article, from the *Los Angeles Times*, discusses the plight of an honor student who unknowingly violated his school's zero-tolerance policy regarding weapons on campus. This story raises important questions about balancing the regulation of individual behavior with the protection of civil liberties, and about the unintended consequences of a well-intentioned law. The second selection, from the *Atlantic*, raises the question of whether President Barack Obama's domestic policies have done enough to help the African-American community. Third, Senate minority leader Mitch McConnell argues that the problem of the national debt resides with President Obama and congressional Democrats. Finally, we provide a transcript of a radio address by President Franklin Roosevelt detailing his actions and plans for combating high unemployment during the Great Depression. In this speech we can see FDR redefining the role of government, setting the stage for many of the policy debates we have today.

• •

16.1 Zero Tolerance Lets a Student's Future Hang on a Knife's Edge

A Utensil Fell into Taylor Hess' Pickup, Dropping Him into a Storm over School Policy

Barry Siegel, *Los Angeles Times*

Why We Chose This Piece

In the aftermath of a wave of school violence that hit a horrible climax with the 1999 Columbine High School shootings, several states and localities decided to clean up

---

Selection published: August 11, 2002

their schools by enacting zero-tolerance laws designed to keep weapons off campus. These laws meant that any transgression of the rules, no matter how seemingly insignificant or unintentional, would result in a student's expulsion.

We chose the following article from the Los Angeles Times *because it shows that the best intentions can result in unexpected consequences that can return to haunt policymakers. This story profiles an honor student who was expelled for unknowingly bringing a bread knife to school. Although he was eventually readmitted to school, the case raised many questions: Why are zero-tolerance policies attractive to policymakers? What are their limitations? How can lawmakers control the unforeseen consequences of the policies they make?*

No big deal. That's what 16-year-old Taylor Hess thought, watching the assistant principal walk into his fourth-period class.

For Taylor, life was good, couldn't be better. He was an honors student. He was a star on the varsity swim team. That morning, he'd risen at 5:30 for practice. It was agonizing, diving into the school pool before sunrise, but Taylor liked getting something done early. He also liked the individuality of his sport, how in swimming you can only blame yourself.

The assistant principal, he now realized, was looking at him. In fact, Nathaniel Hearne was pointing at him. "Get your car keys," Hearne said. "Come with me."

Taylor still thought, no big deal. Maybe he'd left his headlights on. Maybe he'd parked where he shouldn't.

"A knife has been spotted in your pickup," Hearne said.

He'd gone camping with friends on Saturday, Taylor told him. Maybe someone left a machete in the truck.

"OK," Hearne said. "We'll find out."

In the parking lot, beside the 1993 cranberry red Ford Ranger he'd worked all summer to buy, Taylor saw Alan Goss, the Hurst city policeman assigned full time to L. D. Bell High. He also saw two private security officers holding a pair of dogs trained to find drugs and weapons.

Taylor looked at the bed of his pickup. It wasn't a machete after all, but an unserrated bread knife with a round point. A long bread knife, a good 10 inches long, lying right out in the open.

Now it clicked. That's my grandma's kitchen knife, Taylor explained. She had a stroke, we had to move her to assisted living, put her stuff in our garage. Last night we took it all to Goodwill. This must have fallen out of a box. I'll lock it up in the cab. Or you can keep it. Or you can call my parents to come get it.

The others just kept staring at the knife. Taylor thought they looked confused, like they didn't know what to do.

"Is it sharp?" Hearne finally asked.

Officer Goss ran his finger along the blade. "It's fairly sharp in a couple of spots."

Hearne slipped the knife inside his sport coat. Taylor walked with him back to class, wondering what his punishment might be. Saturday detention hall, maybe. He'd never pulled D hall before, never been in any trouble.

"Get your stuff and come to my office," Hearne said. "I've got to warn you, Taylor, this is a pretty serious thing."

Beginnings at Columbine

The Hurst-Euless-Bedford Independent School District, about 12 miles west of Dallas, resembles so many others that have fashioned zero-tolerance policies to combat mounting fears of campus violence. For most districts, it began in 1994 with the federal Gun-Free Schools Act, which required all schools receiving federal aid to expel students who bring firearms to campus. Many states and school boards, appalled by the shootings that culminated in the 1999 Columbine High School massacre in Colorado, adopted policies even wider and tougher than the federal law. Everything from paper guns to nail files became weapons, everything from second-grade kisses to Tylenol tablets cause for expulsion. In countless rule books, "shall" and "must" replaced administrative discretion.

There'd been crazy situations ever since: Eighth-graders arrested for bringing "purple cocaine"—grape Kool-Aid—in lunch boxes; a sixth-grader suspended for bringing a toy ax as part of his Halloween fireman costume; a boy expelled for having a "hit list" that turned out to be his birthday party guests. Pundits clucked and civil rights lawyers protested, but for the most part, parents liked the changes, in fact campaigned for them. They wanted more rules, stricter rules. They also wanted consistency. They wanted students treated equally.

Jim Short, the principal of L. D. Bell High, understood all this as he sat at his desk on Monday afternoon, Feb. 25. Just minutes before, they'd found Taylor Hess' knife. Short's heart told him to ignore the matter. He knew Taylor well, thought him a great kid, a terrific young man. He believed the boy's story, he understood what had happened. He didn't believe Taylor had done anything wrong. Yet as principal, Short didn't think he could turn a blind eye.

Before him he had the Texas Education Code's Chapter 37 and his own school district's student code of conduct. They both told him the same thing: He had no latitude. There it was in the state code: A student shall be expelled . . . if the student on school property . . . possesses an illegal knife. There it was in the district code: Student will be expelled for a full calendar year. . . .

Nothing got people's attention more quickly than weapons on campus. Short appreciated this. He was 50 years old. For 26 years, he'd worked in the Abilene, Texas, schools, the last 15 as a principal, before coming to L. D. Bell this year. He knew schools could be dangerous places. An Abilene teacher had been shot on campus. Kids were good generally, but some just didn't care. If Short ignored an infraction, it could blow up in his face. If he ignored Taylor Hess' knife, people would hear about it. Then he'd be assailed for paying no heed to a big carving knife. He had to follow the rules.

Still—Short had a sick feeling. He kept asking himself, what did he expect Taylor to have done differently?

At 2 P.M. that day, Short met with five assistant principals and the Hurst police officer, Alan Goss. They traded opinions without reaching a consensus. Most, even while hoping Taylor might win a later appeal, thought the state and district codes mandated expulsion.

We don't make the laws, the way Officer Goss saw it. Their hands were tied. If he were working as a street cop, if he had pulled Taylor over and seen an illegal knife in his pickup, Goss had discretion on whether even to write a report. He'd probably let him go with a warning. But he couldn't do that on school grounds. Not under the district's zero-tolerance policy.

Short found himself sounding the most liberal. Yet he saw his colleagues' view-points. It seemed to him they were honorable people with different opinions. Honorable people who all left the meeting with long faces.

More voices soon chimed in. The Texas Education Agency advised that the district had to proceed against Taylor. A county prosecuting attorney said yes, this was a case he'd accept, this was a violation of the penal code.

That made a difference. Officer Goss had been expecting the prosecuting attorney to say no, don't bring it to me. Expecting—and hoping.

At 2:40 P.M., Taylor Hess, summoned from his 11th-grade advanced-placement chem-istry class, stepped into the principal's office. This will all blow over, he'd been telling himself. If no one else knows, they can let it pass. He didn't feel guilty or anxious, the way you did when you knew you'd messed up. Besides, he had a history with this princi-pal. Jim Short had been supportive of the swim team. He'd sat around with them, talk-ing to Taylor, congratulating him for being regional backstroke champ. Short knew him, knew what kind of kid he was.

A non-event. That's what all this was, Taylor figured. A non-event.

He explained again, telling Short about his grandma's stroke, packing up her stuff, driv-ing to Goodwill. Short appeared to believe him but still looked mighty serious. When Taylor stopped talking, Short said, "Taylor, are you aware this calls for mandatory expulsion?"

Parents' Disbelief

Robert and Gay Hess, Taylor's parents, have an unspoken rule. She doesn't call him at work unless it's urgent. She's a physical therapist's assistant at North Hills Hospital; he's a customer service manager for American Eagle airline at the Dallas–Fort Worth airport. At 3 P.M. that Monday, his pager beeped while he sat in a staff meeting. He bolted from the room to call his wife.

"You're not going to believe this," she began, sounding distraught. Taylor's principal had just phoned her. She'd realized right off what this was about. She'd explained every-thing to Jim Short. He'd appreciated her account, Gay thought. After all, she'd corrobo-rated Taylor's story without knowing what Taylor had told them. Yet Gay didn't think she'd swayed the principal. This is very serious, he'd kept telling her. This is very serious.

Robert Hess tried to calm his wife. He was good at solving problems and easing ten-sion. That's what he did all day with aggravated airline travelers. He could fix this. It was a bread knife, after all. Taylor obviously never even saw it. They were all grown-ups, weren't they?

"The school district has competent leaders," Robert told Gay. "Surely they will be fair and logical."

Late that day, he called Jim Short's office and arranged to meet with him the next afternoon. During dinner, the Hess family—Taylor has one older brother, Jordan, 17, then an L. D. Bell senior—talked things over. Gay thought it ironic that their family had always wanted to make schools safer; she'd never expected it would backfire on them. Taylor thought, this just shows that no good deed goes unpunished.

Robert Hess' mind drifted to Sunday, to their hours in the garage packing up his mother Rose's stuff. Going through everything had sparked such memories. The glassware, for instance. He was 46 now, yet there were glasses he remembered drinking from as a child, glasses his mom had used to serve Kool-Aid at Cub Scout meetings. She must have kept them, he imagined, because they took her back to a time when she was a young, beautiful woman with small children. Now 80, she sat in assisted living, unaware of Taylor's plight, for they'd chosen not to upset her.

It was funny. Robert and Gay had debated about the cutlery set. Gay had decided not to keep it, so it went into a box. Dusk fell before they finished. In the dark, Robert and Taylor drove a mile to the Goodwill center, bouncing along on the Ranger's old springs. The night drop-off area was poorly lighted, so they could barely see as they unloaded. They worked fast, eager to get home.

Don't worry, Robert Hess told his family now. Maybe Taylor will have to write an essay. Something like that. Something that fits the event.

A Word Study

Again and again, Principal Jim Short flipped through the penal code, the state code, the school code. He asked himself, how do you define "possession"? He studied the words: "knowingly." .."willingly." .."recklessly." The first two didn't apply, but "recklessly"— there were those in the district, both below and above him, who thought Taylor's conduct reckless.

Another word drew Short's attention: "shall." Shall be expelled, not "may" be expelled. . . .

Ten years ago, he would have handled the Taylor Hess situation by himself. No longer. Now Short had to talk to his district supervisors, who talked to the district superintendent, Gene Buinger. People in Buinger's office had to talk to the Texas Education Agency and local police authorities. The rules and codes kept evolving. Although the federal Gun-Free Schools Act had allowed them "case by case" flexibility, the state refined and the districts refined even further. It was Texas that required expulsion of a student with an "illegal knife," but it was Short's own district that insisted the expulsion be for a full year.

Some school administrators found it insulting or preposterous to lose personal discretion. Zero-tolerance panels at school board conferences often drew overflow crowds. There was always talk of the foolish cases. In recent years in Short's district, there'd been half a dozen as perplexing as Taylor Hess', half a dozen where district Supt. Buinger believed the punishment had been excessive. "Feel-good legislation" is what Buinger called the state laws; legislation that is "supposed to solve, but deep down, everyone knows it just addresses issues superficially."

Still, Buinger had to admit—zero-tolerance rules made life easier. They eased the burden. By applying consistency instead of subjective judgment, you had support for your actions rather than claims of discrimination. If Jim Short disregarded the Taylor Hess case and six months later a different principal responded another way with, say, a Latino student, you would surely hear cries about prejudice.

That, above all, was why Short's supervisors wanted firm formulas. Their school district was in transition, undergoing "a change in demographics." It was one-third minority now, mostly Latino. There was a distinct and growing gap between poorer and more affluent students. For people to have faith in the school system, they had to believe everyone was being treated equally.

Deep down, despite his unease, Jim Short agreed. He had to admit: He derived a certain comfort in not having discretion. He could lean on that. He could then say he followed the formula.

As arranged, Robert Hess appeared in his office at 2:15 P.M. on Tuesday. Assistant Principal Nathaniel Hearne joined them. So did the Hurst police officer, Alan Goss. Hess sat down, ready to settle this as he did most problems. Right off, though, Short handed him a letter and asked him to sign a receipt for it.

For the first time, Hess began to feel a little nervous. "Wait a minute," he said. "Let me read it."

"This letter is to notify you that your son, Ryan Taylor Hess, is being considered for expulsion from L. D. Bell High School. . . . We have scheduled a Due Process Hearing for Friday, March 1 at 9:00 A.M. . . ."

Hess' nervousness grew. This looked more significant than he'd expected. He asked, "Would I be overreacting if I brought an attorney?"

"I can't say," Short told him. "But if you do, you need to notify us so we have ours too."

The principal felt he owed it to Hess to be truthful. Short himself would preside at the due process hearing, he explained. He'd be following the code of conduct. It would be unlikely that he'd be able to recommend anything but expulsion.

Hess, normally easy with conversation, sat speechless. OK, he thought, OK. This has gone a step or two further than he'd expected. But surely they'd resolve this at the hearing. They just needed to prepare; they just needed to get ready.

They needed to do one other thing, Robert Hess decided. They needed to call a lawyer.

Quizzing the Educators

A door at the rear of the principal's office leads into a private conference room. There everyone gathered at 9 A.M Friday, settling around a rectangular table. On the table, a tape recorder turned silently. Facing the Hess family now, along with Short, Hearne and Goss, was Dianne Byrnes, who directs the district's "alternative education programs" for problem kids.

This wouldn't be adversarial, Short had advised. Yet it seemed that way to the Hesses. Taylor felt numb, in shock, ready for anything, He talked little, trying instead to grasp what was going on. Same with his mother, who couldn't believe this was even happening. Mainly, Robert Hess spoke for the family.

He'd been preparing for two days, studying the codes, scouring the Internet, consulting an attorney, drafting specific questions for each person present. Whoever loses his temper, he reminded himself, is at a disadvantage. So he spoke politely, without a hint of antagonism, something that Short noted and appreciated. Yet as they walked through the facts of the case, Hess poured on the questions, unrelenting.

You don't have the knife or a photo of the knife at this hearing? You don't have a copy of the police report? You're sitting here today without any of the evidence? Do you really think these proceedings are fair? Do you really feel you're following the spirit of the law? Do any of you in the least doubt the truth of Taylor's explanation? What are your feelings about the school district's zero-tolerance policies? How do you feel about what you're doing to Taylor?

Dianne Byrnes, who wrote the district's code of conduct and spends most of her time on matters of discipline, took the hardest line. Her stance made the Hess family feel uncomfortable. "Taylor did have a knife visible in his truck . . . ," she said. "Taylor did put students at risk. . . . The spirit of the law is to ensure the safety of students. . . . I think there was a risk factor."

Jim Short sounded much more ambivalent. Where Byrnes resisted questions about personal feelings, he responded. He thought zero-tolerance policies "a two-edged sword." They made it possible for him to "look myself in the mirror and know that I treated the students as equally as I possibly could." On the other hand, the policies "make you feel like you lose some judgment." So it was for him "a love-hate thing."

Short turned to Hess. "I don't know if that answers your question."

Hess said, "Yes, you answered it eloquently. I can appreciate how frustrating it must be to have your hands tied."

Short sighed. "I'd be lying if I said any aspect of this is pleasant. This is a sorrowful experience."

As they talked, Hess kept looking for signs. No one else had files or questions or evidence. They've already made their decision, he concluded. Reading their body language, he believed he saw people eager to go. To him, Dianne Byrnes seemed particularly antsy, glancing often at her watch. She had another appointment, she declared finally. They would have to postpone this hearing.

"No," Robert Hess said. "We're not through."

Short eventually sided with Hess. At 11 A.M., two hours into the hearing, Dianne Byrnes left. Hess seized the opportunity. Again he asked Short how he felt.

"Miserable," the principal said, with a rueful laugh. "How's that?" He paused. "There's not a good feeling in my body about this."

Half an hour later, they all rose. Short usually ruled right away in these situations, but not today. "I want to think about this over the weekend," he told the Hess family.

Doing the "Right Thing"

Late on Monday afternoon, Robert Hess called the L. D. Bell office. "I need another day," Jim Short told him. "I want to make sure we do the right thing for Taylor and for the student population of Bell High."

Hess' heart sank. Right thing for the student population. Oh my God, he thought. They're going to expel Taylor.

That night he warned his family. Taylor reeled. He'd been in turmoil for a week. Like his principal, he'd been wondering why he hadn't just denied any knowledge of the knife. It hadn't occurred to him, though. There'd been no reason to lie. Besides, he'd always been taught to tell the truth.

Taylor had career plans. He wanted to get a private pilot's license; he wanted to study aeronautical engineering. Now what would happen? Taylor couldn't help but think this whole thing made the school administrators look cowardly. Nobody was asking, what should we do? Instead, everyone was asking, what do we have to do?

The call from Short finally came at 3:15 P.M. Tuesday. "I've decided to expel Taylor," the principal told Robert Hess. "You can appeal. I encourage you to appeal. If you do, I'll be one of Taylor's biggest advocates." Short also asked, "Do you want me to tell Taylor, or should you?"

"We'll both tell him," Hess said. "I'm on my way there." . . .

In Short's office. Hess and the principal swapped letters.

Legalese filled Short's: "This is to inform you of my decision to recommend expulsion of Ryan Taylor Hess from L. D. Bell High School."

Hess' cited a federal appellate court ruling in another zero-tolerance case: A school administrator that executed such an action could be held personally liable and would not have the luxury of his qualified immunity.

Hess vainly implored Short to reconsider. Hess said, "Mr. Short, the only thing that can happen from this point on is, this could get bigger and uglier."

Short replied, "I'll try not to take that as a threat." Yet to himself, he thought: This man is just being an advocate for his child. I would do exactly the same.

They called Taylor in. He'd been waiting in the anteroom, summoned once again from his advanced-placement chemistry class. Short explained his decision. Taylor felt gut-punched, stung with pain. All my hard work shot to hell, he thought. Honors classes, the swim team, all a waste of time. He held his tongue, though. Jim Short thought him amazingly courteous.

The principal let Taylor stay at L. D. Bell for two more days, Wednesday and Thursday. Taylor told all his friends now, after keeping things mostly to himself. A couple of teachers had him get up, explain to the class. He asked his English teacher to spread the word wider, to tell other students. Taylor preferred that everyone hear the true story rather than think he'd gone and stabbed someone. . . .

Debate Goes Public

On the Thursday afternoon of spring break, district Supt. Gene Buinger arrived home to find a note on his front door. It was from Monica Mendoza, a reporter for the *Fort Worth Star-Telegram*. Robert Hess had contacted her, she advised, and had provided her a tape recording of Taylor's due process hearing. She'd be writing a story for the Sunday paper. Did Buinger want to respond?

Buinger had heard about the Taylor Hess case. There were 20,000 students in his district, though, 30 schools in all, so he didn't have a complete grasp of the matter. His first response to the reporter's note was surprise—surprise that the Hess family had gone to a newspaper. In his 20 years as a superintendent, that had never happened. Most parents didn't want the notoriety. The Hesses were waiving lots of confidentiality rights.

That didn't mean Buinger believed he could waive confidentiality. He declined to comment to the reporter, explaining that federal law prevented him from responding. Then he braced himself for the article.

Jim Short's phone rang at 4:30 that Sunday morning. You going to call off school? an anonymous voice inquired. Short didn't know what the man was talking about. He was still in bed and hadn't seen the newspaper. The caller explained: They're going to have lots of sharp pencils out.

By 10 that morning, the onslaught had begun, mostly directed at Short. Phone calls, e-mails, radio talk shows, TV cameras, CNN, NBC—from all quarters, pundits and outraged citizens were lambasting him. He'd never imagined being the subject of radio talk shows; he'd never grasped the full might of the Internet.

Zero tolerance is a cop-out. Here my tax dollars are paying a principal to not use his judgment.... Ludicrous.... I am so disgusted.... Not only insane, but cruel and unnecessary.... Any administrator who supports this should resign immediately....

Other messages scared Short even more. The loudest voices came not from civil libertarians but from the antigovernment, right-to-bear-arms crowd. Free men are armed, slaves are disarmed. The Constitution guarantees the right of the people to bear arms.... You're just a bunch of left-wing nazi indoctrinators.... Take away the arms and you break a nation.

Most damaging of all were the Hess family's comments. They were doing back-to-back interviews now, filling TV screens by the hour. It had been their attorney's idea to contact the news media. They agreed, seeing no other alternative, but called only the one Fort Worth reporter. They'd not expected the enormous response. They'd not realized that people would sense this could happen to their own kids, to anyone. The feedback felt good to the Hess family, but also scary. "We're just regular working folks," Robert Hess kept saying. "We're not used to TV trucks and reporters outside our door. This feels so alien."

All the same, they handled it with aplomb. Hess observed that "an act of being a good Samaritan now has this fine young man expelled from school.... Having zero tolerance doesn't mean having zero judgment or zero rights." Taylor, amid bashful shrugs, said, "Somehow a knife had to fall out. A fork couldn't fall out, a spoon couldn't fall out.... It's criminal trespass if I go on campus, which means I can't see my brother graduate."

Gene Buinger and Jim Short realized there was no way to look good. Truth was, they didn't feel good. Buinger thought of his old Marine adage: There's a time when you have to stand at attention and take it.

By Tuesday, though, he'd decided to respond. The school district called a news conference for 2 P.M., timed to make the evening news. Buinger still wouldn't discuss the details of the Hess case, but he wanted to explain the state laws and district codes that mandated their zero-tolerance policy. With printed handouts and a big-screen PowerPoint presentation, he emphasized the "musts" and "shalls."

"We're very limited in what we can do," he said. "I understand the public's frustration. I'm frustrated too.... Individuals opposed to such policies should take their concerns to their respective state legislators."

Watching from the back of the hall, Robert Hess thought Buinger handled himself well. The superintendent had said something about possibly being able to shorten the expulsion because the offense involved a knife, not a gun. Hess sensed that Buinger was trying to find a way out.

The outcry wouldn't stop, though. Hess couldn't believe the momentum. The national newspapers were calling him now, alerted by a story distributed by Associated Press. The school district was getting crucified. The Hurst Police Department had backed away, deciding not to file a complaint with the county prosecutor. So had the Texas

Education Agency, telling AP that local districts did have discretion, that "every case has to be looked at individually."

Enough, the Hess family resolved. For Taylor, the first couple of times on TV had been neat, but the back-to-back interviews lost their sparkle real quick. For his father, it began to feel like piling on. When would it just become cruel? It wasn't his intent to ruin the school system, to hurt these people's careers. He just wanted Taylor back in school.

He would turn down further interviews, Hess decided. He'd take all the reporters' phone numbers, stick them in his hip pocket. If his family lost their appeal, scheduled for Thursday at 11 A.M., he could always pull them out again.

By Wednesday night, that didn't seem likely. Early in the evening, the phone rang at the Hess home. It was an assistant superintendent in Gene Buinger's office. Would the Hesses be agreeable to a 9 A.M. meeting, he wondered, before the scheduled appeal? The district had some ideas. The district thought matters maybe could be resolved.

Finding a Way to Bend

In the end, it all came down to what had been lacking, to what everyone said the law didn't allow: personal judgment.

The federal Gun-Free Schools Act had always included a clause specifying that state laws "shall" allow school superintendents to modify expulsion requirements. The Texas Education Agency, in a letter to district administrators, had made clear that the term of expulsions "may be reduced from the statutory one year." Yet it was the Hurst-Euless-Bedford district's own code that governed in the Hess case—and like many others across the country, the HEB district had handcuffed itself by mandating inflexible one-year expulsions.

Now, one day before the Hesses' appeal, Gene Buinger decided to remove the self-imposed handcuffs. He'd simply waive district policy; he'd rescind the expulsion. Following a conversation with the Texas Education Agency's school safety division, he thought he could do that, especially since the police had never filed a complaint. And if he could do that, why even hold an appeal hearing?

When the Hesses arrived at his office on Friday morning, Buinger began to explain his plan. Just then, however, an assistant came in carrying a newly arrived fax from the state agency's legal department. No, the fax advised, Buinger couldn't rescind the expulsion. He could only reduce the expulsion to time served.

Buinger wasn't sure whether the Hesses would buy this. He shared with them the conflicting advice he'd received. This does call for expulsion, he said, but we can adjust the amount of time. Is that OK with you?

Robert Hess had a typed list of conditions. "Yes," he said. "If we can agree on these."

The Hesses wanted Taylor readmitted immediately to L. D. Bell, his record expunged of any reference to the expulsion, tutorials to help him catch up on missed classes and a public announcement of the resolution. Buinger's staff readily agreed, but since it was already Thursday, they thought Taylor should come back to Bell on Monday.

No, Robert Hess said. Tomorrow.

Applause greeted the announcement, at an 11 A.M. joint news conference, that Taylor Hess would be returning to L. D. Bell the next morning. Taylor said it hadn't been "a pleasant experience, but I hold no personal grudges." Robert Hess said, "What I was hoping for is exactly what I got." Gene Buinger said, "Zero-tolerance policies have become excessive. . . . The school board is now undertaking a complete review of district policy. We want to give as much discretion as possible to local administrators so we don't have to repeat this situation."

In time, the district would revise its policy, among other things ending the mandatory one-year term for expulsions. All that remained unresolved were the fundamental reasons for zero-tolerance policies in the first place. Gene Buinger knew as much; he knew that if another student had lifted the knife from Taylor's pickup and used it in an altercation, they would have endured an even more impassioned response. He knew also what he would hear in the next knife-on-campus case: I want the same as Taylor Hess. If I don't get the same, it's discrimination.

There were no simple answers. Still, returning to L. D. Bell after the final news conference, Jim Short saw one thing clearly. This day happened to be the occasion for another random security sweep of the campus, complete with drug-sniffing dogs. There they were, out on the parking lot, just as they were the morning they spotted Taylor's knife. This crew had never found drugs, hardly ever weapons. Littering and tardiness had been the biggest problems at Bell all year.

"No thank you," Short told the dog handlers. "You're not going to do this today. Stay out of the parking lot. Stay out of our classes."

Consider the source and the audience

- Why would a national newspaper like the *Los Angeles Times* run a story about a small town in Texas?
- This is a human-interest story with lots of personal detail. How does that fact affect your feelings about it? Can you tell where Siegel's sympathies lie?

Lay out the argument, the values, and the assumptions

- Both the people advocating zero-tolerance laws and those opposing them are concerned about "fairness," but they define it differently. What two definitions of "fairness" are at work here?
- How do values like safety, flexibility, due process, and equality figure into the arguments made by each side? What trade-offs among these values is each side willing to make?

Uncover the evidence

- How does Siegel know what happened, who thought what, and who said what to whom? What motives might his sources have had in talking to him?
- What evidence do the two sides bring to bear in making their cases for and against the policy?

Evaluate the conclusion

- The advocates of zero tolerance believe that schools can be safe, and students treated fairly, only if all transgressions of the no-weapons rule are swiftly and evenly met with expulsion. Opponents also want safety and fairness, but they want administrators to be able to use discretion in applying sanctions. Can either side get what it wants?
- What are the implications of this article for zero-tolerance policies? Are such implications stated clearly?

Sort out the political implications

- Ultimately, even with a zero-tolerance policy in place, Taylor Hess was treated differently due to the individual circumstances of his case, his own personal merits, and the advantages his family could bring to his defense. What is the lesson here for the makers of zero-tolerance policies?

· ·

16.2 Has President Obama Done Enough for Black Americans?

George Condon Jr. and
Jim O'Sullivan, *Atlantic*

Why We Chose This Piece

President Obama's election in 2008 was a historic moment in U.S. history. Watching images on television that night made it clear that to many people this was not just an ordinary election. Obama's victory brought with it a sense of hope that the country's racial issues of the past were starting to change and, for many African Americans, the sense that an occupant of the White House was like them—someone who would understand their concerns and would work hard to pass policies that improve their lives. But Obama has always struggled to balance the expectations that many have of him for being the nation's first black president with the fact that he is president of all Americans. Many in the African-American community have criticized him for not doing enough on their behalf. This article raises that very critique. What challenges come with being the first president who is a member of a racial minority?

Selection published: April 5, 2013

Bernard Anderson, a pathbreaking African-American economist, understands the importance of rhetoric. He was up front at the Lincoln Memorial when Martin Luther King Jr. gave his historic "I Have a Dream" speech in 1963. And he was in the audience on the Howard University campus in 1965 to hear President Johnson deliver a grim view of the state of black America and declare war on "past injustice and present prejudice."

So Anderson had high hopes as he sat at home in Pennsylvania watching President Obama deliver his second Inaugural Address this year. He wanted Obama to acknowledge that even five decades after Johnson's stirring oration, African Americans in today's America still struggle against discrimination. And when the president started talking about "We, the people," the veteran civil-rights champion grew excited. "As he was going through 'We, the people' and 'We, the people,' my heart started to beat," Anderson said. But just as fast, his spirits sank. "I didn't find me among the people he was talking about."

Eleven days later, Anderson—an early supporter and fundraiser for Obama, an Obama delegate in 2008, and an expert on economic disparities who has been called to the Obama White House several times—allowed himself to vent his frustration and call for more high-level attention to the black community's economic challenges.

Grumbling that he had heard "not a single blessed word on race" in the Inaugural Address, Anderson told attendees at the fourth annual African-American Economic Summit at Howard, "I believe now is the time for the president to find his voice, summon his courage, and use some of his political capital to eliminate racial inequality in American economic life." To applause, he added, "We cannot let the president off the hook in the second term. Black people gave him a pass in the first term. . . . He is not going to run for anything. He doesn't deserve a pass anymore."

In those few moments at the microphone, Anderson gave voice to the inner turmoil shared by so many African Americans. Thrilled beyond words at seeing a proudly black man in the Oval Office, they almost don't want to admit they want still more. But they know they have to be exceedingly careful in pushing Obama to talk more about—and do more for—black Americans still reeling from a recession that hit them harder than anyone else.

Wanting more is why so many blacks, from the barbershops and street corners to the think tanks and highest levels of academe, are investing so much in the belief that Obama has been liberated by his reelection to become more of a champion for his community. "That's what African Americans out in the world believe," said Rep. Emanuel Cleaver, D-Mo., former chairman of the Congressional Black Caucus. "I can't tell you how often I heard that, particularly during the campaign." Cleaver said he still keeps hearing, "In the second term, we're going to get the 'real' Barack Obama, and by 'real,' they mean that, I guess, he's going to show up in a dashiki."

Just because that view is widely shared in the black community does not make it so, of course. Cleaver responds, "The president was who he was in the first term. And it would be foolish for me or any CBC member to give them the impression that the nation and the world will see some kind of reincarnation of Eldridge Cleaver and Huey Newton." But many African American leaders still hope there is some truth in the widespread belief. "Will President Obama find his voice in this term? My answer is yes," said Lorenzo

Morris, a Howard University political-science professor. "He won't have a big stick to carry with it, but it will be a voice that I think will be a little clearer."

That hope springs from the reality of daily life for many African Americans. The Great Recession may be over for the country as a whole, but they aren't feeling the recovery. Black unemployment remains double that for whites. The median income gap between white and black households has hit a record high. Blacks have half the access to health care as whites. The gap in homeownership is wider today than it was in 1990. African Americans are twice as likely as whites to have suffered foreclosure.

The list goes on: Net wealth for black families dropped by 27.1 percent during the recession. One in 15 African-American men is incarcerated, compared with one in 106 white men. Blacks make up 38 percent of inmates in state and federal prisons. Although only 13.8 percent of the U.S. population, African Americans represent 27 percent of those living below the poverty line.

It is a grim picture—and one that administration policymakers know well. They insist the White House has attacked the stubborn problems with an array of policies, some of them through executive-branch actions and more through legislative proposals.

Avis Jones-DeWeever, executive director of the National Council of Negro Women, thinks there is a chance we will hear more from Obama on these issues now that he has secured another four years. "I do think it is probably realistic that in his first term he was a bit more cautious than one might expect him to be in this term," she told *National Journal* soon after she and other black leaders met with Obama at the White House. "I do see this president as one who now is ready to lay out a legacy. . . . Though he is still facing a significant amount of challenge [from Congress], he has finally—it took him a minute to get it—but I think he has finally got the hang of the effective use of the bully pulpit."

Walking softly

At that White House meeting, which lasted more than two hours on Feb. 21, the Rev. Al Sharpton, president of the National Action Network, drew laughter from Obama and his fellow activists when he found a folksy way to defend the president from charges he didn't talk enough in his first term about black issues:

"I had a friend when we were in school who told me he was going on a kosher diet. He converted his religion. We went to eat, and he ordered a ham sandwich. I said, 'You can't eat that.' He said, 'Why?' I said, 'That is pork.' He said, 'No, no, no. Pork is pork chops or pork loin. I said, 'No, you don't have to call it pork for it to be pork. It is still pork.'" The lesson, Sharpton said, is simple: "Some things he's done, it may not have been called 'black.' But it affected us. It was still pork."

Jones-DeWeever said that Sharpton, who sat directly across the table from the president in the Roosevelt Room, was also very forceful in characterizing much of the criticism of Obama's first term as misguided. "Reverend Sharpton makes a very good point that the president has been critiqued by certain very loud elements of the black community who have argued the president hasn't pursued a black agenda," she said. "And Reverend Sharpton pointed out in this meeting that it is not the president's responsibility to define a black agenda. He is the president. It is the responsibility of advocates to define the agenda and then push it forward. . . . That's what we do."

From the start, Obama has steered clear of the notion that he has any special responsibility to the African-American community. Asked that question in 2011, he told NPR, "I have a special responsibility to look out for the interests of every American. That's my job as president of the United States. And I wake up every morning trying to promote the kinds of policies that are going to make the biggest difference for the most number of people so that they can live out their American dream."

Inevitably, answers like that draw criticism from some African Americans. But the critics have found little traction in a community still in awe of having one of its own win the presidency. Princeton University professor Cornel West drew stinging rebukes when he told the *Democracy Now!* radio program that last year's election had been won by "a Rockefeller Republican in blackface." West and his partner in excoriating Obama, PBS host Tavis Smiley, find themselves increasingly marginalized because their attacks on the president have been so overheated. Their critique has been discounted "because it has been so very personal," said Fredrick Harris, director of the Institute for Research in African-American Studies at Columbia University, who keeps his criticism focused on the issues he believes Obama is giving short shrift.

Harris noted that the president used Martin Luther King's bible at his swearing-in and featured Medgar Evers's widow, Myrlie Evers, at the inauguration. But Harris also craves more substance. "You had all these symbolic gestures that are connected to the civil-rights past," he said. "But there is not enough focus or attention, particularly policy-wise, on addressing the legacies of racial inequality in this country." He noted an ongoing study, conducted at the University of Pennsylvania by professor Daniel Q. Gillion, showing that Obama spoke less about race in his first two years than any other Democratic president since 1961. As Harris noted in *The New York Times* in October, "From racial profiling to mass incarceration to affirmative action, his comments have been sparse and halting."

Anderson, the economist whose heart sank while watching the inauguration, was assistant secretary of Labor in the Clinton administration, in charge of enforcing affirmative action for government contracts. An adviser to the National Urban League and an emeritus professor of economics at the Wharton School, he remains a strong supporter of Obama's. But Anderson yearns for the president to gain his voice on racial issues, as he did during a memorable speech in Philadelphia during the 2008 campaign. He finds it sad that Obama "evidently does not want to be labeled as a president who is consumed by racial inequality in this country." And the view "that an African-American president must remain silent on this issue? That's an abomination," Anderson says. "We can't tolerate that."

It did not go unnoticed that Obama steered clear of inner cities and predominantly African-American communities in his first term and his reelection campaign. An analysis of campaign travel by *National Journal*'s Beth Reinhard ("Beyond the Trail") found that Obama did not campaign in any of the 100 counties with the highest jobless rates. The president went to Cleveland, Detroit, Miami, New York, and Philadelphia during the campaign, but primarily for fundraisers. Typical was his visit to the famed Apollo Theater in Harlem last year for a fundraising event made memorable not for his talk about poverty or race but for his brief riff on an Al Green song.

Of course, a president's campaign schedule is mostly dictated by electoral realities. Obama had already locked up the black vote. The keys to victory were the suburban counties. And that meant more presidential visits to Ohio's Montgomery County around Dayton than to Cleveland's Hough neighborhood.

Even at the White House, Obama shied away from discussing race, with only a few exceptions, in his first term. At a July 2009 press conference, he lashed out at the Cambridge, Massachusetts, police department for arresting Harvard University professor Henry Louis Gates Jr., an African American, as he tried to enter his own home. The police, Obama said, "acted stupidly." To quell the ensuing furor, the president invited Gates and the arresting officer to the White House for a "beer summit" aimed at turning the controversy into a "teachable moment."

Three years later, he reacted to the shooting death in Florida of 17-year-old Trayvon Martin by a private citizen who found the black teen's presence in his neighborhood suspicious. "If I had a son, he'd look like Trayvon," the emotional president said.

But those two statements were just about it for the first four years, when the über-cautious "post-racial" Obama was front and center. Typical was his comment in a 2009 interview with the *Detroit Free Press* and *USA Today*. "The most important thing I can do for the African-American community is the same thing I can do for the American community. Period. And that is to get the economy going again and get people hiring again," he said. "It's a mistake to start thinking in terms of particular ethnic segments of the United States rather than to think that we are all in this together and we are going to get out of this together."

But that is not enough for many in the black community. Anderson still recalls from memory Johnson's stirring speech at Howard. "You do not take a person who, for years, has been hobbled by chains and liberate him, bring him up the starting line of a race, and then say, 'You are free to compete with all the others,' and still justly believe that you have been completely fair," LBJ said. Anderson pointedly asks, "Can you imagine President Obama referring to 200 years of slavery? I cannot imagine him saying anything like that. . . . He has an obligation to address this [economic disparity] that is grinding black people down." While encouraged by parts of Obama's State of the Union address, Anderson asks, "Why has he not revisited the issue since he made that speech during the campaign?"

An old fight

At the White House, there is little patience with the critics and some exasperation at those who want more talk from the president about what he is doing for his "own community." To them, that sentiment is reminiscent of the "Is he black enough?" questions that dogged his campaign in its 2007 infancy. Privately, administration officials bristle when asked why Obama doesn't talk more about race in the ways that Presidents Johnson, Carter, and Clinton did.

"The president gave one of the most powerful speeches about race in history during the 2008 campaign," Valerie Jarrett, senior adviser to the president, told *National Journal*. "He is now interested in results. So he will be judged by his actions. . . . Simply talking about race is not as important as actually working toward equality." As president, she said, Obama does not want to single out one community in his rhetoric. "He is interested . . . in describing our challenges in terms of how we are inextricably linked in mutuality," she said, adding, "The president tries to describe our challenges in ways that are inclusive." That is how he hopes to "keep the broadest possible mandate for moving forward," she said. "He does not intend to polarize; he intends to unify."

Jarrett challenged the notion that the president has been freed by reelection to be himself. "It is liberating in terms of the president's time, because he can spend all of his time now focused on being president," she said. "He had to run a campaign and then his day job, which was pretty all-consuming. So it is certainly liberating in the sense that not having to run for reelection is a burden that is lifted."

But that, she said, does not mean a "new" Obama. "His core values, his principles, and his vision for America are the same in the second term as they were in the first term," she insisted.

Jarrett, 56, is the go-to person in the White House for black leaders and the Congressional Black Caucus. She, like Obama, did not come out of the traditional civil-rights movement. But she has gained the trust of that establishment. "She is very important," Sharpton said. "I have a lot of respect for her because she has never misled us. She does not mind telling you she disagrees with you. She does not mind telling you no. But if she says yes, she stands by it."

Jarrett earned her first scars in Chicago City Hall when that city's first African-American mayor, Harold Washington, was trying to balance the demands of a newly empowered black community and a white population that felt threatened. She understands that nothing is ever simple in matters of race. Today, she hears the demands; she gets the complaints; she goes to the meetings. But she also sees how average African Americans—and even veteran civil-rights leaders—react to the reality that a black son of an African man is the president of the United States and a confident black woman is first lady.

The last time she had the luxury of focusing on that history was election night in 2008, Jarrett said. "Frankly, we're so busy that we don't have that much time to reflect right now on the historical significance," she said. To her, the importance of the 2012 election is that "you didn't hear a lot of conversation about his race. You heard a debate about two different visions of America."

Other black leaders try to put the history aside and concern themselves with the work in front of them. "It's all business, but you do have that pride," said Jones-DeWeever after her White House meeting with Obama. Sitting across the table from the president, she focused on the agenda, fighting for programs that would bring jobs and education and hope to the hard-hit African-American community. But she wasn't prepared for how she reacted when she got home and told her boyfriend about the session. "I left that meeting, and I said to my partner, 'You know what? We have a black president,'" she recalled. "He laughed and said, 'I know.' I said, 'No, you're not hearing me: We have a black president. We have a black president.' You couldn't wipe the smile off my face." It was a moment that surprised her.

For Sharpton, there also are those unexpected moments, such as when he was at the White House to watch the Super Bowl during Obama's first term. He was introducing his daughter to Michelle Obama when he saw a historic portrait of George Washington behind her. "It struck me how far we have come," he said. "But," he quickly added, "those of us who have worked with the administration from the beginning are more sober, because we've been in there enough now where you see the other side of that, [which] is, the expectations are higher."

By any other name

Those expectations include programs that can lift urban areas out of poverty, improve inner-city schools, reform the criminal-justice system, and alleviate sky-high black unemployment. All these numbers, Jarrett acknowledges, have been stubbornly resistant to fixes from Washington, none more so than the jobless figures. African Americans are the only demographic group with higher unemployment today than when Obama took office. White unemployment dropped from 7.1 percent in January 2009 to 6.8 percent in February 2013. Hispanic unemployment dropped from 10.0 percent to 9.6 percent. But African-American unemployment rose from 12.7 percent to 13.8 percent during that time.

A White House official, who asked not to be named, calls those numbers "unacceptably high" but insists that "we have made real progress," with black joblessness on a decline from 16.8 percent in August 2011. "We have seen it come down pretty dramatically over the last couple years, and that is not an accident. That is the explicit result" of administration policies.

"Jobs, jobs, jobs has been the central focus of the president's administration since day one," Jarrett said, and also, she noted, at the heart of the "Ladder of Opportunity" program the president laid out in his State of the Union in February and his follow-up speech in Chicago. In his second term, the president is determined to target the most stubborn pockets of unemployment in urban areas, another White House aide said, pointing out that a part of the American Jobs Act—which remains untouched by Congress—"would provide subsidized employment for the long-term unemployed in this country, which would disproportionately benefit many people of color." The president's new proposals also recognize "that where you live matters, and that in many of our . . . areas of concentrated poverty, we need to take a holistic approach, to really invest." The president talked about investing in 20 selected communities, focusing on education, housing, and crime, but also, according to the aide, "looking at how we create jobs and leverage private capital back into these communities."

As he promoted his new programs in a return to his hometown of Chicago in February, the president added a distinct personal touch that some outsiders took as an indication he could be more open about race in his second term. After meeting with young black men from the Hyde Park Academy, Obama drew some knowing laughter when he noted, "A lot of them have had some issues." But the president stressed his kinship with them. "I had issues too when I was their age. I just had an environment that was a little more forgiving. So when I screwed up, the consequences weren't as high as when kids on the South Side screw up. So I had more of a safety net. But these guys are no different than me."

Reminiscent of his Trayvon Martin remark, this statement resonated in the black community like almost no other presidential words of the past four years. It was, for some, proof that the second term will indeed be different on race. And the president used that Chicago speech to outline what he called his "vision of where we want to be." It was a speech that touched on all the ills that plague urban communities: lack of role models, a too-low minimum wage, guns, violent crime, inadequate education, substandard housing, and the reluctance of businesses to locate in inner cities and hire local workers.

In some ways, it was the shooting in the white suburban community of Newtown, Conn., that provided the impetus for the president to talk about the gun violence that is so endemic to black neighborhoods in Chicago, Minneapolis (where he also traveled recently), and other cities. In Chicago alone, 443 people were killed by guns last year, with an additional 42 homicides by gun this January, the most since 2002. "Too many of our children are being taken away from us," Obama declared emotionally.

Much of what he said on guns in that speech clearly resonated with his audience. And much of what he said in the rest of the speech about economic opportunity and jobs was in sync with the "black agenda" adopted after the election by a group of leaders headed by Urban League President Marc Morial. That agenda, Jarrett said, "is one that the president has embraced from day one." But, not surprisingly for the Obama White House, she adds quickly, "It is important to point out that it isn't just African Americans who benefit from these policies."

Like Sharpton's "ham sandwich" story, she and other administration officials stress that the president has championed policies that aren't called "black programs" but that benefit blacks. Health care reform is at the top of that list. "Approximately 7 million African Americans are without health insurance," Jarrett said. "So, yes, it is a policy that disproportionately does benefit the African-American community. But it also disproportionately benefits poor people." In that vein, the White House cites the president's espousal of voting rights and his opposition to Republican efforts to more tightly regulate voting.

Hilary O. Shelton, Washington bureau director for the NAACP, credits the Justice Department for fighting racial profiling and praises the Dodd-Frank financial-reform law for targeting predatory lending in inner cities. He also mentions the Fair Sentencing Act's reform of punishment for crack-cocaine versus powder-cocaine offenses. "All of these policies don't mention the African-American community one time," Shelton said. "But all of them have our priorities interwoven into the initiative."

At the White House, that caveat always gets added: He isn't doing these things just to help blacks. In this, Georgetown Law professor Paul Butler says Obama is being steadfast. "He doesn't like to talk about race. He does not like to talk about racial justice. He believes in it, but he has a color-blind approach."

It is, perhaps, the strongest evidence of Obama's generational differences with the civil-rights pioneers. But the president has been decidedly consistent. He articulated his philosophy in an interview with the *Chicago Reader* in 1995 when he was launching his political career with a run for the Illinois Legislature. "We have moved beyond the clarion-call stage that we needed during the civil-rights movement," Obama declared. "Now, like Nelson Mandela in South Africa, we must move into a building stage."

Obama had attended the Million Man March that October, but he faulted the organizers for not developing a positive agenda beyond just demanding "our fair share." And he added, "Any African Americans who are only talking about racism as a barrier to our success are seriously misled if they don't also come to grips with the larger economic forces that are creating economic insecurity for all workers—whites, Latinos, and Asians."

A rift in time

It is this reticence to talk specifically about targeting programs for African Americans that privately drives some members of the Congressional Black Caucus to distraction.

That, and the president's odd refusal to meet often with a group he belonged to during his brief Senate career.

The relationship has been challenged from the start. In 2009, caucus members had to watch the president meet with House and Senate Republicans and the Blue Dog Coalition before inviting them to the White House five weeks into his administration. Then, they chafed when forced to accept $60 billion in cuts in stimulus spending they wanted for urban communities. And they were unhappy at his escalation of the war in Afghanistan. When Rep. John Conyers, D-Mich., one of the most senior and respected members of the Black Caucus, criticized Obama for watering down health care reform and taking advice from "clowns," the president called him and pointedly asked Conyers why he was "demeaning" him.

Then, in 2011, Obama delivered a speech to the CBC whose tone privately irked many of the members. "I expect all of you to march with me and press on. Take off your bedroom slippers, put on your marching shoes. Shake it off. Stop complaining, stop grumbling, stop crying," he said. "We are going to press on. We've got work to do, CBC."

The reaction was not good. "It was very condescending," Columbia University's Harris said. "For many people who are sick and tired of the Republican Party, we wish the president would speak in that tone to John Boehner and the Republican Party, which he doesn't. So I find it ironic that he would feel free to speak that way to the CBC."

Obama has not met with the caucus since, sending Jarrett instead. Cleaver admits the CBC would like more access. "Is there frustration sometimes when we can't get in to see the president when we want? Yes. . . . We do want to meet with the president more." But he adds, "So does [Vladimir] Putin," to suggest all the demands on a president's time.

The most recent request for a meeting with Obama came March 11 when CBC Chairwoman Marcia Fudge, D-Ohio, sent a letter to the White House complaining about the lack of African Americans among the president's second-term appointments. Voicing disappointment, she said CBC members are hearing from their constituents. "Their ire is compounded by the overwhelming support you've received from the African-American community," Fudge wrote, adding, "The absence of diverse voices leads to policies and programs that adversely impact African Americans."

Sharpton said he has counseled black lawmakers not to take it personally that Obama holds them at arm's length. "That's his style," Sharpton said. "I work with a lot of the caucus members. I've said to them, if he's meeting with other caucuses and a lot of congressional leaders and not with you, I would say that is wrong, and I would complain. But if that's his style, how do you deal with that, other than argue with his style?"

CBC members' reticence to protest publicly is also tied, as are all things with Obama, to the incredible history he represents. Those who work in the black community simply can't get over what it means to have a black president. They know this isn't a make-believe Hollywood character like Bill Cosby's Cliff Huxtable. This is a strong black man with a loving family who lives in the White House—a real role model, whose image adorns classrooms across the nation.

And Obama understands the need for African-American role models. "There are entire neighborhoods where young people . . . don't see an example of somebody succeeding," he said movingly in his recent Chicago speech. "And for a lot of young boys and young men, in particular, they don't see an example of fathers or grandfathers, uncles, who are in a position to support families and be held up and respected." Black leaders know that Obama powerfully fills that role.

And if they start to take it for granted, they often are reminded in stunning ways that make it smart to mute their frustration over the president's style or his shortcomings. For Jones-DeWeever, it came recently when she was watching a movie with her two sons.

Her younger son, 9, can only remember one president, and he is Obama. "It has made such an indelible mark on his mind that when we watched a movie and there was a white actor playing the president, he said to me, 'Ma, that ain't real.'" Jones-DeWeever was struck speechless. "It is almost inconceivable to him that there was a time that what we see now was unthinkable."

And perhaps, in this case, that reality alone is simply enough.

Consider the source and the audience

- Subscribers to the *Atlantic* are most likely to be white. Why would this article be of interest to them? Is this the audience for whom it is intended? How might this article be different if it were published in a magazine that has a primarily African-American readership?

Lay out the argument, the values, and the assumptions

- Why are some African-American leaders frustrated with President Obama? What do they mean when they say that he needs to find his voice? What issues do they want him to address?
- How does the White House respond to those criticisms? How does it view Obama's role as president differently from many in the black community?

Uncover the evidence

- What kinds of statistics do the authors use to show that African Americans have been hit harder by the recession than whites?
- The authors provide some nonpolicy evidence that seems to indicate that Obama may be ignoring the African-American community. What is it? Why might it be persuasive? Are there other ways to interpret that evidence?
- Do supporters of Obama provide any evidence to show that his critics are wrong?

Evaluate the conclusion

- Has President Obama done enough for the black community? If no, then what might he have done—or do—differently? If yes, then why do the criticisms of Obama exist?
- Being the first of anything often brings with it great expectations. Are the expectations of Obama laid out by many in the black community obtainable? How might he have better tried to meet those expectations?

Sort out the political implications

- How might the fact that Obama does not have to run again for reelection influence the issues on which he focuses, specifically regarding the black community? Or does Obama's vision of what it means to be president make his focus unlikely to change?
- President Obama has faced a divided government during much of his time as president. How might that have prevented him from doing more on behalf of the black community?

16.3 President, Democrats Must Now Focus on the Real Problem: Spending

Mitch McConnell, *The Hill*

Why We Chose This Piece

We chose this op-ed for several reasons. First, few policy issues have received as much attention over the last decade as government spending. Differences in opinion between the parties on this issue are one of the major reasons why Washington is so gridlocked today. Additionally, debates over government spending were responsible for the growth of Tea Party organizations across the country as well as the Occupy Wall Street movement. Second, unlike many of the selections in this book, this one comes directly from a practitioner, and an important one at that. Mitch McConnell is the current Senate minority leader and one of the biggest obstacles to President Obama and congressional Democrats. Third, The Hill is an interesting news source to which students are rarely exposed.

Soon President Obama will take the oath of office for a second time, and as commander in chief he will have a unique opportunity to lay out his vision for the country over the next four years. We all know that America faces many serious challenges, both at home and abroad, but none is more urgent than the massive federal debt that is hanging over the heads of our children and grandchildren.

Given the serious nature of the challenge, I hope the president uses his inaugural address to acknowledge the seriousness of the debt crisis and lays out ways, working with both parties in Congress, to get our profligate spending under control.

Selection published: January 18, 2013

I will be the first to admit that the bipartisan "fiscal cliff" agreement we reached earlier this month was far from perfect, starting with the process. But aside from shielding 99 percent of Americans from tax hikes the president seemed all too willing to impose, it gave us something else—it settled the revenue debate for good. According to the president, those he calls "rich" are now paying their "fair share." So it's time to move on. The president got his revenue, and now it's time to turn to the real problem, which is spending.

We all knew that the tax hikes the president campaigned on were never going to solve the problem. Now that he's got them, he has a responsibility to put his preoccupation with taxes behind him and to work with Congress to actually solve the problem at hand. So it's time to face up to the fact that our nation is in grave fiscal danger, and that it has everything to do with spending. This is a debate the American people want to have. And it's an area where we're more than willing to work with the president to find solutions to Washington's out-of-control spending.

By the end of next month, the president will ask us to raise the nation's debt limit. We cannot agree to increase that borrowing limit without reforms that lower the avalanche of spending that's creating this debt in the first place. It's not fair to the American people. And it's not fair to our children, who we're asking to foot the bill. And the health of our economy requires it.

I recently called on the president, the Senate majority leader and the rest of my Democratic colleagues to start working with congressional Republicans right now—not one hour or one day or one week before we hit the debt limit, but ahead of time for once—so we can pass a bipartisan solution on spending that everyone has had an opportunity to weigh in on in early February. We need a plan that can pass the House and actually begin to get Washington spending under control. And, if we're serious, we will get one done.

With taxes now off the table, the only way to achieve a "balanced" plan is to focus on the spending side of the equation, particularly—as the president pointed out—health-care entitlement programs. Taxes simply can't go high enough to keep pace with the amount of money we're projected to spend on them without crushing our economy. And the best way to reform these programs is to make them work better. The debt isn't exploding because these programs exist; it's exploding because they're inefficient. They were created in a different era, the era of black-and-white TV. They should be updated for the age of the iPad. And we should want to fix them, not just because we want to lower the debt, but because we want to strengthen and improve these programs themselves.

So over the next few months, it will be up to the president and his party to work with us to deliver the same kind of bipartisan and meaningful resolution on spending that we have now achieved on taxes—but it needs to happen before the 11th hour. We addressed the revenue issue; it is now time to address the spending issue and for the president to agree to significant spending cuts.

The president claims to want a balanced approach. Now that he has the tax rates he demanded, his calls for "balance" mean he needs to join us in the effort to achieve meaningful spending reforms. The president may not want to have this debate, but it's the one he's going to have, because the country needs it. Republicans are ready to tackle the spending problem, and we start today.

Consider the source and the audience

- As noted, McConnell is the leading Republican in the Senate. Obviously, one must read this piece with that in mind. But what might Democrats be able to take away from McConnell's argument?
- *The Hill* is a source read mostly by Washington insiders. Why would McConnell choose this outlet for his op-ed?
- Is his audience all insiders or just certain ones? Or is his audience actually much broader than Washington insiders?

Lay out the argument, the values, and the assumptions

- Why does McConnell believe the spending "problem" is in the hands of the Democrats and not his party?
- McConnell keeps coming back to the fact that the revenue debate has been settled. Why?
- According to McConnell, what is responsible for the spending problem?

Uncover the evidence

- What empirical data does McConnell provide to support his argument? Are there any additional data that you need to see in order to evaluate his argument?

Evaluate the conclusion

- What solution does McConnell offer to halt the increasing deficits? How politically feasible is that solution?
- Has McConnell convinced you that government spending is the problem? Why or why not?

Sort out the political implications

- If the national debt continues to grow, how might that affect government services in the future? The economy? The United States' standing as a superpower?
- A common refrain is that budgets should be balanced. However, can some debt be good? What issues might arise if the national government always balanced its budget?

• •

16.4 Fireside Chat
The Work Relief Program
Franklin Delano Roosevelt

Why We Chose This Piece

When President Franklin Roosevelt was inaugurated in the winter of 1933, roughly a third of Americans were unemployed. When he told the nation, in his inaugural address, that the only thing we have to fear is fear itself, he was referring in part to the devastating effects that economic panic had had on the system. Many Americans were fearful that good times had come to an end permanently.

By the spring of 1935, FDR was halfway through his first term. He had already set in motion new legislation, including reforms designed to help heal the American banking system, but he had much more planned in his New Deal for America. In this "fireside chat" he outlined his ideas for a works relief policy—a temporary program to get people back to work at the public's expense—as well as for Social Security, the program for worker compensation and old-age pensions that is still with us, albeit in somewhat rocky financial shape today. We include this speech because it was one of many examples during Roosevelt's presidency that changed the scope of domestic policymaking. In what ways does this speech show how FDR was redefining the way Americans thought about the purpose of government and the role of the presidency? Also, the speech allows for an interesting comparison to the challenges facing President Obama as he entered office during his first term.

Since my annual message to the Congress on January fourth, last, I have not addressed the general public over the air. In the many weeks since that time the Congress has devoted itself to the arduous task of formulating legislation necessary to the country's welfare. It has made and is making distinct progress.

Before I come to any of the specific measures, however, I want to leave in your minds one clear fact. The Administration and the Congress are not proceeding in any haphazard fashion in this task of government. Each of our steps has a definite relationship to every other step. The job of creating a program for the Nation's welfare is, in some respects, like the building of a ship. At different points on the coast where I often visit they build great seagoing ships. When one of these ships is under construction and the steel frames have been set in the keel, it is difficult for a person who does not know ships to tell how it will finally look when it is sailing the high seas.

It may seem confused to some, but out of the multitude of detailed parts that go into the making of the structure the creation of a useful instrument for man ultimately comes. It is that way with the making of a national policy. The objective of the Nation has greatly changed in three years. Before that time individual self-interest and group selfishness were paramount in public thinking. The general good was at a discount.

———
Selection aired: April 28, 1935

Three years of hard thinking have changed the picture. More and more people, because of clearer thinking and a better understanding, are considering the whole rather than a mere part relating to one section or to one crop, or to one industry, or to an individual private occupation. That is a tremendous gain for the principles of democracy. The overwhelming majority of people in this country know how to sift the wheat from the chaff in what they hear and what they read. They know that the process of the constructive rebuilding of America cannot be done in a day or a year, but that it is being done in spite of the few who seek to confuse them and to profit by their confusion. Americans as a whole are feeling a lot better—a lot more cheerful than for many, many years.

The most difficult place in the world to get a clear open perspective of the country as a whole is Washington. I am reminded sometimes of what President Wilson once said: "So many people come to Washington who know things that are not so, and so few people who know anything about what the people of the United States are thinking about." That is why I occasionally leave this scene of action for a few days to go fishing or back home to Hyde Park, so that I can have a chance to think quietly about the country as a whole. "To get away from the trees," as they say, "and to look at the whole forest." This duty of seeing the country in a long-range perspective is one which, in a very special manner, attaches to this office to which you have chosen me. Did you ever stop to think that there are, after all, only two positions in the Nation that are filled by the vote of all of the voters—the President and the Vice-President? That makes it particularly necessary for the Vice-President and for me to conceive of our duty toward the entire country. I speak, therefore, tonight, to and of the American people as a whole.

My most immediate concern is in carrying out the purposes of the great work program just enacted by the Congress. Its first objective is to put men and women now on the relief rolls to work and, incidentally, to assist materially in our already unmistakable march toward recovery. I shall not confuse my discussion by a multitude of figures. So many figures are quoted to prove so many things. Sometimes it depends upon what paper you read and what broadcast you hear. Therefore, let us keep our minds on two or three simple, essential facts in connection with this problem of unemployment. It is true that while business and industry are definitely better our relief rolls are still too large. However, for the first time in five years the relief rolls have declined instead of increased during the winter months. They are still declining. The simple fact is that many million more people have private work today than two years ago today or one year ago today, and every day that passes offers more chances to work for those who want to work. In spite of the fact that unemployment remains a serious problem here as in every other nation, we have come to recognize the possibility and the necessity of certain helpful remedial measures. These measures are of two kinds. The first is to make provisions intended to relieve, to minimize, and to prevent future unemployment; the second is to establish the practical means to help those who are unemployed in this present emergency. Our social security legislation is an attempt to answer the first of these questions. Our work relief program the second. The program for social security now pending before the Congress is a necessary part of the future unemployment policy of the government. While our present and projected expenditures for work relief are wholly within the reasonable limits of our national credit resources, it is obvious that we cannot continue to create governmental deficits for that purpose year after year. We must begin now to make provision for the future. That is why our social security program is an important part of the complete picture. It proposes, by means of old age pensions, to help those who have reached the age of retirement to give up their jobs and thus give to the younger generation greater opportunities for work and to give to all a feeling of security as they look toward old age.

The unemployment insurance part of the legislation will not only help to guard the individual in future periods of lay-off against dependence upon relief, but it will, by sustaining purchasing power, cushion the shock of economic distress. Another helpful feature of unemployment insurance is the incentive it will give to employers to plan more carefully in order that unemployment may be prevented by the stabilizing of employment itself.

Provisions for social security, however, are protections for the future. Our responsibility for the immediate necessities of the unemployed has been met by the Congress through the most comprehensive work plan in the history of the Nation. Our problem is to put to work three and one-half million employable persons now on the relief rolls. It is a problem quite as much for private industry as for the government.

We are losing no time getting the government's vast work relief program underway, and we have every reason to believe that it should be in full swing by autumn. In directing it, I shall recognize six fundamental principles:

(1) The projects should be useful.

(2) Projects shall be of a nature that a considerable proportion of the money spent will go into wages for labor.

(3) Projects which promise ultimate return to the Federal Treasury of a considerable proportion of the costs will be sought.

(4) Funds allotted for each project should be actually and promptly spent and not held over until later years.

(5) In all cases projects must be of a character to give employment to those on the relief rolls.

(6) Projects will be allocated to localities or relief areas in relation to the number of workers on relief rolls in those areas.

... For many months preparations have been under way. The allotment of funds for desirable projects has already begun. The key men for the major responsibilities of this great task already have been selected. I well realize that the country is expecting before this year is out to see the "dirt fly," as they say, in carrying on the work, and I assure my fellow citizens that no energy will be spared in using these funds effectively to make a major attack upon the problem of unemployment.

Our responsibility is to all of the people in this country. This is a great national crusade to destroy enforced idleness which is an enemy of the human spirit generated by this depression. Our attack upon these enemies must be without stint and without discrimination. No sectorial, no political distinctions can be permitted. It must, however, be recognized that when an enterprise of this character is extended over more than three thousand counties throughout the Nation, there may be occasional instances of inefficiency, bad management, or misuse of funds. When cases of this kind occur, there will be those, of course, who will try to tell you that the exceptional failure is characteristic of the entire endeavor. It should be remembered that in every big job there are some imperfections. There are chiselers in every walk of life; there are those in every industry who are guilty of unfair practices, every profession has its black sheep, but long experience in government has taught me that the exceptional instances of wrong-doing in government are probably less numerous than in almost every other line of endeavor. The most effective means of preventing such evils in this work relief program will be the eternal vigilance of the American people themselves. I call upon my fellow citizens everywhere to cooperate with me in making this the most efficient and the cleanest example of public enterprise the world has ever seen. It is time to provide a smashing answer for those cynical men who say that a democracy cannot be honest and efficient. If you will help, this can be done. I, therefore, hope you will watch the work in every corner of this Nation. Feel free to criticize. Tell me of instances where work can be done better, or where improper practices prevail. Neither you nor I want criticism conceived in a purely fault-finding or partisan spirit, but I am jealous of the right of every citizen to call to the attention of his or her government examples of how the public money can be more effectively spent for the benefit of the American people.

I now come, my friends, to a part of the remaining business before the Congress. It has under consideration many measures which provide for the rounding out of the program of economic and social reconstruction with which we have been concerned for two years. I can mention only a few of them tonight, but I do not want my mention of specific measures to be interpreted as lack of interest in or disapproval of many other important proposals that are pending. The National Industrial Recovery Act expires on the sixteenth of June. After careful consideration, I have asked the Congress to extend the life of this useful agency of government. As we have proceeded with the administration of this Act, we have found from time to time more and more useful ways of promoting its purposes. No reasonable person wants to abandon our present gains—we must continue to protect children, to enforce minimum wages, to prevent excessive hours, to safeguard, define and enforce collective bargaining, and, while retaining fair competition, to eliminate, so far as humanly possible, the kinds of unfair practices by selfish minorities which unfortunately did more than anything else to bring about the recent collapse of industries. There is likewise pending before the Congress legislation to provide for the elimination of unnecessary holding companies in the public utility field. . . .

Not only business recovery, but the general economic recovery of the Nation will be greatly stimulated by the enactment of legislation designed to improve the status of our transportation agencies. There is need for legislation providing for the regulation of interstate transportation by buses and trucks, to regulate transportation by water, new provisions for strengthening our Merchant Marine and air transport, measures for the strengthening of the Interstate Commerce Commission to enable it to carry out a rounded conception of the national transportation system in which the benefits of private ownership are retained, while the public stake in these important services is protected by the public's government.

Finally, the reestablishment of public confidence in the banks of the Nation is one of the most hopeful results of our efforts as a Nation to reestablish public confidence in private banking. We all know that private banking actually exists by virtue of the permission of and regulation by the people as a whole, speaking through their government. Wise public policy, however, requires not only that banking be safe but that its resources be most fully utilized, in the economic life of the country. To this end it was decided more than twenty years ago that the government should assume the responsibility of providing a means by which the credit of the Nation might be controlled, not by a few private banking institutions, but by a body with public prestige and authority. The answer to this demand was the Federal Reserve System. Twenty years of experience with this system have justified the efforts made to create it, but these twenty years have shown by experience definite possibilities for improvement. Certain proposals made to amend the Federal Reserve Act deserve prompt and favorable action by the Congress. They are a minimum of wise readjustment of our Federal Reserve system in the light of past experience and present needs.

These measures I have mentioned are, in large part, the program which under my constitutional duty I have recommended to the Congress. They are essential factors in a rounded program for national recovery. They contemplate the enrichment of our national life by a sound and rational ordering of its various elements and wise provisions for the protection of the weak against the strong. Never since my inauguration in March, 1933, have I felt so unmistakably the atmosphere of recovery. But it is more than the recovery of the material basis of our individual lives. It is the recovery of confidence in our democratic processes and institutions. We have survived all of the arduous burdens and the threatening dangers of a great economic calamity. We have in the darkest moments of our national trials retained our faith in our own ability to master our destiny. Fear is vanishing and confidence is growing on every side, renewed faith in the vast possibilities of human beings to improve their material and spiritual status through the instrumentality of the democratic form of government. That faith is receiving its just reward. For that we can be thankful to the God who watches over America.

Consider the source and the audience

- Roosevelt gave this speech to the American public over the radio. He was the first president to regularly sidestep the critical voice of the media to speak directly with his constituency en masse. Why did FDR choose to "go public"?

Lay out the argument, the values, and the assumptions

- What does FDR see as the basic purpose of government in a time of crisis? How does this differ from the view of government as basically an administrative apparatus?
- What does FDR see as the fundamental difference between his Social Security proposals and the work relief program?

- Even though FDR's audience wants him to fix its broken system, the solutions he proposes are unorthodox and even threatening to many Americans. How does he try to diffuse the public's fear?

Uncover the evidence

- To make the point that the public should support his policies, FDR needs to argue that what he has done so far has been effective, but that more needs to be done. What evidence does he offer to support this claim? Is it enough?

Evaluate the conclusion

- Is FDR right in saying that it is government's job to restore economic security, the enrichment of national life, confidence in democracy, and faith in human beings?

Sort out the political implications

- Although obvious exceptions exist, some analysts have drawn parallels between the problems facing Roosevelt and Obama when they entered office. Based on your reading of this speech, what similarities existed? What issues and obstacles did Roosevelt face that Obama did not? Did Obama face any challenges that Roosevelt did not encounter?
- It is now close to eighty years since FDR's New Deal changed our expectations of government and altered the way we perceive the office of the presidency. What would life today be like if we still believed that government should have a narrowly prescribed role and that the president's job is just to be chief among the bureaucrats running the administrative apparatus of government?

17

Foreign Policy

It is clear from Chapter 16 that Americans are split over the role of the national government on domestic issues. Liberals generally want more government involvement, conservatives less. Americans are often just as divided over foreign policy. In fact, some of the most heated political debates deal with issues of foreign policy. In what world affairs should we involve ourselves? Who are our allies? When do we use diplomacy as a tool, and when do international affairs require the use of force?

How do the parties divide on foreign policy issues? Keeping in mind that there are always exceptions, we can say that liberals are more likely to support aid to other countries and efforts to build democratic regimes abroad. Liberals are more willing to support the United Nations (UN) and to engage in multilateral foreign policy—building support among several nations. In matters of war they tend to be doves; that is, they hesitate to use force.

Conservatives, on the other hand, are generally nationalistic. They are more likely to be hawks (they tend to support military action) and are skeptical of the UN. As a consequence, they are more likely to endorse unilateral action, in which the United States goes it alone without the support of our allies or international organizations. They question aid to foreign governments or for building up regimes because of the cost, and they believe that money is better spent on programs at home—or not spent at all.

The United States is the only remaining superpower; no other country in the world has as complex a foreign policy or plays as large a global role. Yet that hasn't always been the case. Not until our belated, reluctant involvement in World War II did the United States emerge as a major player on the world stage.

After World War II the fascist governments of Germany and Italy were defeated, but a new enemy emerged—the totalitarian and communist Soviet Union. The development of hydrogen and nuclear weapons changed diplomacy as well, adding a weapon of mass destruction that the world had never seen before.

In the 1960s and 1970s, controversy surrounding U.S. involvement in Vietnam forced many observers to question the goals of American foreign policy. During the 1980s the arms race heated up as President Ronald Reagan convinced Congress to put millions of dollars into military buildup and the development of missile defense technology. The collapse of the Soviet Union in the late 1980s brought the Cold War to an end but raised a number of new questions regarding U.S. foreign policy. The United States was now the world's only superpower, but that did not mean it was without enemies.

As a result of the terrorist attacks of September 11, 2001, foreign policy issues have emerged once again at the top of a president's issue agenda. The Soviet Union is no longer the enemy (although relations between the two countries are strained)—now it is a group of rogue nations and terrorist organizations, such as al Qaeda, that many people believe present the biggest threat to the United States. The enemy may have changed, but the questions posed earlier have not. In fact, they remain as important and controversial as ever.

In this chapter we tackle some of those foreign policy questions. We begin with an article written by George Packer critical of the foreign policy of President Barack Obama during his first term. Then we examine an article from the conservative *New American*, in which Steve Bonta argues that the events of September 11 have forced us to focus on a new threat—terrorism—and have made us forget about what he still considers the real threat to the country, a nuclear attack. Next, David Petraeus and Michael O'Hanlon encourage Congress not to cut foreign aid. Finally, for this chapter's classic piece, we turn to President Reagan's address to the National Association of Evangelicals, in which he warns that we need to maintain national strength and defense capabilities against "evil empires" like the former Soviet Union.

● ●

17.1 Long Engagements
George Packer, *New Yorker*

Why We Chose This Piece

When Barack Obama tapped Hillary Clinton to be his secretary of state during his first term, a few eyebrows were raised. After all, Obama and Clinton had just emerged from a long, contentious battle to be the Democratic nominee in the 2008 presidential election. Nevertheless, Obama asked Clinton to serve, she said "yes," and they put the bitter rancor of the campaign behind them.

Yet, as George Packer, the author of this article in the New Yorker *argues, Clinton was never really brought into the president's inner circle on foreign policy issues. We include this article because it (1) provides interesting insight into how foreign policy decisions are made inside the current White House, (2) presents an interpretation of President Obama's worldview, and (3) takes a more personal look at the relationship between Obama and Clinton.*

Selection published: February 11, 2013

After four exhausting years, Hillary Clinton leaves the State Department with an impressive record of air miles logged, town-hall meetings held, important but neglected issues highlighted, international crises defused, gaffes avoided, citizens of the United States and the world wowed, and White House policies capably carried out. When Clinton and President Obama recently sat down for an interview on "60 Minutes," they all but held hands, swearing deathless affection and respect, and they seemed to mean it. But Clinton was denied the chance to be a truly great Secretary of State—another George C. Marshall or Dean Acheson—by both history and the President she served.

Last year, Denis McDonough, a top White House adviser, described Clinton's role as "the principal implementer" of Obama's foreign policy. On a few occasions, her advice helped to tip the scales—the 2009 surge in Afghanistan, which she strongly supported, was one—but she and her department were never trusted with the policy blueprints. From Iran and Israel to nonproliferation and human rights, the President has kept policymaking inside the White House, tightly held by a small circle of political advisers.

This shouldn't matter, except maybe to Washington insiders, as long as the policies were the right ones. By the standard of the Hippocratic oath, they have been. Judging from last fall's campaign, the biggest preventable foreign-policy disaster of Barack Obama's first term was the killing in Benghazi of the U.S. Ambassador to Libya and three other Americans. Benghazi was a tragedy for which the State Department bore much responsibility; but, after the Bush years, the rest of the Administration's record is no minor achievement. Obama and Clinton inherited two unwinnable wars, a toxic international atmosphere in which America was reviled where it wasn't ignored, and a badly diminished stock of national power.

The criticism that there is no encompassing "Obama doctrine" misses the point. Geopolitics today is too complex, messy, and various to be bent to America's will by an overarching doctrine like containment, or a massive initiative like the Marshall Plan, or a single breakthrough like Nixon's trip to China. A doctrine was what put the country in a deep hole; climbing out required restraint, flexibility, and opportunism. A first-term Secretary of State with one grand strategic vision wouldn't have matched the demands of the moment, which called for a fox, not a hedgehog. Clinton's true legacy might be the countless public events that she held from Lahore to Kinshasa, where thousands of ordinary people got to question the U.S. Secretary of State, and where the topic was often something like women's rights or access to clean water. These efforts were sometimes derided as soft, and marginal to real foreign policy, but Clinton—who is, after all, a politician—knew that she would have to be seen listening in order to help regain the world's respect. That and four years of carefully calibrated Presidential rhetoric and support for multilateralism have gone a long way to restoring America's legitimacy as the leading global actor.

If there is one idea that sums up Obama's approach to foreign policy, it's engagement. "We will extend a hand if you are willing to unclench your fist," he proclaimed in his first Inaugural, and in his second (which barely touched on foreign policy) he said, "We will show the courage to try and resolve our differences with other nations peacefully. Not because we are naïve about the dangers we face, but because engagement can more durably lift suspicion and fear." But, in his first term, Obama didn't live up to the promise of engagement. When the world proved recalcitrant, the President was too disengaged to do it himself, and he didn't give his Secretary of State the chance.

On Afghanistan, the White House pursued a military strategy for more than two years without enabling the Administration's diplomats to negotiate seriously with the Taliban or work out a regional framework for peace; then Obama announced a deadline for withdrawal, which removed the incentive for America's enemies in Afghanistan to compromise. On Iran, the State Department has played little role, while the President's two-track policy of talks and sanctions soon narrowed to one, bringing Iran no closer to abandoning its nuclear ambitions. On Israel and Palestine, there has been practically no diplomacy at all.

The standard debates in American foreign policy—realism vs. idealism, heavy footprint vs. light footprint—don't get to the heart of the problem with Obama's foreign policy. It's not that diplomatic engagement is the wrong approach; it's just that the President's first four years have given us the idea of diplomacy more than the thing itself. In a forthcoming book, "The Dispensable Nation: American Foreign Policy in Retreat," Vali Nasr, a former adviser under Hillary Clinton and the late Richard Holbrooke, argues that, from North Africa to Afghanistan and Pakistan, the White House has relied too much on the military and the C.I.A. (mainly in the form of drones) to guide policy: "These agencies' solutions were not, and could never be, a substitute for the type of patient, long-range, credible diplomacy that garners the respect of our allies and their support when we need it." In Nasr's view, a White House that feared being called soft and wanted to keep intractable foreign entanglements out of the news turned to Clinton only after things had fallen apart, as in Pakistan at the end of 2011, when she moved to repair a relationship that had degenerated into outright antagonism.

Obama and Clinton wanted to "pivot" away from the Middle East, toward the Pacific, but a bloody hand keeps reaching out to pull America back. Sixty thousand people have died in Syria's civil war, Egypt is on the brink of state collapse, and the region is moving toward Sunni-Shiite confrontation. These are not problems that can be addressed by drone strikes and fitful diplomacy. The President is wise to acknowledge America's inability to solve them by itself—"We are not going to be able to control every aspect of every transition and transformation," he said on "60 Minutes"—but a tragic sense of limitation is not a substitute for real, prolonged engagement, which always carries the risk of failure. Whether Obama believes that America can or should shape the outcome, the greater Middle East will remain an American problem, and he will need to give his next Secretary of State, John Kerry, the authority that he denied his last one, to put the country's prestige on the line by wading deep into the morass.

Consider the source and the audience

- The *New Yorker* is a magazine that often focuses on cultural life in New York City. What might that tell us about the kind of readership the magazine has? Why would its readers care about Packer's argument?
- Packer is a journalist who regularly writes on foreign policy issues, including a book on the Iraq war. How might that shape his views on foreign policy?

Lay out the argument, the values, and the assumptions

- Can you tell from this article what Packer's foreign policy values are? What role does diplomacy play?
- How did the White House use Clinton? Why does Packer believe this kept her from becoming a "truly great Secretary of State"?

Uncover the evidence

- Packer provides little in the way of evidence to support his claims. Instead, he is making a normative argument about how Obama's foreign policy should be. Is it possible for people who disagree with his normative claims to be persuaded? What kinds of evidence could he have presented that might have done so?

Evaluate the conclusion

- As noted, Packer believes the White House's use of Clinton limited her ability to become a secretary of state that history remembers. Does he believe that Obama misused Clinton or that she served an important purpose?
- Can we know what foreign policy outcomes would have been different had Obama relied more on the State Department and less on the military and CIA for advice? How might they have been different?
- How might the White House respond to Packer's criticisms?

Sort out the political implications

- What are the advantages and disadvantages of using Clinton the way Obama did? How might Obama's foreign policy strategy influence the way the rest of the world sees the United States?

● ●

17.2 The Case for Missile Defense

The Fact That America Faces Novel Terrorist Threats Such as Hijacked Planes and Anthrax Spores Does Not Negate the Need for an Effective, Comprehensive Missile Defense

Steve Bonta, *New American*

Why We Chose This Piece

September 11, 2001, brought a new fear to the American public: terrorist attacks on our homeland. Until that point, while terrorism at home may have concerned some,

---

Selection published: December 3, 2001

most people believed that the biggest threat to the United States would come from a foreign missile attack. In the days of the Cold War, the United States and its chief superpower rival, the Soviet Union, had contained the threat posed by each nation with a policy of mutually assured destruction (MAD), based on the idea that if each had the ability to destroy the other, each had an incentive not to guarantee its own destruction by launching the first attack. As part of the principle of MAD, the nations signed the Anti-Ballistic Missile (ABM) Treaty in 1972, promising not to build a missile defense system. Such a system, by protecting one side from nuclear attack, would render the policy of MAD ineffective, and the threat of nuclear war would no longer be contained.

The ABM Treaty did not end discussion of missile defense. In the 1980s Ronald Reagan pushed Congress to authorize billions of dollars to create a missile defense system, nicknamed Star Wars, designed to protect the country from a nuclear strike by the Soviet Union. Although the United States has worked on developing missile defense technology since the early 1980s, it has yet to build a system that works in test situations. Then, in 2001, George W. Bush announced his intention to withdraw the United States from the ABM Treaty, arguing that it prevented the United States from defending itself against possible terrorist or "rogue-state" missile attacks.

We no longer live in a world defined by two nuclear superpowers. The Cold War is over, the Soviet Union is gone, and its nuclear weapons are divided among its former republics, including Russia, now on more or less friendly terms with the United States. Today, many other nations—some friends to the United States, some foes— have nuclear weapons or are attempting to build them, and there is no guarantee that these nations can be "contained" in the same way the United States and the Soviet Union once were.

Since September 11, some Americans have been divided between those who believe we should concentrate our resources on preventing threats like the terrorist attacks on the World Trade Center and the Pentagon, and those, like the author of this piece, who think the reasons for pursuing missile defense are stronger than ever. Although this article was written shortly after 9/11, the issues it raises are still relevant today, as Congress regularly debates missile defense funding and some observers have questioned President Obama's commitment to missile defense systems. Moreover, concerns about nuclear proliferation in places like North Korea have made the debate all the more pertinent.

In an October 28th op-ed piece for the *New York Times*, ex-Soviet dictator Mikhail Gorbachev wrote that, in light of the shocking breaches of American security on September 11th, the United States might begin making a priority out of unilateral national defense. "It would be a cause of great concern," he fretted, "if major nuclear powers abandoned or neglected multilateral forums, or took steps that would endanger the entire structure of arms control treaties, many of which, such as the 1972 ABM Treaty, are of as much value today as they were during the decades of nuclear confrontation."

Gorbachev isn't a lone voice, either. In the aftermath of September 11th, with the Bush administration's intention to scrap the ABM Treaty attracting a lot of political support, a chorus of Establishment voices have been clamoring to keep the 1972 agreement and to nix any national missile defense. "Even in the wake of Sept. 11, Bush clings to the wasteful, improbable Son of *Star Wars*," complained the *Houston Chronicle* on October 23rd. On the same day, the *San Francisco Chronicle* warned, "[N]ow, more than ever, an anti-missile defense system mocks the actual dangers that threaten Americans—as well as the rest of the world. It won't defend against terrorist weapons that, so far, have included boxcutters, planes and anthrax spores. Nor will it protect us from plastic explosives, cyberterrorism, or chemical warfare."

Arguments like these are nothing new. For several decades, since the United States embarked on the suicidal policy of Mutually Assured Destruction (MAD) and underscored it with an ABM Treaty forbidding any substantive missile defense measures, foreign policy experts with more Ivy-League credentials than common sense have been promoting abstract goals like "containment," "stabilization," and "deterrence" rather than national defense per se. In the process, they have successfully convinced a large number of gullible Americans, including congressional leaders, that defense against a missile attack is technologically impossible, politically unwise, and strategically unnecessary—and they have kept the United States pitifully vulnerable to nuclear attack. Exploiting our supposed nuclear Achilles' heel, the fanatical adherents of appeasement and arms control have extracted dangerous concessions in national sovereignty—like the ABM and SALT treaties—that unilaterally limit our ability to defend ourselves.

Changing Climate

With recent terrorist attacks, though, the political climate has changed. Suddenly national defense is a pressing urgency, and momentum is growing to scrap the ABM Treaty and other treasonous agreements with the former Soviet Union. But anti-American globalists, still eager to keep America weakened and vulnerable, have begun a campaign of withering propaganda to prevent this from happening.

The most common argument for continuing to neglect missile defense is that September 11th has shown us that, in the words of the *New York Times*, "the most immediate threat to the nation comes from terrorists, not nations with intercontinental ballistic missiles." Therefore, the critics argue, we should focus our resources on going after the men with the box cutters and the anthrax spores, rather than spend billions developing a system to shoot down Russian missiles.

That is, we should be *selective* in which threats to defend against. This is tantamount to choosing between a burglar alarm and a fire alarm, on the specious premise that we can't defend against both break-ins and fire hazards.

More importantly, a "threat" by its very nature is virtual, not actual. While no modern-day power has yet attempted a full-scale military assault, nuclear or otherwise, against the United States mainland, no one could credibly argue that any terrorist cell, however ingenious or well-equipped, could wreak as much havoc and loss of life as a Russian or Chinese nuclear missile attack. The most effective defense anticipates what might happen, rather than reacting too late to damage already done.

But, reply the critics, no country would dare launch a direct nuclear attack against the United States. As the *Houston Chronicle* put it, "such governments, even at their edge-of-reality looniest, would think twice about such an act because . . . U.S. retaliation would bring annihilation." This argument assumes that the only suicidal enemies of the United States are "non-state actors" like the terrorists who blew up the World Trade Center and the USS *Cole*.

But governments, even those of open societies, frequently act irrationally and against their best interests. The United States itself has done so consistently, under the influence of subversives hostile to American freedoms. And the verdict of history suggests that tyrannical regimes are even less rational. It is now well-known, for example, that some of imperial Japan's military and political leaders warned of the consequences of attacking Pearl Harbor. Saddam Hussein was deluded into believing that the West would not defend Kuwaiti oil fields. During the Gulf War, he even launched a barrage of SCUD missiles at Israel, undeterred by Israel's nuclear capability. The People's Republic of China has gone on record threatening to nuke Los Angeles if the United States comes to the defense of Taiwan in the event of a Chinese invasion. And a hypothetical nuclear regime like North Korea, facing military defeat in a future Korean conflict, might launch a desperation nuclear assault as a last-minute gesture of vengeful defiance. It is dangerously naive to assume that states and their leadership will behave rationally, especially in wartime.

Technological Capabilities

The next line of argument usually leveled against missile defense is the supposed technological limitations. "There is no indication that such a scheme would work and every sign it would cost billions even to find out," opined the *Los Angeles Times*. Wrong on both counts. Not only is a credible missile defense well within our technological capabilities, there is little question that such a system—if deployed—would work very effectively. As Sam Cohen, the inventor of the neutron bomb, wrote in these pages in October 1998, nuclear-tipped missile interceptors would be an extremely effective and easily achievable missile-defense system:

> Real strategic defense requires nuclear interceptors to overcome the huge economic and technical disadvantages of the non-nuclear defense systems that inherently favor attackers. . . . Nuclear explosives of the kind developed for Safeguard [a short-lived ABM system deployed in the '70s] included the six-kiloton Sprint, which could effectively take out attacking missiles within a radius of tens of yards, and the megaton Spartan, which could reach out to a radius of several miles to destroy missiles. These or similar systems could be launched from the ground, sea, air, or space, and a genuine ABM program would utilize a combination of these launch options to provide in-depth defense.

Even leaving aside nuclear ABM defenses, conventional anti-missile missiles like the Patriot have proven effective—especially against obsolescent models like the Iraqi SCUDs, the type of missile most likely to be used by a third-world rogue regime.

For those who insist on some kind of defense against enemy missiles, Establishment liberals have a pat concession: Limited ABM defenses are okay, as long as they don't pose a serious threat to a major nuclear-armed adversary like the Russians. This is, in fact, the position of Bush administration "conservatives" who insist, even as they loudly promote a limited missile defense against rogue regimes, that America will not consider building any significant countermeasures against an all-out nuclear assault by a superpower adversary like Russia or China. The Bush administration's tough-talking Donald Rumsfeld implied as much by announcing on October 25th that the Pentagon had postponed antimissile tracking tests to avoid the appearance of violating the ABM Treaty or provoking the Russians.

But there is evidence that, despite the propaganda smokescreen, many Americans are awakening to America's dangerous vulnerability not only to terrorism but to old-fashioned military assaults. A new poll on internationalist views conducted by the Pew Research Center in conjunction with the Council on Foreign Relations found "growing public support for a missile defense system" since September 11th. The study admitted uneasily that "nearly two thirds [surveyed] favor the development of a missile shield and a growing number say we need such a system now."

Americans must not be deluded by the false alternatives offered by the Establishment on missile defense. They must insist that the excuses and prevarications stop, and that our elected leaders take all steps to defend our country, as completely as possible, from nuclear attack. No government that has frittered away billions of dollars on risky Mars missions, many of which have failed abysmally, can cite lack of technology, risk of failure, or budget shortfalls as excuses for not developing missile defense. And since September 11th, no one with a shred of human decency can justify any but a comprehensive approach to national defense. National defense, after all, is the first responsibility of any moral government. It's time to stop holding Americans hostage by playing games with America's enemies.

Consider the source and the audience

- The *New American* is a conservative magazine with the avowed purpose of protecting our freedom. What (or whom) does Bonta see as the threat to Americans' freedom? Would a liberal publication define freedom in the same way?

Lay out the argument, the values, and the assumptions

- What is Bonta's view of national power and sovereignty? What is the primary purpose of government, in his view? Bonta is worried about our leaders playing games with America's enemies. When it comes to protecting America, would he argue that we have any friends?
- According to Bonta, what was wrong with MAD, and why did it work against national defense? What arguments are frequently used by opponents of missile defense, and why, according to Bonta, are they wrong?

Uncover the evidence

- Bonta cites many newspaper editorials and claims that they lack evidence to back up their arguments. Does he offer evidence to back up his own? What evidence does Bonta provide to counter the objection that the technology does not yet exist to create a successful missile defense system?

Evaluate the conclusion

- Does Bonta successfully make the case that we should expand our missile defense spending? Why or why not?
- Does Bonta successfully refute the claims of opponents of a missile defense system? Does he deal with any of the positive aspects of treaty making? Would he agree that any exist?

Sort out the political implications

- If the U.S. government followed Bonta's suggestion, what trade-offs, if any, would it have to make? Can we deal effectively with all threats facing the United States at the same time?
- How might the rest of the world view our increased spending on missile defense? Should the United States be concerned with the reaction of other countries?

17.3 Fund—Don't Cut—U.S. Soft Power

David Petraeus and Michael O'Hanlon, *Politico*

Why We Chose This Piece

U.S. presidents spend much of their time trying to persuade and influence leaders of other countries to do what they want them to do. One way to do so is through so-called "hard power," which is threatening military action or economic sanctions. These are exceptional uses of power, and ones that presidents normally try to avoid. They prefer carrots rather than sticks. Countries have means at their disposal beyond aggressive threats, including good diplomatic relations, foreign aid, and investment. These assets are types of "soft power," which is to say a country's means of influencing other countries without relying on threats of military action. Reading 17.2 deals more directly with hard power—or at least defending the United States from the use of hard power by others. In this op-ed, David Petraeus, former commander of U.S. forces in Afghanistan and Iraq, and Michael O'Hanlon, senior fellow at the Brookings Institution, argue that the United States should not forget soft power. Specifically, they do not want Congress to cut foreign aid to other countries. Why might the use of soft power be controversial?

Selection published: April 30, 2013

The president's budget proposal is now on the streets of Washington, D.C. Currently, it would protect funding for the State Department and the Agency for International Development and related activities from further cuts. The combined annual budget for development aid, security aid and diplomacy has averaged close to $60 billion over the past half decade. That is now slated to decline to about $50 billion, partly due to reduced war-related costs. But this amount could come under intense scrutiny. Moreover, if there is no grand bargain between the president and the Congress, sequestration could force reductions of a further 10 percent.

Such an outcome would be bad for our nation's security. As each of us has testified on Capitol Hill in past years, America's ability to protect itself and advance its global interests often depends as much on its "softer" power as it does on our nation's armed forces. For example, though Latin American countries were themselves primarily responsible for their progress, the headway many of them made in stabilizing their countries in recent years has been a big plus for American security, too—and American aid had a role in that progress. That is part of why we have supported a budget deal that would repeal sequestration and achieve most further deficit reduction through savings in entitlement spending with similar increases in revenue generation. Implicit in our approach was the thinking that lawmakers should avoid the temptation to gut foreign aid just because it generally lacks a strong constituency in the United States.

America's spending on development and diplomacy and security aid—the so-called 150 account—has strengthened under Presidents George W. Bush and Barack Obama. That has been a positive and long overdue development. Funds for diplomacy and development were starved in much of the 1990s. Some of the reductions in that earlier period were warranted, admittedly, as aid then was not always as productive as it might have been.

Today, we are arguably doing a good deal better. Various forms of development assistance and aid have, in fact, produced impressive results on a host of fronts in recent years. The President's Emergency Plan for AIDS Relief, a major initiative of Presidents Bush and Bill Clinton and now President Obama, has played a significant role in helping to turn the tide against the HIV/AIDS epidemic—even if more work remains to be done. Development assistance has also helped more than 600 million people move out of extreme poverty, achieving one of the United Nations Millennium Development Goals several years before the 2015 target date.

Moreover, as John Podesta has recently written, in this century alone, aid has helped reduce the global childhood mortality rate by one-third—impressive, even if only halfway toward the U.N. goal for 2015. The maternal mortality rate has been reduced by almost half, as well. And progress has been seen in other sectors—such as agriculture, energy and other realms, including many in the combat zones where each of us spent considerable time in the past decade.

America deserves considerable credit for much of this progress, as the U.S. is the world's largest aid contributor, at roughly $30 billion in 2012. The United Kingdom, Germany, France and Japan round out the rest of the top five donors, each providing from $10 billion to $15 billion a year. But relative to our economy's size, America does not do more than its fair share; it provides just 0.19 percent of gross domestic product in development aid, similar to Japan's level but less than half that of the three big European donors listed above, and less than a third the U.N. goal of 0.7 percent of GDP. Private donations improve our net national position somewhat, but only to an extent. The State Department budget is still less than 5 percent of the military's—and the number of Foreign Service officers worldwide is less than half the number of soldiers in a single Army division.

Given our military contributions to international stability and the global economic growth that results from that stability in various areas, American foreign aid doesn't need to grow substantially. But it should not be cut further. Consider some of the ideas we might want to consider in the years ahead. These should not be unconditional offers of help but would require the right kind of cooperation from key nations abroad whose future stability is central to our own security:

- A possible deal to help Egypt revive economic growth and service its debt after a two-year economic downturn following its Arab Spring; this would be contingent on President Mohamed Morsi respecting the Egyptian constitution and helping us with Middle East peace;
- A possible proposal to help Pakistan reinvigorate its energy sector, which currently holds back the country's growth and compromises its quality of life; this would be contingent on Pakistan contributing more to security in the region and to pursuing reforms that reduce disincentives for significant private initiatives in the energy arena;
- A major push with other donors to help countries like the Democratic Republic of the Congo reform and strengthen their security forces;
- Aid for transitional governments in Libya, Yemen and Mali, and perhaps someday Syria, to get on their feet so they can stabilize, develop security forces, police their own territories and prevent terrorists from establishing sanctuaries;
- Ongoing help in future years for Afghanistan's government provided that it takes steps toward better governance and a sound election in 2014.

This agenda need not break the bank; even taken together, development aid and assistance and these initiatives would not remotely add up to another Marshall Plan. But this discussion suggests that our security will be improved by sustaining foreign aid in the years ahead rather than by making further cuts.

Consider the source and the audience

- *Politico* is a newspaper that is regularly read by Washington insiders, including members of Congress and their staffs. Who are the readers that Petraeus and O'Hanlon are trying to convince here?
- Does the fact that Petraeus was the former commander of U.S. forces in Afghanistan and Iraq—two wars that would generally be associated with hard power—make people more likely to listen to his views on soft power?

Lay out the argument, the values, and the assumptions

- According to the authors, what have been the positives associated with soft power?

Uncover the evidence

- The authors provide several examples of what they see as the benefits of soft power. Are these examples persuasive? How do we know that the results can be attributed to aid and not something else?

Evaluate the conclusion

- The authors admit that aid in the 1990s "was not always as productive as it might have been." They also provide several areas where they would like the United States to commit aid. How do we know that it will be productive today?

Sort out the political implications

- What unintended consequences might result from providing aid to foreign governments?

17.4 Speech Before the National Association of Evangelicals

Ronald Reagan

Why We Chose This Piece

Along with tax cuts, less intrusive government, and increased defense spending, Ronald Reagan made winning the Cold War a central part of his presidency. He believed that America needed to defend itself against a communist threat, promote free governments, and limit Soviet power and aggression. In this speech before the National Association of Evangelicals, Reagan made an impassioned plea to keep the "evil empire" in check and promote democracy throughout the world. Specifically, he argued that it would be foolhardy for the West to freeze its development of nuclear forces because it is only by being strong and armed that the United States can bring about peace.

Although the United States' adversaries have changed, the issues raised in Reagan's speech remain pertinent today. Indeed, Reagan's views presented in this speech guided much of George W. Bush's philosophy on foreign policy. Moreover, as Reading 17.1 made clear, the issues raised here are issues that President Obama must grapple with as well.

(The beginning of this speech focused on President Reagan's views on the place of faith in public life. Toward the end of his talk he turned his attention to the role of faith in foreign affairs. We pick up the speech at that point.)

Selection delivered: March 8, 1983

And this brings me to my final point today. During my first press conference as president, in answer to a direct question, I pointed out that, as good Marxist-Leninists, the Soviet leaders have openly and publicly declared that the only morality they recognize is that which will further their cause, which is world revolution. I think I should point out I was only quoting Lenin, their guiding spirit, who said in 1920 that they repudiate all morality that proceeds from supernatural ideas—that's their name for religion—or ideas that are outside class conceptions. Morality is entirely subordinate to the interests of class war. And everything is moral that is necessary for the annihilation of the old, exploiting social order and for uniting the proletariat.

Well, I think the refusal of many influential people to accept this elementary fact of Soviet doctrine illustrates a historical reluctance to see totalitarian powers for what they are. We saw this phenomenon in the 1930s. We see it too often today.

This doesn't mean we should isolate ourselves and refuse to seek an understanding with them. I intend to do everything I can to persuade them of our peaceful intent, to remind them that it was the West that refused to use its nuclear monopoly in the forties and fifties for territorial gain and which now proposes a 50-percent cut in strategic ballistic missiles and the elimination of an entire class of land-based, intermediate-range nuclear missiles.

At the same time, however, they must be made to understand we will never compromise our principles and standards. We will never give away our freedom. We will never abandon our belief in God. And we will never stop searching for a genuine peace. But we can assure none of these things America stands for through the so-called nuclear freeze solutions proposed by some.

The truth is that a freeze now would be a very dangerous fraud, for that is merely the illusion of peace. The reality is that we must find peace through strength.

I would agree to a freeze if only we could freeze the Soviets' global desires. A freeze at current levels of weapons would remove any incentive for the Soviets to negotiate seriously in Geneva and virtually end our chances to achieve the major arms reductions which we have proposed. Instead, they would achieve their objectives through the freeze.

A freeze would reward the Soviet Union for its enormous and unparalleled military build-up. It would prevent the essential and long overdue modernization of United States and allied defenses and would leave our aging forces increasingly vulnerable. And an honest freeze would require extensive prior negotiations on the systems and numbers to be limited and on the measures to ensure effective verification and compliance. And the kind of a freeze that has been suggested would be virtually impossible to verify. Such a major effort would divert us completely from our current negotiations on achieving substantial reductions.

A number of years ago, I heard a young father, a very prominent young man in the entertainment world, addressing a tremendous gathering in California. It was during the time of the cold war, and communism and our own way of life were very much on people's minds. And he was speaking to that subject. And suddenly, though, I heard him saying, "I love my little girls more than anything." And I said to myself, "Oh, no, don't. You can't—don't say that." But I had underestimated him. He went on: "I would rather see my little girls die now, still believing in God, than have them grow up under communism and one day die no longer believing in God."

There were thousands of young people in that audience. They came to their feet with shouts of joy. They had instantly recognized the profound truth in what he had said, with regard to the physical and the soul and what was truly important.

Yes, let us pray for the salvation of all of those who live in that totalitarian darkness—pray they will discover the joy of knowing God. But until they do, let us be aware that while they preach the supremacy of the state, declare its omnipotence over individual man, and predict its eventual domination of all peoples on the earth, they are the focus of evil in the modern world.

It was C. S. Lewis who, in his unforgettable *Screwtape Letters*, wrote: "The greatest evil is not done now in those sordid 'dens of rime' that Dickens loved to paint. It is not even done in concentration camps and labor camps. In those we see its final result. But it is conceived and ordered (moved, seconded, carried and minuted) in clean, carpeted, warmed, and well-lighted offices, by quiet men with white collars and cut fingernails and smooth-shaven cheeks who do not need to raise their voice."

Well, because these "quiet men" do not "raise their voices," because they sometimes speak in soothing tones of brotherhood and peace, because, like other dictators before them, they're always making "their final territorial demand," some would have us accept them at their word and accommodate ourselves to their aggressive impulses. But if history teaches anything, it teaches that simpleminded appeasement or wishful thinking about our adversaries is folly. It means the betrayal of our past, the squandering of our freedom.

So, I urge you to speak out against those who would place the United States in a position of military and moral inferiority. You know, I've always believed that old Screwtape reserved his best efforts for those of you in the church. So, in your discussions of the nuclear freeze proposals, I urge you to beware the temptation of pride—the temptation of blithely declaring yourselves above it all and label both sides equally at fault, to ignore the facts of history and the aggressive impulses of an evil empire, to simply call the arms race a giant misunderstanding and thereby remove yourself from the struggle between right and wrong and good and evil.

I ask you to resist the attempts of those who would have you withhold your support for our efforts, this administration's efforts, to keep America strong and free, while we negotiate real and verifiable reductions in the world's nuclear arsenals and one day, with God's help, their total elimination.

While America's military strength is important, let me add here that I've always maintained that the struggle now going on for the world will never be decided by bombs or rockets, by armies or military might. The real crisis we face today is a spiritual one; at root, it is a test of moral will and faith.

Whittaker Chambers, the man whose own religious conversion made him a witness to one of the terrible traumas of our time, the Hiss-Chambers case, wrote that the crisis of the Western world exists to the degree in which the West is indifferent to God, the degree to which it collaborates in communism's attempt to make man stand alone without God. And then he said, for Marxism-Leninism is actually the second-oldest faith, first proclaimed in the Garden of Eden with the words of temptation, "Ye shall be as gods."

The Western world can answer this challenge, he wrote, "but only provided that its faith in God and the freedom He enjoins is as great as communism's faith in Man."

I believe we shall rise to the challenge. I believe that communism is another sad, bizarre chapter in human history whose last pages even now are being written. I believe this because the source of our strength in the quest for human freedom is not material, but spiritual. And because it knows no limitation, it must terrify and ultimately triumph over those who would enslave their fellow man. For in the words of Isaiah: "He giveth power to the faint; and to them that have no might He increased strength. . . . But they that wait upon the Lord shall renew their strength; they shall mount up with wings as eagles; they shall run, and not be weary. . . ."

Yes, change your world. One of our Founding Fathers, Thomas Paine, said, "We have it within our power to begin the world over again." We can do it, doing together what no one church could do by itself.

God bless you, and thank you very much.

Consider the source and the audience

- President Reagan gave this speech to the National Association of Evangelicals. Would he have emphasized the same factors in a speech to a political group?

Lay out the argument, the values, and the assumptions

- What, for Reagan, is the relationship among freedom, democracy, peace, and a belief in God? What defines the differences between "good" and "evil"? Why is the Soviet Union the "evil empire"?
- What does Reagan think is the route to peace? What is the role of arms and national strength? What is the role of faith in God?
- Who is Reagan arguing against here? What do his opponents want the United States to do? How do they think our problems with the Soviets can best be handled?

Uncover the evidence

- Reagan claims that the best way to bring about world peace is by increasing America's strength and refusing to take part in a nuclear freeze. What evidence or logic does he offer for this claim?
- Does Reagan offer any evidence for the link between freedom and faith in God? Is it a link that can be verified? What kind of evidence would support it?

Evaluate the conclusion

- Can you accept Reagan's conclusions about the relationship of belief in God with freedom and democracy if you don't share his faith? What conclusions can nonbelievers take from his speech?

Sort out the political implications

- President George W. Bush also used the word *evil* to refer to the United States' enemies. Did it have the same meaning for him as it did for Reagan?
- What are the advantages of framing one's political struggles in terms of good and evil? What are the disadvantages?

Credits

Chapter 1: Introduction to American Politics

Chapter 2: Political Culture and Ideology

Chapter 3: Immigration and American Demographics

Chapter 4: Federalism and the Constitution

Chapter 5: Civil Liberties

Chapter 6: Civil Rights

Chapter 7: Congress

Chapter 8: The Presidency

Chapter 9: Bureaucracy

Chapter 10: The Courts

180: Reprinted by permission of the author. **187**: Copyright © 2009 Condé Nast. From *The New Yorker*. All rights reserved. Articles by Jeffrey Toobin. Reprinted by Permission. **201**: From *The New York Times*, © 2013 *The New York Times*. All rights reserved. Used by permission and protected by the Copyright Laws of the United States. The printing, copying, redistribution, or retransmission of this Content without express written permission is prohibited. **204**: From The New York Times, © 2013 The New York Times. All rights reserved. Used by permission and protected by the Copyright Laws of the United States. The printing, copying, redistribution, or retransmission of this Content without express written permission is prohibited.

Chapter 11: Public Opinion

218: "Party on Dudes!" by Matthew Robinson © The American Spectator, March/April 2002. **226**: From Chronicle of Higher Education, November 5, 2012 © 2012 Chronicle of Higher Education. All rights reserved. Used by permission and protected by the Copyright Laws of the United States. The printing, copying,redistribution, or retransmission of this Content without express written permission is prohibited. **231**: Copyright 2009 *The Hill*. **233**: Reprinted with permission from *The Washington Monthly*. Copyright by Washington Monthly Publishing, LLC, www.washingtonmonthly.com. **241**: Reprinted with the permission of Simon & Schuster, Inc., from *The Pulse of Democracy* by George Horace Gallup and Saul Forbes Raw. Copyright © 1940 by George H. Gallup and Saul F. Race. Copyright renewed © 1986 by George H. Gallup. All rights reserved.

Chapter 12: Political Parties

252: From reuters.com © 2013 reuters.com. All rights reserved. Used by permission and protected by the Copyright Laws of the United States. The printing, copying, redistribution, or retransmission of this Content without express written permission is prohibited. **256**: From CNN.com, © 2012 Cable News Network, Inc.. All rights reserved. Used by permission and protected by the Copyright Laws of the United States. The printing, copying,redistribution, or retransmission of this Content without express written permission is prohibited. **259**: From *Politico*, November 11, 2012 © 2013 *Politico*. All rights reserved. Used by permission and protected by the Copyright Laws of the United States. The printing, copying, redistribution, or retransmission of the Material without express written consent is prohibited. **262**: © 2006 by Kurt Anderson. Reprinted by permission of William Morris Endeavor Entertainment, LLC on behalf of the Author.

Chapter 13: Interest Groups

276: From *The New York Times*, © 2013 *The New York Times*. All rights reserved. Used by permission and protected by the Copyright Laws of the United States. The printing, copying, redistribution, or retransmission of this Content without express written permission is prohibited. **282**: From *The Huffington Post*, © 2011 *The Huffington Post*. All rights reserved. Used by permission and protected by the Copyright Laws of the United States. The printing, copying, redistribution, or retransmission of this Content without express written permission is prohibited. **295**: From *Politico*, September 25, 2012 © 2012 *Politico*. All rights reserved. Used by permission and protected by the Copyright Laws of the United States. The printing, copying, redistribution, or retransmission of the Material without express written consent is prohibited.

Chapter 14: Voting and Elections

306: From *Slate* © 2012 The Slate Group. All rights reserved. Used by permission and protected by the Copyright Laws of the United States. The printing, copying, redistribution, or retransmission of this Content without express written permission is prohibited. **310**: From reuters.com © 2013 reuters.com. All rights reserved. Used by permission and protected by the Copyright Laws of the United States. The printing, copying, redistribution, or retransmission of this Content without express written permission is prohibited. **314**: Reprinted with permission of the Sunlight Foundation.

Chapter 15: The Media

332: Reprinted by permission of the author. **329**: © 2012 Buzzfeed, Inc. All rights reserved. Used with permission. All rights reserved. Used by permission and protected by the Copyright Laws of the United States. The printing, copying, redistribution, or retransmission of the Material without express written consent is prohibited. **332**: From *Politico*, February 19, 2013 © 2013 *Politico*. All rights reserved. Used by permission and protected by the Copyright Laws of the United States. The printing, copying, redistribution, or retransmission of the Material without express written consent is prohibited. **335**: From *Politico*, February 18, 2013 © 2013 *Politico*. All rights reserved. Used by permission and protected by the Copyright Laws of the United States. The printing, copying, redistribution, or retransmission of the Material without express written consent is prohibited. **340**: Reprinted with permission of Ryan Holmes and HootSuite. **342**: *SAN FRANCISCO CHRONICLE* (1865-) by William Randolph Hearst. Copyright 1935 by *SAN FRANCISCO CHRONICLE*. Reproduced with permission of *SAN FRANCISCO CHRONICLE* in the format Other book via Copyright Clearance Center.

Chapter 16: Domestic Policy

Chapter 17: Foreign Policy

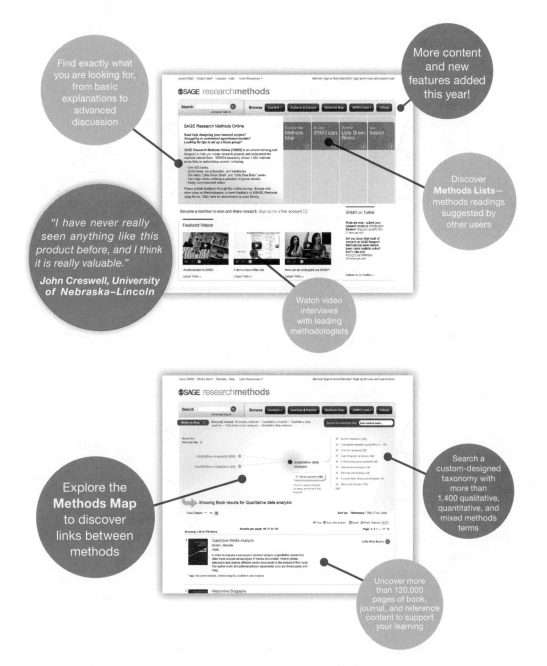

$SAGE researchmethods

The essential online tool for researchers from the world's leading methods publisher

Find exactly what you are looking for, from basic explanations to advanced discussion

More content and new features added this year!

Discover **Methods Lists**—methods readings suggested by other users

"I have never really seen anything like this product before, and I think it is really valuable."

John Creswell, University of Nebraska–Lincoln

Watch video interviews with leading methodologists

Explore the **Methods Map** to discover links between methods

Search a custom-designed taxonomy with more than 1,400 qualitative, quantitative, and mixed methods terms

Uncover more than 120,000 pages of book, journal, and reference content to support your learning

Find out more at
www.sageresearchmethods.com